PAYMENT SYSTEMS

Examples and Explanations

Second Edition

James Brook
Professor of Law
New York Law School

ASPEN

PUBLISHERS

1185 Avenue of the Americas, New York, NY 10036
www.aspenpublishers.com

Printed in the United States of America

1 2 3 4 5 6 7 8 9 0

ISBN 0-7355-3974-X

Library of Congress Cataloging-in-Publication Data

Brook, James, 1946-
    Payment systems : examples and explanations /James Brook—2nd ed.
      p. cm.
    Includes index.
    ISBN 0-7355-3974-X
      1. Sales—United States. 2. Payment—United States. 3. Checks—United States. 4. Point-of-sale systems—Law and legislation—United States. I. Title.

KF933.B76 2004
346.7307'2—dc22
                                                   2003062980

PAYMENT SYSTEMS

Examples and Explanations

About Aspen Publishers

Aspen Publishers, headquartered in New York City, is a leading information provider for attorneys, business professionals, and law students. Written by preeminent authorities, our products consist of analytical and practical information covering both U.S. and international topics. We publish in the full range of formats, including updated manuals, books, periodicals, CDs, and online products.

Our proprietary content is complemented by 2,500 legal databases, containing over 11 million documents, available through our Loislaw division. Aspen Publishers also offers a wide range of topical legal and business databases linked to Loislaw's primary material. Our mission is to provide accurate, timely, and authoritative content in easily accessible formats, supported by unmatched customer care.

To order any Aspen Publishers title, go to *www.aspenpublishers.com* or call 1-800-638-8437.

To reinstate your manual update service, call 1-800-638-8437.

For more information on Loislaw products, go to *www.loislaw.com* or call 1-800-364-2512.

For Customer Care issues, e-mail *CustomerCare@aspenpublishers.com;* call 1-800-234-1660; or fax 1-800-901-9075.

Aspen Publishers
A Wolters Kluwer Company

For my parents

Contents

Preface

I start with a simple assumption. You come to this book because for one reason or another you want to learn the basic law covering modern payment systems as those systems are governed by Articles 3, 4, and 4A of the Uniform Commercial Code and various federal regulations. Most likely you are in a course — either a course devoted distinctly to payment systems (also sometimes called "negotiable instruments") or a more expansive survey course in commercial transactions that will necessarily devote a great deal of time to the subject. This book may have been assigned or recommended as additional reading by the professor teaching the course, or you may have come to it on your own as a means of review. You may find it helpful to think of it as a kind of workbook, giving you an organized way of *working through* the various sections, definitions, concepts, and controversies that make up the modern law of payment systems as set forth in the Uniform Commercial Code and a series of federal regulations.

This volume is not a substitute for having your own copy of the Uniform Commercial Code (including Official Comments) and the relevant regulations. I will be quoting from these sources from time to time. At other points I may simply suggest that you "recall the rule of §4-401(a)" or "look to §3-104(c)." The law you are learning is to be found in, not merely suggested by or illustrated through, the exact language of the Uniform Commercial Code as it has been enacted into law by the states and by particular federal regulations. I assume throughout that as you work through these chapters you will always have at your side and at the ready the primary texts for the study of the law of payment systems: the Code itself and the necessary federal regulations.

The general organization and sequence of chapters follows a fairly standard order in which these topics are taken up in courses on Payment Systems, although different professors may vary in how they work through the material. If this book has been assigned or recommended by your professor, you will want to follow his or her instructions about what chapters to look at when and which examples to do and which to leave for another day. If you are working your way through the book on your own and trying to coordinate it with your course, you will be able to navigate using the chapter headings, the Table of U.C.C. Citations, and the Index.

Each chapter is structured in the same way: introductory text is followed by a set of examples and then by my explanations of the questions asked and the issues raised in the examples. You will obviously only get the maximum benefit out of using this book by first *working through* the examples thoroughly on your own. You may want to write out a detailed and carefully constructed answer to each problem. I recommend that you at least jot down what you believe to be the correct answer or what you see as the central issue being presented, and how your reading of the primary materials suggests it should be handled.

One final note on the examples: It will not surprise you if, when you get to my analysis in the explanations, you find I will not always offer a simple yes or no in many cases. This subject, like any other you have already studied, has its irresolvable questions and "subtle" difficulties — places where the U.C.C. provisions or federal regulations seem to be of little or no help. On the other hand, don't think that just because this is the study of law that the answer to even the simplest question must necessarily be open to argument or subject to competing analyses. Sometimes, perhaps most of the time, a question can and indeed should be answered in a word or two, directly and without hedging. If the answer is *yes* you should say *yes*. If *no*, say *no*. Beyond that, of course, you should go on to say *why* you respond as you do — citing the Code or regulation, chapter and verse.

I hope that you find this book to be both helpful and enjoyable.

James Brook

January 2004

Acknowledgments

This is one of my three contributions to the Examples and Explanation series. As before I have to give special thanks to the good people at Aspen Law & Business including Carol McGeehan, Eric Holt, Melody Davies, Carrie Obry, and especially Jessica Barmack, without whose regular encouragement and gentle prodding it's questionable whether the trilogy (and now its regular updating) ever would have been completed. I also have to once again acknowledge the work of Joe Glannon, who was a friend long before either of us even thought of going to law school much less making a career out of teaching law. His initial work on the Examples and Explanation format was the genesis for all that followed, including my own works in the series. Joe remains a valued friend.

I would also like to thank former Dean Harry Wellington and Associate Dean Ellen Ryerson during whose tenure the bulk of the work on this project was undertaken. Their unfailing support for this effort as well as for all of my other endeavors at New York Law School was always much appreciated. I am fortunate to have found a similarly supportive atmosphere under our current Dean Rick Matasar and Associate Dean Steve Ellmann. Thanks as well to my colleagues at New York Law and to the large number of students at that school with whom I first got a chance to work over and test out many of the Examples that have found their way into this book.

Portions of the Official Text and Comments to the Uniform Commercial Code reproduced and quoted herein are Copyright 2002 by the American Law Institute and the National Conference of Commissioners on Uniform State Laws and are reprinted with the permission of the Permanent Editorial Board for the Uniform Commercial Code.

A Note on "the Revisions"

Articles 3 and 4 of the Uniform Commercial Code, with which we will be dealing in Part One through Part Five of this volume, were present in the Code at its creation and promulgation under the joint auspices of the American Law Institute and the National Conference of Commissioners on Uniform State Laws, leading to its eventual enactment in all of the states by the late 1960s. The Official Version of Article 3 was totally revised and Article 4 significantly amended by these powers-that-be in 1990. This set of revisions, the so-called 1990 Revisions, were fairly quickly adopted by almost all of the states, and it is the resulting versions of Articles 3 and 4 that I will be citing, quoting, and discussing here. This is the text, along with its accompanying commentary, that I assume you have available in whatever statutory supplement you are using in conjunction with your study of commercial law. You should be aware, however, that as of this writing, two states — New York and South Carolina — have *still* not adopted the 1990 revisions. Actual controversies governed by the laws of those states would still have to be analyzed with reference to the original versions of Articles 3 and 4, and even recent cases from those states will still be citing, naturally enough, from the original Articles 3 and 4.

In 2002, the ALI and NCCUSL adopted another set of amendments to these two Articles, making for what we will now have to call the "2002 versions" of Articles 3 and 4. These latest amendments may be in your statutory supplement as an appendix to the U.C.C. text or, by the time you are reading this, they may have made their way into the front of the book relegating the articles as they stood as of 2001 and prior to the proposed amendments to an appendix. This latest set of amendments is, as it turns out, relatively modest in scope. Furthermore it has, as of this writing, been adopted only by the state of Minnesota and nowhere else. Given this state of affairs, I decided that the better course for this edition would be to reference them only in a series of what I have designated *Revision Alerts* inserted at the end of some of the chapters. Should you be studying from the "newest" Articles 3 and 4, be sure to check out whether there is such an Alert at the end of a chapter before you delve too deeply into the material. You should then be able to make the adjustment easily enough so that this edition can still serve your purposes. Until, that is, another edition comes along.

Adding a bit more spice to the mix is the promulgation in 2001 of a revised version of Article 1 of the Uniform Commercial Code. This article, comprising the General Provision of the Code, including an important set of definitions and general principles, ends up coming into play and being cited in any work dealing with any aspect of commercial law. The "new Article 1" has, as of this writing, been adopted only in the U.S. Virgin Islands, Virginia, and Texas. At the same time, I have found that the statutory supplements used in most courses have begun putting the new version of Article 1 at the front of the book. As a practical matter, there is no real difference in substance between the original and the new versions of this article, at least as far as I'll be using it here, but the definitions have been renumbered and other important passages moved around, which can lead to a good deal of confusion. The cites to Article 1 in this volume are few enough that I have followed the path of least resistance and given parallel cites to both versions. So, for example, Original §1-201(39) is for all intents and purposes the same as Revised §1-201(b)(37) [or "O§1-201(39) = R§1-201(b)(37)"]. You should be able to use this edition no matter which version of Article 1 your professor, or your own predilection, asks you to follow.

PAYMENT SYSTEMS

Examples and Explanations

PART ONE

The Basic Law of Negotiable Instruments

1

What Is a Negotiable Instrument?

Introduction to Payment Systems

I would be among the last to suggest that when it comes to what really matters the most in life, wealth heads or ranks very high on the list. As far as the study of payment systems is concerned, however, there's no way around the fact that wealth *is* what it's all about. Payment systems, as a topic falling within the wider classification of commercial law, does not deal with how individuals and organizations accumulate and hold onto their share of the aggregate wealth generated within the society, although for those with an acquisitive nature a good understanding of the topic certainly doesn't hurt. The field of payment systems is concerned with how wealth can be and is *moved around* from place to place and from person to person: what means will shift some specific amount of money from one person's or organization's stash of wealth — from that legal entity's pocket so to speak — into that of another?

To narrow the focus considerably, we observe that payment systems deal only with how wealth gets moved around, shifted from one owner to another, when the transfer is made in terms of an amount of cash. Wealth is transferred, of course, any time an individual deeds or gives some measure of legal rights in an identified parcel of real estate to another or hands over and gives good title to a particular piece of personal property. Such transactions in themselves are covered in other parts of the legal curriculum. The area of payment systems, however, deals exclusively with promises to pay or payments that are actually made by one party to another of *an amount of money.*

Although what has become in recent years the conventional designation for this area of commercial law — *payment systems* — does feature the word *payment*, not all transfers of money with which we deal in our lives or which we will see in this volume necessarily involve a party's attempt to "pay" for something that he or she has received, some property transferred, or some services rendered. Such transactions are no doubt the background for a great majority of payments made through the means that we will study, but they do not cover the entire field. Each of us probably, at some time, has been moved to make a gift of cash to a friend or relative on some special occasion or to write out a check to a favored charity, such as (of course) an alma mater's alumni fund. Whatever the underlying reason, what we were attempting to do was move some of our money into the hands of another. We were participating in the wonderful world of payment systems.

Undoubtedly, the earliest form of payment mechanism, and that which is still used most frequently, is straightforward payment by cash. You may have paid cash for this book. You most likely have paid cash to a merchant over the past few days to buy pens or pencils with which to take notes, or a sandwich to eat or a soda with which to wash it down. Simply in terms of the number of transactions that occur each day, payment by cash still ranks as by far the most common type of payment transaction. As we will see later, however, in terms of the aggregate value of money that moves from one place to another in the course of a given day, the direct delivery of cash accounts for a small — though not insignificant — amount of the payments being carried out. However often it may be proclaimed that we are heading toward a "cashless society," people still tend to feel comfortable making payment by cash, at least for smaller amounts, and are apparently in no great hurry to drop the practice.

Once larger sums have to be transferred, however, payment by cash turns out to be a much less attractive option. It is easy to understand the reasons behind this. Few of us feel at ease carrying around large amounts of cash, because of the risk of theft or loss, which we quite understandably want to avoid. Once the question is how to make a payment, a gift, or a donation to a party in some far-off location, and the answer seems to be that we will have to send it via the mail or some similar carrier, it would be a rare individual who would eagerly stuff a large amount of cash into an envelope and blithely send it on its way. We search for other ways of getting the cash into the hands of the distant party without actually having to travel the distance ourselves with a large quantity of cash on our persons or sending that same amount of cash out into the world on its own, trusting (or perhaps we have to say hoping) that it will make its way to the intended recipient untouched.

In just the past few decades, mechanisms have been devised for transferring cash over great distances using modern means of electronic telecommunications. In Parts Six and Seven of this book, we will deal with the systems now in place for the electronic transfer of funds, both in the consumer context, where someone like you or me has a paycheck automatically deposited in a specified bank account or pays a bill by computer; and in the world of high finance, where major commercial entities are increasingly turning to the use of computerized mechanisms for large-scale *wire transfers* of incredibly large sums back and forth around the country and the world. We start, however, and spend the majority of our time with the modern version of a distinctly low-tech system for making payment by means other than cash. This system, which has a long and venerable history, relies on private parties creating, issuing, passing from hand to hand, and in the process taking on obligations and securing rights under some very distinctive pieces of paper with some unique properties. These special pieces of paper, which under modern parlance and the law of the Uniform Commercial Code (the "U.C.C.") now go by the name of *negotiable instruments*, are more than just contractual promises to pay that have been reduced to writing, like a simple I.O.U. scratched out on a paper napkin. To say that a given piece of paper qualifies as a negotiable instrument under the U.C.C. is to say quite a lot about it: how it should properly be passed from one party to the next, what rights are conveyed to the one taking such an instrument, what defenses are available against anyone asserting rights based on the instrument, and so much more. Ultimately, of course, we are interested in how reliance upon such negotiable instruments can serve as a payment mechanism substituting for payment in cash, as well as how payment in this manner is similar to and different from the paradigm of payment by cash. Our first order of business is therefore, quite naturally, to understand what exactly a negotiable instrument is. For this we turn first to the following section and then to the Examples and Explanations with which the chapter concludes.

The Definition of a Negotiable Instrument

Let's start at the very beginning. Section 3-101 of the Uniform Commercial Code states that, "This Article may be cited as Uniform Commercial Code — Negotiable Instruments." Nothing terribly exciting there, but at least it assures us that we've come to the right place if what we are interested in is the law relating to negotiable instruments. This is confirmed by the first sentence of §3-102(a): "This Article applies to negotiable instruments." The rest of §3-102 deals with possible overlaps or conflicts between Article 3 and other articles of the U.C.C., as well as with Regulations and other pronouncements of the Federal Reserve System, but nothing here need concern us for the moment.

Section 3-103 is, as you can see, a fairly lengthy compendium of definitions, some of which are given in subsection (a) and others of which appear in other sections of Articles 3 and 4 (with which we'll be dealing later) as indexed in subsections (b) and (c). Subsection (d) further reminds us that Article 1 of the U.C.C. contains still other definitions, as well as principles of construction that are applicable to all issues arising under any article of the Code. There is certainly no reason now to linger over any of these definitions. As a particular definition becomes relevant to the topic or issue we are considering at the moment (and some will become crucial within just a page or two), I will point you back to the definition or definitions you will need. Just observing the length and detail of §3-103, however, should serve as notice that the study of the law of negotiable instruments is replete with a whole set of special terms — a distinct lingo all its own. If, as you go through this material, you ever find yourself stymied by a question that doesn't seem to make any sense or seems harder than it should be, the first thing to do is read the question and any relevant Code sections over again, paying particular attention to the exact wording used. Now is the time to commit yourself to being as precise and meticulous in the use of the special terminology relating to negotiable instruments you will be learning as you will find the drafters of the Code were in their crafting of Article 3 and its compatriot Article 4.

Moving on in our tour of Article 3, we finally hit the Code provision directly relevant to the question we have first to address: What exactly *is* a negotiable instrument? This is answered in subsection (a) of §3-104. Stripped of a lot of language around the edges, which we will consider later on, the core language of §3-104(a) on which you should now focus is as follows:

> "[N]egotiable instrument" means an unconditional promise or order to pay a fixed amount of money.

Note also that in subsection (b) we are instructed that whenever the Code uses the single word *instrument*, it is referring to a negotiable instrument as that term is defined in subsection (a).

We can now make use, for the first time, of a couple of crucial definitions from §3-103(a), in particular the definitions of *promise* and *order*. Look at (a)(9):

> "Promise" means a written undertaking to pay money signed by the party undertaking to pay. An acknowledgment of an obligation to pay by the obligor is not a promise unless the obligor also undertakes to pay the obligation.

Similarly, we see in (a)(6) that the term

> "Order" means a written instruction to pay money signed by the person giving the instruction. . . . An authorization to pay is not an order unless the person authorized to pay is also instructed to pay.

So a promise is a promise and an order is an order. The first thing you notice in these two definitions is that for a promise to be a "promise" and for an order to be an "order" for Article 3 purposes, the given promise or order must be *in writing*. A *writing* is defined for purposes of the U.C.C., in §1-201(46) of the original Article 1 (which I'll cite as "O§1-201(46)") or §1-201(b)(43) of the recently revised version of that article ("R§1-201(b)(43)"), as including not only verbiage rendered by hand but also "printing, typewriting or any other intentional reduction to tangible form." Thus, a negotiable instrument, whether it be based on a promise or an order, is first and foremost a tangible thing: a piece of paper. But then, of course, it's not just any old piece of paper, but only one that meets the §3-104(a) definition as we are exploring it.*

A second important point that comes out of the definitions of *payment* and *order* is that for a writing to qualify as a negotiable instrument, it must be *signed* either by the party making the promise or the one issuing the order. For the Code's definition of *signed*, look to O§1-201(39) or R§1-201(b)(37). Signing includes "using any symbol executed or adopted by a party with present intention to adopt or accept a writing." What this means, among other things, is that if a particular person chooses to sign his or her name to a writing of this type with what seems to us a perfectly indecipherable scrawl, or with a simple "X" if that is his or her choice, that mark can be sufficient to meet the signature requirement — as long as that scrawl or that X is being adopted by the party in question "with present intention to adopt or accept" the writing.

The first three Examples of this chapter ask you to examine some simple pieces of paper that may or may not be negotiable instruments according to the definition as we've discussed it so far, and furthermore to identify what subspecies of negotiable instrument that paper would be. (See Figures A–C.) Negotiable instruments come in two main varieties, the *note* and the *draft*, on which see §3-104(e). You will certainly want to know a *check* when you see one. See §3-104(f). These initial examples will also help you to identify some principal characters in the negotiable instruments game, the parties as they are identified by role either as *maker*, *drawer*, or *drawee*. You'll find these terms defined as you need them in §3-103(a).

The following examples then explore the criteria, in addition to those we've already mentioned, that must be satisfied if a particular piece of paper

---

* As a matter of fact, and as you may have noticed, nothing in the Code says that this particular type of writing must actually be written on a piece of paper, although that clearly is the convention and one we can happily live with. Within the world of commercial law, there are any number of stories, some of them probably true and others no doubt apocryphal, of some wiseacre (for what must have seemed like a good reason at the time) writing a negotiable instrument not on a sheet of paper but on some other tangible medium: something like a check written on the side of a watermelon, or on a tamale, or welded onto a sheet of heavy metal. For our purposes it seems perfectly legitimate, and will make our lives that much easier, if we assume that all the negotiable instruments with which we deal are pieces of paper with the right kind of writing on them. We'll assume that a "writing" is a writing on paper, and leave the watermelons and the tamales to the commercial folklore.

is to qualify as a negotiable instrument. When we first looked at the crucial definition of that term in §3-104(a), we set aside for the moment a lot of the language around the edges to focus on the fact that a negotiable instrument must be, at its core, a written and signed promise or order to pay a sum of money. Beginning with Example 4, we look at the several other criteria laid out in §3-104(a). In particular we explore the requirements that:

- the purported negotiable instrument must be based on an "unconditional" promise or order,
- the promise or order must be "to pay a fixed amount of money, with or without interest or other charges described in the promise or order,"
- the purported negotiable instrument must be payable "to bearer or to order" at the time it is issued or first comes into the possession of a holder,
- the instrument must be payable on demand or at a definite time, and
- the instrument must not also state "any other undertaking or instruction by the person promising or ordering payment to do any act in addition to the payment of money," with only a narrow set of exceptions.

The concluding examples deal with some other definitions that we'll be needing soon enough — that of *certified check*, the *cashier's check*, and *teller's check* — and also with the particular issues that arise when we are dealing with what is termed an *incomplete instrument* under Article 3. There is plenty to look forward to in this first set of Examples and Explanations. They set the stage for all that is to come. Right now there is nothing for it but to set in on the first of them.

EXAMPLES

1. Examine the writing pictured in Figure A.
   (a) Does this qualify as a negotiable instrument under §3-104(a)? If so, what type of negotiable instrument is it?
   (b) Is its status as a negotiable instrument jeopardized by the fact that it does not indicate the date on which Horace Rivers created or purported to create the writing? See §3-113 and in particular subsection (b).
   (c) What term does Article 3 use to describe Horace Rivers?
   (d) The party in Jennifer Lake's position is conventionally referred to as the "payee" of the instrument, but as a matter of fact Article 3 never defines that term. An interesting question remains, however. We have to assume that there are some number of people out there with the name Jennifer Lake. To what person, to *which* Jennifer Lake, does this promise run? See the first sentence of §3-110(a).

2. Professor Brook owes Sarah Student $1,000 for work she did in helping him to prepare the manuscript of a book he is writing. Brook tells Sarah that

Figure A

I promise to pay $2,000 to the order of Jennifer Lake on January 15, 2006.

<u>*Horace Rivers*</u>
Horace Rivers

Figure B

TO: Arnold Moneybucks   January 12, 2004

Pay to the order of Sarah Student $1,000 on February 15, 2004.

<u>*James Brook*</u>
Prof. James Brook

Figure C

First National Bank
123 Main Street
Brookville, New York   *January 12, 2004*

Pay to the order of _____*Stewart Student*_____   *$1,000*
_____*One Thousand and 00/100*_____ Dollars

James Brook

he does not have the cash at the moment to pay her, but that he has arranged for her to get the money the next month from one Arnold Moneybucks, a prominent (and wealthy) local businessperson. On January 12, Brook prepares and signs the writing pictured in Figure B and hands it over to Sarah.

    (a) Does this qualify as a negotiable instrument under §3-104(a)? If so, what type of negotiable instrument is it?

    (b) What terms does Article 3 use to identify Brook and Arnold Moneybucks as of January 12?

3.   Professor Brook also owes another research assistant, one Stewart Student, the sum of $1,000. He decides to pay Stewart in a more conventional manner, out of a checking account he maintains at the First National Bank in his hometown. He takes out a blank check and fills it out as pictured in Figure C.

    (a) Does this qualify as a negotiable instrument under §3-104(a)? If so, what type of negotiable instrument is it?

    (b) What terms does Article 3 use to describe each of Brook and First National Bank as of January 12?

    (c) Suppose that Brook, prior to handing the writing over to Stewart, had struck out the preprinted phrase "Pay to the order of" preceding the space on which he inserted Stewart's name, or that the company that had printed up the forms had through some oversight failed to include these words on the preprinted check form? Does this change your analysis of the situation at all? See §3-104(c).

4.   Jason Jones signs a writing dated August 4, 2003, stating that, "I promise to pay to the order of Roberta Rogers $12,450 if she conveys to me title to her 1998 Mercury Cougar automobile one week from this date."

    (a) Is this writing a negotiable instrument? See §3-106(a).

    (b) What if the writing signed by Jones had read, "In consideration of her agreement to convey to me title to her 1998 Mercury Cougar automobile, I, Jason Jones, promise to pay to the order of Roberta Rogers $12,450 one week from this date?" Would this writing be a negotiable instrument?

    (c) Suppose that the writing had initially stated only that Jones "promises to pay to the order of Roberta Rogers" the sum on the date set. It also contains a sentence, however, stating that, "This note and any rights or obligations arising hereunder are subject to a Contract of Purchase and Sale entered into between Jason Jones and Roberta Rogers on the same date as the date hereof." Would this writing qualify as a negotiable instrument?

    (d) Finally, consider the following possibility. The writing Jones signs reads, "In accordance with a Contract of Purchase and Sale entered into between myself and Roberta Rogers on this date, I promise to pay to the order of the said Roberta Rogers $12,450 one week from the date hereof." Is this a negotiable instrument?

5. Lili McCue signs a dated writing stating, "I promise to pay to the order of Colin Danforth that which I owe him by delivering to his place of address a ruby of at least one carat three months from the date hereof."

    (a) Is this a negotiable instrument?

    (b) Even if this writing does not qualify as a negotiable instrument under Article 3, does that mean it has no legal significance?

6. Isabelle Inkster is able to obtain a small business loan from the First Federal Bank of New York. The note she signs in 2002 states that she must repay, on a specified schedule, "to the order of the First Federal Bank of New York" the principal amount, along with interest to be calculated as "three percent (3%) over the Prime Rate charged by First Federal of New York, to be adjusted monthly." First Federal's prime rate, which is the rate of interest it charges its most favored and creditworthy customers, is regularly reported in the financial press. Assuming that all the other criteria of §3-104(a) are met, does this writing qualify as a negotiable instrument under Article 3? See §3-112(b).

7. Consider in each of the following, using as your guide §3-109(a) and (b), whether the language in what purports to be a note or a draft satisfies the requirement of §3-104(a)(1) that at the time of its creation the writing be "payable to bearer or to order." In each case, if the writing does qualify as a negotiable instrument at the time of issuance, is it an instrument initially payable to bearer or to order?

    (a) "I promise to pay to Rachelle Roe . . ."

    (b) "I promise to pay to bearer . . ."

    (c) A check directing the drawer's bank to "Pay to the Order of Rachelle Roe."

    (d) A check made out "Pay to the Order of Cash."

    (e) A check, otherwise complete, that is made out "Pay to the Order of _____ . . ." with no name filled in on the line where the payee's name usually goes.

8. Consider, using as your guide §3-108, whether each of the following would satisfy the requirement of §3-104(a)(2) that the writing be "payable on demand or at a definite time."

    (a) "Pay to the order of Rachelle Roe on demand."

    (b) "Pay to the order of Rachelle Roe on sight."

    (c) "Pay to the order of Rachelle Roe" but with no date given.

    (d) "Pay to the order of Rachelle Roe on December 15, 2006."

    (e) "Pay to the order of Rachelle Roe thirty (30) days following sight."

    (f) "I, Allan Adare, promise to pay to the order of Rachelle Roe $40,000 within six months following the death of my Uncle, Adrian Adare."

9.   A writing, dated February 3, 2004, reads "I, Otto Olson, promise to pay to the order of Manuel Marquez the sum of $16,000 and also to deliver him title to the estate known as Whiteacre one month from the date hereof." Does this qualify as a negotiable instrument?

10. Joseph Byers of Boston and Suzanne Sellers of Seattle both collect antique porcelains. Byers has for several months been negotiating over the telephone with Sellers for the purchase of a particular piece she owns, which he very much wants to add to his collection. It is finally agreed that she will sell him the piece for $12,000, delivery to be made in exchange for that price when the two meet the next week at a porcelain collectors' convention in Chicago. Byers obviously does not want to have to carry that much cash with him on his journey from Boston to Chicago, so he tells Sellers he will pay her by check. Sellers has completed her study of payment systems and hence is aware, as you will be soon enough, of the problems she might encounter if she were to take a simple personal check from Byers in a situation such as this, such as that the check might bounce for insufficient funds or that Byers might stop payment on the check before she gets to cash it. Therefore, Sellers tells Byers that she wants him to pay the purchase price to her by some other, more secure (for her) means.

    (a) Byers has a checking account with the Bay State Bank in Boston. He writes out a check payable to the order of Sellers for $12,000. He then takes this check into his branch of Bay State Bank, where he gets a representative of the bank to apply to the back of the check a stamp bearing the name of Bay State Bank and to place her initials by the mark she has made with the stamp. What term would you now use to characterize this check? See §3-409(d).

    (b) Suppose instead that Byers had gone into Bay State and arranged for the withdrawal of the $12,000 from his account. Instead of taking this amount in cash, he requests that the bank prepare a check of the following type: Bay State Bank directs itself, Bay State Bank, to "pay to the order of Suzanne Sellers" the sum of $12,000 on demand. What term does Article 3 use for such a check? See §3-104(g). Notice that Byers is neither the drawer nor the drawee of this check. What term characterizes Byers in this situation? See §3-103(a)(11).

    (c) As a third possibility, suppose that Bay State Bank itself has a checking account with Seaside Bank of Seattle, in which it keeps a sizeable balance. Byers uses the $12,000 he withdraws from his account at Bay State to purchase a check drawn by Bay State on its account with Seaside Bank "to the order of Suzanne Sellers" for the right amount. What term does Article 3 use for such a check? See §3-104(h).

11. Coincidentally, Byers has also come upon another piece of antique porcelain that he wants to buy, this one in a small antique shop in Boston

not far from his home. The owner of the shop, which is called "The Antique Attic," is a woman named China White. The last time Byers looked in the store, the piece in which he is interested was marked with a tag giving its price as $3,500.

(a) Byers takes a blank check from his checkbook and fills in the name of the payee as "The Antique Attic" and the amount as $3,500. He does not sign the check, but puts it in his wallet as he heads out the door on his way to the shop. As it now sits in his wallet, is this paper an "incomplete instrument" as that term is used in §3-115?

(b) Suppose instead that Byers has in fact signed the check, along with filling in the amount. However, because he is not sure in what name Ms. White will want the check to be made out, he leaves the payee space blank. He gives the check to his assistant, Murphy, instructing Murphy to purchase the item from the store and fill in the name of the payee as whatever Ms. White requests. Would the paper now in Murphy's possession be an incomplete instrument? Would it be a negotiable instrument under §3-104(a)? To carry on with the story, when Murphy gets to the shop, Ms. White is more than happy to take the check in exchange for the item, and asks that he fill in the name of the payee as "China White Antiques, Incorporated," which is the legal name under which she carries on the business. Murphy does so and hands the check over to her. What is its status now?

(c) As a third alternative, suppose that Byers is well aware, from prior dealings, of the correct name to put on the check. He fills in the payee as "China White Antiques, Incorporated" and signs it. He does not fill in the amount of the check, however, thinking that through Murphy he may have some chance to cut a deal at a lower price with Ms. White. He gives the paper filled out in this fashion to Murphy. Is it at this point an incomplete instrument? Is it a negotiable instrument under §3-104(a)? As it turns out, the valued assistant Murphy is able to get Ms. White to accept $3,000 for the piece, so he completes the check form by filling in this amount and hands it over to her. What is the status of the paper now?

EXPLANATIONS

1a. Yes. This is a negotiable instrument under §3-104(a). You should verify that it meets all the criteria of that definition. It expresses a promise to pay, is in writing, and is signed by the person making the promise, Rivers. There is not a hint of a condition on this promise. It is a promise to pay a fixed amount of money, $2,000. As we will later see in more detail, it is "payable to order" in that the promise is stated as an obligation to "pay to the order of" an identified person. It is payable in this case not on demand, but at a definite time, January 15, 2006. Finally, there is simply nothing in this uncomplicated writing that states an "undertaking" by Rivers to do any act in addition to the payment of money. It is a negotiable instrument all right, and because the core language is that of promise it is the type of negotiable instrument we call a *note*. See §3-104(e).

1b. No. There is no requirement that a writing include or exhibit a date in order for it to be a negotiable instrument. Under §3-113(b), should the issue ever arise, the "date" of this instrument would be "the date of its issue [a concept we will get into in the Chapter 2], or in the case of an unissued instrument [ditto], the date it first comes into the possession of a holder [ditto again]."

1c. Horace Rivers is to be referred to as the maker of the note (§3-103(a)(5)).

1d. Under §3-110(a) the particular Jennifer Lake to whom this note is initially payable is determined by the intent of Horace Rivers when he put that name, "Jennifer Lake," into his promise. The Jennifer Lake to whom this money is initially promised is the Jennifer Lake that Horace had in mind when he wrote out the promise. No other Jennifer Lakes need apply.

2a. Yes. This is a negotiable instrument under §3-104(a), as you can confirm for yourself. Because the language is that of an order, this is a draft (§3-104(e)).

2b. Professor Brook is the drawer of the draft (§3-103(a)(3)) and Arnold Moneybucks is the drawee (§3-103(a)(2)). Note that the creation of a valid draft does not require the participation, the approval, or even the knowledge of the drawee. In Chapter 3, we will pick up on this example, and see what happens when Sarah tries to get Moneybucks to follow the order which Brook has written out and addressed to him. For the moment, it is enough to see that Moneybucks, the drawee, plays no part in the drawing of the draft. His part in the story comes later.

3a. The paper that Brook has handed over to Stewart is indeed a negotiable instrument. It is a draft. Furthermore, as you can confirm by a reading of §3-104(f), it is, unsurprisingly, what we and more to the point Article 3 call a *check*. "'Check' means (i) a draft . . . payable on demand and drawn on a bank." As to what constitutes a "bank" for these purposes, see §4-105(1), a definition made applicable to Article 3 via §3-103(c).

3b. Professor Brook is the drawer of the check and the Main Street branch of First National Bank is the drawee. Again, as in Example 2's case of the draft Brook made payable to Sarah Student, the drawee — in this case the bank — is not involved in the creation of the draft.

3c. Under §3-104(c), this is still a check, even though it fails to display what we will soon discover to be the crucial words of negotiability ("to the order of" or "to bearer"), which are in all other cases absolutely essential for the creation of a negotiable instrument. The reasons why the drafters of the 1990

Revised Version of Article 3 thought it appropriate to put in this subsection (c) are given at the end of the first paragraph of Comment 2 to §3-104.

4a. No. This is not a negotiable instrument. Under §3-106(a), the promise made is not unconditional for purposes of the basic definition of §3-104(a), because it states "an express condition to payment," that condition being Rogers's conveyance of title to her car by August 11. See, for example, *Reid v. Pyle*, 51 P.3d 1064, 48 U.C.C.2d 1066 (Colo. App. 2002), where what professed to be a note was correctly held not to be a negotiable instrument as the promise to pay was expressly conditioned on "the sale or transference" of a particular piece of real estate.

4b. Yes. This is a negotiable instrument. Jason Jones has expressed no condition on his obligation to pay Roberta Rogers the set sum on the given date. The introductory phrase, "In consideration of . . ." is read as explaining, if you will, the genesis of the promise — it is a bit of background information — but it does not express a condition on Jones's promise as he has made it. See the first paragraph of Comment 1 to §3-106.

4c. No. Here the promise is deemed, under §3-106(a), other than an unconditional one because it is "subject to or governed by another writing."

4d. Yes. The last sentence of §3-106(a) tells us that, "A reference to another writing does not of itself make the promise or order conditional." Here there is reference to the Contract of Purchase and Sale that Jones and Rogers have entered into, but nothing in the language of the note suggests either that the promise is "subject to or governed by" that contract document nor that "rights and obligations with respect to the promise" are stated in it. See the second paragraph of Comment 1. Note the rationale for the distinction between this example and something like what we saw in 4c: "[T]he holder of a negotiable instrument should not be required to examine another document to determine rights with respect to payment."

The slight differences in language that we are exploring in this Example may not seem like much, but just such distinctions can be crucial to the determination of whatever rights the parties are trying to assert, or any defenses they are or may be subject to, on a particular written promise or order. For an example, see *Telerecovery of Louisiana v. Gaulon*, 738 So. 2d 662, 38 U.C.C.2d 853 (La. Ct. App. 1999). In that case the Court of Appeals of Louisiana concluded that the presence of the language "I agree to payment according to the terms of the Credit Payment Agreement previously executed by the undersigned" found on the writing under dispute (a so-called casino marker for gambling debts in the amount of $10,000) did not render the writing, which otherwise met all the requirements for being a check, nonnegotiable. The court wrote:

> Examining the language at issue in this case, we conclude it does not destroy negotiability of the marker. Its location on the last line of the

instrument as well as its use of "according to" simply references another document but does not make payment conditional.

Another interesting example is *Sheppard v. Stanich*, 749 N.E.2d 609, 46 U.C.C.2d 773 (Ind. App. 2001). There the parties entered into an agreement in April 1993 under which Sheppard was to purchase all of Stanich's stock in a company called 21st Century Holdings. In accordance with that agreement Sheppard executed what was presumably intended by both to be a note in which he promised to pay the amount of $38,000 plus interest on or before April 15, 1994. Following Sheppard's signature there appeared on the paper a handwritten sentence: "If value exceeds 6 percent interest Jon agrees to split profits." The court took this last sentence to be a reference to an aspect of the underlying Agreement of Purchase under which the seller would split the profits of the business in a defined way based on a valuation that was to be made of the stock being sold. The addition of this sentence was held by the court to render the "note" nonnegotiable "because it was not an unconditional promise of one party to pay the other, but a bilateral agreement. . . . The Note [that is, the piece of paper that purported to be a note] was evidence of Sheppard's promise to pay the purchase price and contained an additional term of the agreement [Stanich's promise to take less than the $38,000 under some condition laid out in the Agreement of Purchase]."

Here we confront for the first time what will become the principal notion lurking behind all the subsidiary rules to be applied when we must answer the question of whether a specific piece of paper is a negotiable instrument. Whether a writing constitutes a negotiable instrument should be determinable by the person we will end up referring to as the *holder* — or by anyone else examining it for that matter — by what is to be found *within the four corners* of the writing itself. Whether a writing satisfies the requirements to be a negotiable instrument for Article 3 purposes, and if so what type of instrument it is; who is promising or ordering whom to pay how much and when; and (as we have yet to see) whether the drawee of a draft has accepted — all this information should be available from taking a good look at the writing itself. Should we conclude, after examining the writing itself, that we would have to consult another document to answer any of these questions, or would have to question a party for crucial information or to discern that party's or a set of parties' "intention" (heaven forfend!), we are dealing with something that isn't a negotiable instrument to begin with. Any negotiable instrument is a special type of document that carries all the pertinent information about it right on its face or, as we will begin to see, on its flip side. The negotiable instrument is a very tangible thing; it is a piece of paper. Its importance, however, is that the instrument and the information it carries are, at least metaphorically speaking, one and the same.

5a. This is not a negotiable instrument. Under §3-104(a), the promise or order must be one "to pay a fixed amount of money. . . ." Look at the definition found in O§1-201(24) R§1-201(b)(24), the heart of which is the statement that: "'Money' means a medium of exchange authorized or adopted by a domestic or foreign government. . . ." That a note or a draft may be payable in foreign currency is confirmed by §3-107, as you can check, but a promise to deliver a ruby, even a fairly pricey one, will not do.

5b. Even though this piece of paper turns out not to be a negotiable instrument, that certainly does not mean that it has no legal significance. McCue apparently is indebted to Danforth for some amount and has promised, to pay him not in cash but by the delivery of a gem of a certain type and by a given date. McCue will presumably be obligated to do as she has promised; her legal obligation arises under the common law of contracts and is governed by its principles. This paper is a contract document and may turn out to be very important to Danforth if McCue fails to carry out her promise or tries to deny that she ever made such a promise. It just doesn't happen to be a negotiable instrument.

6.   By the test of §3-112(b), the way the interest term is expressed in the note Inkster signs — as a variable rate of interest keyed to First Federal of New York's Prime Rate, when that rate is readily available by consulting generally available sources of information, even though these are extrinsic to the instrument — does not render the note nonnegotiable. Note from the Comment 1 to §3-112 that the same would of course not be true if the *principal* amount were not given as a "fixed amount."

You should be aware that the answer to this question is as easy as it is because the note was signed by Inkster in 2002 and hence is governed by the Revised Version of Article 3 and its very helpful §3-112(b). The prior version of Article 3, adopted by the states in the 1960s, had no section comparable to what we now see in §3-112(b). This was no huge oversight on the part of the drafters; at the time, the so-called variable-interest-rate note was virtually unknown. Notes were almost without exception written in terms calling for a fixed rate of interest. Only in the following decades did the idea of the variable-interest-rate note come into general use, to the point where today such notes probably account for a majority of all notes signed by borrowers.

The earlier version of Article 3 not only lacked a section specifically providing for the negotiable status of this type of variable-interest-rate note (such as we now have in §3-112(b)), but in fact was so written as to lead most courts to hold that any note providing for interest calculated in this manner was definitely *not* a negotiable instrument. The original version of §3-104 required that, for a writing to be a negotiable instrument, the writing had to contain a promise or order to pay "a sum certain" — but the Article did not go on to define this term. In fact, a comment to the old §3-106, which dealt with (even if it never actually defined) *sum certain*, stated that, "The computation [of how much is promised or ordered] must be one which can be made from the instrument itself and without reference to any outside source." Even though faced with such language in the then-effective version of Article 3, some courts did find their way to a reading of the Code that allowed variable-interest-rate notes to be true negotiable instruments. However, the majority of courts, as I have indicated, did not. See, for example, *Taylor v. Roeder*, 234 Va. 99, 360 S.E.2d 191, 4 U.C.C.2d 652 (1987). The note in question called for interest to be charged at "[t]hree percent (3.00%) over Chase Manhattan Prime to be adjusted monthly." The Supreme Court of Virginia concluded that this was not a negotiable instrument under the then-applicable version of Article 3:

> We conclude that the drafters of the Uniform Commercial Code adopted criteria for negotiability intended to exclude an instrument which requires reference to any source outside the instrument itself in order to ascertain the amount due, subject only to those exceptions specifically provided for in the U.C.C.
>
> . . . Although the rate may be readily ascertained from published sources, it cannot be found within the "four corners" of the note.

In a number of jurisdictions in which the variable-interest-rate note was held not to be a negotiable instrument subject to the old Article 3, the legislatures quickly stepped in and adopted a nonuniform amendment to cover the situation. In others, the legislatures did nothing and the situation remained as the courts of those jurisdictions had held: The variable-interest-rate note, however much it might be used and accepted in day-to-day business affairs and treated just as a note conventionally would be, was not a true negotiable instrument — a conclusion that might later come as an unpleasant surprise to some party down the line if things got dicey and litigation ensued.

Thus, the situation prior to the 1990s was anything but uniform. In some jurisdictions the variable-interest-rate note was simply nonnegotiable. In others it was negotiable under that state's courts' reading of the original Article 3. In others it was negotiable due to legislative initiatives amending Article 3. I would like to say that the whole controversy has been rendered moot by the promulgation and near-uniform passage by the states of the Revised Version of Article 3, but unfortunately that isn't entirely the case. Notes are typically term instruments and in some instances the terms are quite long. Plenty of notes still out there were entered into prior to the adoption of the 1990 revisions, and hence they are still subject to the rules, whatever they may be for the particular state, of the original Article 3. See, e.g., *Barnsley v. Empire Mortgage Ltd. Partnership*, 142 N.H. 721, 720 A.2d 63, 37 U.C.C.2d 1069 (1998) and *Amberboy v. Société de Banque Privée*, 831 S.W.2d 793, 35 Tex. Sup. J. 621, 17 U.C.C.2d 145 (1992).

For notes entered into today, of course, we have the rule of §3-112(b) to consult and to make our lives a lot easier. This subsection doesn't make any purported note a negotiable instrument no matter how weirdly or in what complex fashion the interest terms are stated, but it does give a clear criterion by which this question is to be addressed.

7a. This writing, because it is not payable to bearer under any of the possibilities given in §3-109(a) nor to order under (b), is not a negotiable instrument. Your initial reaction might be that Article 3 is being unnecessarily finicky (or downright silly) in requiring that either the exact six-letter word "bearer" or the five-letter word "order" appear in just the right way on the writing in order to make the writing a negotiable instrument. What magic do these words, sometimes referred to as the *language of negotiability*, work on a simple piece of paper? But that is exactly the point. These words serve as neat, and one might say, elegant markers of negotiability, placed right there on the document itself. Recall the fundamental notion that whether or not a writing constitutes a negotiable instrument should be determinable from the face of the writing itself, from within its "four corners." What better way to do this than to make at least one criterion the presence of at least one of these two distinctive words? If the language of negotiability is not on a writing, then it can't be a negotiable instrument (with that one odd but necessary exception dealing with preprinted checks of §3-104(c)). The fact that certain words, and these two in particular, set off a negotiable instrument from all the other writings that people sign is (as I have a feeling you've already surmised) not a recent innovation of the Uniform Commercial Code. Just as the notion and nature of negotiable instruments has a long and distinguished history, the use of these particular words as the touchstone language of negotiability are a central part of that history.

Don't be misled. The fact that any particular promise to pay, stated *without* the language of negotiability, appears in a writing doesn't make the promise illegal, immoral, or anything like that. More to the point, it certainly doesn't render the promise unenforceable. The result is only that any enforcement of the promise will be enforcement under the traditional common law of contract, unless some other regime of legal rules can be successfully invoked. What the enforcing party cannot do is enforce the promise as an obligation *on a negotiable instrument*; as I have promised before and will promise again, what differences exactly that makes will be apparent soon enough.

7b. This promise will make the writing a negotiable instrument under §3-109(a)(1). Not surprisingly, this writing has been created as what we would term a *bearer instrument*.

7c. This check is a negotiable instrument payable to order under §3-109(b), because it is written as payable to the order of an identified person. It is classed as an *order instrument*.

7d. This is a bearer instrument under §3-109(a)(3).

7e. This is a bearer instrument under §3-109(a)(2). It is also what we will discuss as an "incomplete instrument" in Example 9. There is some language in the middle of Comment 2 accompanying §3-109 that confirms this result, if you aren't willing to take my word for it.

8a. This is (obviously) payable on demand.

8b. An instrument using this language is also payable on demand (§3-108(a)(i)).

8c. This is also payable on demand (§3-108(a)(ii)).

8d. This is payable at a definite time under §3-108(b) because it is payable at a fixed date.

8e. This is also considered to be payable at a definite time under §3-108(b), because it is "payable on elapse of a definite period of time after sight."

8f. This promise could not be the basis of a negotiable instrument, as it is neither payable on demand nor payable at a definite time. Who could tell from a good look within the four corners of the instrument, or even the most careful look at Uncle Adrian himself and his medical records, when the promised payment will become due?

9. No. Under §3-104(a)(3), a negotiable instrument must "not state any other undertaking or instruction by the person promising or ordering payment to do any act in addition to the payment of money," with some limited exceptions not relevant here. Olson's promise to convey Whiteacre in addition to paying the money renders the entire writing a nonnegotiable one.

You should read through the listing of exceptions to this general rule that concludes §3-104(a)(3). You'll see that they certainly don't cover a promise to convey a piece of real estate, and, in effect, don't really deal with any type of undertaking or order to take any action in addition to or independent of the core obligation to pay money which is what the note or draft is all about. Any promise to give or maintain collateral to support a monetary obligation, for example, doesn't have an independent life, so to speak, other than as it relates to the promise to pay the money. Similarly, an authorization or power given to the holder of the instrument to confess judgment or to take other acts to enforce the monetary obligation can't be thought of as anything distinct from or in addition to the monetary obligation itself. There is no reason to worry, unless an actual case comes your way in which the matter arises, about this latter part of §3-104(a)(3). The fundamental principle is what we are after here: A negotiable instrument is a promise or order to pay a sum of money and the maker or the drawer cannot, if his or her creation is to retain its negotiable status, tack on any additional promises or instructions unrelated to that fundamental monetary obligation.

10a. This check is now a *certified check* under §3-409(d). Byers was from the outset the drawer of the check, and he remains so. Bay State Bank was the drawee, and when an authorized representative of the bank stamps its name on the check the bank becomes what we will term the acceptor as well.

10b. This is a *cashier's check* under §3-104(g). Bay State Bank is *both* the drawer and the drawee of the check. Byers is the *remitter* in this situation

(§3-103(a)(11)), as he was the person who purchased the instrument from its issuer, Bay State Bank, when the instrument was payable to an identified person other than himself, that person being Suzanne Sellers.

10c. This instrument is a *teller's check* under §3-104(h). Bay State Bank is the drawer and Seaside Bank of Seattle is the drawee. Byers is once again the remitter.

11a. No. Under §3-115(a), an incomplete instrument must be a signed writing. We can stop right there. The check now in Byers's wallet has not been signed. It is not an *incomplete instrument* as that term is used in Article 3.

11b. Under this set of facts, the check in Murphy's possession is an incomplete instrument as he makes his way to the antique shop. It is signed and its contents indicate "that it is incomplete but that the signer intended it to be completed by the addition of words or numbers." The more interesting question is whether this incomplete instrument is in its present state a negotiable instrument under §3-104(a) criteria — and the answer is yes. Recall that a draft is payable to bearer if it states that it is payable "to the order of . . ." but then has no name appearing in the space provided for naming (if one chooses to) a specific person as payee (§3-109(a)(2)). Murphy carries to the shop a check payable to bearer for $3,500. Once Murphy fills in the correct name of the payee as Ms. White gives it to him, and then hands the paper over to her, she has in her possession an order instrument, a check payable to the order of a corporate entity named China White Antiques, Incorporated.

11c. Once again, the check Murphy is holding onto as he makes his way to the antique shop is an incomplete instrument, but in this case it is not a negotiable instrument. The price is left blank. It does not include an order to Byers's bank to pay "a fixed amount of money," and so it fails to meet that criterion of negotiability of §3-104(a). Once the figure of $3,000 is filled in, the paper does become a negotiable instrument. See the second sentence of §3-115(b). When the check is handed over to Ms. White, she is in possession of a check payable to the order of her corporation for $3,000.

See Revision Alert on the following page.

Revision Alert

The basic definitions with which we have been working in this chapter have been moved around a bit in the 2002 Revisions to Article 3 — for example the definition of *order* is now found in Revised §3-103(a)(8) and that of *promise* in R§3-103(a)(12) — but the definitions themselves have not been changed, not even by a word. And the singularly important definition of what is a *negotiable instrument* in §3-104(a) remains the same. In fact that entire section has not been tampered with at all by the Revision drafters.

In all the chapters that follow, you may assume that this latest Revision of Articles 3 and 4 has not made any change, or at least not any change of substance, in what we have studied unless I indicate otherwise by an "alert" such as this at the end of the chapter.

2

Principles of Negotiation and Becoming a Holder

The Life Story of a Negotiable Instrument

A negotiable instrument, once it is created by the maker of the note or the drawer of the draft, doesn't just sit there. If it is going to play out whatever function the maker or the drawer intended for it, it must start moving from hand to hand. The life of a negotiable instrument, at least metaphorically and in most cases quite literally, is a life on the move. The tale of any particular negotiable instrument unfolds as a series of events. The first of these events is termed *issuance* of the instrument. As §3-105(a) tells it,

> "Issue" means the first delivery of an instrument by the maker or the drawer, whether to a holder or nonholder, for the purpose of giving rights on the instrument to any person.

We'll deal with the nature of issuance in the first example of this chapter.

The life cycle of the instrument typically ends with its *presentment* by some party seeking to enforce the promise or order it contains back to the party who in the normal course of events is expected to pay it: the maker in the case of a note or the drawee in the case of a draft. Presentment is defined in §3-501(a), and is something we will look at more closely in Chapter 3. Presentment gets the instrument to the party who is supposed to pay up on the promise or order, and in the vast majority of cases (even the most cynical would have to admit) the demand that payment be made is honored. The presentment results in the instrument turning into the correct amount of cash. The role of the negotiable instrument in moving wealth in the form of money from one party to another has been played out just as it was intended.

It is perfectly possible that the person to whom the instrument is initially issued will himself or herself directly present it for payment. In many instances, however, there are some intervening steps — often quite a few — and additional parties involved between the issuance of the instrument and its presentment. Any such intervening step is referred to as a *transfer* of the instrument. Notice that by the definition of *transfer* found in §3-203(a), issuance of an instrument is not a transfer.

> An instrument is transferred when it is delivered by a person *other than its issuer* for the purpose of giving the person receiving delivery the right to enforce the instrument.

Also, as you can see, presentment is not a transfer because the instrument is not being delivered to the maker or drawee "for the purpose of giving the person receiving delivery the right to enforce the instrument." The maker or the drawee does not enforce the instrument; the whole idea of the instrument is that it is to be enforced *against*, not *by*, the maker or drawee.

There you have, in broad outline, the life cycle of the negotiable instrument, at least as it runs if all goes according to plan. The instrument is issued; it may be transferred anywhere from zero to some significant number of times; and all is wrapped up when the final transferee (or the party to whom it was issued if there have been no transfers subsequent to issue) makes a presentment to the maker or drawee. Of course, as you would expect, the real world being what it is, in some small but still meaningful number of cases everything doesn't go just as it should. Parties don't do what they are supposed to; ambiguities arise that need clearing up; or people who should have nothing to do with the instrument (such as the thieves and forgers we will eventually be meeting) try and often succeed in getting their hands on money that by no stretch of the imagination is meant for them. The legal rules for sorting all of this out are what give Article 3 (and Article 4, which we will later add to the mix) and the large middle portion of this book their heft.

The Process of Negotiation

The primary topic of this chapter, after an initial look at issuance of the instrument, is transfer of a negotiable instrument: how it is to be done and what effect it will have. Of prime importance is that some transfers qualify to be distinguished by a special term and confer specific rights on the transferee. We call such a transfer a *negotiation* of the instrument. Negotiation is defined in §3-201(a) as

> a transfer of possession, whether voluntary or involuntary, of an instrument by a person other than the issuer to a person who thereby becomes a holder.

Which reasonably leads us to inquire: Who or what is a *holder*? For that we have to look at O§1-201(20) (or its equivalent in the revised Article 1, R§1-201(b)(21)(A)):

> "Holder" with respect to a negotiable instrument, means a person in possession of the instrument if the instrument is payable to bearer or, in the case of an instrument payable to an identified person, if the identified person is in possession.

This is not as gracefully written as it might be, but its meaning has never been in question. First and foremost, to be a holder of a particular instrument one must be in actual physical possession of that instrument. If at the moment the instrument is in "bearer" form — either because it was initially issued as a bearer instrument or it has become so through the rules of negotiation, which we will explore in the examples — then possession is *all* that is required to make the possessor the holder of the instrument. If, however, the instrument is at the time in question an "order" instrument, that is, payable to the order of an identified person, then that person and that person only will be the holder *if* he or she is in possession of the instrument.[*]

It is important to make clear at the outset that the conclusion that a person qualifies as a holder of an instrument is not necessarily to say that the person is a rightful holder or the lawful owner of the instrument. As we will see in the examples, a thief of an instrument may, under the right circumstances (for the thief), be the holder of that instrument even if he or she clearly has no legal right to that which he or she has stolen. Who is the rightful owner of the instrument, and the problems that person will encounter in trying to avoid the loss due to the theft, are issues that make up a large part of what is to come. For our present purposes, it is sufficient to recognize the importance of being able to determine who is and who isn't the holder of a given instrument, whether rightfully so or otherwise.

The term *negotiation* is defined in §3-201(a) by its result. A transfer is a negotiation if the transferee thereby becomes a holder. This still leaves the question of *how* exactly a negotiation is carried out. For that we look to subsection (b). Putting aside the special case of negotiation by a remitter,

> if an instrument is payable to an identified person, negotiation requires transfer of possession of the instrument and its indorsement by the holder. If an instrument is payable to bearer, it may be negotiated by transfer of possession alone.

Now we need only identify a few other key sections and the terms they contain before we put all these pieces together in the examples that follow. The term

---

[*] This is as good a place as any to point out that, under O§1-201(30) or R§1-201(b)(27), as used in the U.C.C. the word person "includes an individual or an organization." You may have questions at this point about how an organization can give its signature, the act that we have already seen is crucial to the creation of a negotiable instrument and which we will explore in this chapter as ofttimes essential for a valid negotiation. We will deal with such problems in Chapter 4.

indorsement is defined in §3-204(a). Notice that indorsement requires the signature of the indorser on the instrument itself and that this signature must be done for one of a set of purposes — and indeed is assumed to have been done for such a purpose — which include negotiating the instrument. You should also look over the definition of the terms *special indorsement* in §3-205(a) and *blank indorsement* in §3-205(b). Finally, look back to §3-109. We previously looked at subsections (a) and (b) of this section to determine whether a writing purporting to be a negotiable instrument was "payable to bearer or to order" at the time of its creation. Now look at subsection (c):

> An instrument payable to bearer may become payable to an identified person if it is specially indorsed pursuant to Section 3-205(a). An instrument payable to an identified person may become payable to bearer if it is indorsed in blank pursuant to §3-205(b).

So an instrument as it passes from hand to hand on its journey through life may, if certain conditions are met, be not merely transferred but also negotiated by one party to the next. As it is negotiated, it may change character from a bearer instrument to an order instrument or the other way around. All very interesting for a relatively simple piece of paper. And all worthy of study through the following examples and explanations.

EXAMPLES

1. Ms. Boss runs a small business with about a dozen employees. At the end of the year she decides to give each employee a bonus, and on the day before the Christmas holiday is to begin she writes up a set of checks. Included in this set is one payable "to the order of Louie Lacky," Lacky being one of her oldest and most trusted employees. She puts this check along with the others in a pile on the top of her desk.

    (a) As of this moment, has Boss issued the check?

    (b) Boss puts out the word around the shop that each of the employees should stop by her office before the end of the day "for a pleasant surprise." When one of them, Terry Toady, comes into Boss's office, he is given his bonus check and thanks Boss profusely. Toady happens to comment that Lacky is not at work that day but is home sick. In fact, Toady is planning on dropping by Lacky's home after work to see how his friend is doing. Boss hands to Toady the bonus check made out to Lacky, instructing Toady to give it to Lacky and commenting, "Maybe this will make him feel better." Toady takes this check out of Boss's office. As of this point, has the check been issued? Is Toady the holder of the check?

    (c) Suppose instead that Lacky has come into work that day. He comes into Boss's office, but before she has a chance to thank him for all the work he has done over the year and give him his bonus check, he launches into a tirade about how much he hates "this stinking job"

and also how little (to put it mildly) he thinks of Boss and her operation. Boss tells Lacky that if that's how he feels, he is fired on the
spot — then she storms out of the room. When Boss later returns to
her office, Lacky is gone. Also gone is the bonus check made out to
Lacky, which he must have spotted on the desk and taken with him
as he left. In this situation, is it correct to say that the check has been
issued? Is Lacky a holder as he walks out of the office and out of
Boss's place of business with the check in his pocket?

2. Able draws a check "to the order of Baker" which he hands over to Baker.
    (a) Is Baker the holder of the check?
    (b) Baker then gives the check to Charlene in exchange for a rare set of old
        law books that he has been craving, but he does not place his signature
        anywhere on the check. Is Charlene now the holder of the check? If
        not, what can Charlene do about the situation? See §3-203(c).

3. Dora draws a check "to the order of Ervin," which she gives to Ervin.
    Ervin signs the back of the check under the legend "Pay to Felice." Ervin
    puts the check in his pocket.
    (a) As of this moment, is Ervin the holder of the check? Is Felice?
    (b) Later in the day, Ervin runs into Felice and hands her the check. Is
        Felice now the holder of the check?
    (c) Would Felice's ability to negotiate this check later to another party
        have been diminished in any way had Ervin written not simply "Pay
        to Felice" over his signature but instead either "Pay only to Felice" or
        "Pay to Felice only upon her completion of certain construction work
        now being done for me under contract?" See §3-206(a) and (b).

4. Greg writes a check on his account for $400 payable to "Cash." He
    loses this check, which is found by one Hannah.
    (a) At this stage, is Hannah a holder?
    (b) This check is stolen from Hannah by Thad the thief. Was the trans-
        fer of the check in this way a negotiation from Hannah to Thad? Is
        Thad now the holder of the check?
    (c) Thad transfers this check to Isaac, of Isaac's Liquor Store, in return
        for $360 in cash. Is Isaac a holder?

5. Jason writes a check on his account for $300 payable "to the order of
    Katherine." He gives this check to Katherine. Before she can do anything
    with it, it is stolen from her by Thelma, another thief. Thelma then takes it
    to Isaac's Liquor Store, where she writes "Pay to Isaac" on the back of the
    check and signs "Katherine" underneath. She hands it over in return for
    $270 in cash. Is Isaac a holder of this instrument?

6. Leroy writes a check "to the order of Maria" and gives it to Maria.
    Maria signs her name on the back of the check. The next thing she knows,
    the check is missing. It has either been stolen or lost.
    (a) Is the thief or finder a holder of the check?

(b) What if Maria had signed her name on the back of the check under the legend "Pay to Natalie" before the check went missing? Would any thief or finder of this check be a holder?

7. Oscar writes a check "to the order of Patricia" and gives it to her. Patricia signs just her name on the back of the check and hands it over to Quincy. Quincy writes "Pay to Quincy" above Patricia's signature on the back of the check. What effect, if any, does this have on the status of the check? See §3-205(c).

8. Ralph signs a note (identified on the note as #SBT12345) for $10,000 payable "to the order of State Bank and Trust" on December 31, 2004. Soon after taking the note, an authorized representative of State Bank writes "Pay to Tremont Financial Services" on the note and signs below this legend on behalf of State Bank. She delivers the note to Tremont.

(a) Is Tremont now the holder of the note?

(b) Assume instead that the representative of State Bank delivered the note to Tremont together with a separate document, signed on behalf of the Bank, containing the statement, "State Bank and Trust hereby transfers and negotiates to Tremont Financial Services a note for $10,000 (#SBT12345) made by Ralph and stated to be payable to the order of State Bank and Trust on December 31, 2004." Would Tremont become a holder through this procedure? What if this document prepared by State Bank had been securely attached to the note itself, either at its bottom or on its reverse, by the use of a hefty application of glue?

9. Uma owes money to Victor Verdun for some work Victor did for her. Never terribly good at names, Uma makes out a check for the correct amount payable "to the order of Victor Verdone" and mails it to Victor at his correct address. Is Victor the holder of this check? When he goes to negotiate it to another, or to sign it for deposit in his bank account, how may or must he sign his name in order for it to be all nice and legal? See §3-204(d).

10. Walter writes a check "to the order of Xavier or Yolanda Zendel."

(a) Who will have to sign this check to make for a valid indorsement? See §3-110(d).

(b) What if the check had been made out "to the order of Xavier and Yolanda Zendel"?

(c) What if the check had been made out "to the order of Xavier Zendel/Yolanda Zendel"?

EXPLANATIONS

1a. No. Ms. Boss is here the drawer of the check and it is pretty clear that she has not "delivered" it to anyone for any purpose whatsoever. Under §3-105(a), the instrument has not been issued.

1b. Yes, the check has been issued. No, Toady is not a holder of the check. It is an order instrument payable to Lacky as the specified person, so although Toady is in possession of it he cannot be a holder. Of course, as of this moment Lacky is not the holder of the instrument either, because he is not in possession of it. As long as Toady retains the check, there is no holder of it. Still, this does not preclude our determining that the check has been issued by Boss. Subsection 3-105(a) defines *issuance* as including delivery (on which see O§1-201(14) or R§1-201(b)(15)) "to a holder or nonholder" as long as the delivery is carried out "for the purpose of giving rights on the instrument to any person." As of Boss's delivery to Toady, it's fair to say that Boss intended Lacky to have rights in the instrument — in particular the right to have it handed over to him by his friend Toady.

Perhaps a more typical example of an instrument being initially issued by deliverance into the hands of a nonholder is suggested by Comment 1 to §3-105. A remitter purchases a cashier's or teller's check payable to someone else from an issuing bank. The remitter would not be a holder any more than Toady is a holder of Lacky's bonus check, but we would still say the check has been issued when it has been sold and delivered to the remitter.

1c. No, the check was never issued because Boss never "delivered" it to anyone. Lacky, however, is by definition a holder of the check, as he has the check made out to his order in his possession. Where does that leave us? Well, notice in §3-105(b) the statement that "nonissuance is a defense." This means that if Lacky or anyone else to whom he has negotiated the check tried to present it for payment or were to bring an action against Boss when the presentment for payment did not succeed, Boss would have a defense based on the fact that the instrument was never issued in the first place. Would this defense on Boss's part succeed? The answer — as we will see when we get into Part Two of this volume and the important principles surrounding the central figure of what is termed the holder in due course — is that the defense will sometimes be good as against the claimant and sometimes not. Don't worry about this for the time being; just be sure you see why, in the situation as I have presented it here, we are bound to the conclusions that the instrument was never issued and yet Lacky is truly a holder of it.

2a. Yes. Baker is the holder of the check because he is in possession of an order instrument that is, as of the moment, payable to the order of him as the "identified [on the check itself] person."

2b. No. Charlene is not the holder. She is in possession of the instrument, but it is still an order instrument running to the order of Baker. And she's not Baker. The holder's signature on the instrument is no mere technicality, but absolutely essential for a proper negotiation of an order instrument; see *Town of Freeport v. Ring*, 1999 Me. 48, 727 A.2d 901, 38 U.C.C.2d 1225 (1999). As a matter of fact, although Charlene is not now a holder of the instrument, she will have the rights of a holder under what is referred to as the *shelter principle* of §3-203(b): "Transfer of an instrument, whether or not a negotiation, vests in the transferee [here Charlene] all and any right of the transferor [here Baker] to enforce the instrument. . . ." Therefore, because Baker was a holder and had the rights of a holder, Charlene here has acquired the *rights* of a holder, those rights which Baker her transferor had, even though the transfer to her was not a negotiation.

As a practical matter, it would be wise for Charlene to become the check's actual holder and not have to worry about relying on the shelter principle if she is planning to cash the check any time in the future. Under §3-203(c), because the check was transferred for value (remember those rare and presumably valuable old law books?), "the transferee has a specifically enforceable right to the unqualified indorsement of the transferor, but negotiation of the instrument does not occur until the indorsement is made." So Charlene is going to have to find a way of actually putting into practice this "specifically enforceable right" against Baker and getting his unqualified indorsement on the check. Then she can rest comfortably as a full-fledged holder of the instrument.

3a. As the check sits in Ervin's wallet, after his having specially indorsed it over to Felice, Ervin is no longer the holder of the check. He is in possession of it, but as it stands it is payable to the order of Felice, not him. Note, by the way, that the special indorsement under §3-205(a) required only that Ervin, as the then holder, sign below his identification of "a person [in this case Felice] to whom it [the act of specially indorsing] makes the instrument payable." Thus, it was enough that he wrote "Pay to Felice" above his signature. It was not necessary for him to use a special word of negotiability, as, for instance, by writing "Pay to the order of Felice" over his signature. Once the writing is created as a negotiable instrument by having met the criterion (among others) that it bear the crucial words of negotiability at the time of its origination, there is no need for the words to be used again in any subsequent negotiation, as long as the negotiation otherwise meets the requirements of §§3-201, 3-204, and 3-205.

But what about Felice? Is she the holder of the check now payable to her order as of this moment? Of course not. She is not in possession of it, and that is enough to defeat any argument that she is the holder.

3b. Yes. Once Felice comes into possession of the check — which we are assuming has been specially indorsed by the previous holder Ervin in the proper way — she becomes the holder of it.

3c. Any such attempt by Ervin to restrict what Felice is able to do with the check, and particularly to prevent her from freely negotiating it to another or presenting it for immediate payment, by this type of restrictive endorsement is ineffective. That's the clear message of the first two subsections of §3-206 and of Comment 2 to this section. The type of *restrictive indorsement* with which you are probably more familiar, where the holder writes

"For Deposit Only" on the check and identifies a particular account of his or hers into which the funds are to be credited, is dealt with in subsection (c) and Comment 3. We don't go into it here, because it requires some familiarity with the check collection system, which is a subject yet to come. Suffice it to say, however, that this type of restrictive indorsement does have the effect you would hope. The check can now not be effectively indorsed to any nonbank party, and the bank to which the check is first delivered in an attempt to get it paid must, in the words of the Comment, "act consistently with the indorsement."

4a.   Yes. The check is a bearer instrument and Hannah is in possession of it. That's enough to make her a holder.

4b.   Yes and yes. Because this is still bearer paper, the transfer from Hannah to Thad was a negotiation and Thad is now the holder of the check. Refer back to §3-201(a), which says that negotiation is "a transfer of possession, *whether voluntary or involuntary,* by a person other than the issuer to a person who thereby becomes a holder." Thad, however he came by the instrument, is in possession of it and, because it is in bearer form, is the holder of it. If you have any questions or qualms about this result, see the concluding part of Comment 1 to §3-201.

4c.   Yes, Isaac is a holder, and this would be true whether Thad just handed over the check to him (keeping it as bearer paper) or specially indorsed it with the words "Pay to Isaac" over Thad's signature (converting it to a piece of order paper payable to Isaac). In either case, as long as Isaac remains in possession, he remains the holder.

The principal lesson of this example is an important one: Even if the person in possession of an instrument happens to be so totally by accident (as with Hannah) or has stolen it (like the ignominious Thad) — or if the instrument has passed through the hands of a finder or thief somewhere up the line before it ends up in the hands of someone who gives true value for it (Isaac) — the possessor of the instrument can qualify as a holder for Article 3 purposes, *if* the paper was in bearer form when it was lost or stolen. (We will compare this result to what happens when a forgery is involved; see the next example.) Thad was never what we would want to call the rightful owner of the instrument. Nor was Hannah, for that matter, unless you want to call on some primitive notion of "finders-keepers." The check was rightfully the property of Greg from the start. But Greg has learned a simple truth about carrying around bearer paper: If you lose it or if it is stolen from you, you stand a good chance of never seeing it again. Furthermore, it may end up in the hands of a total innocent, such as Isaac, who will be able to cash the check and keep the money. Carrying around bearer paper is like carrying around cash. Don't carry more than you can afford to lose.

5.   No. Isaac does not qualify as a holder of the check. He could become a holder only if the check were negotiated to him by the previous holder.

When Thelma steals the check from Katherine, she does not become a holder, because she has stolen an instrument payable to Katherine. Thelma is in possession of the check, but the check is payable to "an identified person" and that person is someone other than her. Isaac, we will assume, is innocent and maybe nonnegligent, as he has no sure way of checking if the "Katherine" who indorsed on the back is who she purports to be (given that the kind of people inclined to steal checks are also not necessarily averse to getting their hands on some fake ID when the need arises). Notwithstanding his innocence, Isaac stands in possession of the check but is not its holder.

Contrast this result with what we saw in the previous example: When a thief makes off with an order instrument, he or she does not become its holder. If the thief tries to pass it on to someone else, he or she is necessarily going to have to forge the true owner's signature, and the person who takes thereby does not become a holder. Once a negotiable instrument bears a forged indorsement of someone to whose order the instrument had been specifically made payable (either because it was initially issued as an order instrument or had later been specially endorsed), no one who subsequently gains possession of the instrument can ever qualify as a holder.

6a. Maria, by placing her signature and nothing else on the back of the check, has converted it into a check payable to bearer. When it is either lost or stolen, the finder or the thief comes into possession of bearer paper and hence becomes its holder. What words of advice would you have for Maria?

6b. By specially indorsing the check over to Natalie as she has, Maria has converted it into an order instrument payable to the order of Natalie and Natalie only. Maria, by so doing, is no longer herself a holder, even though she is in possession, but at least when the check goes missing she can be sure that the thief or finder could not be a holder either. (That is, of course, unless the thief or finder just happens to be the Natalie in question.)

7.   Patricia has indorsed in blank before handing the check over to Quincy, so Quincy becomes the holder of a bearer item. Quincy, who may have been talking to our friend Greg of Example 4, does not like the idea of carrying around a bearer item that could be lost or stolen. His actions, under the rule of §3-205(c), convert Patricia's blank indorsement into a special indorsement identifying him, Quincy, as the person to whom the instrument is now payable. Quincy is now in possession of an order instrument running to his order. He is still its holder, but now it is in order form and he can rest more comfortably knowing that should it ever slip out of his possession, the person who "finds" it would have to forge Quincy's signature to do anything with it, and neither that person nor anyone who took from that person could become a holder of this particular check.

8a. Yes. This is just a reminder that notes can be — and in fact must be — indorsed and negotiated according to the same rules we have been applying in the earlier examples to checks. By State Bank's special indorsement of the note to Tremont and its delivery to that firm, Tremont becomes the holder of the note.

8b. If the indorsement was written up and signed on a completely separate piece of paper that was not attached to the note in any way, it would not be effective. Note in the first sentence of §3-204(a) the requirement that an indorsement be a signature made "on an instrument."

If this separate document containing the authorized signature of State Bank had been glued to the note itself, then it would be effective as an indorsement and the transfer to Tremont would be a proper negotiation. Note the last sentence in §3-204(a): "For the purpose of determining whether a signature is made on an instrument, a paper affixed to the instrument is a part of the instrument." A piece of paper so affixed to a negotiable instrument as to become "a part of" it, and hence worthy of bearing indorsements, is referred to historically and to the present day as an *allonge* (apparently from the French for "extension" or "to elongate"). See the last short paragraph of Comment 1 to §3-204.

9. Victor is the holder of the instrument. Recall the rule of §3-110(a) that the person to whom an instrument, in this case the check, is initially payable is determined by the intent of the issuer. The second sentence of that section explicitly states, "The instrument is payable to the person intended by the signer even if that person is identified in the instrument by a name or other identification that is not that of the intended person." There is no question here that Uma intended Victor to be the payee of the check, so it is initially created as a check payable to his order. Being in possession of it, Victor is the holder of the check. As to how Victor should sign the back of the check properly to indorse, see §3-204(d). His indorsement may be made "in the name stated in the instrument or in the holder's name or both, but signature in both names may be required by a person paying or taking the instrument for value or collection." So he can sign as Victor Verdun or Victor Verdone or both. In some instances, he may be asked and will be required to sign as both, which he should have no qualms about doing. This situation is covered in Comment 3 to §3-204.

10a. Under §3-110(d), because the check is payable to the two Zendels in the alternative, it is payable to either of them individually and may be negotiated by either without the signature of the other.

10b. When the check is written in this way, it is payable to them "not alternatively" and hence is payable to both of them. An effective negotiation would require the signatures of both.

10c. Checks or other negotiable instruments that name the payees in this fashion or something similar had, prior to the effectiveness of the 1990 Revisions to Article 3, caused some problem for the courts. Should this check be treated like that in subpart (a) or subpart (b) of this Explanation?

The court in *Danco, Inc. v. Commerce Bank/Shore, N.A.*, 675 A.2d 663, 29 U.C.C.2d 513 (N.J. App. Div. 1996), for example, concluded that what is called a *virgule* ("/") was equivalent to the word "or" when placed between two names and unambiguously indicated that signature in the alternative was called for. The court did go on to suggest that it would have reached the same result even if the use of the virgule had been "deemed to have resulted in ambiguity." Note that new §3-110(d) now contains an express rule as to the result when the multiple payees of an instrument are named in such a way that it is "ambiguous as to whether it is payable to the persons alternatively." The result is that the ambiguity is resolved in favor of the named persons alternatively. So either Xavier or Yolanda may negotiate this check by his or her signature alone. See Comment 4.

What if, instead, the check had been made payable to "Xavier Zendel – Yolanda Zendel," with their names being separated by a hyphen? At least one case held that this would require the signature of only one of the Zendels, not both — but it took a trip to the supreme court of the state to get to this result. In *J.R. Simplot, Inc. v. Knight*, 139 Wash. 2d 534, 988 P.2d 955, 40 U.C.C.2d 57 (1999), the trial court had concluded that a hyphen between two payees' names created an ambiguous situation, and that therefore the check could be cashed with the signature of only one. The court of appeals reversed, stating that,

> [a] hyphen is an indicator that words are to be read as a compound or together. Unlike the virgule which separates, a hyphen joins. We hold that a hyphen between the names of two payees on a check unambiguously means "and" so that the check is payable to all of them and may be negotiated only by all of them.

The Supreme Court of Washington granted a petition for review and reversed the court of appeals, reinstating the trial court's determination. Following a lengthy section of its opinion entitled "Interpreting the Hyphen," the Supreme Court of Washington came to the conclusion that "the use of a hyphen to separate multiple payees on a negotiable instrument is patently ambiguous"; this being so, the check was, under the rule of §3-110(d), payable in the alternative.

In a number of recent cases, courts have had to decide who could effectively indorse an instrument on which a set of dual or multiple payees were listed with *no* grammatical connectors whatsoever separating their names, the situation of so-called stacked payees. The payees may be stacked either vertically, as in:

> Pay to the order of:
> Xavier Zendel
> Yolanda Zendel

Or horizontally:

> Pay to the order of Xavier Zendel Yolanda Zendel.

The cases have pretty uniformly concluded that such an instrument is ambiguous under §3-110(d) and as a result they could effectively be indorsed by any one of the named payees individually. See, for example, *Harder v. First Capital Bank*, 332 Ill.App.3d 740, 775 N.E.2d 610, 48 U.C.C.2d 1069 (2002), or *The Hyatt Corp. v. Palm Beach Nat. Bank*, 840 So.2d 300, 49 U.C.C.2d 1039 (Fla. App. 2003).

In the world of negotiable instruments, as you are no doubt coming to appreciate, little things (or the absence thereof) mean a lot.

3

Liability on the Negotiable Instrument

Introduction

At the core of any negotiable instrument lies a promise or order to pay a sum of money. In the great majority of cases, the promise made by the maker of a note is kept, or the order to a draft's drawee is followed, as a matter of course. The person entitled to payment on the instrument gets that payment and is thereby satisfied, just as we would hope and expect to be true. The note or draft has served its purpose, and that's the end of that.

There are instances, however, when not everything goes so smoothly. For one reason or another, rightly or wrongly, the maker of the note does not keep the promise he or she has signed, or the drawee of the draft does not accept and pay as he or she has been commanded. In such cases someone is left holding the instrument, literally, and left holding the bag, figuratively, when the money expected is not forthcoming. What is this person to do? It will not surprise you to discover that Article 3 sets out, in some detail, the ways in which the party with the right to payment under the instrument, but who has been frustrated in getting that payment as due, may enforce his or her rights to get the amount owed. Enforcement may in some circumstances end up calling for suit by the aggrieved party. Other times a satisfactory result can be achieved just by calling to the attention of the relevant obligor his or her responsibility as set out by the U.C.C. In this chapter we are concerned not with the procedural niceties of any potential suit but with the underlying rules of liability. To whom does the obligation represented by the negotiable instrument run, and what party or parties must meet that obligation? As we will see, the present version of Article 3 is written in terms of "the obligation" on the instrument of any person who has become, in one role or another, a party to the instrument. Traditional usage invokes the same notion when we speak of a party's "contract liability" on the instrument itself.

The Person Entitled to Enforce

The first question to address is to whom is this obligation or contractual liability — liability on the instrument — owed? For that we look at §3-301 and its delineation of just who is a *person entitled to enforce* an instrument. For most situations it is enough to look at part (i) of the definition and use as a working rule the idea that the person entitled to enforce at any given moment is the holder of the instrument at that moment. The slight expansion of this term in subparts (ii) and (iii) to cover some possible, if uncommon, situations need not detain us here. One thing seems clear: At the very minimum a person seeking to enforce an instrument must have actual physical possession of it and be able to produce it in court. See *In re Sheskey*, 263 Bankr. 264, 46 U.C.C.2d 475 (N.D.Iowa 2001).

It is therefore very much worth pausing to reflect on the dilemma of a person seeking to enforce who would in all rights be the holder of the instrument but for the fact that the instrument has been lost, destroyed, or stolen. Can a person who has been deprived of physical possession of an instrument by such misfortune simply assert the facts of the loss as he or she knows them to be and then proceed to enforce the instrument as if the piece of paper itself were still on hand? Far from it. Read §3-309(a). The unfortunate soul who has lost an instrument, seen it destroyed, or from whom it has been stolen must satisfy a set of fairly strict criteria before he or she can go forward with enforcement of the instrument. Beyond that, as you read in §3-309(b), he or she will have to *prove* "the terms of the instrument and [his or her] right to enforce" to a court before being allowed to proceed. A court entering a judgment under this section in favor of a party seeking to enforce an instrument, who does not have physical possession of it but can meet the requirements of §3-309(a), may not enter judgment allowing the suit to proceed unless the court "finds that the person required to pay the instrument is adequately protected against loss that may occur by reason of a claim by another person to enforce the instrument."

Return now to §3-301 and read its last sentence:

A person may be a person entitled to enforce the instrument even though the person is not the owner of the instrument or is in wrongful possession of the instrument.

In a variety of situations we will encounter in later chapters, we will have to remind ourselves of this distinction and come to terms with its consequences. The person entitled to enforce under the definition of §3-301 is most typically a holder, and whether or not someone qualifies as a holder is, as we saw in Chapter 2, a matter requiring careful evaluation of his or her position under the definition of *holder* in O§1-201(20) or R§1-201(b)(21) and the rules of negotiation set forth in Article 3. In a given situation, a person may be a holder even if he or she is not the true owner of the instrument or in rightful possession; for example, if he or she is a thief of bearer paper or has taken from such a thief. At the same time, a person who should rightfully be considered the owner of the instrument but is not the holder of it, because he or she is not in possession or an indorsement critical to a negotiation is missing, will not be a person entitled to enforce.

Enforcement Against Whom?

Once we have established that a given person qualifies as a person entitled to enforce a particular instrument, *against whom* may he or she enforce it? What requirements must he or she satisfy to set out a valid prima facie case for enforcement against the party in question?* The first point to be made in addressing this issue is the prime directive laid out in §3-401(a):

> A person is not liable on an instrument unless (i) the person signed the instrument, or (ii) the person is represented by an agent who signed the instrument and the signature is binding on the represented person under §3-402.

We will deal with the problems pertaining to signature through a representative agent in Chapter 4. For the moment, the all-important point is that no person (natural or corporate) can be held to obligation on an instrument unless that person's signature appears on the instrument itself. The signature can be made by the person himself or herself, or through an authorized agent, but it must be physically present on the piece of paper. As Comment 1 to §3-401 states, "Obligation on an instrument depends on a signature that is binding on the obligor." Obligation of the type we are concerned with here is in the nature of contractual obligation of the most classic sort, and a party cannot and will not be bound to such contractual obligation unless and until that party has

---

* Our concern in this chapter is how and when a prima facie case of liability on the instrument is established. As you may imagine, even when all the elements of a prima facie case are present, the defendant may under certain circumstances assert affirmative defenses that, if effective, will relieve it from obligation on the instrument. We deal with the types of defenses available to a party who is being charged to meet its obligation on the instrument — and when and whether such defenses will be valid under the particular circumstances of the case — in Chapters 8 and 9. For the moment, we are interested only in the basic criteria of the prima facie case for obligation on the instrument.

exhibited his or her assent to be bound. In the law of negotiable instruments, such assent is manifested in one and only one way: by the party's placing of his or her signature on the instrument itself. On the nature of the signature required for these purposes, see §3-401(b) and Comment 2.

Once it is established that a party may be obligated on an instrument, because his, her, or its signature appears thereon, the key to all that follows is to recognize that the U.C.C. authority for any such obligation (and the place we look to determine the extent of, any exceptions to, or preconditions on such obligation) depends upon the role in which that party affixed its signature to the instrument in question. Any signature appearing on an instrument must of necessity be the signature of either a maker of a note, a drawer or an acceptor of a draft, or an indorser of either type of instrument. There are simply no other alternatives. Furthermore, the obligation of the signatory depends upon the capacity in which the signature was made.

The one character in this list whom we haven't met before is the *acceptor* of a draft. Look at §3-409(a):

> "Acceptance" means the drawee's signed agreement to pay a draft as presented. It must be written on the draft and may consist of the drawee's signature alone. Acceptance may be made at any time and becomes effective when notification pursuant to instructions is given or the accepted draft is delivered for the purpose of giving rights on the acceptance to any person.

We have already seen that the creation and issuance of a draft does not require the cooperation or even the knowledge of the drawee of that draft. As we will see in this chapter, the drawee has no liability on the instrument simply because he or she is named thereon as drawee. If, however, the draft is presented to the drawee who then accepts the draft, the drawee will by that act become the acceptor of the draft and will have committed himself, herself, or itself to liability on the draft. As to what constitutes *presentment*, look at subsection (a) of §3-501.

You should now take an introductory look at the following sections, which set out the rules in each of the possible situations:

Section 3-412: Obligation of Issuer [Maker] of a Note or [Drawer of a] Cashier's Check

Section 3-413: Obligation of Acceptor [of a Draft]

Section 3-414: Obligation of Drawer [of a Draft]

Section 3-415: Obligation of Indorser

In each of the following examples, the first order of business will be to determine the capacity in which the party whose obligation or lack thereof is being questioned signed the instrument. That should lead you to the correct U.C.C. section of those set forth in the preceding list and to the explanation you are seeking.

EXAMPLES

1. Andrea borrows $5,000 from Bart in 2001. In return for the loan she gives Bart a note promising to pay "to the order of Bart" on June 1, 2004, the amount of $5,600. When June of 2004 comes around, Bart still has the note in his possession. He has not, however, been paid any money by Andrea.

   (a) Does Article 3 create a legal obligation to Bart on Andrea's part? For how much?

   (b) Suppose instead that sometime in 2003 Bart negotiated the note over to Carol in exchange for, say, $5,300 in cash. It is now June 2004 and Carol remains in possession of the note. To whom, if anyone, does Andrea owe an obligation on the note, given these facts?

2. Professor Brook owes Sarah Student $1,000 for work she did in helping him to prepare the manuscript of a book he has written. Brook tells Sarah that he does not have the cash at the moment to pay her, but that he has arranged for her to get the money the next month from one Arnold Moneybucks, a prominent (and wealthy) local businessperson. On January 12, Brook prepares and signs a draft ordering Moneybucks to "pay to the order of Sarah student $1,000 on February 15, 2004." He hands this draft over to Sarah.

   (a) Would it be proper to say that as of January 12 Moneybucks is the acceptor of the instrument?

   (b) On January 13, Sarah heads over to the offices of Arnold Moneybucks in the impressive Moneybucks Tower building. With persistence, she is able to make her way into the office suite of Mr. Moneybucks himself. She tells the secretary guarding the door, "I come bearing an order from Professor Brook." The secretary understandably looks puzzled, but upon speaking with Moneybucks on the intercom, is told to usher Sarah directly into the great man's office. Sarah hands the writing over to Moneybucks. He examines it and then says, "If Brook wants me to pay you $1,000 on February 15, that is certainly what I'll do. We go back a long way and I owe him a lot. Any order from him like this is one I'm more than willing to follow." Moneybucks signs his name to the writing and hands it back to Sarah, telling her to come back on February 15 for her money. As of this point, would it be correct to characterize Moneybucks as the acceptor of the instrument? What would your answer be if Moneybucks showed every willingness to follow the order and committed himself orally to do so, but never actually signed the paper?

   (c) Suppose instead that, even though Sarah is able to make her way into Moneybucks's inner sanctum and present him with the writing, his reaction is quite different. He bellows, "Who the heck is this James Brook, and why does he think he can order me to do anything, much less pay out some of my hard-earned money? This is all very amusing, but take your silly piece of paper and get out of here!" He hands the writing back to Sarah, who quickly leaves the office and the Moneybucks Tower. How would you characterize the situation as of this point?

3. Professor Brook owes one of his research assistants, Stewart Student, the sum of $1,000. Stewart agrees to take payment by a personal check for this amount, which Brook draws payable "to the order of Stewart Student" on Brook's checking account at the First National Bank in Brook's hometown. Stewart decides that the quickest way to get his money is to go directly to the branch of First National Bank where Brook has his account. He hands the check to a teller and demands that he be given $1,000. The teller looks the check over, makes some inquiries of the bank's computerized accounting system, and then hands the check back to Stewart, telling him, "Sorry, I can't cash this for you."

    (a) Can Stewart make the argument that the bank is under a legal obligation to him for its refusal to take the check and exchange it for cash? See §3-408.

    (b) Stewart still has the check but not the cash. To whom do you suggest he look for legal satisfaction, citing which section of Article 3?

4. Seymour Sellers agrees to sell a quantity of high-quality widgets to Bertha Byers, who uses such widgets in her manufacturing operations, for the price of $12,000. On March 1 Sellers delivers the widgets to Byers. He does not ask for cash payment immediately, but does ask Byers to sign a draft that Sellers has drawn up. The operative language of the draft states that Sellers orders Byers to pay "to the order of Seymour Sellers" the amount of $12,000 "sixty days from sight" of the draft. In exchange for getting her hands on the much-needed widgets, Byers signs the draft.

    (a) By signing as she does, has Byers taken on any obligation on the instrument? To whom does the obligation run? What is the extent of the obligation?

    (b) Assume that soon after getting Byers's signature on this draft, Sellers sells the draft to the firm of Friendly Factors. He does so by negotiating the draft over to Friendly Factors in exchange for $11,300 cash in hand. To whom does Byers's obligation now run? If by the end of the 60-day period Byers has not paid the $12,000 to Friendly Factors, does that firm have a cause of action against Byers?

5. Let us return to the situation presented in Example 1b. In 2001 Andrea delivers to Bart a note promising to pay "to the order of Bart" on June 1, 2004, the amount of $5,600. In 2003 Bart negotiates this note over to Carol in exchange for $5,300. It is now June 2004. Carol remains in possession of the note and has not received any payment on it.

    (a) Would Carol be within her rights immediately to sue Bart, as an indorser of the instrument for the amount due?

(b) Suppose that Carol does first make a presentment for payment to Andrea for the amount due, but that Andrea is unable or unwilling to meet her obligation as set forth in the note. She refuses to pay. Carol immediately notifies Bart of what has happened. Would Carol now be within her rights to hold Bart responsible for paying the amount due on the note?

(c) Suppose that Carol had not immediately informed Bart of Andrea's failure to pay on the instrument when called upon to do so, but had instead waited something like two months to let Bart know what had happened. Would your answer to the previous question be any different?

(d) If Bart is legally obligated to Carol for the amount due on the note and is made to pay up, is there anyone against whom Bart may then proceed to recover what he has been forced to pay Carol?

6.   Richard writes a check payable to "Cash" and delivers it to Stella. Stella deposits this check into her own checking account with the Depot National Bank. When doing so, the teller insists that Stella sign the back of the check with her own name. Under her banking agreement with Depot, and because she is such a good customer, the bank allows Stella immediately to withdraw the amount of money represented by the check. The check itself is then forwarded to Richard's bank for collection, but is returned to the Depot Bank unpaid, as Richard does not have enough money in his own checking account to cover the check. Depot Bank notifies Stella immediately that the check has been returned.

(a) Is Stella obligated to Depot for the amount of the check under her contract of indorsement?

(b) Would your answer be any different if the bank had waited three days to inform Stella that this check had been returned dishonored by Richard's bank?

7.   In return for some work done for him, Damon draws a check payable to Fred First and delivers it to First. First negotiates the check over to Suzanne Second in exchange for cash. Second then takes the check to the Third Avenue Liquor Store where she in turn cashes it, negotiating it over to the store. The store deposits the check in its account with Depot National Bank. When the check is sent to Damon's bank for collection, it is returned to Depot unpaid because Damon does not have enough in his account with his bank to cover the check. Depot immediately notifies the liquor store of the bounced check and physically returns it to the store. Third Avenue Liquor is now in possession of a bounced check and is out the money that it gave to Second.

(a) Against whom does the store have a right of action on the check to obtain relief?

(b) Assume that Third Avenue is able to find Second and get her to pay the amount of the check. Third Avenue then surrenders the check back to Second. Against whom may *she* then proceed to make herself whole?

(c) Would it make any difference to your analysis if any of the indorsers (First, Second, or the Third Avenue Liquor Store) had added the words "without recourse" to his, her, or its signature at the time of indorsement?

(d) What if Damon, the drawer of the check, had added the words "without recourse" to his signature at the time he initially issued the check? See §3-414(e).

8.   Garson draws a check payable to Harry and delivers it to him on February 1. On February 2, Harry indorses the check over to Isadora. Isadora puts the check on a pile of papers accumulating on her desk and does not get around to depositing it in her checking account until March 30. The check is returned unpaid to her bank, which immediately returns the check to Isadora along with a notice that the amount represented by the check has not been added to her account balance. Does Isadora have the right to go against Harry on his contract of indorsement? See §3-415(e).

9.   Bertha Byers is in need of a particular type of widget connector, which is a critical component of her manufacturing operation. She finds a firm, Critical Connections, that is willing to deliver her the parts in question, but on a "cash only" basis. This means that the seller will hand over the merchandise only in exchange for cash or its equivalent. Byers draws a check, for the purchase price called for in the sales contract, payable to Critical Connections, on the checking account she has with Commerce Bank and Trust. She then takes the check to that bank, where she has it certified. She turns this check over to Critical Connections in exchange for the widget connectors. If for some reason this certified check is not paid when presented to Commerce Bank and Trust, does Critical Connections have the right to sue Byers as drawer of the dishonored instrument? See §3-414(c).

EXPLANATIONS

1a. Andrea's obligation to pay the amount due on the note, $5,600, is found in §3-412, which reads in relevant part, "The issuer of a note . . . is obliged to pay the instrument (i) according to its terms at the time it was issued." This a perfectly straightforward example of the primary obligation of the maker of a note — who has, after all, signed a promise to pay a certain amount of money on specified terms — to keep that promise. Notice, as the final sentence to this section makes absolutely clear, that this obligation "is owed to a person entitled to enforce the instrument." Bart is the current holder of the note, and hence under §3-301 a person entitled to enforce it.

As you see when you read through the full text of §3-412, the drafters included language to deal with those instances when a note somehow comes into the hands of a holder even if it was never technically issued, as that term is defined in §3-105, or when the note was initially issued as a so-called incomplete instrument under §3-115. Neither of these more unusual circumstances is before us at present, so there is no need to look further at the precise way in which the section deals with them. It is worth remembering, however, that §3-412 gives clear guidance on the question of a maker's obligation on an unissued instrument or an instrument initially issued but as an incomplete instrument. For the moment, we are dealing with the most common case. The maker of a note has not kept the promise embodied in the note. Section 3-412 is clear and to the point: The maker has an obligation to keep the promise.

1b. Again there is nothing tricky or ambiguous about the question. Andrea owes the obligation to pay the instrument according to its terms — that is, to pay $5,600 on June 1, 2004 — only now the person to whom this obligation runs is not Bart (who is no longer the holder of the note and hence not a person entitled to enforce) but instead the current holder, Carol.

2a. No. As of January 12, Moneybucks is the drawee named on the draft, but he has not accepted it.

2b. Once Moneybucks, for whatever reason, signs his name to the instrument, he has accepted, and as of the moment he hands the draft back to Sarah he is the acceptor of this particular draft. What Sarah has done in her determined way is to present the draft to Moneybucks. In this case, because the money is not yet due, this would be referred to as *presentment for acceptance*, as opposed to a presentment for immediate payment. Moneybucks has responded to the presentment by signing his name to the draft, which is all that is required for an acceptance under the second sentence of §3-409(a). Having accepted as of January 13, Moneybucks is now obligated to carry out the order conveyed to him by Brook through the means of the draft. Sarah will have to return to Moneybucks Tower on or after February 15 with the draft and present it once again to Mr. Moneybucks himself, this time making a *presentment for payment* under the language of subpart (i) of §3-501(a). Moneybucks will then be obligated to pay the draft according to its terms under §3-413(a), and Sarah will finally have her money. Notice that Moneybucks will be legally responsible for paying this amount, but not because of Brook's writing out a draft with Moneybucks's name as drawee. The drawer by his or her will alone cannot obligate the drawee to do anything. In this scenario, Moneybucks becomes obliged to pay the stated amount on February 15 because *he* willingly took on this obligation by his voluntary act of accepting on January 13. It is the drawee's acceptance, if acceptance there be, that obligates him on the draft, not the creation of the draft itself or his being named therein as drawee.

If Moneybucks did indicate to Sarah his willingness to follow the order put before him but never signed the paper, he would not have accepted (see again the definition of *acceptance* in §3-409) and would not be committed in any way to do anything for Sarah, now or in the future.

2c. The situation is very easy to characterize, if not one about which Sarah will necessarily feel very happy. Moneybucks has been presented with the draft but has refused to accept it. There is nothing Sarah can do, legally or practically, to make him accept. She sensibly leaves the building, knowing there's no more she can do there, with an unaccepted draft drawn by Brook still in her possession. The question for Sarah then becomes what she can do now, other than curse the day she agreed to work for Brook or to accept payment in this strange fashion. She still has the right to the money, but she's going to have to get it from someone other than Moneybucks. She will have to go against Brook himself. Note that he will be liable as the drawer on an unaccepted draft under §3-414(b). As we will see in Chapter 6, Sarah could also decide to ignore the draft entirely and sue Brook directly on the contract for services that she initially entered into with him.

3a. First National has been presented, as drawee, with a demand draft and has made the decision not to accept (or, as we tend to say in the banking context, not honor) the check. The reality is that in the vast majority of cases the standard personal check (especially one written by Professor Brook) is honored as a matter of course. The money flows to the person entitled to enforce the instrument, either directly, as cash paid over the counter; or by an addition to his or her own checking account into which the check has been deposited once the check has cleared. There are instances, of course, even if their number be relatively small, when a check is dishonored. The drawee bank decides, for one reason or another, not to honor the check, but to return it dishonored.

The question here is whether Stewart has any rights *against First National* for its dishonor of the check, and the answer is clearly no. As §3-408 makes clear:

> A check or other draft does not of itself operate as an assignment of funds in the hands of the drawee available for its payment, and the drawee is not liable on the instrument until the drawee accepts it.

First National has, for whatever reason, refused to accept the check. Its signature appears nowhere on the check. First National cannot and does not have any obligation on the instrument itself as a drawee who refuses to accept. Stewart has no way of enforcing the instrument against First National. He has no rights against that bank whatsoever. The holder of a draft presents the draft to the drawee (in this case First National) in the hope and expectation that the drawee will accept and then pay the draft as it has been ordered to do, but the holder has no right to *insist* that the drawee accept. And if it hasn't accepted it can't be made to pay.

Two recent cases, which you might want to take a look at, serve as powerful reminders (at least they should have to the losing parties) of the importance of this result. *Outdoor Technologies, Inc. v. Allfirst Financial, Inc.*, 44 U.C.C.2d 801 (Del. Sup. Ct. 2001), reads in the words of one of the judges who had to deal with it "like a payment systems hypothetical written by a law school professor." Like at least some law school hypotheticals, however, the answer turns out to be perfectly straightforward: "Article 3," the court notes, "does not provide a basis for relief when the drawee bank has not accepted the negotiable instrument." In *Harrington v. MacNab*, 163 F.Supp. 2d 583, 45 U.C.C. 2d 697 (D. Md. 2001), the one to learn this lesson was someone whom the court described as "an experienced real estate attorney" who found himself "bamboozled" by a couple of real estate buyers who convinced him to take a personal check that later bounced instead of the conventional certified check as part of a real estate closing. The plaintiff's argument that the drawee bank had in effect orally accepted the check in the course of a phone call made during the course of the closing was to no avail. "Acceptance requires," the court reminded him, "as it has since Lord Mansfield's day, the formality of the drawee's signature on the check."

You may naturally wonder why a bank, such as First National in our hypothetical, would decide to dishonor a check written on an account held at the bank. There are, as you may expect, plenty of perfectly good reasons why it might do so: Brook may no longer have an active account at the bank; he may not have enough in his account to cover the check; or by the time Stewart makes it to the bank, Brook may have issued a stop-payment order on the check. Note that even if the bank has made a mistake in dishonoring this particular check written by Brook on his account with First National — if it dishonored the check when it had no legitimate reason to do so — its failure (what we will end up discussing in Chapter 13 as *wrongful dishonor* by the bank) is a wrong against Brook as the bank's customer, not against Stewart as a holder of the check. Brook has entered into a contract with the bank (much more about which in Part Four of this volume) under which the bank has agreed to honor his checks unless certain defined reasons not to do so are present. A bank's wrongful dishonor of a check written by its customer (that is, its failure to abide by the terms of the agreement it entered into when the customer opened the account) can create a cause of action *for the customer* against the bank. All of this creates no rights for the holder of the check, in our case Stewart, however. For whatever reason, rightly or wrongly, the bank has decided not to honor the check and there is nothing Stewart can do about it vis-à-vis the bank. He is going to have to look elsewhere for relief.

3b. This is where §3-414(b) swings into play. The check has been dishonored. Therefore, under this subsection, "[t]he drawer [Brook] is obliged to pay the draft . . . according to its terms at the time it was issued." This obligation is owed to "a person entitled to enforce the draft," which definitely means Stewart in our case. So, given that the check has been duly presented to the drawee bank and has been dishonored, Stewart now is in the position of demanding that Brook as drawer pay on the instrument itself. He also has the option, as did Sarah in the final part of Example 2, of bringing suit against Brook, not on the instrument but on the underlying contract for services into which he and the good professor had at one time entered.

4a. This example is meant to give you a look at a typical use of the noncheck draft in the commercial context, one that you are frankly much more likely to encounter in the real world than the situation we examined in Example 2. By signing the draft addressed to her as drawee by Sellers as drawer, Byers has become an acceptor of the draft. Byers is now obligated, not merely on the contract to pay for the widgets, but also on the draft that Sellers has made her sign, to pay Sellers $12,000 within 60 days of the date on which Byers accepted the draft by her signing of it.

4b. After the sale and negotiation of the accepted draft over to Friendly Factors, that firm becomes the holder of the instrument and hence a person entitled to enforce it. So Byers's obligation under §3-413 runs from that point forward to Friendly Factors. If the amount due on the accepted draft is not paid as and when due, Friendly Factors can invoke this section in bringing a suit against Byers for her failure to meet her Article 3 obligation to act as an acceptor is supposed to act — that is, to follow the order which, by accepting, she has committed herself to obey.

5a. The obligation of an indorser to pay on an instrument is governed by §3-415. Carol does not have the right immediately to sue for payment from Bart as an indorser. At least two things have to be checked out. For one, the indorser's obligation under subsection (a) is predicated on the instrument's having been dishonored. Has this note been dishonored merely because the date for payment has passed and Andrea has not made payment? Look at §3-502(a), comparing parts (2) and (3). The answer would depend on whether the note in question "requires presentment." If presentment is required, then Carol would first have to formally present the note to Andrea and demand payment. Only if payment is then not forthcoming would Carol be able to proceed against Bart as indorser. As Comment 2 to §3-502 points out, in most cases the note will be written so as to waive any requirement of formal presentment or demand for payment upon the maker. "If payment is not made when due, the holder usually makes a demand for payment, but in the normal case in which presentment is waived, demand is irrelevant and the holder can proceed against indorsers when payment is not received." Still Carol, who after all has the note in her possession, will want to inspect its language carefully to determine whether the terms of the particular note in question require presentment to establish a dishonor under §3-502(a)(2).

Even if no formal presentment to Andrea is required of Carol, however, this does not mean she may proceed directly against Bart as indorser without question. Bart's obligation under §3-415(a) is specifically made subject to a series of other subsections, of which (c) is of present concern:

> If notice of dishonor of an instrument is required by Section 3-503 and notice of dishonor complying with that section is not given to an indorser, the liability of the indorser under subsection (a) is discharged.

Needless to say, we now want to look at §3-503. Subsection (a) states that:

> The obligation of an indorser stated in Section 3-415(a) . . . may not be enforced unless (i) the indorser . . . is given notice of dishonor of

the instrument complying with this section, or (ii) notice of dishonor is excused under Section 3-504(b).

You can look at §3-504(b) to find out about the unusual instances in which notice of dishonor is excused. If not excused, then it will be necessary for Carol to give notice to Bart of Andrea's dishonor. The manner of giving such notice is laid out in §3-503(b). As you can see, notice of dishonor will be deemed effective if given by any person and "by any commercially reasonable means." It need not even necessarily be in writing. As to the amount of time the holder of a dishonored instrument has to give an indorser of the instrument notice of the dishonor, so as not to jeopardize the case for holding the indorser liable on the instrument, see subsection (c), which we will apply in the next two parts of this example.

5b. Carol has made a presentment for payment to the maker of the note, whether or not that presentment was technically called for by the provisions of the Code. The maker has dishonored. Carol's right to hold Bart liable as an indorser is, under §3-415(c), subject to her complying with her responsibility to give effective notice of dishonor to Bart under §3-503. We can assume that the manner of notice complies with the criteria of §3-503(b). Was the notice timely under §3-503(c)? The first lengthy sentence of this subsection applies only to instruments "taken for collection by a collecting bank," which is not the case here. The Andrea, Bart, and Carol situation is governed by the final, shorter sentence of (c): "With respect to any other instrument, notice of dishonor must be given within 30 days following the day on which the dishonor occurs." Given that we are told in this part of the example that Carol immediately notified Bart, Carol has apparently met all of the preconditions for holding Bart "obliged to pay the amount due on the instrument . . . according to the terms of the instrument at the time it was indorsed," under §3-415.

5c. If Carol waits two months to give Bart notice of dishonor, then under the last sentence of §3-503(c) she has failed to give timely notice. Thus, unless the late notice of dishonor can for some reason be excused under §3-504(b), the notice is ineffective, and under §§3-415(c) and 3-503(a) Carol would not be able to enforce any obligation against Bart as an indorser of the note.

5d. Bart may sue Andrea as the maker of the note, who still has not paid what she promised to. Look again at §3-412, the section in which we found the responsibility of the maker of a note to meet the obligation undertaken by the making of the note. "The obligation," the last sentence of this section reads, "is owed to a person entitled to enforce the instrument *or* to an indorser who paid the instrument under §3-415." This last phrase covers Bart's case if he is made to pay Carol on the contract of indorsement. It gives him the right to sue Andrea on the contract of the maker.

6a. Yes. When Stella signed the back of the check, her signature was an indorsement. Look again at §3-204(a). You see that *indorsement* means any signature on an instrument other than that of a maker, drawer, or acceptor (none of which Stella is) that, alone or accompanied by other words, is made for the purpose, among others, of "(iii) incurring indorser's liability on the instrument." Because what Stella was depositing was a bearer instrument, her signature was not necessary for a valid negotiation of the check over to the bank, but the bank asked for her signature anyway, and now you can appreciate why. Here Depot National Bank insisted on this indorsement, not just because it likes to collect signatures of those with whom it deals, but because the indorsement allows the bank to enforce the contract of indorsement against Stella should events take an unfortunate turn and such enforcement become necessary to protect the bank's interests. Remember, had her signature not been placed on the check itself, Stella would never have incurred any contractual obligation under the instrument.

As an indorser, and again looking to §3-415(a), Stella is obligated to pay the amount of the instrument according to its terms at the time of her indorsement provided first of all that the instrument has been dishonored — which we know is true here because Richard's bank has been presented with the check and has refused to accept it — and that the bank has given Stella as an indorser proper notice of this dishonor, as called for in §§3-415(c) and 3-503. To see whether notice of dishonor by the bank to Stella was timely, we look to §3-503(c), but this time to the first sentence, as the situation involves an instrument (the check) taken (by Depot National Bank) for collection. Unless the time for notice of dishonor is extended by one of the excuses for delay set out in §3-504(c), notice of dishonor must be given by the bank "before midnight of the next banking day following the banking day on which the bank receives notice of dishonor of the instrument." We are told in this portion of the example that Depot immediately notified Stella of this check's dishonor, so the bank should be able to hold Stella to the contract of indorsement.

6b. If Depot National Bank had instead waited three days to let Stella know of the check's dishonor, you can see that under §3-503(c) it would have failed to give timely notice to Stella, and any liability it might hope to impose on her as an indorser will be discharged for failure to give prompt and proper notice under §3-503.

7a. Third Avenue Liquor would have the right under §3-414(b) to go against Damon, as the drawer of a dishonored check; or against any of the two prior indorsers, Fred First or Suzanne Second, on their contracts of indorsement of that same dishonored instrument, via §3-415(a). Third Avenue would be a person entitled to enforce the instrument. Its only problem being that, in order to make sure that the obligation of either of the indorsers is not discharged, it must give proper notice of dishonor according to the rules of §3-503 to either or both of the prior indorsers whom it might contemplate later going against on the contract of indorsement. Looking again at §3-503(c), we can see that Third Avenue would be well advised to give notice of dishonor to First or Second (or preferably both) within 30 days following the day on which it receives notice from the Depot National Bank that the check has been returned dishonored.

7b. If Third Avenue is able to enforce the contract of indorsement against Suzanne Second, that leaves her holding the bag. She could then try to enforce the drawer's contract against Damon, or she could choose instead to go against First, whose indorsement was prior to hers. Notice that in §3-415(a), last sentence, the obligation of the indorser is owed not only to "a person entitled to enforce the instrument," but also "to a subsequent indorser who paid the instrument under this section." So Second, as a subsequent indorser who has been made to pay the instrument, may sue on the contract of indorsement anyone who indorsed the instrument *prior to* her in the temporal chain of indorsements. So, just as Third was entitled to sue either of the prior indorsers, First or Second, on the contract of indorsement once it had been left holding the bag (provided, of course, it had given proper and timely notice of dishonor), Second — once the loss has been shifted to her — can herself sue not only the drawer but also any previous indorsers. If she brings a successful action against First, then First is left only with the possibility of a suit against Damon on Damon's obligation as the drawer of the dishonored draft. If all goes well, First should be able to make Damon pay up, which is only right when you think of it. The genesis of the check in the first place was the fact that First did some work for Damon and was to be paid for it. First initially got his money not by presenting the check directly to Damon's bank, but by negotiating it over for cash to Second. Second, having paid First cash for the check, was able to come out even by selling the check to Third Avenue. Third Avenue then deposited the check in its account with Depot National Bank. Had the check been good — had it not been dishonored by Damon's bank — then Third would have come out even, as the amount in its account at the Depot bank would have been increased by the amount of the check. Simultaneously, the amount in Damon's own checking account would have been decreased by the amount of the check. Thus, by what is admittedly a fairly circuitous route, Damon would have paid First for the work done. The amount of the check would have been deducted from Damon's store of wealth in his checking account and First would have had the money he agreed to take for the work done.

The trouble comes in an example like this one when the check is not accepted for payment by the drawee bank but is instead dishonored. The game for the parties involved then becomes one of attempting to pass the check back, retracing the steps it took in reverse order to parties who had signed, and thereby taken on the role either of drawer or indorser, prior to themselves. The holder who tries to collect by presentment but is rebuffed through dishonor of the check is able to sue either the drawer or anyone who indorsed the instrument on its way to the current holder. If the holder is able to get paid by one of these parties — either because the earlier party voluntarily agrees to abide by the obligation it took on by signing the instrument or through a suit enforcing the obligation — then that party in turn can look up the chain of signatures to determine against whom to proceed. Eventually, if all goes as it should in an ideal world, the ultimate responsibility to pay the amount of the check comes to rest on the drawer, Damon, as indeed it should. (Of course, were this an ideal world, the check would not have been dishonored in the first place, and none of this analysis, talk of obligation, and threatened lawsuits would be necessary.)

If at the end of it all the check does not clear *and* Damon cannot otherwise be made to pay the amount, the ultimate outcome is that Damon will have received something of value (here services from Fred First) and will not have paid a penny for them. Some innocent party will be left to absorb the loss.

7c. If any of the indorsers had signed "without recourse," then they could not be liable under the contract of indorsement. You see this in §3-415(b). This provision allows the holder of an instrument to sign the instrument as necessary to make for an effective negotiation over to another party, but to avoid binding himself or herself to the contract of indorsement to the party to whom the instrument is negotiated or to anyone who later takes it.

In our particular example, if all three of the indorsers (First, Second, and Third Avenue) had signed without recourse, then Depot Bank, once the check was returned to it unaccepted, would have recourse only against Damon as drawer.

7d. Under §3-414(e), although the drawers of certain other types of drafts may sign "without recourse" and thus avoid taking on the obligation of the drawer of a dishonored draft, this opportunity does not extend to the drawer of a check. "A disclaimer of the liability stated in subsection (b) is not effective if the draft is a check." This makes sense. When a person takes a personal check in payment, it is expected that the check will turn into actual cash money in one way or the other. In the vast majority of cases, the check is honored by the bank on which it is drawn and that's the end of the story. If the check is dishonored (if it bounces, as we say), it is only natural that the payee will look to the drawer to make good and pay up what is still owed. For someone to draw a check and at the same time, by adding a few words to his or her signature, disavow any responsibility for that check being any good or for paying up in some other fashion if it is not would undermine the whole check payment system. It is this system that makes people willing to take personal checks in payment with some confidence. As Comment 5 to §3-414 states, "There is no legitimate purpose served by issuing a check on which nobody is liable."

8. No. Under §3-415(e):

> If an indorser of a check is liable under subsection (a) and the check is not presented for payment, or given to a depositary bank for collection, within 30 days after the indorsement was made, the liability of the indorser under subsection (a) is discharged.

In this case the indorsement was made on February 2. Isadora does not deposit the check into her bank for collection under March 30, more than 30 days later. Harry can no longer be held to his contract of indorsement.

9. No. Under §3-414(c) once a check is accepted by a bank — and recall that under §3-409(d) a *certified check* is one that has been accepted by the bank on which it is drawn, as is true here — the drawer is discharged from any potential liability under §3-414. Critical Connections, the seller here, has specifically refused to take a personal check in payment for the valuable widget connectors it is handing over. It has insisted upon and has received a bank check. As a party taking a bank check, it will have only the bank to look to for payment. Of course, this should not cause it any grief. The main feature of a bank check, be it a certified check, a cashier's check, or a teller's check, is that there should be absolutely no trouble turning it into cash. The bank has accepted this check already and hence it is bound by the unconditional contract of an acceptor from the very beginning. We will deal in later materials with the exceptionally rare situation in which a bank that has either certified a check or issued its own cashier's or teller's check argues that it has the right to refuse payment on such an item. The relevant point here is that such instances will be exceedingly uncommon; rarer still will be those when the bank is ultimately successful in avoiding its liability on such a bank check. The party who takes a bank check is relying, and not unreasonably, on the fact that the bank will as a matter of course be ready, willing, and able to pay on that check. For that reason Byers, as the drawer of the check that she has had accepted by the bank prior to handing it over to her supplier, is let off the hook by §3-414(c). She has already done her part in making sure that the seller will be paid.

4

Issues of Agency

Signature by a Representative

As we already seen, contractual liability of a party to a negotiable instrument necessarily requires that the party in question have signed the instrument in one capacity or another. The signature is the key to obligation on an instrument. It's worth the effort to look at §3-401(a) again, now reading it in its entirety and giving special attention to the language of subpart (ii).

> A person is not liable on an instrument unless (i) the person signed the instrument, or (ii) the person is represented by an agent or representative who signed the instrument and the signature is binding on the represented person under Section 3-402.

As subsection 3-401(b) assures us, a document may be signed in a variety of ways (look to O§1-201(39) or R§1-201(b)(37) for a definition of *signed*). As the concluding language of subsection (a) reminds us, however, the actual act of signing for a party, whether a manual signature is used or some other "device or machine," in the language of subsection (b), is employed, is not always done by the party himself, herself, or itself. People and organizations, in the course of going about their business, in many instances rely upon the actions of their employees or other agents to get things taken care of for them. A given individual burdened with running a complex business operation, for instance, may delegate to others under her command the right to enter into contracts on her behalf or otherwise affect her legal rights and responsibilities by the acts those others undertake.

Once we get to something like a corporation or a trust, however, the use of a representative to sign an instrument — or to do any other act, for that matter — becomes more than an issue of convenience. Such a legal entity is able to bind itself to even the most complex of legal obligations, but among the perfectly mundane activities that it can't do for itself is the simple act of signing something. A signature can be made only through action taken by an individual, a real live human being. A corporation, General Motors for example, for all its power and prestige, cannot *itself* physically sign the simplest document. It must necessarily work through others, authorized representatives who are actual he's and she's, who sign on its behalf. Subsection 3-402(a) acknowledges this reality by providing that a *person* — which under the definition of O§1-201(30) or R§1-201(b)(27) includes an individual or an organization — can become bound himself, herself, or itself through the signature of an agent or representative, signing on that person's behalf.

This chapter deals with two significant issues that can arise when a signature on an instrument is made by someone acting, or purporting to act, in a representative capacity. The first thing to notice is that the drafters of Article 3 have chosen to use the terms *represented person* and *representative* for the two main players in this story. You may be more familiar (indeed, you most definitely should be familiar by the time you've finished your legal studies) with the more conventional common law terms *principal* and *agent*. The terms you find in Article 3 may be meant to connote slightly different concepts, but if so the differences are very slight and certainly not something that we need worry about. Indeed, as you will see, the comments to the two sections with which we'll be concerned in this chapter, §§3-402 and 3-403, immediately slip into the language of principal and agent without any apology or explanation.

When Does the Representative Bind the Represented Party?

The first issue that presents itself when a signature is made on a negotiable instrument by some person who purports to be acting, as a legitimate representative or agent, for another, the represented person or principal, is whether the signature (in the words of §3-401(a)(ii)) "is binding on the represented person." It will come as no surprise to you that in many instances a person will claim to be acting for another but have no legal authority to do so. The reason may be simple mistake on the purported agent's part or something much more sinister. For Article 3 purposes, the crucial language pertaining to this issue is found in §3-402(a):

> If a person acting, or purporting to act, as a representative signs an instrument by signing either the name of the represented person or the name of the signer, the represented person is bound by the signature to the same extent the represented person would be bound if the signature were on a simple contract.

As the second sentence to Comment 1 makes clear, the intention of this language is to defer to the law of agency, which will presumably be common law of the state governing the transaction, for determination of when the purported agent's signature binds the principal.

The law of agency is a whole area of study unto itself. A large part of any systematic review of agency law deals with just the kind of question we have here: When does the act of the purported agent bind the principal? This covers a lot of territory, and its importance is definitely not confined to the effect of signatures on negotiable instruments. It is not my intention here to review all of the intricacies of the general law of agency, nor even the subset of rules devoted to the all-important question of when the act of the agent serves legally to bind the principal. A few words on the subject, however, are not out of order.

We say that the act or acts of one person, the *agent*, are effective legally to bind another, the *principal*, in whatever way the principal would be bound if he or she personally took those acts if and only if the act or acts in question are authorized by the principal. *Authority*, as the word is used in agency law, comes in a variety of forms depending on the circumstances involved. The first and easiest to deal with is the case of what we refer to as *actual authority*, or sometimes, to be even more precise, *actual express authority*. This type of authority is present when the principal expresses — using whatever words and through whatever means are appropriate to the situation — to the agent directly that the agent has the legal power and right to do such-and-such a thing on the principal's behalf. Actual authority arises out of direct communication between the principal and the agent. The principal informs the agent that the agent has the authority to take some action on the principal's behalf and that the agent is thereby empowered and authorized to do so. Notice that the agent's express authority necessarily extends only to those acts and only so far as the principal has, by its communication to the agent, given the agent reasonably to believe. If the principal, for instance, tells an employee that he or she has the authority to sign checks on the principal's account for the purpose of buying supplies and only if the checks do not exceed $2,000, then the agent has no actual authority to sign checks for any other purpose nor in any greater amount.

A second type of authority recognized by the traditional law of agency is termed *implied authority*. Implied authority, like actual express authority, arises out of communication or an understanding between the principal and the agent, but here the agent's reasonable understanding of what he or she may do on the principal's behalf arises not out of any direct unequivocal statement by the principal to the agent. Implied authority can be vested in the agent when statements or other manifestations by the principal, even if not directed expressly to the precise act that the agent ends up taking, have led the agent reasonably to understand that such an act would be within the scope of the agent's duties and conform to his or her principal's desires as to what can be done to bind the principal legally. The principal who expressly authorized an employee to issue checks to pay for supplies would also, it seems fairly clear, have impliedly authorized the same employee to issue a stop-payment order on any such check when the situation so warranted and the employee could reasonably conclude that the principal would want this action to be taken.

The third source of authority which I'll mention in this terribly brief abstract of agency principles is the notion of *apparent authority*.* Apparent authority is grounded not on any dealings or communication between principal and agent, but rather on manifestations the principal has made to the third party who is dealing with the agent. If the third party is led by such manifestations to the reasonable belief that a given person is in fact empowered to act in such-and-such a way as an authorized agent for the principal, then that given person (the person whom the principal has led the third party to believe is acting as the principal's agent) has the apparent authority to take the action and consequently to bind the principal even if he or she was never actually or impliedly (by manifestations made to this agent) authorized by the principal to do so. A reasonable belief in the mind of the third party that the agent is in fact an agent of the principal authorized to take certain action — if that reasonable belief is created by the doings of the principal — creates apparent authority. A person with the apparent authority to take action on behalf of another is able to bind the other just as if he or she had the actual or implied authority to do so. The principal is bound by the act of this other, not because of any intention to authorize the agent to act, but because the third party has been led by the principal reasonably to believe that the agent has in fact been authorized to act on the principal's behalf in the way that he or she does.

So, for example, suppose that Ted, a seller of business supplies and equipment, pays a call on a store owned and operated by one Paula. As he is beginning his sales pitch, Paula cuts him short by telling him, "Talk to my assistant Adam. He takes care of all those decisions for me." Paula points Ted in the direction of Adam's office. Ted is eventually able to convince Adam to purchase a piece of equipment for use in Paula's enterprise. Adam signs a contract committing Paula to purchase the equipment in question for a purchase price of $3,418 and writes Ted a check out of Paula's business

---

* Those who have already studied the basics of agency law in some other context, even if not in a separate course in agency law (which I'd urge you to take as a general matter if such a course is available to you), will no doubt already have observed how superficially I am skimming the surface here of concepts that are nowhere near as easy, neat, and straightforward as this text might suggest. A full discussion of this topic would probably also include, beyond what I am outlining here, the notions of inherent agency power and even agency by estoppel. For our purposes in this chapter, however, I hope that the introduction offered in the text will suffice — or at least give you a elementary understanding of the deeper issues, and often quite difficult complicated analyses, that lie just below the surface. Given that §3-402(a) directs us to the law of agency of the jurisdiction involved, much of the substance of a full-blown agency course comes into play. I can only present the highlights here.

account for this amount. Assuming that it is reasonable for Ted to believe that Adam has the power to enter into such a deal and to write a check in this amount for the purpose of acquiring equipment to be used in the business, then both the acts of signing the contract of sale and writing the check on Paula's behalf would, under the rubric of apparent authority, be binding on Paula as principal. This would be true even if in fact Paula had expressly told Adam that he was not authorized to enter into any deals for equipment or supplies or to write checks covering such expenses when the amount being spent was over $2,000 without first checking the deal out with Paula and getting her specific approval for the contract in question. Ted's success in holding Paula bound, both to the contract of sale and to the obligation of a drawer on the check, all depends on his being able to establish that he was reasonable in believing, based on what he had been told by Paula and given all the other circumstances surrounding the transaction, that Adam had been authorized by Paula to commit her to such a purchase and to write such a check. If we imagine that Ted and Adam had gotten along so well that their conversation ended with an agreement that Ted would purchase Paula's whole business — lock, stock, and barrel — for a sum in the hundreds of thousands, Adam might eventually sign all kinds of documents purporting to commit Paula to the scheme, but it is doubtful, to say the least, that Adam's signature on even the most finely drawn papers would bind Paula in any way. Ted would be hard-pressed to prove that he was reasonable in believing that Paula had authorized Adam to conduct any transaction of this type or on such a scale on Paula's behalf.

As I'm sure you can imagine, in many situations the facts are such that an agent's power to bind the principal could be established under any or all of the notions of express authority, implied authority, and apparent authority. These three variants or types of authority — express, implied, and apparent — will in the simpler situations overlap to a great degree. In a trickier setting, the third party who hopes to hold the principal accountable based on the acts of another may have a tough time showing that even one of these concepts can rightfully be brought to bear. To narrow our focus considerably, and to return to the issue with which we are concerned in this chapter, the important point to remember in the negotiable instruments context is that the question of whether the signature of a representative (returning now to the language of Article 3) is effective to bind the represented person is, by virtue of §3-402(a), to be answered by reference to this general law of agency, not by resort to any distinct rules treating the signature of negotiable instruments differently from any other acts that an agent may purport to do on behalf of another. This treatment is confirmed by looking at the definition in O§1-201(43) or R§1-201(b)(41) which, appearing as it does in the set of Article 1 definitions, applies wherever the defined term appears in the Code.

"Unauthorized" signature means a signature made without actual, implied, or apparent authority. The term includes a forgery.

Some special rules pertaining to the consequences of application of an unauthorized signature to a negotiable instrument are covered by §3-403, to which you will have to refer (along with §3-402) in considering some of the examples of this chapter.*

When May the Representative Be Personally Bound by His or Her Signature?

The second distinct issue we have to address when a signature is made on a negotiable instrument by someone acting in a representative capacity is whether that person can himself or herself be held *personally* obligated on the instrument. The presence of one's signature on an instrument in whatever role — maker, drawer, acceptor, or indorser — is, after all, the key to obligation on the instrument under §3-401(a). The representative has himself or herself signed the instrument. Will the representative ever be obligated on the instrument through the act of signing? If so, when?

This question is, as you can imagine, of more than academic interest. The representative, if he or she intends to bind the represented party but to do no more, will want to be sure that his or her form of signature cannot later be argued by someone entitled to enforce the instrument to have given rise to personal liability on the representative's part. At the same time, in some circumstances the person who is taking the instrument or asking for and relying upon the signature of the representative is perfectly reasonable in wanting to ensure that *both* parties (the represented party and the representative himself or herself) can be held to the effect of the signature should something go wrong and suit (or at least arguments of legal liability) be necessary. Neither outcome — obligation of the represented party only or personal obligation of the representative as well — is necessarily right or wrong. It depends on what is called for in the situation; what obligation, if any, the representative is willing to take on; and what the party asking for the

---

* It is interesting and important to note that the term *unauthorized signature* includes but is not limited to a forgery. We will see, in chapters to come, any numbers of situations of forgery, where someone signs the name of another to the instrument with the intention that it be taken as the actual signature of that party, and it can be tempting to conclude that the only type of unauthorized signature is the forgery. But look at the first sentence of Comment 1 to §3-403. An unauthorized signature includes not only a forgery but also a signature made by one exceeding his or her actual (which would mean either express or implied) or apparent authority. In the example used earlier, for example, should Adam sign his name to a check from Paula's account for $1 million, this is not a forgery. Adam signs Adam's name, and there is no attempt to pass it off as a signature of anyone else. It would, however, be an unauthorized signature if Adam had never been authorized (expressly or impliedly) to write a check for such an amount out of Paula's account nor could any apparent authority be shown on his part to do so.

signature is willing to accept. In the ideal situation, the signer and the party relying on the signature should have no doubt about whether, if at all (and if so, when) the representative could be held liable on the instrument by virtue of his or her signature on it. To the extent there is doubt as to the ramifications of the representative's signature in this regard, §3-402(b) and (c) present rules under which such doubt is to be resolved. If you read the beginning of Comment 2 to this section, you'll see that the original version of Article 3 took an approach which the drafters of the 1990 revision found "unsatisfactory." Hence, the rules under the revised §3-402 differ in style and in some instances in result from what was previously to be found in the prerevision §3-403.* The rules of the revised §3-402(b) and (c) are meant to be easier to apply and to lead to more certain and consistent results. Whether this is so we will test in the following examples.

As you can see under paragraph (1) of §3-402(b):

> If the form of the signature shows unambiguously that the signature is made on behalf of the represented person who is identified in the instrument, the representative is not liable on the instrument.

Note the two criteria here that must be satisfied for the representative to avoid liability on the instrument. The form of the representative's signature must show *unambiguously* that the signature has been made on behalf of another, the represented person. Furthermore, that represented person must be *identified* in the instrument itself.

If either of these criteria fails to appear from a reading of the instrument, the representative may still avoid personal liability, but the situation becomes much more problematic. We have to consult paragraph (2) of §3-402(b). The rule then is that

> the representative *is* liable on the instrument to a holder in due course who took the instrument without notice that the representative was not intended to be liable on the instrument. With respect to any other person [than a holder in due course], the representative *is* liable on the instrument unless the representative proves that the original parties did not intend the representative to be liable on the instrument.

You no doubt noticed that in application of §3-402(b)(2) the question may turn on whether the person seeking to enforce personal liability on the part of the representative is that special breed of holder referred to in Article 3 as a "holder in due course." We will have much to say in later chapters

---

* If you were ever confronted with this issue as it pertains to a signature made on an instrument prior to the effective date of the revised Article 3 in the governing jurisdiction, you would of course turn to the old §3-403 and to cases decided under it for guidance. Be aware that there are still plenty of notes of older vintage outstanding, and for those notes the question here presented would have to be dealt with by reference to that former §3-403, because the newer version of Article 3 is generally held not to be retroactive in effect.

about who does and who does not qualify for this impressive title and the special status of the holder in due course of any particular instrument. For me to attempt, at this juncture, even the crudest nutshell version of just who qualifies as a holder in due course and what exactly the consequences of this may be seems unwarranted and unwise. For the purposes of this chapter, I beg your indulgence and your trust. If I say that someone does not qualify as a holder in due course, take my word for it. The party may be a holder and a person entitled to enforce the instrument, but he or she is not a holder in due course. If I say that someone will in fact be able to establish that he or she holds that special status, take my word for that as well. Once we have dealt in the proper fashion with who or what is a holder in due course, you will able to review this chapter and §3-402(b)(2) to appreciate with even greater sophistication and respect the rules as we find them there.

EXAMPLES

1. Xavier and Yolanda Zendel are a happily married couple. When a large tax refund check, made out "to the order of Xavier Zendel and Yolanda Zendel," arrives at their house, Yolanda is out of town on an extended business trip. Xavier would like to deposit the check in their joint checking account as soon as possible. When they speak by telephone that night, Yolanda tells Xavier that, yes, he should indorse the check on her behalf and deposit it in that account. The next day Xavier takes the check to the bank. On the back of the check he signs his own name and under it signs "Xavier Zendel, as Agent for Yolanda Zendel."

  (a) Has the check been effectively indorsed?
  (b) Would the result be any different if under his own signature Xavier had signed "Yolanda Zendel" in his own script?
  (c) What if, instead, Xavier never tells Yolanda that the refund check has arrived. He takes it to a bank where he has an account in his name only. In depositing it he signs his own name and also Yolanda's. Has the check been properly indorsed under this set of facts?

2. Minisoft Corporation is a thriving and well-known enterprise with its main headquarters located in Washington state. Someone introducing herself as Willa Bates, the President of Minisoft, rushes into an office of Empire State Bank located in New York City and is quickly ushered into an office of one of Empire's senior loan officers. Willa hands this officer a copy of her business card, which bears all the markings of a card of the type a representative of Minisoft would be expected to have and identifying her as "Willa Bates, President." Willa tells the officer that she is in town on other matters but has just been presented with the possibility of acquiring some property in New York that she thinks would be particularly good for her corporation. The seller is in a rush, however, and is demanding a $20,000 deposit in the form of a bank check by the end of the day. Willa would like to arrange to

borrow this money on behalf of Minisoft from Empire State. The loan officer is more than eager to comply. He has a cashier's check in the form Willa requests drawn up. He gives this to Willa, asking only that she sign a standard form note naming Minisoft Corporation as the borrower. Willa signs this note, promising to repay the $20,000 at a stated rate of interest, as "Willa Bates, President, Minisoft Corporation." The bank soon becomes aware, but not before the cashier's check it has issued has been paid, that the person who presented herself as Willa Bates, President of Minisoft, is not who she claimed to be. She is, instead, one up-and-coming and until now little-known con artist named Connie. The business card that Connie presented to the bank was not issued by Minisoft, but had been cleverly printed up by Connie herself to appear to be a Minisoft business card.

(a) Can Empire State Bank hold the Minisoft Corporation obligated on the note signed, as it turns out, by Connie?

(b) Is anyone obligated to pay the money due on the note? See §3-403(a).

3. Paula Pratt owns and operates a large business that relies heavily on the most advanced, state-of-the art computerized equipment. Paula gives one of her employees, Adam Archer, the title of Purchasing Director and tells him that he is authorized to acquire any new piece of such equipment that he deems appropriate for the use of the business, paying either in cash or on reasonable credit terms, as long as the price of the equipment does not exceed $50,000. Archer arranges for Pratt to buy a particular piece of equipment from the Zippy Computer Company, the cost of which is $30,000. Zippy agrees to take payment in the form of a note payable in a series of 36 monthly installments over a period of 3 years, with the monthly payments being calculated on the basis of the purchase price and a reasonable market rate of interest. The form of the note states that "Paula Pratt, as purchaser, agrees to pay to the order of Zippy Computer Company" the monthly payments. At the bottom of the note, on a line labeled "Purchaser/Borrower," Archer signs by writing "Adam Archer, as agent for Paula Pratt."

(a) Is Pratt obligated on the note? Is Archer?

(b) Suppose instead that Archer had signed by writing simply "Adam Archer, Purchasing Director." Does this change either of your answers to the questions asked in (a)?

(c) Finally, suppose that Archer has written only "Paula Pratt" in script on the line designated for the borrower. Would Paula be bound by this signature? Could Archer be personally held liable on the note?

4. The basic situation is as in the previous example. Paula Pratt is running a business and Adam Archer is her purchasing director. Archer decides to buy another piece of equipment on Pratt's behalf, this time from the Xeroff Copier Company for $15,000. A note presented to Archer for signature to complete the deal states only that "the undersigned Borrower(s) agrees to pay to the order of the Xeroff Copier Company" the sum of $15,000 within

60 days from its date. Archer signs with his own name, Adam Archer, only. Sixty days go by and Xeroff has not been paid on the instrument, which is still is in its possession.

    (a) Assuming that Xeroff would not qualify under the circumstances as a holder in due course, would Archer be personally bound to pay the note that he signed?

    (b) Would your answer be any different if Archer had signed, "Adam Archer, as agent?"

    (c) What if Archer had filled in the signature line on the note by writing "Paula Pratt" and signed below in his own name, Adam Archer?

    (d) In each of the three preceding cases, would your answer be any different if by the time the 60 days had passed the note in question had been sold and duly negotiated to a firm, Friendly Factors, for the price of $13,750? You should assume that, by this negotiation, not only did Friendly Factors become the holder of the note, but also that it met the criteria for being considered a holder in due course of the instrument.

5.   We have one more situation to consider in which the industrious Paula Pratt obtains some equipment through the activity of her purchasing director, Adam Archer. In the deal for this final piece of equipment, a super-sophisticated computer printer from the firm of Izod Printers Incorporated, the note presented to Archer for signature reads, "Paula Pratt as purchaser and borrower promises to pay to the order of Izod Printers Incorporated" a set sum of money at a definite time. Archer signs with his own name only.

    (a) May Archer be personally liable on the note if Izod itself (which you should assume would not be a holder in due course) tries to enforce the note against him?

    (b) How would your answer change if the party trying to hold Archer to personal responsibility on the note was some party other than Izod, one that would rightly be considered a holder in due course?

6.   Cosmo Graphics starts a small enterprise that he incorporates (with himself as president, naturally) and runs under the name of Graphics Surprise, Incorporated. Cosmo arranges with a local bank, Main Street Bank and Trust, to borrow an amount of money that he needs to begin operations. One of the documents that the bank prepares and presents to him to finalize the loan is a note, the text of which gives the name of its maker as "Graphics Surprise, Incorporated." The note is signed by Cosmo under a line that has been filled in with the language, "Graphics Surprise, Inc. by Cosmo Graphics, President."

    (a) Can Cosmo Graphics be held personally responsible on this note?

    (b) Graphics has signed not only as above, but in addition has been asked by the bank's representative to add his signature devoid of any other identification below this on the instrument. Graphics does so sign a second time. Does this affect his potential personal liability on the note? Why might the bank in a situation such as this want, and indeed insist upon, this second signature?

7.   Carlos Martinez has been appointed director of the accounts payable department of the Minisoft Corporation. It is his job, once all appropriate internal corporate accounting procedures have been observed and the proper authorization forms reach his desk, to issue and dispatch checks drawn on that corporation's account with the First Bank of Washington State. The preprinted check forms used by Carlos clearly identify the checks as being drawn on Minisoft's checking account and coming from that corporation. Before sending off any such check, Carlos personally signs his name on the line provided on the check form for the drawer's signature. Nowhere on the check does he indicate that he is signing in a given capacity or "as agent" for the corporation. Can Carlos be held personally liable on any of the Minisoft checks he signs with his name alone? Refer to §3-403(c).

EXPLANATIONS

1a.   Yes. We know from our previous look at §3-110(d), in which we last met up with the Zendels, that when an instrument is payable to two parties in this fashion it may be properly negotiated only by both of them. Thus, a valid signature of each, Xavier and Yolanda, is necessary. Here we have both. Xavier has signed for himself, and in addition has been given express authority by Yolanda to sign the check on her behalf and to deposit it in their joint account as he has done. Under §3-402(a) Yolanda is the represented person, bound by the signature of Xavier as her representative.

1b.   The result would be the same if Xavier, in addition to signing his own name, signs for Yolanda in this fashion. Section 3-402(a) says that the effect of a signature by a representative is the same whether the representative, or one purporting to be an authorized representative, "signs an instrument by signing either the name of the represented person or the name of the signer." In the prior example, Xavier signed for Yolanda using his own name. Here he signs by signing the name of Yolanda, the represented person. The issue is still the same: Did Xavier have the authority to sign on Yolanda's behalf and thereby bind her to the same extent as if she had personally signed the instrument? In this example there is no doubt; Yolanda expressly authorized Xavier to act as her representative for the purpose of indorsing the check and depositing it into their joint account. Xavier has not forged Yolanda's name. He has signed on her behalf as an authorized representative.

1c.   It is doubtful that anyone later trying to rely on this indorsement would be able to establish its validity. The issue, of course, is whether there is any basis to argue that under the facts Xavier was authorized in any way to sign Yolanda's name as he did and then to deposit the check, not into the couple's joint account, but into his own individual account. Xavier has certainly not been given any express authority to do so by his wife. Xavier could argue that he had the implied authority to do as he did, but that would require him to establish that he was reasonable in assuming (perhaps based on how the couple dealt with similar tax refund checks in previous years), that Yolanda would want him both to sign her name to the check and to deposit it in his personal account. This would seem to be a hard case to make, but it would ultimately have to be resolved by the particular facts, not just about how the couple acted here but also about their past practices and communications.

It would similarly seem a hard case to make that Xavier had the apparent authority to sign as he did. Yolanda was not even aware of the receipt of this particular check, and so she certainly could not have made any direct manifestations to any third parties that could lead them reasonably to believe that Xavier was authorized to do as he did, diverting their joint tax refund into an account under his exclusive control. Again it would all be in the facts. Under the common law of agency, to which §3-402(a) defers on such points, issues of whether someone purporting to act for another has the authority to bind the purported principal, and if so to what particular acts the authority extends, depend to a great degree on the particulars of the situation and the present and past dealings of the parties involved. This is especially true when the argument being advanced is that the agent acted not with express authority but rather with implied or apparent authority. In the particular example before us — with Xavier signing Yolanda's name to a check made payable to them jointly and depositing it into his personal account, all without informing her — I think it highly unlikely that this would be found to be an effective indorsement by Yolanda and hence an effective negotiation made, as it would have to be, by the two of them.

2a.   There is no basis to argue that Minisoft has signed the note in question, and hence it cannot be held obligated on the note. The facts here at least are not in dispute, and the conclusion is unavoidable (for the bank) that this person Connie was not authorized in any manner to sign for the Minisoft Corporation. She had never been given any authority, either express or implied, by that company, which does not even know of her and certainly wouldn't be happy with what she's up to. Whatever indicia the loan officer was relying upon that allowed him to come to the conclusion that the person before him was in fact Willa Bates, president of Minisoft — and what's more, that she had the authority to sign a note on the corporation's behalf promising to pay $20,000 — all emanated from the supposed Willa herself. Connie was the one who said she was the famous Willa Bates. Connie was responsible for printing up the (phony) business cards. There were no actions at all that could be traced back to the Minisoft Corporation itself, which contributed to the loan officer's belief that Connie was who she claimed to be. That being so, there is no way that it could be argued that Connie had the apparent authority to act on behalf of Minisoft in any way whatsoever. The signature purporting to be that of Minisoft is an unauthorized signature, pure and simple. Minisoft is in no way bound to any obligation on the note by what Connie did here.

2b. Connie herself is obligated as a maker of the note promising to pay Empire State Bank the $20,000 on the terms and conditions set forth in that note. At first this might seem strange. We know that any obligation on an instrument must be based on a person's signature appearing thereon, and we don't seem to have Connie's signature anywhere on the note. Under §3-403(a), however, an unauthorized signature such as we have here, though ineffective to bind Minisoft in any way, *is* effective "as the signature of the unauthorized signer [Connie] in favor of a person who in good faith pays the instrument or takes it for value." Empire State Bank has indeed taken the instrument for value; it has given a cashier's check for $20,000 in exchange for the note. The bank may have been, at least as we view it in retrospect, awfully gullible here and not terribly prudent in how it handled its affairs, but there is nothing to indicate that it was lacking in good faith (as that term is defined in §3-103(a)(4), a definition we will concentrate on in greater detail in later material) in taking the note for value as it did. By signing the note with the words "Willa Bates, President" as she did, when she knew for certain that she was not authorized to do so, Connie in effect signed the note herself. Because her signature appears on the note in the place where the maker's signature is to be found, Connie is bound to pay as the maker when called upon to do so. The prospects of Empire State actually getting repaid by Connie are, of course, pretty dim at best. Con artists like Connie, if they are any good at what they do, tend to disappear into the woodwork fairly quickly once a con has been pulled off. They don't, as a rule, hang around to follow up on their legal obligations to make whole those parties they have defrauded. Good luck to the bank in its efforts to find Connie and make her pay up. The Code at least is on the bank's side, if not the laws of human nature.

This example obviously brings to the fore the much larger question of how someone getting the signature of a representative on an instrument can be sure, or at least maximize the likelihood, that the person with whom he is dealing is in fact who she claims to be. Beyond that, although we did not even have to reach the issue in this example, how can the party relying on the signature reach a desired level of confidence that the person, even if she is without doubt who she says she is and not an impostor or phony, is *authorized* to sign and commit the represented party in the way and to the extent that she is doing? Even if a bank's loan officer were dealing with someone who was in fact the real Willa Bates, President of Minisoft, and there was no doubt about it, if Willa said she was authorized to sign a note for $10 million on behalf of that corporation, would you suggest the loan officer simply take her word for it? I have not tried to incorporate into this chapter all the issues dealing with when and whether an agent has the requisite authority to act for the principal as he or she maintains that he or she has. This is rightly the stuff of a large part of the study of agency law as that law applies to all sorts of activities and transactions, not just dealings in negotiable instruments. There is, obviously, no way we could cover all, or even any large measure, of that material here and come close to doing it justice. I trust that you will at some time get a chance to treat such issues in agency, and particularly the significant issue of when a purported agent is empowered to bind the principal by his or her deeds, more generally at some time in your legal studies.

3a. Pratt is obligated on the note. She has authorized Archer to act as he has, entering into the contract to buy the equipment and signing a note to serve as payment under that contract. His signature binds Pratt under the basic principle of §3-402(a) and common law of agency. The more interesting issue here is whether Archer has in any way obligated himself to pay on the instrument. After all, he has appended his signature to the note. We consult §3-402(b). First we note that the precondition stated at the beginning of §3-402(b) has been met: Archer as representative has signed his own name to an instrument and that signature is an authorized signature of Paula Pratt as the represented person.

The question then becomes whether the case we are looking at falls within the rule of paragraph (1) or (2) of this subsection. As you should confirm, we are here safely within the bounds of subsection (b)(1). Here the form of the signature, "Adam Archer, as agent for Paula Pratt," does show unambiguously that Archer is signing on behalf of Pratt; furthermore, Pratt is "identified" in the instrument, here both in the body of the instrument and in the form of signature as well. Archer cannot be held personally liable on the instrument.

3b. If Archer signs in this manner, the result should be the same as it was in Example 3a. Pratt is obligated by the authorized signature of her representative, Archer. Archer would be able to argue that the form of signature, "Adam Archer, Purchasing Director," shows unambiguously that he is not signing for himself but for another, and furthermore that the other (the represented person) is identified within the instrument — if not at the bottom where the signature is placed, more importantly in the body of the note itself. The critical text of the note reads that Pratt and only Pratt is the party agreeing to pay and hence is the maker of the instrument. In this context it seems unambiguous that Archer's signature, followed as it is by his title, indicates that he is signing in a representative capacity only.

3c. Assuming as we are that Archer is authorized to sign this note for Pratt, his signature of her name will be effective to bind Pratt just as if she had herself signed, under the introductory language of §3-402(a), whether he carries through on his authority by signing in his name or in hers. So Pratt is bound to the obligation of the maker on the note. Is Archer bound? No.

Notice that he himself never signed the note. His scrawling of "Paula Pratt" on the line designated for the borrower was his act of signing *her* signature, as he was authorized to do. Neither his name nor his signature appears anywhere on the note, so there is no way he could ever be liable on it. Note also that the rule of §3-403(a), which we looked at in Example 2b, does not come into play here: It applies when an *unauthorized* signature is placed on the instrument. In this case Archer was authorized to sign for Pratt as he did. If for some reason Archer were not so authorized and his signing of "Paula Pratt" to the note were deemed to be an unauthorized signature, then and only then would his actions amount to his own signature, even though not literally in his own name, of the instrument, creating possible obligation for him on the instrument itself.

4a. This example differs from the previous one in that the form of signature does not "show[ ] unambiguously that the signature [was] made on behalf of the represented person," nor is the represented person, Pratt, "identified in the instrument" itself. Neither of these conditions being present, Archer cannot rely on §3-402(b)(1) to relieve him of any potential liability on the instrument. The case then comes within the rule of paragraph (b)(2) to this same section. We are to assume that the person trying to enforce obligation on the instrument is not a holder in due course. That being so, the operative rule is that "the representative is liable on the instrument unless the representative proves that the original parties did not intend the representative to be liable on the instrument."

   In the particular case, it may not be too difficult for Archer to meet his burden of proving that the intention of the parties was to bind his employer Pratt to the instrument (via §3-402(a)) and Pratt only. After all, the note was signed to pay for a Xeroff copier machine, which machine presumably was delivered to Pratt's place of business and is being used by her. The Xeroff representative dealt with Archer not because she believed him to be the kind of person who would buy an expensive copier in his own right, but because he was the purchasing director for the enterprising Paula Pratt. Of course, it does not necessarily follow just because Xeroff, in taking the note, wanted Pratt to be obligated on it, that it did not also want to have Archer as a second person liable to pay the note. There are certainly instances, as we will soon see, in which the party relying upon a signature by a representative will most definitely want to see that the represented party and the representative are *both* obligated on the instrument. That does not seem to be the case here, however. Xeroff, in agreeing to sell to Pratt on credit, was presumably making some determination about her creditworthiness and what decree of risk it was willing to take in allowing her some time to pay. It's doubtful that the possibility of having Paula's director of purchasing personally liable as well was something that Xeroff even considered.

   It seems likely here that Archer would be able to prove that the original parties to this instrument did not intend him to be liable on it. Still, the lesson, at least as far as Archer the agent is concerned, should not be over-looked. Had he been careful and made sure both that the note he was signing on Pratt's behalf identified her and that the form of his signature left no room for doubt that he was signing in a representative capacity only, he would then have been able to rely on §3-402(b)(1), where the rule is simple and straight-forward. He would not have been liable on the instrument and he would have needed no proof beyond what was on the face of the instrument itself to assure himself of this result. Having signed this note written out as it was, and with his simple signature devoid of any clear indication of his signing as a representative only, the result is that he is prima facie liable on the instrument unless he can prove through facts extrinsic to the instrument itself that there was no intention on the part of the original parties that he be bound. Even if he is eventually able to satisfy his burden of proof in this regard and thereby escape personal liability should some problem develop and litigation ensue, he'll no doubt be struck by (and probably cursing himself with) the realiza-tion that the necessity of his taking on and meeting this burden could all have been avoided had he been a little more careful about looking over and insist-ing on a more clearly worded form of note at the time of signing, and then signing unambiguously in his representative capacity only.

4b. The applicable rule is the same as in 4a. We and Archer are still going to have to look to subsection (b)(2) of §3-402. Subsection (b)(1) is reserved for instances where both the form of signature is unambiguously that of someone signing in a representative capacity *and* the represented person is identified in the instrument. In this case Archer has met the first criterion: the form of his signature shows unambiguously that he was signing in a representative capac-ity. However, the represented person, Paula Pratt, is still not identified in the instrument. Recall that the body of the note refers only to "the undersigned Borrower(s)." Archer will be able to avoid personal liability on the note, as against a person other than a holder in due course, only by taking on and meeting the burden of proving that the original parties to the instrument (that would be Pratt and Xeroff) did not intend him to be liable on it.

4c. The situation remains the same. Archer is still stuck as far as §3-402(b)(2) is concerned. Here the represented person *is* identified in the instrument, but Archer's representative capacity is not unambiguously shown by the way he signed. Again, he will be prima facie liable to one not a holder in due course unless he can prove that the original parties to the instrument did not intend him to be personally obligated on it.

4d. Once the party trying to hold the representative liable qualifies as a holder in due course, the rule changes, and it will become that much harder for Archer to avoid liability. Subsection (b)(2) states that a representative in Archer's situation — where either his representative status does not unam-biguously appear from the form of his signature *or* the represented party is not identified in the instrument — is liable to a holder in due course "that took the instrument without notice that the representative was not intended to be liable on the instrument." There is no requirement that the type of notice that would bar the holder in due course from holding the representative personally liable be found on the instrument itself, or even that it be in writing — but note the language at the end of the first long paragraph of Comment 2 to §3-402 to the effect that "[a] holder in due course should be able to resolve any ambiguity against" the representative. (I know John Doe and Adam Archer may not be one and the same person, but it may not have escaped your notice that the three examples I have used in 4a, 4b, and 4c just happen to parallel Cases #1, #2, and #3 of this Comment.)

In our Example 4a, but now assuming that the note is in the hands of Friendly Factors, a holder in due course, Archer would probably have a very hard time escaping personal liability. Note that at the time Factors bought the note and took as a holder in due course, all that appeared on the face of the note was the promise that "the undersigned Borrower(s)" would pay the promised amount; Adam Archer's signature appears, devoid of any hint of representative capacity, at the bottom of the note. It is going to be very hard for Archer to prove that, at the time it took the note, Factors had notice that Archer was not "intended to be liable on the instrument." We have to assume that Factors would not have paid all it did for the note unless it thought *someone* was committed to paying it, and no name other than Archer's even appears on the note. Perhaps Archer would be able to come up with compelling proof that, at the time it took the note, Factors had the requisite notice that the note had been signed on behalf of Pratt, with no intention that Archer be bound on it, but this may not be easy and it is most assuredly not something that Archer can count on when he signs the note in this fashion. Remember that a negotiable instrument such as this may have passed through the hands of several parties before it ended up in the possession of Friendly Factors. How is Archer to prove what notice Factors had when it took the note? Also, as a practical matter, a firm like Friendly Factors will often pay for and take negotiation of notes such as this from a merchant not on an individual basis but in large quantities. Factors may have purchased this note directly from Xeroff, but perhaps as one of a group of dozens or even hundreds. If this were the case, Factors would have examined the notes to make sure each looked satisfactory within its four corners and asked for some general information from Xeroff, but it is highly doubtful that a person from Factors would have sat around chatting with someone from Xeroff to learn about the nature of each note and the underlying transaction that gave rise to it. Xeroff would have no way of knowing that someone like Adam Archer could not possibly have been buying a Xeroff copier for himself, much less that he was doing so only on behalf of one Paula Pratt. I wouldn't count on Archer's being able to escape personal liability on the note once it is in the hands of a holder in due course like Friendly Factors, no matter how Friendly that firm may be.

The situation in Example 4b, where Pratt is not identified in the instrument but Archer has signed "as agent," is a little more hopeful for Archer, but it still is unclear that he could escape personal liability. True, the addition of these words definitely suggests that Archer was acting in a representative capacity for someone when he signed the note, but nowhere on the note does it identify *who* that someone is. It may be hard for Archer to establish that Factors had, at the time it took the note, notice that he "was not intended [by whom?] to be liable on the instrument." If it had such notice, whom did it think would be liable as maker of the note? Perhaps if Factors had been more careful it would not have taken this instrument until this matter had been cleared up. But then Archer could have avoided the whole problem simply by signing, "as agent for Paula Pratt," identifying his principal. This kind of messy situation, which comes up all too often, could have been avoided with a little more care and attention to detail by the representative who has no intention of taking on personal responsibility, looking out for his or her own interests as well as those of the principal.

The situation in Example 4c would probably find Archer liable to Friendly Factors as a co-maker along with Pratt of the note. There are two signatures on the note, that of Pratt (made by Archer acting as her agent) and that of Archer himself. Nothing distinguishes one as the mark of a principal and the other as that of an agent or representative. There is, of course, the possibility of Archer's proving that Friendly Factors, at the time it took the instrument, had notice of who was whom and of what exactly was going on here in more detail, but it will be a hard burden for Archer to meet.

5a. This case also comes within (b)(2) of §3-402 — here not because the represented party is not identified in the instrument, which she clearly is, but because Archer the representative has not signed with a form of signature unambiguously showing that his signature was made in a representative capacity only. If Izod tries to enforce the note against Archer, he will be put to the test of proving that Pratt and Izod are to be considered the "original parties" to the instrument and furthermore that they did not intend Archer to be liable on it. Fortunately for Archer, the way Pratt is identified in the instrument, along with other facts he will be able to bring into the picture, may well allow him to meet this burden. But again, think of how much easier life would be for Archer (at least on this one particular matter) had he signed, "Adam Archer, as agent," or "Adam Archer, Purchasing Director for Paula Pratt." Had he done so, the situation would be governed by (b)(1), not (b)(2), of §3-402, and Arthur would have been, by the language of the Code itself, "not liable on the instrument" without having to make any additional showing.

5b. Should Archer be confronted with a holder of the note who qualifies as a holder in due course, he would (again under (b)(2)) be liable unless he can establish that the holder took the instrument with notice that there was no intention that Archer be bound. The case here doesn't look as bleak for

Archer as some we have been considering, even if the party seeking enforcement is a holder in due course, because the text of the note itself refers to Pratt as the "purchaser" of the printing equipment and "borrower" of the money to pay for it. Still, should Pratt not pay on the instrument, and especially if her financial condition makes it unlikely that she will ever be able to pay, the holder in due course may find it has no choice but to go against Archer, and the result will depend on who can prove what about what the holder had notice of at the time it took the instrument. That holder could properly point out that just because one person, Pratt, had clearly taken on obligation on the instrument, it does not follow that another signer, in this case Archer, had not also taken on responsibility. In plenty of situations, two or more parties will jointly take on the obligation to pay a note when due. Archer may eventually win this one, but he can't just walk away from any such suit or the argument that the original intention was that he, in addition to Pratt, was to be obligated on the instrument.

6a. No. This situation fits within §3-402(b)(1). Cosmo has clearly signed in a representative capacity, as the president of the corporation, and the represented party, the corporation itself, is clearly identified in the instrument.

6b. If Cosmo signs a second time using his name only, it seems appropriate to interpret this as his signing as a co-maker (and, as we will see in Chapter 5, being considered an "accommodation party," with all that implies) of the instrument. Two parties are obligated to pay as promised: the corporation as a distinct legal entity and Cosmo as an individual. A court should, and most courts have, found this to be the legal effect of the second personal signature in a situation such as this, but if you represented the bank you could do a bit more to make this outcome crystal clear and beyond doubt. You could create the note to read so that the corporation and Cosmo were both unequivocally identified as makers, each jointly and severally liable. On the bottom of the note you would be sure there were two distinct lines labeled "Borrower." On one you would fill in the name "Graphics Surprise, Inc." and have Cosmo sign under this in his representative capacity, "by Cosmo Graphics, President." On the second borrower line you would have Cosmo sign his name alone. This would make evident beyond any question the intention that both the corporation, signing through its representative, and Cosmo personally were to be liable on the instrument.

It is not difficult to see why, in a situation such as this, a lender such as Main Street Bank and Trust would not merely hope for, but also (if it knew its business) insist upon, the personal obligation of Cosmo, the president of this small closely held corporation, in addition to the obligation of the corporation. It is lending to the corporation, and if all goes well the corporate business will thrive and Graphics Surprise, Incorporated, will have no trouble keeping up with any loan payments it has agreed to make. The bank, however, has to be aware that not all businesses flourish, and that there is some nonnegligible chance that the corporation will run into trouble and not be able to meet its obligations. The corporation may even be forced to declare bankruptcy and dissolve. Where does that leave the bank? When lending to a small business entity, especially a newly formed one, the bank will necessarily want to have the ability to go against the people who put that business together, those we sometimes refer to as the *principals of the business.* One way of doing that is to make sure that those people can be held personally obligated on any notes signed on behalf of the business. Someone like Cosmo Graphics here, who may be incorporating his business for perfectly valid and noble reasons, still has to recognize that others will be concerned that, should the corporation run into difficulty, Cosmo will not automatically be liable for its debts just because he is the president or even the sole shareholder of the corporation. In fact, the general rule, as you should know, is just the opposite. Those such as Main Street Bank and Trust, in our example, who deal with a corporation — the form of which legally limits liability to the entity itself and insulates its owners and officers from responsibility for the corporation's obligations — have to take reasonable precautions. A lender such as the bank will do so by making sure that the form of any note it takes from the corporation and the way that note is signed makes it possible for the corporate principal or principals to be held personally liable if the corporation goes belly-up.

7.   Carlos is free from any worry that he could be held personally liable on the checks, even though he has signed them and even though he may not have signed with any clear indication that he did so in a representative capacity. The 1990 revisions to Article 3 added the provision we find in §3-402(c):

> If a representative signs the name of the representative as drawer of a check without indication of the representative status and the check is payable from an account of the represented person who is identified on the check, the signer is not liable on the check if the signature is an authorized signature of the representative.

As you can read in Comment 3 to this section, the prerevision version of Article 3 contained no such provision, and some courts had found the person signing, as Carlos is doing here, to be personally obligated on the instrument for lack of any showing of a representative capacity. The revision drafters meant to and did address what they obviously thought to be an incorrect and unfortunate outcome with the new §3-402(c), for which Carlos can be thankful.

Carlos is, of course, a fictional character. For a recent case showing how the new §3-402(c) worked to the benefit of one Janet V. Andrew — the real life secretary treasurer of Storage Solutions, Inc., a Connecticut corporation — who has signed checks on behalf of the corporation but was found not to have incurred any contractual liability on the checks, and hence never to have "transacted business" in Massachusetts so as to be subject to personal jurisdiction in that state, see *Raid, Inc. v. Andrew*, 47 U.C.C.2d 633 (Conn. Sup. Ct. 2002).

5

Accommodation Parties

Introduction

A creditor is typically someone like a lender, who has exchanged money lent in the present for a promise of repayment in the future, or a seller of goods who has taken as payment not cold hard cash but a promise of payment at some later date. The creditor is necessarily living at risk. To some greater or lesser degree, the possibility always exists that, when time comes for the loan to be repaid or the goods paid for, the promise upon which the creditor has been relying will not be kept and the money that is due the creditor won't be forthcoming. A creditor can try to reduce, if never totally eliminate, this risk in a variety of ways. One possibility is for the creditor to insist that the debtor, in addition to making his or her promise of payment, put up some collateral — some property of the debtor's — to secure the amount of credit that has been extended. If the property put up as collateral is real property, the situation is that of the traditional real estate mortgage, and the law governing this aspect of the transaction is the common law governing mortgages as it has developed over time in each of the several states. If the collateral that backs up the debtor's promise of payment is in the form of personal property, the creditor and debtor will have entered the world of the secured transaction, now governed not by common law principles but by Article 9 of the Uniform Commercial Code as adopted in each of the several states.

Putting up some property (collateral) is only one way in which a debtor may "back up" the promise made to the creditor and ease the creditor's anxiety about whether it will be paid in the future. Another possibility is for the debtor to bring in another party, someone who agrees to stand behind the promise made to the creditor and become legally committed to making payment if the debtor does not do so. This third party is commonly referred to as a *guarantor* or a *surety* of the debtor's obligation. The surety stands behind the debtor's obligation to the creditor. In general, the rules governing

75

the relationship between the creditor, the debtor (now referred to as the *principal debtor*), and the surety constitute a special body of common law — and a particularly intricate and oft-times perplexing body of law it is — referred to as the law of *suretyship*. The basic framework of suretyship — this tripartite arrangement involving the creditor, the principal debtor, and the surety — and the issues that may arise in its application are not limited to deals in which negotiable instruments play a part. The possibility of a third party being brought into a deal to act as surety for one of the more active players exists in a wide variety of situations. We limit our examination in this chapter to those special cases in which the surety takes on that role by affixing his or her signature to a negotiable instrument for the purpose of giving assurance that some other party to the instrument (someone who has already signed as either a maker, a drawer, an indorser, or an acceptor) will fulfill the obligation assigned to that role under the rules of Article 3 (which have already been examined in Chapter 3).

Although Article 3's treatment of suretyship does not differ radically from the general common law of suretyship as you would study it elsewhere, the drafters chose not to simply refer to that law and incorporate it by reference. Instead, they set forth the operative rules with regard to the role of the surety, in the context of negotiable instruments law, in detail (often, it has to be admitted, in what initially reads as excruciating detail) in the text of the Code itself. These rules are to be found principally in two sections, §3-419 and §3-605, on which we will focus in this chapter.*

Who or What Is an Accommodation Party?

The first thing we have to be aware of when looking at this topic through the lens of the law of negotiable instruments is that Article 3 adopts a vocabulary entirely distinct from that of the common law of suretyship. To see this, look at §3-419(a):

> If an instrument is issued for value given for the benefit of a party to the instrument ("accommodated party") and another party to the

---

* This is one situation where I do not suggest that you immediately try to read through the entire text of these two sections, much less the rather voluminous Official Commentary with which the drafters have provided us, on your own at the outset. The twists and turns in this area of law, whether as a general matter of common law or as the drafters of Article 3 have attempted to pin them down, are many. Our goal in this chapter is not to go through all of the minutiae of this material or these sections in all their agonizing (or mesmerizing, depending on how you look at these things) detail. It will be enough for you to get a good grasp of the basics and an appreciation of what kinds of further problems might have to be addressed and where to look for guidance when reference to the finer technicalities becomes necessary.

instrument ("accommodation party") signs the instrument for the purpose of incurring liability on the instrument without being a direct beneficiary of the value given for the instrument, the instrument is signed by the accommodation party "for accommodation."

So Article 3 refers to the surety, who has become a party to the instrument as an *accommodation party*. The party we have been referring to as the debtor or the principal debtor is the *accommodated party*. The third party in the picture, the creditor with whose concerns we started out this whole discussion, does not appear in subsection (a), but he, she, or it will be, in Article 3 lingo, the "person entitled to enforce" the instrument in question, a character whom we have already met.

Notice that under §3-419(a) no one can become an accommodation party to an instrument unless he or she has actually signed the instrument. The general rule remains true: A person cannot become a party to an instrument — accommodation party or otherwise — unless he or she has signed on the paper itself. As the second paragraph to Comment 3 makes clear:

> An accommodation party is always a surety. A surety who is not a party to the instrument, however, is not an accommodation party. For example, if M [for maker] issues a note payable to the order of P [for payee], and S [surety] signs a separate contract in which S agrees to pay P the amount of the instrument if it is dishonored, S is a surety but is not an accommodation party. In such a case, S's rights and duties are determined under the general [common] law of suretyship [and not under the provisions of Article 3].

In this chapter we will be dealing with accommodation parties only, and not even attempting to cover the law of suretyship in general. And whether a person is an accommodation party is first and foremost to be determined by whether that person's signature appears on the instrument. The circumstances of how and why that person's signature came to be affixed to the instrument will determine whether he or she is an accommodation party instead of a regular nonaccommodation party, but the fact of that party's signature appearing on the instrument is an absolute prerequisite to accommodation party status.

The fact that a party signs as an accommodation party does not alter another of the basic principles with which you should already be familiar: Anyone signing an instrument does so in a particular capacity. Once again, there are only four possibilities. Anyone whose signature appears on an instrument must have signed either as a maker of a note, the drawer or acceptor of a draft, or an indorser. This is no less true for an accommodation party. Any accommodation party will necessarily be either an accommodation maker, an accommodation drawer, an accommodation acceptor, or an accommodation indorser.

As Comment 1 to §3-419 points out, and as we will explore in the earlier examples, by far the most common situations (and the only two we will consider here) are those of the accommodation co-maker of a note and the accommodation indorser of either type of instrument. The comment actually refers to the second situation as that of the *anomalous indorser*, for which we need to turn back for a moment to §3-205(d):

> "Anomalous indorsement" means an indorsement by a person who is not the holder of the instrument. An anomalous indorsement does not affect the manner in which the instrument may be negotiated.

In the material we have already covered (particularly in Chapter 2), we saw that the purpose of an indorsement on an instrument was to fulfill a requirement so that instrument could be effectively negotiated. The holder was required, if the note was as held payable to the holder as an identified person, to sign the instrument either with a blank or a special indorsement in order to negotiate it to the next person down the chain of title by the act of transfer of possession.

You should be able to convince yourself that any signature on an instrument that isn't clearly the signature of a maker, drawer, or acceptor, and is furthermore not an indorsement made by a holder for the purposes of negotiating the instrument to the next person in the chain of title, is necessarily and simply by process of elimination an anomalous indorsement. As Comment 3 to §3-205 states:

> The only effect of an "anomalous indorsement" . . . is to make the signer liable on the instrument as an indorser. Such an indorsement is normally made by an accommodation party. Section 3-419.

All this still leaves us with the ultimate question: On what basis do we determine whether a party to an instrument can correctly be characterized as an accommodation party in whatever role that party signed the instrument? As we will see as we work through the examples, in most instances there should be no trouble making this determination. In some instances, however, a party may claim accommodation status, for reasons we have yet to see, and the party seeking to enforce the instrument against that party will contest the claim. Should the question of whether a party qualifies as an accommodation party arise, the ultimate test is as stated in §3-419(a): Did the party "sign the instrument for the purpose of incurring liability on the instrument without being a direct beneficiary of the value given for the instrument?" In some situations, as you can imagine and as we will examine in the examples and explanations to follow, the distinction between a direct and an indirect benefit can be a difficult line to draw.

The Consequences of Accommodation Status

It is all well and good to consider in the abstract who is and who is not an accommodation party to an instrument, but the answer to this question must be of more than theoretical interest. What difference does it make if a party to an instrument can successfully maintain that he or she is not simply a party to the instrument, but is rightfully to be considered an accommodation party? The first thing that has to be pointed out is one way — and a very significant way at that — in which an accommodation party is no different from any other party to an instrument. Any person signing an instrument as an accommodation party, remember, signs as either a maker, drawer, acceptor, or indorser. We have already seen that any party to an instrument, whatever that party's role, takes on the obligation to pay what is due on the instrument under certain well-defined rules supplied in §§3-412 through 3-415. The accommodation party is no different in this crucial regard. Recall that part of the definition of *accommodation party* in §3-419(a) is that the accommodation party "signs the instrument for the purpose of incurring liability" on it. Subsection (b) of §3-419 could not be clearer:

> An accommodation party may sign the instrument as maker, drawer, acceptor, or indorser and, subject to subsection (d) [a special and very limited case, that we'll look at in Example 3c], is obliged to pay the instrument in the capacity in which the accommodation party signs.

Whatever else may be true of the person who can establish signature of the instrument as an accommodation party, the basic rules controlling when the signatory must pay a person entitled to enforce the instrument remain the same. The accommodation party who tries to escape liability on the instrument by arguing that he or she signed "only" in an accommodation capacity, and received no benefit or value in exchange for his or her signature, will get nowhere with this argument. The accommodation party signs the instrument in one capacity or another — either as a drawer or acceptor or, more typically, as a maker or indorser — and is obliged as any nonaccommodation party would be to pay on the instrument if the conditions, and the rules of Article 3, call for payment by a party signing in that capacity.

Other consequences of accommodation status, however, do confer special benefits on the accommodation party. First, we note that if an accommodation party does have to come up with the cash to pay the instrument, he or she will be doing so because some other person, the accommodated party, has failed to meet its own obligation. The accommodation party has agreed to stand as surety for the accommodated party and to pay if and when the accommodated party fails to pay as it is expected to do. The accommodation party has committed itself to "backing up" the accommodated party's obligation, but it is clear that the ultimate obligation to pay rests on the accommodated party. The accommodation party certainly never agreed to pay whatever is due by the accommodated party and leave it at that. The accommodation party that has been forced to pay on the instrument because of the accommodated party's failure to do so will have what is referred to in the law of suretyship as a *right of recourse* against the accommodated party; that is, the right to payment by the accommodated party of what the accommodation party has paid on the other's behalf. Section 3-419 incorporates this general principle in subsection (e): "An accommodation party who pays the instrument is entitled to reimbursement from the accommodated party and is entitled to enforce the instrument against the accommodated party."

A second significant way in which a party that can establish signature in an accommodation status only may gain some benefit involves a series of defenses to liability, which are traditionally referred to as the *suretyship defenses.* These special defenses, available only to a surety, and only when the most exacting of criteria have been established, traditionally go by the names of *discharge, material modification* (which Article 3 treats as two separate situations, extension of the due date and all other material modifications), and *impairment of the collateral.* The specifics and exact contours of each of these defenses, both as they have evolved in the common law of suretyship and as they are incorporated into Article 3 via §3-605, are (to put it mildly) complex and dense with detail. In the examples I will not even attempt to get into all of the subtleties, but I do think it important and entirely possible for you to get some basic understanding of what the suretyship defenses involve and how they work, at least in broad relief.[*]

At the outset we can recognize the type of problem that the suretyship defenses are intended to address. When a party agrees in whatever manner to act as a surety, such as when a party agrees to sign a negotiable instrument as an accommodation party, that party is agreeing to lend not just its name but also its credit to a particular situation. It is agreeing (one would hope only after due deliberation) to act as surety for a defined obligation or set of obligations that the principal debtor has to the creditor as of the particular time when the suretyship obligation is assumed. In the cases with which we are concerned, the accommodation party agrees to meet certain obligations of the accommodated party — should the accommodated party fail to do so — to the extent and under the conditions as they exist as of the time when the accommodation party signs the instrument. Suppose that at some later date the principal debtor and the creditor agree between themselves, without

---

[*] You need not worry about the separate reference to the indorser in the caption to or other parts of §3-605, which we will cover. In some instances an indorser acts as a surety even though it does not technically fit within the definition of an accommodation party under §3-419(a). The drafters did their best to cover all the bases and capture each and every detail in their careful rendition of §3-605 and the comments thereto. Even after all that work was done, they were called upon to reexamine some 11 distinct issues related to the general matter of suretyship under the new Article 3, in a Commentary No. 11 issued in 1994 by the Permanent Editorial Board for the Uniform Commercial Code. This Commentary in turn revised some of the Official Comments. The degree of embellishment and complexity here can be truly daunting. Fortunately, it is not our goal here to master the field in all of its sophisticated variations. We are interested in getting a general appreciation of the main lines and contours of what §3-605 and the accompanying commentary cover in such loving detail. For our purposes, it will be more than sufficient to deal with only the simple situations and leave the seemingly endless variations on the principal themes to another day.

either informing or getting the agreement of the surety, to make some change from their original agreement. Suppose further that the surety is later called upon to come up with money to pay the creditor off when the principal debtor is unable to do so and that because of the debtor's financial position there is no chance that the surety will be made whole by the debtor through the right of recourse. If the surety can establish that it would not have been placed in this position — having to pay the principal debtor's obligation and being unable to get reimbursed for doing so — had the principal debtor and the creditor not made this readjustment to the terms and conditions of the principal debtor's obligation *after* the surety signed on and without getting the surety's agreement to the newly configured deal, then the surety should certainly have the right to argue that it should not be held to its initial agreement to back up the principal debtor's obligation, because that obligation has changed from what the surety originally agreed to support. The surety agreed to stand behind and guarantee the debtor's obligations as they were known to the surety at the time of the initial agreement. If the subsequent change in circumstances, agreed to by the creditor and the debtor but not the surety, can be shown to have placed a greater risk on the surety than it originally agreed to accept, the surety in all fairness should have some argument that its suretyship obligation can no longer be enforced against it, or at least that its potential liability on its agreement to stand as surety should be limited in some fashion to reflect the terms and conditions on which it did originally agree to take the responsibility and risks of suretyship.

Trying to make sense of the suretyship defenses in the abstract is, as you may be feeling at this point, a difficult proposition. This is just the type of problem with which a concrete example or two or three should help enormously. The final examples in this chapter are not intended to address every detail or variation on the theme, but if you work through them carefully you should be able to pick up the fundamentals of how the suretyship defenses may affect the potential liability of an accommodation party to a negotiable instrument. The availability of these defenses under the right circumstances is a significant consequence of accommodation status.

EXAMPLES

1.   Cosmo Graphics starts a small enterprise that he incorporates under the name of Graphics Surprise, Incorporated, with himself as sole shareholder and president. Graphics arranges with a local bank, Main Street Bank and Trust, to borrow on behalf of the corporation an amount of money that Cosmo needs to begin operations. One of the documents that the bank prepares and presents to him in order to finalize the loan is a note, the text of which gives the name of its maker as "Graphics Surprise, Incorporated." The note is signed by Graphics under a line that has been filled in with the language: "Graphics Surprise, Inc. by Cosmo Graphics, President." The bank also insists, because

the corporation is a new enterprise with few assets of its own, that Graphics add his signature, devoid of any other identification, a second time to the bottom of the instrument. Has the notion of accommodation signing of an instrument been invoked here? If so, who or what is the accommodation party? Who or what is the accommodated party?

2.   Upon her graduation from college, Lisa desires to buy a car. She finds just the kind she is looking for at Wiggum's Autorama. Wiggum is willing to sell the car to Lisa on credit, but since she has not had the opportunity to build up any kind of positive credit history, he says that he will do so only if Lisa finds someone to co-sign the note, which is of the type he asks all credit buyers to sign. Lisa's father, Homer, is more than willing to act as co-signer. The note is prepared, saying that "Lisa, as purchaser and borrower, promises to pay to the order of Wiggum's Autorama" specified monthly payments over the next three years. Lisa signs at the bottom of the note. Homer also signs at the bottom. Lisa takes delivery of the car and registers it in her own name.

(a) Who is the accommodation party here? Who is the accommodated party?

(b) What if the text of the note had read only that "the undersigned Borrower(s)" promise to make payment on the note? Both Lisa and Homer each sign at the bottom of the note with no other language indicating status. Does this change the situation?

(c) What if the note refers in its text only to "the undersigned Borrower(s)," but Homer adds the words "as Guarantor" after his signature?

(d) Finally, what if Lisa signs on the bottom of the note and Homer signs his name only on the reverse? How would you characterize this situation?

3.   Bart also wants to buy a car from Wiggum's Autorama, but because of his poor credit rating is told by Wiggum that he will be able to do so only if he gets a co-signer for the note he will be asked to sign. Bart convinces his mother, Marge, to act as co-signer. She does so by signing at the bottom of the note with her signature only. Bart takes delivery of the car and registers it in his name. From the beginning Bart falls behind on the monthly payments called for in the note, and eventually he stops paying altogether.

(a) May Wiggum go directly against Marge for failure to pay on the instrument as due, or is he obligated first to try to collect from Bart?

(b) If Wiggum does bring an action against Marge on the note, can she use as a defense the fact that she personally never received anything of value for her agreement to sign the note?

(c) Suppose Marge had signed with her name followed by the legend "Collection Guaranteed." Would this change the analysis? See §3-419(d).

(d) If Marge does have to make good to Wiggum on the payments not made by Bart, has she any course open to her other than to bear the loss and curse the day she ever agreed to help Bart buy the car on credit? See §3-419(e).

4.   Selma and Patty are sisters. Selma loves boating and contracts to buy a small but far from inexpensive yacht from The Skipper's Marina. The Skipper agrees to the sale only on the condition that Selma get a co-signer for the note she will be giving to him. Patty agrees to and does co-sign the note. Selma takes possession of the boat and registers it in her name. She arranges for it to be docked at a nearby yacht club that she has joined and regularly pays for the boat's fuel and other maintenance expenses. Patty, as it happens, doesn't like boating at all. She consistently turns down Selma's invitations that she "come out for the day" on the yacht.

(a) Is Patty an accommodation party under this set of facts?

(b) What if Patty were as enthusiastic about boating as is Selma? Patty joins Selma on the boat often and agrees to share the expenses of paying for, docking, and maintaining the craft. Patty also feels free to, and does on occasion, take the yacht out on her own. Can Patty still claim to be an accommodation party under these facts?

(c) What if the facts are somewhere in between those given in (a) and (b)? Patty doesn't avoid the yacht entirely, but goes out on it only occasionally and then only when Selma is at the helm. Should the issue arise, can Patty be classified as an accommodation party and take advantage of any special rights she may have deriving from that status?

5.   Seller agrees to deliver a quantity of goods to Buyer on credit. Buyer is required to sign a note promising to pay the purchase price within a year from the date of delivery. Seller also insists, as part of the arrangement, that Buyer have some independent party, Guarantor, sign the note as an accommodation party. Buyer and Guarantor both sign the note. When the goods are delivered, it turns out that they are totally substandard and without question fail to meet the requirements of what Seller was bound to deliver under the contract of sale. Buyer returns the goods to Seller. A year goes by and the note is still in the hands of Seller. You may assume that if Seller attempted to sue Buyer on its obligation as a maker of the note, Buyer would have a complete defense based on the quality of the merchandise delivered.

(a) If instead Seller were to sue Guarantor under its contractual obligation on the note, would Guarantor be able to rely upon the same defense based on the poor quality of the goods? See §3-305(d).

(b) What if instead the goods as delivered were just what was ordered? Buyer keeps the goods, but when the time comes for it to pay on the note, it has undergone such financial problems that it has been forced to declare bankruptcy and thus will be able to avoid payment on the note. Will Guarantor be off the hook as well in this situation?

6.   In April 2003, Homer arranges to borrow $45,000 from the Springfield National Bank, to set him up in a small business that he is sure will make him a ton of money. To get the loan from the bank, Homer has to ask his friend and neighbor Flanders to co-sign the note given to the bank. Flanders agrees to do so. The note that both of them sign calls for payment of the $45,000 plus interest on April 15, 2005. By early 2004, it has become apparent that Homer's get-rich-quick scheme is going nowhere and is steadily losing money. Homer contacts the bank, which agrees that if he will pay it $30,000 immediately it will release him from any further obligation on the note. Homer scrapes up this amount of cash and takes it to the bank, which gives him in exchange a signed writing renouncing all further rights against Homer on the note.

    (a) Can the bank later reverse its decision and sue Homer for the remainder due on the note when it comes due in April 2005? See §3-604.

    (b) Is the bank barred from suing Flanders on the note for what is due on April 15, 2005, minus the $30,000 previously paid on the obligation by Homer? See §3-605(b).

7.   The basic situation remains the same: Homer signs a note agreeing to pay Springfield Bank and Trust the sum of $45,000 plus interest on April 15, 2005, and Flanders signs the note as an accommodation to Homer. When Homer approaches the bank in early 2004, telling it of his financial troubles, it agrees not to release him from his obligation on the note but rather to extend the time he has to pay on it. Homer is now given until April 15, 2007, to come up with the $45,000 plus interest, which will continue to accumulate at the same rate as it has previously. Flanders is not informed of this renegotiation by Homer and the bank. By the time April 2007 comes around, Homer is flat broke. He is unable to pay the bank, or anyone else for that matter, a penny. The bank brings suit against Flanders as a co-maker for the full amount due on the note.

    (a) What argument does Flanders have that he may not be held fully liable for the amount due on the note? By what measure may his potential liability be reduced? See §3-605(c).

    (b) Would your analysis of the situation be any different if it were shown instead that Flanders had in fact been informed at the time the extension was granted by the bank to Homer and that Flanders made no objection to the bank's decision to grant Homer more time to repay the loan? See §3-605(i).

    (c) Suppose that there was language in the note, signed by both Homer and Flanders in the year 2003, to the effect that "any party hereto waives any defenses based on that party's status as surety for the obligation of another on this instrument." How, if at all, does this affect the situation?

8.   Moe owns a tavern. He approaches the Springfield National Bank, wanting to borrow $70,000 for the purpose of making improvements to his

establishment. The bank agrees to make the loan only on two conditions: (1) Moe must put up as collateral all of the equipment of his business, and (2) he must get a co-signer on the note he will be giving the bank. Moe enters into an agreement granting to the bank a security interest in "all of his equipment, now held or hereafter acquired," to secure repayment of the loan; he also signs all other papers requested of him by the bank in connection with this security agreement. In addition, he gets his friend Barney to co-sign the $70,000 note that he gives to the bank. Before the note comes due, Moe's business has taken a nose dive and he is forced to declare bankruptcy. The bank, it turns out, has through its own carelessness failed to file an Article 9 financing statement covering the collateral. As a result of this oversight, the bank is not able to establish a perfected interest giving it any special right in the equipment at the time of the bankruptcy. The bank is reduced to the position of a general (rather than a secured) creditor and as a result gets none of the $70,000 it is owed by Moe at the distribution of the bankruptcy estate.

(a) The bank goes against Barney as the accommodation party on the note. Assuming that the value of Moe's equipment was around $38,000, how much is the bank entitled to collect from Barney?

(b) What would the bank be able to collect from Barney if the value of the equipment at the time of the bankruptcy was nearer the $100,000 mark?

EXPLANATIONS

1.   This is most definitely an example of an accommodation signature. The first time Graphics signs, he signs as president of the corporation and binds the corporation as the principal debtor on the note. The second time he signs with his name only, and his signature binds him personally as an accommodation party, in this case an accommodation co-maker. The accommodated party is the corporation, Graphics Surprise, Incorporated.

You might have been tempted to say that Graphics could not be an accommodation party, as he will personally benefit from the loan "his" corporation has been able to obtain, and indeed in various ways he will benefit. He is, after all, the president of the corporation, and what's more important its sole shareholder and probably an employee as well. The key, however, is that all of this would be classified, at least in the minds of the U.C.C. drafters (as we will soon confirm) as indirect rather than direct benefit to Graphics personally. A signer can be an accommodation party under §3-419(a) as long as he is not "a *direct* beneficiary of the value given for the instrument." As Comment 1 to this section explains,

> Subsection (a) distinguishes between direct and indirect benefit. For example, if X cosigns a note of Corporation that is given for a loan to

Corporation, X is an accommodation party as long as no part of the loan was paid to X or for X's direct benefit. This is true even though X may receive indirect benefit from the loan because X is employed by Corporation or is a stockholder of Corporation, or even if X is the sole stockholder so long as Corporation and X are recognized as separate entities.

For a recent decision that follows the lead of this language in the commentary, see *Plein v. Lackey*, 149 Wash.2d 214, 67 P.3d 1061, 50 U.C.C.2d 234 (2003), a case otherwise most instructive because the plaintiff did not think of invoking Article 3 and §3-419 in particular until the final stage of a lengthy litigation in his petition for review before the Supreme Court of Washington. The plaintiff eventually won, but how much more smoothly things would have gone had he or his counsel picked up earlier on the obvious fact that Article 3 governed — and easily resolved — the situation, we can only guess.

In our example, as long as Graphics makes sure that all the loan proceeds go directly into the corporate treasury, are used for legitimate corporate purposes, and are not carelessly commingled with his own personal funds, he should be able to characterize himself as an accommodation co-maker should the need ever arise in the future for him to do so.

The basic scheme we see in this example — of one and sometimes several of the principals of a small corporation acting as surety, and in this case as an Article 3 accommodation party, for an obligation taken on by the corporation directly — is a very common one in business. Can you appreciate why a lender would not be comfortable getting the assurances of the corporate borrower alone that the loan will be repaid?

2a. Homer is the accommodation party. Although Homer might want to argue, if for some reason it would make a difference, that his signature was an indorsement and not that of a maker, he would almost assuredly lose on this point. It is technically true that under Article 3 there is no requirement of *where* an indorsement must be placed on an instrument. However, the courts have generally ruled that someone signing at the bottom of the front of a note is signing in just the space conventionally reserved for the signatures of makers and will, unless there is very clear language to the contrary, be so classified. Homer is an accommodation co-maker. Lisa is the accommodated party.

2b. This should not change the situation. As long as all of the direct benefit of the loan is going to Lisa, and Homer is receiving only indirect benefit from his signature (such as the pleasure he gets from being of assistance to his daughter, not having to drive her wherever she has to go, and perhaps just getting her out of the house), he is still signing as an accommodation party. The fact that his accommodation status is not clearly evident from a full reading and examination of the instrument alone is not decisive. As Comment 3 begins: "As stated in Comment 1 [where exactly?], whether a person is an accommodation party is a question of fact." Here the facts all point to Homer's being an accommodation party only. A separate question — and one that is important only in limited circumstances of the type we get into when we later touch on the suretyship defenses and §3-605 — is whether any particular holder of the instrument would have notice that Homer signed for accommodation only. In our situation Wiggum would certainly have notice. He was the one who told Lisa that for her personally to obtain the loan and get the car, she'd have to get a co-signer to back up her signature. Should Wiggum sell the note to another party, that party would not necessarily have any way of knowing, at least not from the face of the instrument itself, that Homer's signature was intended to make him an accommodation co-maker only. Homer might still be able to establish himself as an accommodation party, but the burden would be on him to show that this person who took from Wiggum had either actual knowledge or reason to know that Homer had signed without receiving a direct benefit.

It's skipping ahead a bit, but take a look at §3-605(h). On the question of notice, this section refers us to §3-419(c). The important language in that section for our purposes is its first sentence:

> A person signing an instrument is presumed to be an accommodation party and there is notice that the instrument is signed for accommodation if the signature is an anomalous indorsement or is accompanied by words indicating that the signer is acting as a surety or guarantor with respect to the obligation of another party to the instrument.

If Homer just signs his name below that of Lisa on a note that speaks only of "the undersigned Borrower(s)," as he has done here, he may later be able to establish that he was signing as an accommodation party only, and furthermore that whoever is trying to enforce the instrument against him had notice of his accommodation status, but he won't be able to take advantage of the exceptionally helpful presumption of §3-419(c) working in his favor to make his case.

2c. Homer has done better to sign in this fashion. Should the issue ever arise of whether he was signing for accommodation only, he has the presumption of §3-419(c) to lean on. Here his signature is not an anomalous indorsement, however it is "accompanied by words indicating that the signer [Homer] is acting as surety or guarantor with respect to the obligation of another party to the instrument [Lisa]." Assuming, as we have been, that all the direct benefit of the loan proceeds have gone to Lisa, Homer is an accommodation party and should have little trouble establishing that anyone who might later come into possession of the note had notice of the status in which he signed.

2d. A signature on the reverse of an instrument is conventionally assumed to be an indorsement, and there is nothing to suggest that this intention was not present here. Homer is once again an accommodation party, but now an accommodation indorser. Lisa is, as always, the accommodated party.

3a. Marge has signed as an accommodation co-maker. Bart is the accommodated party. Wiggum as the holder and person entitled to enforce the instrument is perfectly within his rights to go against Marge directly as one of the two makers of the instrument, without trying first to collect from Bart. Recall the general rule of §3-419 that the accommodation party "is obliged to pay the instrument in the capacity in which the accommodation party signs." Marge signed as one of two makers, and as such her obligation to pay on the instrument is as set forth in §3-412.

3b. Marge has no defense that she signed merely as an accommodation party, that she received no direct benefit from the value given (that is what an accommodation party is all about, after all), nor that she received nothing in exchange from Bart or anyone else for her agreement to act as an accommodation party to help Bart out. See the very last part of §3-419(b): "The obligation of the accommodation party may be enforced . . . whether or not the accommodation party receives any consideration for the accommodation." She may very well have agreed to co-sign the note only out of the kindness of her heart, to help Bart out. Even so, that in no way lessens her obligation on the negotiable instrument she signed.

3c. Yes, the situation is different if the accommodation party signs in a way indicating that her signature is "guaranteeing collection rather than payment of the obligation of another party to the instrument." For an accommodation party to fall within the special rule of §3-419(d), the signature must truly and "unambiguously" (as the subsection makes clear) show that only collection and not payment was guaranteed. An accommodation party who signs simply as "Guarantor" or with the words "Payment Guaranteed" would clearly not be unambiguously guaranteeing collection only.

In this part of our example, Marge was very careful and signed with the legend "Collection Guaranteed." This being the case, under subsection (d) Wiggum will have to go against Bart first. Marge can be called upon to meet her obligation on the instrument only after Wiggum has obtained a judgment against Bart and attempted to enforce it. If (i) the execution of judgment against Bart has been returned unsatisfied, (ii) Bart is insolvent or in insolvency proceedings, (iii) Bart cannot be served with process, or (iv) it is otherwise apparent that payment cannot be obtained from Bart, then and only then can Wiggum go against Marge. This obviously puts Marge much less at risk of having to pay on the instrument, or at the very least delays considerably the time when she conceivably might have to pay. In contrast, a "Collection Guaranteed" accommodation such as this is of much less value to the lender, who was willing to proceed only on the condition that Bart get someone to "stand behind" his obligation and co-sign his note. It is fairly unlikely that someone in Wiggum's position, at least if he knows what is good for him, will accept a guarantee of collection only and not a full guarantee of payment as a suitable co-signature allowing Bart to buy the car on credit. In other, more complex financial arrangements, of course, the guarantee of collection only by someone other than the principal debtor may be perfectly appropriate and all that the lender wants, or can expect to obtain, in order for the deal to go through.

3d. If Marge does have to fork over the money due to Wiggum, she is entitled under §3-419(e) "to reimbursement from the accommodated party and is entitled to enforce the instrument against the accommodated party." This last language, allowing her "to enforce the instrument" against Bart, is not just a duplication of the right to reimbursement (also provided for). Reimbursement would entail Marge's getting from Bart (if she can find him) just the amount she had to pay out of her pocket to Wiggum. Often a straightforward reimbursement will be enough to satisfy the accommodation party who has been made to pay on the instrument — and indeed, in many cases the accommodation party will feel lucky if she can get just this. The provision permitting the accommodation party who has had to make payment to "enforce the instrument," however, allows for more than mere reimbursement. The accommodation party who pays the instrument then, in effect, takes up the instrument and can assert any of the rights that the initial obligee (here Wiggum) had on the instrument against the accommodated party (Bart). So, for instance, if the terms of the note allowed the holder to accelerate the amount due upon a default, or to charge some reasonable penalty against the defaulting borrower, or to recover its attorney's fees involved in collection, Marge would succeed to those rights once she has paid Wiggum. Also, assume that Wiggum had initially, in addition to insisting that Bart get a co-signer to back up his obligation on the note, taken a security interest in the car he was selling to Bart as collateral to further ensure the payment of Bart's debt. Marge, once she has paid off Wiggum, would step into his shoes, obtaining such rights as he had against Bart; this would include the rights to consider the car (if she can find it) as collateral supporting Bart's obligation to pay her what he owes on the note. See Comment 5 and the *Plein v. Lackey* case cited earlier.

The situations in this and the previous example — where a parent agrees to act as surety for his or her child for whom credit is understandably hard to obtain — are typical of a whole other group of transactions in which the nature of accommodating another on a note is employed. All kinds of circumstances are possible, of course. For a rarer case in which a high-school-age son signed a note to accommodate his mother without reading it (because he had come into the house "tired from work"), see *Ruane v. Jancsics*, 2001 Mass.App.Div. 103, 44 U.C.C.2d 1122. What school he was in or what job he was working when he was held liable as an accommodating party the court does not tell us.

4a. Yes. Patty, whatever her motives for agreeing to sign the note, receives no "direct benefit," as that term is used in §3-419(a), from the value given for the instrument, the boat. As this example is meant to explore, it is not necessarily crystal clear in all cases whether someone claiming to be an accommodation party has in fact received what would amount to a direct benefit for the purposes of this subsection, and hence would not meet the test for being an accommodation party. The Code nowhere provides a definition of the term nor a standard for distinguishing a direct benefit from an indirect one. In this part of the example, however, Patty — who chooses to have nothing to do with the boat in question or boating in general — clearly has gotten no direct benefit, however that term should be understood, from Selma's acquisition and will qualify as an accommodation party.

4b. Patty can still claim to be an accommodation party, but under this set of facts it is far less clear that she should or would be so characterized. Even though the boat may be registered in Selma's name only, so that she is technically the owner, Patty seems to be getting the same benefit from its acquisition as is Selma. Patty could try to argue that she is only receiving the "indirect benefit" of having a sister who owns a yacht and is generous about inviting her aboard and letting her use it on occasion, but the picture here seems to show that Patty is a direct beneficiary of the purchase of the boat in the same way that Selma is, if not exactly to the same degree. Whether or not a person is an accommodation party is always a question of fact, and the facts here could make it hard for Patty to prove that she had accommodation status.

Notice that the result would not necessarily be different even if Patty had signed with the notation "as Guarantor" under Selma's unqualified signature. True, under §3-419(c) Patty's signing in this manner would create the presumption that she is an accommodation party, but this is only a presumption and is subject to rebuttal. The first paragraph of Comment 3 to §3-419 reminds us of the basic proposition that whether a person qualifies as an accommodation party is always a question of fact. Subsection (c) creates the presumption of accommodation status in certain circumstances, but it is a presumption only and can be overcome by the right evidence. This paragraph of the comment concludes, "A party challenging accommodation party status would have to rebut this presumption by producing evidence that the signer was in fact a direct beneficiary of the value given for the instrument." If Patty is truly using the boat as if she were a co-owner, as the facts here suggest, anyone later trying to hold her liable on the instrument might well be able to rebut any presumption that she is an accommodation party, no matter how she signed the instrument.

4c. The facts are now somewhere in between those of parts (a) and (b), and it will not surprise you that being confident of the correct answer is just that much harder. Patty is deriving *some* benefit from Selma's purchase of the boat, but does it rise to the level of a direct benefit, or is it merely, as Patty will argue, an incidental and indirect benefit? Perhaps further investigation of the facts would clarify the matter, but even with all the facts at hand the issue can be a close call and there is simply no bright-line test that will resolve it. The cases that have had to address situations such as this (under the prerevision version of Article 3, which employed slightly different language to define an accommodation party but did not seem to be aiming for a different analysis) have done the best they could in sorting out direct from indirect benefit, but, as we would expect for such a fact-specific issue, the results have not been noted for any great consistency.

5a.   Yes. We have not yet had the opportunity to explore the defenses that a party to an instrument will be able to assert, and then with what success, when that party is sued on the obligation it undertook by signing the instrument in one capacity or another. The rules, as we will see, depend on the nature of the defense and furthermore on who is seeking enforcement. I trust, however, that you didn't find it hard to accept what I asked you to assume for the purposes of this question. If the note is still in the hands of Seller, and Seller tries to enforce it against Buyer, Buyer's defense here — what would amount to a total failure of consideration — would be good against Seller. The relevant point for our present purposes is, as you saw in §3-305(d), that Guarantor as surety would be able to assert this same defense against Seller if Guarantor, rather than Buyer, were being sued on the note. With certain limited exceptions of which we will soon take note, any defense that the accommodated party would be able to assert is also available to the accommodation party being sued on the instrument.

What we are seeing here is not an example of the so-called suretyship defenses. We come to those in the next example. Those are defenses available only to an accommodation party and then only under very distinct circumstances. Here the defense of failure of consideration, which Buyer would be able to assert if it were being sued by Seller, is available to Guarantor as a *derivative defense*. Guarantor has agreed, by becoming an accommodation party, to stand behind and act as surety for whatever obligation the accommodated party may legitimately owe. Buyer does not owe Seller anything — not on the underlying contract for sale and not on the instrument given as payment — for the goods that were not up to the contract specifications and that in fact were returned to Seller. The accommodated party having no obligation to Seller under the circumstances, Guarantor has every right to assert and prove this to be so and that therefore it has no duty to pay what the accommodated party does not itself owe.

5b.   No, Guarantor will not be able to use as a defense the accommodated party's bankruptcy. As you saw when you read §3-305(d), the accommodation party may assert against the party seeking enforcement any defense that the accommodated party would be able to assert "*except* the defenses of discharge in insolvency proceedings, infancy, and lack of legal capacity." This makes sense. These three defenses might well be available to the accommodated party in some situations, but they do not arise because that party has no obligation to pay what he or she has promised. Rather, they cover situations in which, because of special rules of law, the obligation of the accommodated party cannot be enforced against it, even though it truly does owe some amount of money. It is just these situations that potential creditors find most worrisome — that the principal debtor may owe money that it cannot be made to pay (because of a discharge in bankruptcy, for example) — and exactly the reason why such a creditor is apt to ask for a personal guarantee from some other party. In case the principal debtor, the accommodated party in our story, does go bankrupt, the creditor wants to have some other solvent party against whom it can proceed to collect on the debt. If the surety — or as we say in the negotiable instrument context, the accommodation party — were to be able to avoid obligation when the accommodated party goes bankrupt, it would greatly undermine the very assurance with which the creditor is seeking to provide itself by insisting that someone sign in accommodation for the principal debtor. From the creditor's point of view, what's the value of getting someone else to back up the debtor's obligation if the back-up is immune from suit in just those eventualities about which the creditor is most concerned, and in which being able to proceed against the surety will be most necessary?

6a. No. Under §3-604(a), the bank as the person entitled to enforce the instrument may, as it has done here, "discharge the obligation of a party [Homer] to pay the instrument." The bank in this instance has done so by a signed writing renouncing any rights against Homer. In return it has received consideration of $30,000 cash from Homer, but as you can see in §3-604(a), a person entitled to enforce can discharge a party to an instrument by its voluntary act even if no consideration is given. Homer has no further obligations on the note.

6b. No. Under §3-605(b), discharge of Homer *does not* discharge the obligation of Flanders, an accommodation party having a right of recourse against Homer, the discharged party. The bank can hold Flanders responsible for what is still due, above and beyond the $30,000 it earlier received from Homer, on the instrument. Once Flanders pays this amount, he has of course a right of recourse against Homer, the accommodated party, for reimbursement, but if Homer is unable to pay Flanders will have to bear the loss. That's the kind of thing that can happen when you agree to serve as an accommodation party on an instrument. Flanders can take comfort in the fact that he has acted as a good friend and neighbor, but in doing so he took on a risk that came back to haunt him.

At first it might strike you as strange that the holder of the instrument and the accommodated party, here the bank and Homer, can agree between themselves to release the accommodated party from any further liability on the instrument and at the same time allow the holder to retain all of its rights against the accommodation party, Flanders. Note that this result does not depend on the bank and Homer getting Flanders's agreement to the discharge transaction; Flanders need not even be made aware of it. What is to keep the bank and Homer from agreeing to a discharge of Homer for little or nominal consideration, comfortable in the fact that the bank can then collect the full value of the note from the friendly and solvent Flanders when the time comes for payment? One response to this question is that, like all other actions under any article of the Code, the discharge transaction is subject to the general obligation of good faith found in O§1-203 or R§1-304. We will need to consider the notion of good faith in various topics yet to come, but do look at the definition of *good faith* as it appears in §3-103(a)(4) or now in R§1-201(b)(20): "'Good faith' means honesty in fact and the observance of reasonable commercial standards of fair dealing." Were the bank to discharge Homer from any further responsibility on the note for no good reason other than to put Flanders in the hot seat by shifting the obligation to pay onto him, Flanders would doubtless have a strong argument that the bank had not acted in good faith in so doing.

Although the legal obligation of good faith offers Flanders protection against some type of collusive effort on the part of the bank and Homer to shift the principal responsibility for paying on the note onto him, it is unlikely that the issue of good faith would ever even arise. As a practical matter, Flanders's real protection against the bank's too cavalierly discharging Homer from future liability on the note is the simple fact that creditors just don't do that sort of thing. We have to assume, unless the bank is unlike any lender we have run into in the past, that it is not going to release *anybody* from *any* obligation owed to it without a very good reason. In agreeing to release Homer from any further obligation in return for an immediate payment of $30,000 in early 2004, the bank must have made a calculated business determination that Homer's financial situation would simply deteriorate further and the prospects for the bank's getting even this much from him in the future would only diminish as time went on. By taking the $30,000 from Homer when it did, the bank was making a cold-hearted decision that this was the most it would ever be able to get from Homer on the note, and that it would be better to take what it could at the time rather than risk further loss in the future. We have to assume as well that the figure of $30,000 was not picked out of thin air, but was the result of a negotiation in which the bank aimed at squeezing as much out of Homer as it possibly could at the time. Just as the prudent and professional lender is not about to release any party without what it deems at the time to be a good reason, it is not going to do so for any less in return than it can possibly get that party to come up with. Of course Homer has the sense to agree to pay $30,000 prior to when it is due only in exchange for being released from any further obligation on the note, but that is only to be expected.

Flanders, as we know, remains liable as an accommodation party for the remainder of what the bank is due. He of course has a right of reimbursement from Homer, but if the bank's prognosis of Homer's financial future is correct, it is unlikely that Flanders will have much success in getting reimbursement from Homer of what Flanders is eventually made to pay to the bank. The point to be made, however, is that if the bank was taking care of its own business properly, it was at the same time really acting in a way compatible with and not contrary to Flanders's interests. True, Flanders is almost assuredly going to lose some money, but had the bank not made the earlier settlement with Homer, the amount due from Homer on April 15, 2005, would have been the full $45,000 plus interest, and the possibility that Homer could have been made to pay even $30,000 toward this amount would have been all the more remote. Remember that the reason the bank agreed to release Homer earlier for less that the full sum due was not just to be nice; it had made a pragmatic determination that Homer's get-rich-quick scheme was not working out as planned, that his financial situation was worsening, and that his ability to pay anything on the note would only lessen over time. Homer might have been flat broke by the time April 15, 2005, rolled around. Flanders would have had to pay the full amount due on the note with little hope of getting anything in the way of reimbursement from the now-penniless Homer. So Flanders has to take some comfort in the fact that had the bank not entered into the discharge agreement with Homer earlier, he would in all probability have been required to pay even more on account of his having agreed to act as an accommodation party than the liability he now faces. The first paragraph of Comment 3 to §3-605 calls upon this same line of thinking to justify the rule of §3-605(b). As the penultimate sentence in that paragraph concludes, "Settlement [between the creditor and the principal debtor] is in the interest of sureties as well as the creditor."

7a. Flanders would invoke §3-605(c), asserting the suretyship defense available to him because of the bank's agreement with Homer to extend the due date on Homer's obligation. As that subsection states, when the due date has been extended in this way by agreement between the person holding the instrument and the accommodated party,

> the extension discharges an . . . accommodation party having a right of recourse against the party whose obligation is extended to the extent the . . . accommodation party proves that the extension caused loss to the . . . accommodation party with respect to the right of recourse.

Flanders would first have to establish that he signed the note as an accommodation party only, but that should not be hard in this instance. He would then bear the burden of proving the extent, if any, to which the extension caused a loss to him "with respect to the right of recourse" against Homer. What might such proof entail? Suppose that Flanders could prove that although Homer was in dire financial straits at the time of the initial due date, he could somehow have come up with the full measure due (the $45,000 plus interest) to pay off the note had the bank not extended the time for him to pay. If this were true, then but for the extension Flanders would have had to pay nothing as an accommodation party. Even if the bank, rather than fight Homer tooth and nail, had agreed to take, say, $40,000 flat from Homer in exchange for releasing him from obligation on the note as of April 15, 2005, and had then gone against Flanders for the remainder at that time (as we saw it could under

§3-605(b) in the previous example), Flanders would have been able to assert his right of recourse against Homer for what Flanders would have had to pay the bank and would have come out whole. As it turned out, however, by its agreement to extend the time for Homer to pay, all the bank did was allow the situation to degenerate to the point where Homer could not pay a thing. The bank will collect the full amount due on the note from Flanders, but Flanders's right to reimbursement from Homer has been rendered valueless by the passage of the extra time until April 2007. Suppose that Flanders could prove the facts to be as we've just assumed them: that, in effect, the bank's agreement to extend the due date of the instrument turned the situation from one in which Flanders would not have had to lose anything as an accommodation party (if the original due date had not been tampered with and Homer had been made to pay in 2005) to one in which Flanders was made to pay the entire amount due in 2007, with no hope of reimbursement from a now-destitute Homer. You can see how Flanders could argue that the extension caused him a loss in the full amount of what the bank is demanding he pay in 2007 in his accommodation role on the instrument. Had the bank not agreed to the extension, Homer would have scraped up the money to pay in 2005 and Flanders would have been off the hook entirely. With the bank having agreed to the extension, and Homer's financial condition further deteriorated, Flanders now stands potentially liable for the full debt with no chance of reimbursement from Homer. In the face of such proof by Flanders, the general law of suretyship and §3-605(c) discharges the surety or accommodation party to the extent that the extension of time granted by the creditor (the bank in this instance) actually caused loss to the surety. If the facts are as we have been assuming them to be, Flanders would be fully discharged, in light of the extension, from having to pay anything on the note.

Assume the facts to be otherwise. In particular, assume that Homer was already out of money by 2005. Had the bank not agreed to the extension, it would have attempted to collect from Homer but gotten nowhere. It would then have collected the full amount due from Flanders as the accommodation party. Flanders would, of course, have sought reimbursement from Homer, but if Homer doesn't have the money in 2005 to pay the bank then he's not going to have it to pay to Flanders. Under this assumption, Flanders would have ended up paying the full amount due on the note with no reasonable prospect for reimbursement in 2005. The extension of the due date on the note to 2007 doesn't really cause him any further loss. He can be made to pay the full amount because of his agreement to accommodate Homer on his neighbor's obligation to the bank, but he would have had to do so and pay just as much even if the extension had not been granted by the bank. The extension does not cause any additional loss to Flanders. By the end of the term initially agreed to (April 15, 2005) his fate was sealed. Under this scenario, Flanders cannot prove any loss to him caused by the extension.

(If anything, there was at least the possibility, even if it didn't pan out here, that if Homer had been given some more time to come up with the money, he might have been able to pay all or at least a portion of what was due on the note by 2007, thereby decreasing the amount Flanders would have to pay on his accommodation contract.) Because Flanders would be unable to prove, under this set of facts, that the extension caused him any loss with respect to his right of recourse, he would not be discharged at all from what he now will be obligated to pay the bank in 2007.

Of course, all kinds of situations can arise where the facts are not as all-or-nothing as I have presented them in the two previous paragraphs. The principle remains the same. Assume that Flanders can prove that, had the extension not been granted by the bank, Homer would have been forced to pay, either to the bank or by way of reimbursement to Flanders, some amount X, perhaps less than all he owed but a significant sum nonetheless. As it turns out, the extension is granted and the most that can be gotten out of Homer in 2007, either by the bank or by Flanders, is some other sum Y. If X is less than Y, Flanders has not suffered any loss as a result of the extension, and he will have no right to any discharge under §3-605(c). If, however, X is greater than Y, Flanders is discharged from the amount he will have to pay the bank in 2007, to the extent of X minus Y. In practice, of course, the trick — or rather, the subject of what may turn out to be extensive litigation — is to determine the true value in dollars and cents of the Xs and Ys of the situation.

I did not think it advisable to lengthen this chapter still further by giving you an example on point, but you should be aware that §3-605 deals, in subsection (d), with a different but related set of circumstances. That subsection sets forth the rule when the creditor and the accommodated party agree "to a material modification of the obligation of [the accommodated] party other than an extension of the due date." So, for example, the bank and Homer could agree to keep the due date on the note as is but to increase the principal or to raise the rate of interest, either of which could obviously end up having some detrimental effect on Flanders's position as an accommodation party. The way subsection (d) deals with such situations is basically the same as what subsection (c) does when the alteration is only that of an extension of the due date on the instrument: the accommodation party is discharged from obligation on the instrument to the extent the material modification causes it actual loss. The one significant difference between (c) and (d), however, and the reason the drafters chose to cover the different situations in two distinct subsections, has to do with burden of proof. In subsection (c), which is concerned with modifications the only effect of which is to extend the accommodated party time for payment, the burden of proof is on the accommodation party to show loss caused to it by this modification, and its obligation is discharged only to the extent of the loss it can prove. In subsection (d), which deals with modifications other than extensions of time, the presumption is that such a modification effects a loss to the accommodation party, and the rule is that there is a full discharge "unless the person enforcing the instrument proves that no loss was caused by the modification or that the loss caused by the modification was an amount less than the amount of the right of recourse." The reason for the drafters' decision to treat the two cases differently in this respect is given in Comment 5:

> The rationale for having different rules with respect to loss for extensions of the due date and other modifications is that extensions are likely to be beneficial to the surety and they are often made. Other modifications are less common and they may very well be detrimental to the surety. Modification of the obligation of the principal debtor without permission of the surety is unreasonable unless the modification is benign. Subsection (d) puts the burden on the person seeking enforcement of the instrument to prove the extent to which loss was not caused by the modification.

7b. If Flanders had been made aware of the extension entered into between Homer and the bank and had not objected, he would be barred from later asserting any suretyship defense otherwise available to him under §3-605. The bank could point to §3-605(i) and show that Flanders's failure to object to a modification of which he was aware constituted consent to the modification.

7c. Such a clause in the note, or in any other writing signed by Flanders at the time he took on the obligation of an accommodation party, would deprive him of the right to assert any of the suretyship defenses of §3-605 should the need or the hope of doing so ever arise. Under §3-605(i), a party may not be discharged under §3-605 if "the instrument or a separate agreement of the party provides for waiver of discharge under this section either specifically or by general language indicating that the parties waive defenses based on suretyship or impairment of collateral" (the situation we deal with in the last example). As a matter of fact, such clauses generally and prospectively waiving any and all suretyship defenses are quite common. As Comment 2 notes,

> The importance of the suretyship defenses is greatly diminished by the fact that they can be waived. The waiver is usually made by a provision in the note or other writing that represents the obligation of the principal debtor. It is standard practice to include a waiver of suretyship defenses in notes given to financial institutions or other commercial creditors. Section 3-605(i) allows waiver. Thus Section 3-605 applies to the occasional case in which the creditor did not include a waiver clause in the instrument or in which the creditor did not obtain the permission of the surety to take the action that triggers the suretyship defense.

See, for example, *Decatur County Bank v. Smith*, 40 U.C.C.2d 1236 (Tenn. App. 1999).

8a. Springfield National Bank should be able to collect $32,000 from Barney but no more. The bank could sue Barney for the full $70,000, but Barney should know enough to assert the suretyship defense of so-called impairment of the collateral, provided for in §3-605(e). (This all assumes, of course, that at the time of the initial transaction Barney did not sign anything waiving for all time his right to assert such a defense under §3-605(i).) Under subsection (g), impairing the value of an interest in collateral includes "failure to obtain or maintain perfection or recordation of the interest in collateral," and that is exactly what the bank did here. Under Article 9 of the U.C.C., the bank's failure to file with the proper public records office a financing statement covering the collateral in question rendered its security interest unperfected. Had it done what it was supposed to and filed, it would have had a perfected interest in this equipment, and upon Moe's bankruptcy would have been able to turn this interest into $38,000, which it would then have applied against the debt. Instead, it got nothing of value from its security interest, because of its own failure to protect its interest as it should have, and as Barney could reasonably have expected it to have done.

Under §3-605(e), this impairment of the collateral by the bank discharges the obligation of the accommodated party "to the extent of the impairment." The language of the subsection on how to measure the extent of the discharge to which the accommodated party is entitled in such a situation is fairly dense and not the easiest to read, but the basic principle is not that hard to follow, and it will do for our purposes. In the situation we have before us, had the impairment of the collateral not occurred the bank could have gotten $38,000 of what it was owed from enforcing its rights in that collateral. That would have left it unpaid to the tune of $32,000, and it would have gone against Barney for only that much. Barney would have had to pay the $32,000 to the bank on his accommodation contract. He would of course have a right of recourse against Moe for this amount, but as Moe is bankrupt it is highly unlikely that Barney will ever see a penny from him. The bank, having impaired the value of the collateral right down to zero dollars, can sue Barney for the $70,000, but Barney will be able to argue that he has been discharged to the extent of $38,000 of this obligation, due to the bank's impairment of the collateral.

8b. If the collateral that the bank, through its own failure, let slip through its hands was worth something like $100,000, or anything over $70,000 for that matter, then Barney would be able to argue total discharge of his obligation based on the accommodation signature. Had it not impaired the value of the collateral, the bank would have been able to walk away from the bankruptcy fully satisfied, thanks to its judicious decision to take a security interest in collateral to protect its position and the fortunate fact that when the time came for it to rely on that interest the value of the collateral exceeded the obligation it was owed by Moe. The bank would have had no reason to come against Barney for anything; even if it had, and Barney had been made to pay $70,000 to the bank, Barney would then have a right of recourse against Moe. And Barney's right of recourse would then automatically have been secured by the security interest initially taken by the bank. See Comment 5 to §3-419:

> Since the accommodation party that pays the instrument is entitled to enforce the instrument against the accommodated party, the accommodation party also obtains rights to any security interest or other collateral that secures payment of the instrument.

Barney, now owed $70,000 by Moe under §3-419(e), would be able himself to go against the collateral. Because it is worth more than what he is owed by Moe, Barney will be made whole that way. This all depends, of course, on the rights in the collateral not having been impaired. Once the bank impairs the value of the collateral, neither the bank nor Barney (if he is made first to pay the bank and then later look to Moe for reimbursement) can get any value out of the equipment to lessen the amount due from Moe. Moe is not able to pay anybody anything. So the bank's failure to protect both itself and the surety, Barney, by properly taking, perfecting, and maintaining perfection of a security interest on equipment that would be of some value in the bankruptcy proceeding, has by its impairment of the collateral discharged Barney in this case from having to pay anything on his contract as an accommodation party. For a case of this type, when an accommodation party alleged, but had offered no evidence to prove (thus denying her the right to summary judgment in her favor), impairment of the collateral by the lender, see *J.B. Allen, Inc. v. Pearson*, 31 S.W.2d 256, 43 U.C.C. 2d 360 (Mo. App. 2000).

See Revision Alert on the following page.

Revision Alert

Revised §3-419 now contains a subsection explicitly stating what we have been assuming all along, that a person signing an instrument "accompanied by words indicating that the party guarantees payment or the signer signs the instrument as an accommodation party in some other manner that does not unambiguously indicate an intention to guarantee collection rather than payment, . . . is obliged to pay the amount due on the instrument . . . in the same circumstances as the accommodated party would be obliged, without prior resort to the accommodated party by the party entitled to enforce the instrument." Nothing terribly novel here.

In contrast, R§3-605 has been totally rewritten, right down to all the accompanying comments. This major overhaul is intended, as the drafters inform us in the Prefatory Note to the Amendments to Article 3 and 4 constituting the 2002 revision, to conform this provision to the language and rules of the recently issued (in 1995) and well-received (if they do say so themselves) *Restatement of Suretyship and Guaranty*. The amendment to this one section alone, in fact, makes up something like one-half of the length of the entire set of amendments. With all this rewriting, no doubt there are substantive changes here and there, but this is certainly not the place to go into them in all their gory detail. Should a question arise that needs to be addressed by R§3-605, you should find help in the new commentary, even more copious than what it replaces, which has already been described by some as a "mini-treatise," not just on the workings of this section but on suretyship law in general.

6

Effect on the Underlying Obligation

Introduction

Negotiable instruments are, as you are by now no doubt more than ready to concede, distinct and utterly fascinating pieces of paper. Their importance, of course, lies not in the pure beauty of the form, nor in the intricate rules by which they are distinguished from other types of writings, nor in the specialized mechanics governing how they may be passed from hand to hand, nor even in how the rules pertaining to them both create and simultaneously record a special breed of legal obligations as these fascinating bits of paper move from party to party. Negotiable instruments take on their true importance because of the function they serve in the real world of commerce.

It is perfectly possible, of course, for a negotiable instrument to be issued with the issuer having no business purpose in mind; we have already noted that one may draw a check, for example, for the purpose of making a gift to a friend or a donation to a charitable institution. In the vast majority of cases, though, the reason a negotiable instrument has been called into being is so that the issuer can use it to pay for something. The genesis of the typical negotiable instrument, if you will, is some duty arising under some other area of law — the duty to pay under contract law for goods or services received, the duty to repay a loan, the duty to pay a judgment rendered against the issuer, or any other duty that can be and has been reduced to the obligation to pay a sum of money — which duty the obligor is intending to fulfill by handing over to the obligee not a pile of cash, but some negotiable instrument to serve in its stead. It is customary to refer to this background debt or other duty to pay as the *underlying obligation* explaining why the instrument was issued in the first place. The issuer's intention in creating and handing over to another the negotiable instrument is to satisfy the underlying obligation. When and how this objective is met, and what the consequences are when it is not (if, for example, the instrument is dishonored), are our concerns in this chapter. Fortunately, Article 3 covers the issues involved directly in a single section, §3-310, which you should read over carefully before you proceed to the examples.

EXAMPLES

1. Boris enters into an agreement to buy an expensive antique porcelain figurine from Sonya. As agreed, she hands the valuable object over to him in exchange for a cashier's check for $25,000, which he has obtained from the Independent Republic Bank. By the time Sonya gets around to depositing the check, this bank is experiencing financial difficulty and may not be able to pay on the cashier's checks it has outstanding.

    (a) If Sonya runs into trouble trying to collect on the cashier's check, may she sue Boris for what she will argue is $25,000 due her on the original contract of sale?

    (b) How, if at all, would the situation be different if, in addition to obtaining physical possession of the cashier's check at the time of the transaction, Sonya had gotten Boris to sign the back of the check before he turned it over to her?

2. Bert buys a used stereo system from Sarah. As agreed, he takes delivery of the stereo and promises to send her a personal check for $200. He makes out a check for this amount to Sarah's order and mails it to her. It is apparently lost in the mail and never arrives at Sarah's address. Can Sarah bring an action on the check against Bert? Can she sue Bert for breach of the original sales contract for his failure to pay the purchase price?

3. Bert also agrees to buy a large collection of used compact discs from one Stuart. Stuart delivers the box of CDs to Bert's house and receives in return a personal check made out by Bert to Stuart's order for the agreed purchase price.

    (a) Assume that Stuart immediately deposits this check in his own checking account. Within a few days he is able to confirm that Bert's bank has honored the check and that the amount of the check has been permanently credited to Stuart's own account with his bank. What is the situation now? Does Bert have any further obligation to Stuart, either on the underlying contract of sale or on the check?

    (b) Assume instead that a few days after Stuart deposits the check in his own account, he is informed by his bank that the check has been returned by Bert's bank unpaid and marked "NSF" (for Not Sufficient Funds, meaning that Bert didn't have enough in his account to cover the check). The dishonored check is returned to

Stuart. Does he have a right to bring an action against Bert based on the contract of sale? On the obligation of Bert as drawer of this dishonored check?

4.   Bert further enters into an agreement to buy a valuable collection of vintage long-playing records from Stella. Stella is willing to take payment for this pricey set of LPs by Bert's delivery to her of a check made payable to Stella, issued not by Bert himself but by a friend of his, Carlos. Stella deposits this check in her bank account, and her bank sends it on for collection from the bank on which it has been drawn by Carlos.

(a) Assume the check is honored and paid by Carlos's bank. What is the result?

(b) Assume instead that the check is dishonored and returned unpaid. Does Stella have a cause of action against either or both of Bert and Carlos, and if so on what basis?

5.   Bertha is indebted to a local store, Smallville Office Supplies, for the sum of $1,435. She writes out a check for this amount payable to the store and mails it to the address indicated on the most recent invoice she has received. This check is received by Smallville Office Supplies, but before the store has a chance to deposit the check in its own bank for collection, the check is apparently stolen or mislaid. No one at the store can find the check or figure out what has happened to it. A month goes by and this particular check has never been presented to Bertha's bank for payment.

(a) Can the store simply ignore the fact that it received the check and sue Bertha for the amount of supplies she purchased, under the original contract for sale?

(b) Can the store insist that Bertha issue it another check for the same amount?

6.   Tenant, a freelance artist, lives in a rented loft. According to his lease, he is obligated to pay rent of $1,000 on the first of every month. When his commission work is slow at the beginning of the year, he is concerned that he will not be able to pay the rent. He gets Landlord to agree to take a promissory note for $4,500, payable on April 1, to substitute for the rental payments due on the first of January, February, March, and April of the year.

(a) By the middle of February, Landlord is beginning to doubt the wisdom of her having taken this note and desires to evict Tenant. Assuming that the laws of the jurisdiction allow eviction of a tenant who has not paid rent for two months in a row, can Landlord evict this Tenant?

(b) Assume that Landlord does not try to evict Tenant. Instead, she sells the note in question to a local lender, Financial Services, in the middle of February, negotiating the note over to that firm in exchange for $3,700 cash. Tenant is informed of this transaction.

When April 1 comes around, Tenant does not pay the $4,500 due on the note to Financial Services. He writes to Landlord indicating that he has every intention of beginning to pay the monthly $1,000 rental again starting with the rent due at the beginning of May. Does Landlord now have any right to insist on payment for the first four months of the year? Does Financial Services have any rights against Tenant?

EXPLANATIONS

1a. No. Boris's contractual obligation to pay $25,000 for the pricey piece of bric-a-brac is totally discharged once Sonya takes the cashier's check in payment. As §3-310(a) makes clear, unless otherwise agreed (of which there is no evidence in this example), if a bank check is taken for an obligation, "the obligation is discharged to the same extent discharge would result if an amount of money equal to the amount of the instrument were taken in payment of the obligation."

Notice that Sonya does not have any cause of action against Boris on the instrument either; this was a cashier's check and Boris's signature does not appear anywhere on the check. The bank is both drawer and drawee. Boris has his figurine and has paid for it, presumably by coughing up $25,000 in cash to purchase the cashier's check from the bank. Sonya sought to ensure that she would be paid for the item she was giving up in sale by insisting on payment by a bank check. In the overwhelming majority of situations, such checks really are "the equivalent of cash" or "as good as cash," as we tend to say, from the seller's perspective and the taker will have absolutely no trouble collecting on the item. In the exceptionally rare case such as I have posited here, where the issuing bank itself runs into financial difficulty and is failing to meet its obligations, the holder of the bank's check (such as Sonya) will be left holding the bag.

Notice too that the outcome would be no different if Boris had paid with a certified or a teller's check, as opposed to the cashier's check he used. Under §3-310(a), his obligation on the underlying contract for sale would have been totally discharged by Sonya's taking of the cashier's check in payment. She might hope that she could hold Boris obligated on the instrument itself, as the drawer of a dishonored draft under §3-414. Recall, however, subsection (c) of that section. As we saw in Chapter 3, once a draft is accepted by a bank — as would be true when Boris got his check certified — the drawer is discharged from any obligation on the instrument. So once again Boris has been discharged from his underlying contractual obligation to pay for what he has purchased and has been discharged as well from any Article 3 obligation he might have had on the instrument given in payment. Boris is off the hook (or should I say both hooks?) when a certified check is taken for the amount he owed under the contract of sale.

Sonya's one hope of getting the money due her under this scenario is to go against Independent Republic Bank for the amount due on the cashier's check it issued. Even if the bank is experiencing difficulty in meeting its obligations, Sonya would be considered a customer of the bank protected by Federal Deposit Insurance Corporation (FDIC) insurance if the bank is FDIC-insured. If the bank cannot make the $25,000 payment, the FDIC would be obligated to do so.

1b. If Boris had signed his name to the cashier's check prior to turning it over to Sonya, he would have become an indorser of the instrument. See the last sentence of §3-310(a): "Discharge of the [underlying] obligation does not affect any liability that the obligor [Boris] may have as an indorser of the instrument." Sonya cannot sue Boris on the underlying contract for purchase and sale. She has no right against him as drawer of the dishonored draft, because, this being a cashier's check, he is not in fact the drawer. She will, however, in this instance be able to go against him as an indorser of the dishonored draft.

2. Sarah cannot bring an action against Bert on the check because the check never came into her possession. We don't know where the check ends up, but we do know that Sarah is not now a person entitled to enforce the instrument. Sarah can, and presumably will, sue Bert for breach of the underlying contract of sale, unless he quickly issues her another check that does come into her possession or in some other way pays up. Section 3-310 never comes into play. That section delineates the effect of an instrument when that instrument is "taken" by the obligee in payment. Nowhere in the Code is the word *taken* defined, but it seems clear that at the very least a person, Sarah in this instance, would not be held to have "taken" a check that never even arrived at her address. As far as Sarah and the Uniform Commercial Code are concerned, Bert has never paid for the stereo system, and his obligation to do so has been neither discharged nor suspended by his putting a check in the mail when that check never makes it into Sarah's possession. Bert had better pay up or Sarah can sue him on his obligation undertaken in the sales contract.

Other situations can arise in which the question of whether an instrument has been "taken" for an obligation is somewhat trickier. Suppose, for example, that a contract of sale calls for the buyer to pay with a cashier's check. The buyer sends a personal check to the seller. The seller does receive it, but, wishing to insist on its rights under the sales contract, immediately returns the personal check to the buyer. It seems fair to say that the seller has not taken the check in payment. In contrast, if the seller immediately deposits and tries to collect on the personal check, even if it would have been perfectly within its rights to return the check, the seller would presumably be held to have taken the check in payment for the buyer's obligation, triggering the rules laid out in §3-310. What if the seller neither returned the personal check nor immediately deposited it? The seller just holds onto the check for a time, either because it feels it gains some advantage (but what?) by doing so, or more likely because it just is lackadaisical or downright sloppy in handling its accounts. Would it be right to say that, after a certain period of time has passed, the seller has taken the check in payment of the buyer's obligation, even if perhaps unintentionally so? There is no easy or obvious answer to this question, but it highlights the important point that only when an instrument is "taken" for an obligation may it possibly have an effect on the underlying obligation under the principles laid out in §3-310.

3a.   The result here is as you would expect. Bert has paid Stuart for the CDs and the story is at an end. When Stuart took Bert's personal check in payment of Bert's payment obligation, this resulted (under §3-310(b)(1)) not in the discharge of the underlying obligation, but in its *suspension* "to the same extent the obligation would be discharged if an amount of money equal to the amount of the instrument were taken." From that point forward until the suspension is lifted, one way or another, Stuart would have no right to go against Bert on the underlying obligation. At the same time, it is not as if the underlying obligation has been finally discharged. The final discharge of Bert's obligation to pay for what he has bought comes only when the check is paid. Under (b)(1):

> In the case of an uncertified check, suspension of the obligation continues until dishonor of the check or until it is paid or certified. Payment or certification of the check results in discharge of the obligation to the extent of the amount of the check.

In the case we have before us, the check is paid. Bert has no further obligation to Stuart on the instrument itself. Nor is Bert under any further obligation on the underlying contract, as you see in the last sentence of subsection (b)(1) just quoted. Payment of the check transforms the suspension of Bert's obligation for which the check was taken into a discharge of that obligation. The transaction is wrapped up neatly, just as we expect both Bert and Stuart intended it to be. Bert has his CDs, free and clear from any further obligation to pay for them. Stuart has his money, the purchase price, in the bank. End of story.

3b.   If the check is not paid, as here, the story has not come to an end. The suspension of Bert's obligation on the underlying contract of sale — which came into effect with Stuart's taking of the personal, uncertified check in payment — is lifted once the check is dishonored. Because his obligation was not discharged by payment of the check, Bert is once again under a contractual obligation to pay the purchase price. At the same time Bert is now also the drawer of a check that has been dishonored, the check that has been returned to Stuart. Stuart could enforce Bert's obligation on the instrument arising under §3-414(b). So, once a personal check is dishonored and the suspension is lifted, the person who took the check as payment of an underlying obligation (Stuart in our example), has two ways to go: He can either proceed against the obligor on the original contractual obligation as if no payment had ever even been offered, or he can go against the obligor on that's party's obligation on the dishonored instrument itself. Quoting from Comment 3:

> If the check or note is dishonored, the seller may sue on either the dishonored instrument or the contract of sale if the seller has possession of the instrument and is the person entitled to enforce it.

We have to assume that Stuart, like any reasonable person, would want to avoid the hassle of litigation if he can. So his first effort would be to contact Bert, inform him that the check has bounced, and do what he can to convince Bert to pay what is owed as quickly as possible. Only if this appeal to Bert's conscience — and of course Bert's own natural desire to avoid being hit with a lawsuit, which would mean having to deal with lawyers and their own peculiar (and usually expensive) ways of settling such disputes — fails would Stuart resort to litigation. If he is forced by the circumstances to sue, as we've seen, he has two ways to proceed: He can sue via basic contract law on the buyer's obligation to pay for goods, or he can sue under Article 3 to enforce Bert's obligation on the dishonored check. Which route Stuart (or more realistically Stuart's expensive lawyer) chooses to take may not make that much difference, but in some situations the basis on which the suit is brought can be significant and some thought will have to be given on how to proceed. (That's why Stuart's lawyer charges the quite reasonable fees that she does.)

In most instances a suit on the instrument will be the more direct and easier way to go. If Stuart were to sue on the contract of sale, he would have to allege and prove the existence of the contract, its terms, the fact of Bert's breach, the measure of his damages, and so on. It may not be hard for Stuart to establish each of these elements, but then, even what appears at first blush to be the simplest suit on a contract can have its nasty twists and turns, as no doubt you remember from your contracts course. Suit on an obligation arising under a negotiable instrument has some special features that can make it an easier operation. Many states have special streamlined procedures designed especially for enforcement of obligations owed on instruments; the person entitled to enforce need only produce a copy of the instrument itself and allege nonpayment to make out a prima facie case for relief.

Note also the special rules on pleading and proof of §3-308, which essentially give to the person enforcing an obligation on an instrument the benefit of a presumption of "the authenticity of, and authority to make, each signature on the instrument." In more complicated situations, when the terms of the contract are laid out in a complex document and the instrument is other than a simple check, comparison of the terms of the underlying contract and of the instrument is in order. A successful suit on the contract, for instance, may entitle the disgruntled seller to recovery of its attorney's fees when suit on the instrument would not. In other circumstances, the contract would not allow the seller to recover its cost of collection, but the instrument might. Such considerations will, naturally, weigh heavily in the decision of whether to proceed on the initial underlying obligation or the rights created by the dishonor of the instrument given in payment.

4a. The result here is that Bert's obligation to pay for the LPs, created by the contract of sale, was suspended when Stella took the uncertified check, even if it was a check written by Carlos rather than Bert, in payment (§3-310(b)). This suspension of the obligation continued until the moment when the check was paid, as happily it was here, at which time Bert was discharged from his obligation to pay on the contract (§3-310(b)(1)). Bert has paid for the records, and that's that.

4b. If the check is dishonored, two things are true. First of all, the suspension of Bert's obligation under the contract of sale to make payment for the LPs is lifted, because, under §3-310(b)(1), the check has been dishonored. Stella could sue Bert on the contract of sale. Could Stella sue Bert on the dishonored check? No. Nothing in the fact pattern suggests that Bert has signed the instrument, and so he has no obligation on it whatsoever. (This should suggest to you why Stella would have been wise to insist that Bert sign the back of the check issued by Carlos, thereby becoming an indorser against whom Stella could proceed on the instrument if all else fails. Unfortunately for Stella, there is no indication here that she took that precaution.) Secondly, Stella could bring suit against Carlos on the instrument, as the drawer of a dishonored check. She could not, of course, sue Carlos on the obligation to pay for the LPs created by the contract of purchase and sale. Carlos was not a party to that contract and never took upon himself the responsibility to pay the purchase price.

This example just highlights the fact that the two sources of potential legal liability — the obligation on the underlying contract and the obligation or obligations arising under the instrument — remain distinct even if they are temporarily "merged," as you will sometimes hear said, by the taking of the instrument in satisfaction of the contractual obligation. Once this "merger doctrine" comes into play, the underlying obligation is not just merged metaphorically into the instrument, but is suspended as a legal obligation pending the obligee's attempt to obtain payment on the instrument. If payment on the instrument is forthcoming, both the underlying obligation and of course any obligations on the instrument are discharged. If the instrument is dishonored, both sources of legal liability revive. Whatever obligation there was on the underlying obligation, whatever its source (which need not necessarily be a contract of sale such as we've seen in our examples) and whoever was so obligated, comes back into existence. At the same time, any obligation or obligations on a dishonored instrument, of the type we investigated in Chapter 3, come into being by virtue of the dishonor.

5a. No. Once the store took the check for the obligation owed to it by Bertha, that obligation (to pay for what she bought from the store) is suspended under §3-310(b)(1); because this was an uncertified check, the suspension continues "until dishonor of the check or until it is paid or certi-fied." None of these events has occurred. The check has not even been presented for payment, so it certainly can't be said that it has been dishon-ored. Nor has it been paid or certified.

5b. No. The store has no right to another check from Bertha. Look at the final paragraph of Comment 4:

> If a creditor takes a check of the debtor in payment of an obligation, the obligation is suspended under the introductory paragraph of subsection (b). If the creditor then loses the check, what are the credi-tor's rights? The creditor can request the debtor to issue a new check and in many cases the debtor will issue a replacement check after stop-ping payment on the lost check. In that case both the debtor and the creditor are protected. But the debtor is not obliged to issue a new check.

You can understand why Bertha should be under no obligation to issue a new check just because the store asks her to. Should she do so and not issue a stop-payment order on the original check, she would just be asking for trouble. That first check could later turn up, perhaps in the hands of a thief, and be presented to and paid by her bank. Bertha would have paid the same bill twice. As we will see in material to come, she would presumably have rights to recover for the wrongful payment on the first check, but, as we will also see, these rights are not always easy to assert, nor are they foolproof or cost-free. At the very least, Bertha would want to issue a stop-payment order on the first check and make sure that the stop-payment mechanism is effec-tively in place before she even considers issuing the store — not as a matter of right, but just to be helpful and to keep up good business relations — a second check. She might also want the store to absorb whatever fee she'll have to pay to put the stop-payment on the first check in place.

The more interesting question is why an obligor such as Bertha should not be *obliged* to respond to a reasonable request by the store that she go through this routine of stopping payment on the first check and issuing a replacement. Our first response to this is the simplest: The store's current problem is all of its own making. It has either mislaid the check or allowed it to be stolen from the store's offices. Bertha has done nothing to cause the store's present predicament. If she had dropped by the store and paid the $1,435 she owed for supplies in cash, she would not be responsible (nor probably terribly sympathetic) if the store later misplaced the cash. Nevertheless, if the store offers to pay whatever it might cost Bertha to put a stop payment on this check, why should she not be required to go along with what seems like a perfectly reasonable request and then issue a second check? The reality of the matter, however, is that the proper issuance of a stop-payment order, and the oversight to ensure that the order is actually observed and effective to stop payment on a check, is not always as easy as one might initially imagine. If Bertha issues two checks to pay for the same stuff, even if she has attempted to stop payment on one, she could be at some nontrivial risk, at least initially, of paying for the same stuff twice. True, she might eventually be able to sort everything out, and if the rules of Article 3 work just as they are supposed to, she should be able to get back what has been deducted from her account because both checks were paid. But meanwhile, during the course of all the investigation and possible litigation, her bank account balance will be lower than it should be — all thanks to the store's failure adequately to take care of its own affairs. It is even possible that, whatever the carefully crafted rules of Article 3 might say about the situation in the abstract, practical difficulties and mounting costs of litigation could stand between Bertha and what is technically due her.

In the majority of cases, a debtor in Bertha's position will probably do what she can to help out the creditor, and will issue a second check under the right circumstances even if it is not legally obligated to do so. If not, however, what is the creditor to do? We return to the conclusion of Comment 4 to this section:

> If the debtor refuses to issue a replacement check, the last sentence of subsection (b)(4) applies. The creditor may not enforce the obligation of debtor for which the check was taken. The creditor may assert rights only on the [lost or stolen] check. The creditor can proceed under Section 3-309 to enforce the obligation of the debtor, as drawer, to pay the check.

Section 3-309 does give the creditor the possibility of proving itself a "person entitled to enforce the instrument," but as you can see subsection (a) places on the creditor a set of criteria for reaching this status. Note also that under (b),

> The court may not enter a judgment in favor of the person seeking enforcement unless it finds that the person required to pay the instrument is adequately protected against loss that might occur by reason of a claim by another person to the instrument. Adequate protection may be provided by any reasonable means.

So Article 3 places upon the creditor who finds itself without the instrument in hand the cost and bother of undertaking legal proceedings to get what it feels is owed to it. Even then, the court must be sure that the party who could potentially be subjected to a loss due to the creditor's problem be given "adequate assurance" that it will be protected from such a loss. Once the creditor, Smallville Office Supplies in our example, has obtained a court order under §3-309 entitling it to enforce the check, its obligation physically to present the (still lost) check for payment will be excused under §3-504(a)(i). The store can then treat the check as dishonored and, as Comment 4 to §3-310 has told us, "enforce the obligation of the debtor [Bertha], as drawer, to pay the check."

6a.   No. Landlord's taking of the note in substitution for Tenant's obligation to make those particular four monthly rental payments results, under

§3-301(b), in the suspension of Tenant's obligation to make those payments. Under (b)(2), this suspension of Tenant's underlying obligation under the lease continues "until dishonor of the note or until it is paid." As of the middle of February, the note has been neither dishonored nor paid, so the suspension is still in place. Landlord cannot assert any legal default on the lease (at least with respect to Tenant's obligation to pay the monthly rent) and so has no grounds for eviction.

6b. Although I can nowhere find it spelled out as clearly in the statutory text of §3-310 as the drafters of this provision seem to think they have done, the intended result is this: because the note is now in the hands of a holder who is other than the original obligee (the Landlord), the only remaining possible action is by that holder, Friendly Finance, on the note. We find this in the language at the end of the first paragraph of Comment 3. Following its statement to the effect that when an instrument other than a bank check is taken for an obligation and then dishonored, the seller (or whoever is the original obligee) may sue "on either the dishonored instrument or the contract of sale if the seller has possession of the instrument and is the person entitled to enforce it." This case we have already seen in Example 3b. This paragraph concludes, however,

> If the right to enforce the instrument is held by somebody other than the seller, the seller can't enforce the right to payment of the price under the sales contract because that right is represented by the instrument which is enforceable by someone else. Thus, if the seller sold the note or the check to a holder and has not required it after dishonor, the only right that survives is the right to enforce the instrument.

If this Comment is correct — and there seems every reason it should be, despite the fact that the result is never laid out as clearly in the text of §3-310(b) as the Official Commentators seem to think it is — then once Landlord sold the note to Financial Services for $3,700 cash, she lost forever any right to sue Tenant for the rent due for those months. This seems only fair, as she has actually received $3,700 in cash. The only right that continues thereafter is the right of Financial Services as purchaser and now holder of the note to enforce it. If Tenant fails to meet his obligation on the note, his only legal obligation (not to diminish its importance) is under §3-412 to Financial Services as the person now entitled to enforce the instrument.

PART TWO

The Holder in Due Course

7

Who Qualifies as a Holder in Due Course?

Introduction

The holder in due course is an especially important character in the law of negotiable instruments. Whether a particular party attempting to enforce an instrument qualifies not merely as a holder of the instrument but as that special and particularly favored type we identify as a holder in due course can and will have far-reaching consequences. This chapter makes no attempt to cover exactly what those consequences are. That will come in Chapter 8. For the moment, let me just suggest in broad outline the paramount and often highly significant effect of a party's being able to establish itself as a holder in due course of an instrument. One suing on an instrument who can legitimately assert holder in due course status is immune from many of the most common defenses that the party being sued would otherwise be able to assert to lessen or totally eliminate his or her obligation on the instrument were he or she being sued by someone who does not qualify as a holder in due course. The possibility of a potential plaintiff's being insulated from a whole set of defenses that might otherwise stand in the way of recovery on an instrument is, to put it mildly, no small matter and should be enough to pique your interest in the fundamental question to be explored in this chapter: Who qualifies as a holder in due course under Article 3?

The basic definition of *holder in due course* is found in §3-302(a). Note first of all that one can be a holder in due course only if what one is holding is an "instrument" under Article 2, which we know from §3-104(b) means a "negotiable instrument" as that term is defined in (a) of the same section. We dealt with what pieces of paper meet the standards for being negotiable instruments in Chapter 1. As it turns out, a large number of cases have had

115

to deal with a controversy about whether some paper that does not clearly and unambiguously fall within the definition of §3-104(a) may still be classified as an Article 3 negotiable instrument. These courts are confronted with the issue precisely because some party is claiming not merely the right to enforce the promise or order the paper articulates, but also the right to enforce the obligation as a holder in due course of a negotiable instrument, free and clear of certain pesky defenses the obligor may want to put in his or her way. A party cannot expect to get any special recognition as a holder in due course, or any special benefit from being so classified, unless a negotiable instrument is the basis of that party's suit.

A second basic prerequisite for any party's being able to establish holder in due course status is that the party be a holder of the instrument. As we saw in Chapter 2, whether a party qualifies as a holder of the instrument (assuming that it is a negotiable instrument under Article 3) depends on a complex series of rules and definitions. Again, much of the litigation involving the problem of who is and who is not a holder has as its background the desire of a plaintiff to prove holder status, so that plaintiff can then go on and claim to be a holder in due course, with all the advantages that will bring. There is no need for us to recapitulate here all of what we dealt with in Chapter 2. It is enough to highlight the fact that for a party to become a holder in due course of an instrument, it is essential that the party first establish that it qualifies as a holder of the instrument under the rules we have already studied.

Beyond the need to prove that a negotiable instrument is involved, and that he or she is a holder of that instrument, anyone claiming holder in due course status must prove that the conditions laid out in both (1) and (2) of §3-302(a) are met. (There is no need for us to concern ourselves at the moment with the exceptions of either §3-302(c) or §3-106(d).) It is worth pointing out from the very beginning that the burden of establishing holder in due course status is on the party making the claim to be such. Under §3-308(b),

> If a defense or claim in recoupment [a concept explored in Chapter 8] is proved [by the party being sued on the instrument], the right to payment of the plaintiff is subject to the defense or claim, except to the extent *the plaintiff proves* that the plaintiff has rights of a holder in due course which are not subject to the defense or claim.

So, what exactly must a party prove to establish itself a holder in due course, beyond the fact that it is the holder of the negotiable instrument? Under subpart (1), the holder must show that the instrument, when issued or negotiated to the holder, did not "bear such apparent evidence of forgery or alteration or [was] not otherwise so irregular or incomplete as to call into question [the instrument's] authenticity." This criterion did not appear in the prerevision version of Article 3, although, as Comment 1 explains, it did have a precursor in the Negotiable Instrument Law, which was in effect even earlier, prior to the adoption of the original Uniform Commercial Code in the 1960s. As a result, we have no modern cases interpreting the language of this first criterion. As a practical matter, though, it probably covers only the grossest circumstances, in which no one would have thought a holder could successfully claim to be a holder in due course no matter what the exact language of the definition. In the examples to follow, we will first look at a couple of situations in which this first criterion could be invoked, at least to deal with some simple cases easily and effectively.

The criterion now articulated in part (2) of §3-302(a) was, until the recent revision of Article 3, the sole standard by which the question of who was and who was not a holder in due course was to be determined. Even today it must be consulted when the more interesting and subtle cases emerge, so we will have to put more time into it. This language is what lawyers, judges, and teachers of negotiable instruments law had become used to as the sole test for settling questions of holder in due course status under the original version of Article 3, which served so well for so many years. Thus, there is some tendency to rush to §3-302(a)(2) even if (1) is now available and might be appropriately applied to the instance at hand. Whatever the case, criterion (2) is of such importance and raises sufficient questions that we cannot — nor would we want to — avoid going into it in depth.

To set the stage, observe that what is stated in §3-302(a)(2) really lists a series of conditions, each of which must be met if the party trying to prove itself a holder in due course is to satisfy its burden. To meet the test for being a holder in due course, the holder must (in addition to satisfying the rather straightforward test stated in subsection(a)(1)) have

- taken the instrument for "value" (on which see §3-303),
- taken it in "good faith" (as that term is defined in §3-103(a)(4) or now in R§1-201(b)(20)),
- taken it without notice of its being overdue (on which see §3-304) or having already been dishonored,
- taken it without notice that it contained an unauthorized signature or had been altered,
- taken it without any notice of a claim to the instrument by another (as provided for in §3-306), and
- taken it without any notice that any party has a defense or claim in recoupment of the type described in §3-305(a).

With respect to what constitutes a legitimate claim by another to an instrument of the type recognized by §3-306, I must beg your indulgence for a while. Similarly for the nature of any defense or claim in recoupment provided for under §3-305(a). We will look at the contents of these sections in their full glory in Chapter 8. For the examples of this chapter, it will be necessary for me to make use of some simple examples of the type of thing we will explore in more detail soon enough, and ask you to accept as given what I say about any particular claim or defense falling within the scope of these important provisions.

On the Good Faith Requirement

The concept of *good faith* plays a large part in determining whether a holder can qualify as a holder in due course. Historically, the question of what exactly was required for a holder to establish his or her good faith has always been troubling for the law of negotiable instruments. Prior to the adoption of the 1990 revisions to Article 3, there was no definition of the phrase *good faith* in the text of Article 3 itself. This meant that the general definition of the term in O§1-201(19) was, by default, to be applied whenever the term was used in Article 3; in particular, it was crucial to the definition of *holder in due course*. Under O§1-201(19): Good faith was defined to mean "honesty in fact in the conduct or transaction concerned." Thus, under the prerevision version of Article 3, the presence or absence of good faith was to be determined under what we generally term a purely subjective standard. Did the party whose conduct was being scrutinized act dishonestly in doing what it did under the circumstances? The standard makes no reference to what others in the position of the party in question might have done, nor to what it would have been "reasonable" to do under the circumstances. This standard came to be referred to by many as the "pure heart and empty head" standard or test. If the party could not be shown to have behaved dishonestly in the light of some fact or facts that it actually *knew* at the time of the transaction, its failure to inquire into why it was able to obtain the particular instrument on what might seem incredibly favorable terms would not in and of itself have meant that the party lacked good faith.

Given this situation, the courts were often urged to temper the purely subjective definition of *good faith* supplied by the Code with judicial incorporation of an objective component to the concept of good faith, to be applied in some or all situations. With only some exceptions, the courts refused to do so, and the subjective standard stood alone. In some particularly egregious cases, a court would allow a determination of whether a party had acted dishonestly, and thus failed to meet the subjective standard of good faith, if the facts already known to that party permitted the inference that it must have been suspicious to some degree of what was going on and that its failure to inquire further was evidence of a deliberate desire to avoid gaining further information that it must have feared would damage its position. The result under the prerevision Article 3, even taking these cases into account, was summarized as follows:

> "Good faith" is defined as "honesty in fact in the conduct or transaction concerned." The good faith standard does not require the holder

of an instrument, regular on its face, to inquire as to possible defenses unless facts known to the holder are such that failure to inquire discloses a desire to evade knowledge for fear that it would reveal a defense to the instrument.

Dalton & Marberry, P.C. v. Nationsbank, N.A., 34 U.C.C.2d 748 (Mo. App. Ct. 1998).

One of the more significant changes wrought by the 1990 revision process was the incorporation into Article 3 itself of a distinct definition of *good faith*. Look at §3-103(a)(4):

> "Good faith" means honesty in fact and the observance of reasonable commercial standards of fair dealing.

Under our present version of Article 3, then the purely subjective standard of good faith has been jettisoned and an objective standard has taken its place. (The objective standard has also recently worked its way into the revision of Article 1. See R§1-201(b)(20).) As the Supreme Court of Maine first observed, the inclusion of this new definition in Article 3

> signals a significant change in the definition of a holder in due course. While there has been little time for the development of a body of law interpreting the new objective requirement, there can be no mistaking the fact that a holder may no longer act with a pure heart and an empty head and still obtain holder in due course status. The pure heart of the holder must now be accompanied by reasoning that assures conduct comporting with reasonable commercial standards of fair dealing.

Maine Family Federal Credit Union v. Sun Life Assurance Co., 199 Me. 43, 727 A.2d 335, 37 U.C.C.2d 875 (1999). As the court in this case was quick to point out, the determination of whether a party has observed "reasonable commercial standards of fair dealing" will not always be easy to make. If nothing else, as the court observed,

> The most obvious question arising from the use of the term "fair" is: fairness to whom? Transactions involving negotiable instruments have traditionally required the detailed level of control and definitions of roles set out in the U.C.C. precisely because there are so many parties who may be involved in a single transaction. If a holder is required to act "fairly," regarding all of the parties, it must engage in an almost impossible balancing act of rights and interests. Accordingly the drafters [of the 1990 revision] limited the requirement of fair dealing to conduct that is reasonable in the commercial context of the transaction at issue.

The Maine Supreme Court concluded that application of this new objective standard of fair dealing required a two-step analysis.

> The factfinder must therefore determine, first, whether the conduct of the holder comported with industry or "commercial" standards applicable to the transaction and, second, whether those standards were reasonable standards intended to result in fair dealing.

I have spent so much time on the *Maine Family* case not because I think it is the last word on the question of how the new objective test of good faith, now part of Article 3 via the recently introduced §3-103(a)(4), is to be applied. In fact, as the Maine Supreme Court itself was aware, the case is better understood as something like the first word on the subject, the first major case to have put some thought into exactly how the changes brought about by the introduction of the objective standard into the definition of *holder in due course* work out in practice. To my mind it was a good start.

A noteworthy recent case that adopts and applies the *Maine Family* approach to the objective standard of good faith is *Any Kind Checks Cashed, Inc. v. Talcott*, 830 So.2d 160, 48 U.C.C.2d 800 (Fla. App. 2002). The court there upheld a trial court's findings that on the facts presented the check-cashing firm had *not* acted in good faith in cashing a check for $10,000 but *had* been in good faith in later cashing another for $5,700. Both of the checks were issued by Talcott, a ninety-three-year-old Massachusetts resident, and made payable to one Salvatore Guarino on the advice of Talcott's "financial advisor," D. J. Rivera. Rivera was soon discovered to be, in the words of Guarino, "a cheat and a thief," but meanwhile he had made off with cash received from Any Kind for each of the checks, and that firm naturally enough wanted to recover the sum from the check's drawer. Talcott ended up responsible for the $5,700 even though the check had been clearly obtained from him by fraud, but not for the $10,000. What made the difference between the two checks? In the case of the check for $5,700, a manager at the check-cashing company, whose authorization was required for the cashing of any check over $2,000, had actually called Talcott and gotten his oral approval for cashing the check. The check for $10,000, on the other hand, had been cashed earlier (minus a fee, of course) by the company, the manager apparently relying on her "instinct and judgment" even though she had not been able to reach Talcott by phone to get his approval. The Florida District Court of Appeals upheld a finding by the trial court that in so doing the check-cashing firm had not acted in good faith.

> There was no evidence at trial concerning the check cashing industry's commercial standards. Even assuming that Any Kind's procedures for checks over $2,000 met the industry's gold standard, we hold that in this case the procedures followed were not reasonably related to achieve fair dealing with respect to the $10,000 check, talking into consideration all of the participants in the transaction, Talcott, Guardino, and Any Kind.

Any Kind had argued that this result would put too great a burden upon itself and other check-cashing operations, but the court manifested little sympathy under the circumstances:

> Against this [factual] backdrop, we cannot say that the trial court erred in finding that the $10,000 check was a red flag. The $10,000 personal check was not the typical check cashed at a check cashing outlet. The

size of the check, in the context of the check cashing business, was a proper factor to consider under the objective standard of good faith in deciding whether Any Kind was a holder in due course. [Citing *Maine Family*]

It will be interesting to see, as time goes on, what further explication of the objective good faith standard we will be given by the courts. What no one would doubt is that the move in the 1990 revision of Article 3 from a purely subjective to an objective test for good faith was meant to work a significant change in how that term was understood and applied wherever it appears in Article 3 — and in the definition of *holder in due course* most particularly.

On Notice

A second concept that is extremely important to the definition of *holder in due course* is that of a holder's having or not having notice of this or that being true. It is worth taking time now to become acquainted with the definition of *notice* as first defined in O§1-201(25):

> A person has "notice" of a fact when
> (a) he has actual knowledge of it; or
> (b) he has received a notice or notification of it [on which see subsections (26) and (27)]; or
> (c) from all of the facts and circumstances known to him at the time in question he has reason to know that it exists.

In the revised Article 1 you'll find the same ideas in R§1-202. Having duly taken notice of what "notice" is, we may now move on to some examples to explore more fully just who is and who is not a holder in due course of a negotiable instrument.

EXAMPLES

1. Paul approaches Jennifer and shows her a check for $400 made out to him, drawn by one Darren on Darren's account with the Payson National Bank. The numeral "4" in the space where the amount of the check has been written has a funny look to it and appears to be written in two different inks. Also, the word "Four" on the line where the amount is set forth in words is written over a very discernible smudge and also happens to be written in an ink darker than all of the other writing on the check, such as Darren's signature. Paul convinces Jennifer to cash this check for him. He indorses the check over to her in exchange for $400.

   (a) Does Jennifer qualify as a holder in due course of the check?
   (b) What if there were no such glaring irregularities on the face of the check, but it is apparent that it had once been ripped or cut in half and then taped back together? If she takes the check from Paul by

way of negotiation, could Jennifer successfully claim to be a holder in due course under this set of facts?

2. Andrew issues a check for $1,000 to Belinda. Belinda negotiates this check over to Carlos, taking and asking for nothing in return. Belinda is making a gift to her friend Carlos.

(a) Can Carlos qualify as a holder in due course of the check?

(b) What if Belinda negotiated the check to Carlos in exchange for a used car, the title of which Carlos then transferred to Belinda?

(c) What if the reason Belinda negotiates the check to Carlos is to pay him for some services Carlos has already performed for her?

(d) What if Carlos is given the check in exchange for his promise to perform certain services in the future for Belinda, but which he has not yet performed?

3. Darla issues a note to Ernest in 2004 in exchange for a valuable painting that Ernest is selling to her. The note calls for Ernest to be paid the amount of $10,000 on a date in 2007. In need of some ready cash, as soon as he gets the note Ernest takes the note to Friendly Finance. That firm agrees to buy the note from him for $3,000 payable immediately and another $5,000 to be paid on the due date in 2007. Ernest accepts these terms and negotiates the note over to Friendly Finance, which gives him the initial payment of $3,000. By the time 2007 rolls around, Friendly Finance has become aware, as it had not been initially, that the painting Ernest sold Darla in the transaction giving rise to the note was a fake and not an original as Darla had been led to believe. Can Friendly Finance claim and benefit from holder in due course status when it tries to collect, in 2007, the $10,000 payable by Darla on the note it is holding? See §3-302(d).

4. Grant issues a note to Helena payable on March 1, 2005. On April 1, 2005, Helena negotiates this note over to Irwin in exchange for cash. Can Irwin qualify as a holder in due course of the instrument?

5. Janice writes a check to Kirk dated January 5, 2004. On June 1 of that same year, Kirk negotiates the check to Lena. Can Lena qualify as a holder in due course of the check?

6. Manny, a college student, shows his friend Naomi a check for $18,000, written to Manny and drawn on an account of the Microtough Corporation, a large public company. The check is written on an official preprinted check of the corporation and the signature at the bottom is that of Manny himself. Naomi knows that her friend has been working as a summer intern in the bookkeeping department of Microtough. Without asking any questions, Naomi takes this check in exchange for a used car that she has been trying to get off her hands. Can Naomi qualify as a holder in due course of the check?

7. Oscar is strolling along the street one day when he happens to spy a piece of paper lying on the ground. He picks it up. It turns out to be a check, written by one Boss Industries and payable to a Louie Lackey, and the back

of it bears what appears to be the signature of Louie himself. Is Oscar a holder of this instrument? Is he a holder in due course? You may assume that Louie Lackey, the unlucky loser of the check, would have a valid claim to it as his property under §3-306.

8. Quincy contracts to buy what he believes to be a valuable antique vase from Roberta. In payment for the vase, Quincy writes Roberta a check for $12,500. Roberta negotiates this check over to her friend Steve as partial payment of a larger debt that Roberta owes to Steve. Steve, being a friend of Roberta's, is well aware that the vase she has sold to Quincy is not an original, but rather a reproduction worth nowhere near the amount Quincy paid for it. Roberta has often complained to Steve about how she herself was initially fooled by the vase, but there is no doubt it's a reproduction only. You may assume that the sale of the vase as an original when it is known by the seller to be a modern reproduction would provide Quincy with a defense under §3-305(a) to payment of the instrument, should he become aware of the fact before the check is paid.

    (a) Does Steve qualify as a holder in due course of the check?

    (b) Would your answer be the same if Steve had no knowledge or any reason to believe that the vase was other than original? Roberta was aware that it was a reproduction, but she kept this information to herself and did not share it with anyone, even her friend Steve.

9. Thomas is invited to invest in what he is assured by its promoter, Horace Underwater, is going to be a fast-growing and highly profitable real estate venture, Underwater Estates. In 2005 Thomas acquires an interest in this company by giving a note to Underwater Estates for $50,000, payable five years from the date of signing. On behalf of the venture, Horace immediately sells this note to one of the major banks in the community, Little Rock Bank and Trust. Little Rock pays $40,000 for the note, an amount reflecting a customary discount for purchase of this type of note, given the underlying nature of the enterprise, the time the bank will have to wait for payment, and so forth. You may assume that the bank has no knowledge or reason to know of any defenses that the maker, Thomas, might be able to assert when the time comes to pay the note. It knows that the maker is investing in a real estate deal and that such deals always involve some degree of risk, but it has no reason to believe that the Underwater Estates project is any more risky or suspect than it now appears to be.

    (a) Does the Little Rock bank qualify as a holder in due course of the note?

    (b) Would your answer be the same if Horace had agreed to sell the note to the bank for $22,000? The officials at the bank were surprised that the price they were being asked to pay was so low, but decided not to look a gift horse in the mouth. They eagerly took up the $50,000 note for $22,000 in cash.

10. This example starts with the same situation as in Example 9a. Thomas makes a note promising to pay $50,000 to Underwater Estates in five years. This note is immediately sold at a reasonable discount to Little Rock Bank and Trust, which has no notice of any irregularities in the transaction between Thomas and Underwater that gave rise to the note. About a year later, it is discovered that Horace Underwater had been convincing people, including Thomas, to invest in this project by knowingly giving them false information and projections as to its future profitability. You may assume that this kind of fraud in the transaction would give rise to a defense on Thomas's part, should he ever be sued on the note, of the type described in §3-305(a). After all the facts of Horace's skullduggery become widely known, the Little Rock bank negotiates the note to the Instrument Enforcement Corporation (IEC) for $35,000.

   (a) When the due date of the note arrives, can IEC, in suing for the full $50,000 due on the note from Thomas, prove itself to be a holder in due course of the instrument?
   (b) Even if IEC cannot itself claim to be a holder in due course under the circumstances, can it assert *the rights of a holder in due course,* including the right to enforce Thomas's obligation on the instrument free and clear of any defense Thomas might have were the note still held by the deceitful Horace? Give careful attention to §3-203(b).

EXPLANATIONS

1a. No. This appears to be a particularly clumsy job on Paul's part of attempting to change a check for $100 into one for $400. This is an alteration of the instrument (see §3-407(a)). We don't have to look any further than §3-302(a)(1) to find that Jennifer will not qualify as a holder in due course. At the time the check was negotiated to her, it certainly did bear "such apparent evidence of forgery or alteration . . . as to call into question its authenticity."

1b. I think not. Again, under (a)(1), although there was no apparent evidence of a forgery or alteration made to the instrument, it was in my opinion at the time of negotiation to Jennifer "so irregular or incomplete as to call into question its authenticity." That would be enough to prevent Jennifer from acquiring holder in due course status. The drafters of the revision of Article 3 did not include a definition of the word *authenticity* that they use here, but note the following language from Comment 1:

> The term "authenticity" is used to make it clear that the irregularity or incompleteness must indicate that the instrument may not be what it purports to be. Persons who purchase or pay such instruments should do so at their own risk.

It is important to point out that in this and the previous example the conclusion is not that Jennifer isn't a holder of the instrument. She is, and may enforce it for all it is worth — whatever, if anything, that may turn out to be. The conclusion is only that she would not qualify for the special status as holder in due course of the check, which could very likely affect her ability to enforce it for the full $400 she has supposed it to be worth when the time comes to turn this piece of paper into cash.

2a. No. Carlos has no trouble meeting the criterion of §3-302(a)(1), but he must also fulfill the requirements of (a)(2). The first of these, and the one which we explore in this example, is that for a person to qualify as a holder in due course, that person must have taken the instrument "for value." Section 3-303(a) is used to determine whether an instrument is issued or transferred for value. This case is easy. The check was transferred to Carlos as a gift. Carlos becomes the holder of the check, but he does not become a holder in due course of it. He has not given value for it.

2b. If Carlos gave Belinda a used car in exchange for the check, then he has given value and, assuming that he meets all the other criteria of (a)(2), he takes the check as a holder in due course. It's interesting (and frustrating) that the drafters didn't provide any clear language covering this simplest of situations in §3-303(a), although there is no doubt that we are meant to find Carlos to have given value in such a case. Subparts (2) through (5) of §3-303(a) relate to specific situations, none of which is involved here. Probably the best way to look at this case is to consider it under (a)(1) and conceive of it as follows: Belinda transferred the check to Carlos in exchange for a promise by him to transfer the car to her and he has performed his promise. Thus, Carlos has given value for the instrument and has met this qualification for obtaining holder in due course status.

2c. Carlos took the instrument for value and could be a holder in due course. You can support this conclusion with §3-303(a)(1), reasoning that Carlos had presumably at some time made a promise to Belinda that he would perform these services, and he has given value to the extent the promise has been performed, which in this case is to the full extent of the promise.

2d. Carlos would be a holder of the instrument, but not a holder in due course. Look once again at §3-303(a)(1). An instrument is taken for value if it is taken in exchange "for a promise of performance, *to the extent that* the promise has been performed." Here Carlos's promise to furnish service in the future has not been performed at all, and as a consequence — under the definition found in §3-303(a), which we must apply to §3-302(a)(2) — he has not yet given any value for the instrument. He cannot qualify as a holder in due course of it.

For a case that hinges on just this distinction between a promise already performed and one that has not yet been performed, *see Carter & Grimsley v. Omni Trading Co.*, 306 Ill. App. 3d 1127, 716 N.E.2d 320, 39 U.C.C.2d 484 (1999). Omni Trading Company issued a couple of checks to Country Grain Elevators, Inc., for grain it had purchased. Country Grain soon thereafter negotiated these checks over to the law firm of Carter & Grimsley as a retainer for future legal services. The law firm deposited the checks, but by the time it did so Omni Trading had stopped payment on them and the checks were returned unpaid. Carter & Grimsley later brought suit against Omni on the checks, asserting that it held each of them as a holder in due course. The firm produced no evidence that it had performed any legal services for Country Grain Elevators prior to its receiving the checks. The checks represented a retainer for future services; such future services, the court held, could not constitute value given by the law firm so as to allow it to benefit from holder in due course status.

> This retainer was a contract for future legal services. Under section 3-303(a)(1), it was a "promise of performance," not yet performed. Thus, no value was received, and [the law firm] is not a holder in due course.

3.   Friendly Finance is of course a holder of the note to its full extent. Under the special rule of §3-302(d), however, it will be able to rely on the rights of a holder in due course with respect to only 3/8 of the value of the note, or $3,750. At the time it gave the initial $3,000 of the total $8,000 it agreed to pay for the note, it had no notice of any defense that would be good against its transferor, Ernest, of the type described in §3-305(a). Thus, as of that point and forevermore, Friendly Finance may "assert rights of a holder in due course of the instrument to the fraction of the amount payable under the instrument [$10,000] equal to the value of the partial performance [$3,000] divided by the value of the promised performance [$8,000]." As to the other 5/8 or $6,250, its rights will be those of a holder but not those of a holder in due course. If it had made the other promised payment to Ernest (and let's hope for its sake it did not), that would not increase the extent to which Friendly Finance held the note as a holder in due course. Although more value would have been given, this additional value beyond the $3,000 would have been given by Friendly Finance under circumstances that prevent it from acquiring any further holder in due course rights; it would have had notice, at the time of the giving of this additional value, that the party Darla "had a defense . . . described in Section 3-305(a)." A similar example to the one I've given here can be found as Case #5 in Comment 6 to §3-302.

4.   No. At the time Irwin took the instrument, he had notice that it was overdue. Hence he does not meet all of the requirements of §3-302(a)(2), in particular the criterion stated under (iii) thereof. We know that the note was overdue because §3-304(b)(2) decrees, "With respect to an instrument payable at a definite time . . . [i]f the principal is not payable in installments and the due date has not been accelerated, the instrument becomes overdue on the day after the due date." Irwin certainly had notice that the note was overdue. The due date was written right on the instrument, so he had all the opportunity in the world to know that the particular note was overdue as of

March 2, 2005. He knew he was taking it on April 1, 2005. Look again at the definition of *notice* in O§1-201(25) or §R1-202. Can there be any question that "from all the facts and circumstances known" to Irwin, he had plenty of reason to know that he was taking an overdue instrument?

Remember, although we have just concluded that Irwin will not obtain the rights of a holder in due course in the instrument, this does not mean he is not a holder and is not entitled to enforce the instrument. Everything may turn out just fine for him. If, however, Grant interposes certain defenses to payment when Irwin attempts to enforce it, Irwin as a holder but not a holder in due course may be subject to those defenses in a way he would be not had he taken as a holder in due course. Irwin, by taking the instrument with knowledge that he would hold it not as a holder in due course, was taking a greater risk that he would never be paid all that was supposedly due on the instrument. So Irwin, if he knows what he's about, is not necessarily acting foolishly or unwisely here, at least if the amount of cash he gave Helena for the overdue instrument was low enough to reflect the increased risk that he was knowingly incurring by purchasing this instrument under this set of circumstances.

5.   No, Lena cannot qualify as a holder in due course of the check. Under §3-304(a)(2), a check becomes overdue 90 days after its date. Lena took the check with notice that it was overdue. Don't fall into the trap of concluding that the check Lena took from Kirk was "no good" or anything like that. There would be nothing unusual here if Lena deposited the check in her account and it cleared with no problem. If, however, it doesn't clear and she later has to sue Janice on Janice's obligation as the drawer of a dishonored check, Janice may be able to successfully interpose defenses against Lena that she could not were Lena a holder in due course. There is nothing wrong, in and of itself, with taking a check that was written some time ago, but as Lena may learn to her dismay, it is an inherently riskier proposition than is taking a check that was issued only a few days ago. Most checks are, naturally enough, cashed or deposited for collection soon after they are issued. The fact that a check has been hanging around for some time without its being cashed or deposited doesn't necessarily mean that there will be any difficulty collecting on it, but it does suggest a greater likelihood of some trouble lurking, some messiness surrounding the transaction that gave rise to the check or the route it has taken since that point that would account for its still being outstanding some 90 days after issuance. Any person taking it in such a situation should be aware of the greater riskiness associated with this particular item. Article 3 reflects this simple reality by providing that someone who takes a check more than 90 days old may not become a holder in due course of it.

6.   Naomi will qualify as a holder in due course only if she can show that she took the check "without notice that the instrument contained an unauthorized signature" pursuant to §3-302(a)(2)(iv). Refer again to the definition of

notice that we have to work with. Do you think it likely that Naomi could satisfy her burden of proving that she had no "reason to know" that Manny was not authorized to sign a check for $18,000 payable to himself from his temporary employer, the Microtough Corporation, "given all the facts and circumstances" known to Naomi? Even if she didn't know for certain that Manny had taken advantage of his position in the bookkeeping department to write up this check payable to himself, despite his having no authority to do so, what do you make of the fact that she took this highly dubious item without asking a single question about how Manny came to have it?

As you can see, the determination of when and whether the person taking an instrument has "notice" of a particular infirmity of the type that would, under (a)(2), disqualify the taker from becoming a holder in due course is not always free from dispute. There have been and will presumably continue to be plenty of cases in which a judge or jury has to decide who did or did not have notice of one thing or another at the time that person took an instrument. Each case has to be decided on its facts, of course. As to the case before us, my guess would be that Naomi will have a good deal of trouble meeting her burden of proof that she was without notice of the unauthorized signature of Manny on a check of the Microtough Corporation. Interns in the bookkeeping department aren't usually, at least in my experience, given the authority to sign checks for the employer, especially not checks made out for large amounts and payable to themselves. Naomi may not have "knowledge" of the improper signature, but it's important to note that the definition of *notice* goes beyond this to encompass facts that a person should have "reason to know" under the circumstances. I wouldn't bet on Naomi's being able to establish holder in due course status under the facts as we have them here.

7. If the signature is truly that of Louie, then Oscar qualifies as a holder of the instrument. Louie, by making a blank indorsement on the back of the check payable to him, has turned it into a bearer instrument. Oscar, in physical possession of a bearer instrument, is a holder of it. Oscar, however, would not qualify as a holder in due course. He has notice that another, Louie, would have a claim to the instrument of the type described in §3-306. Under §3-302(a)(2)(v), this prevents Oscar from becoming a holder in due course.

8a. No, Steve is not a holder in due course under this set of facts. He is a holder. Furthermore, he has given value for the instrument; under §3-303(a)(3), an instrument is transferred (here from Roberta to Steve) for value if it is transferred "as payment of . . . an antecedent claim against any person." Steve fails to qualify as a holder in due course, however, because at the time he took transfer of the instrument he had notice that Quincy had a defense against payment of the instrument of a type described in §3-305(a). Hence, Steve does not meet the criterion of §3-302(a)(2)(vi).

You might have been tempted by this example also to consider the question of whether Steve, knowing what he did about how Roberta acquired the check, could appropriately be considered to have acted in "good faith" in taking it as he did. After all, there is a distinct requirement under §3-302(a)(2)(ii) for someone claiming holder in due course status to prove that he took the instrument in good faith. Here Steve did not himself actively participate in the con job that Roberta pulled on Quincy, but he seems more than willing to turn a blind eye to what Roberta did and in an indirect way to profit by it. If Roberta was able to get $12,500 for a vase worth nowhere near that much and then use the money to pay off part of her debt to Steve, then he benefits from the initial purchase and sale transaction and the fraud that Roberta has committed against Quincy. Can Steve, fully aware that this is the source of the check written in this amount, be said to have taken it in good faith?

There is, as you might expect, no easy answer to this question. We will look at the good faith requirement of §3-302(a)(2)(ii) in more detail in the following example, where we will see how difficult it often is to know just when that requirement has been met. For the moment, the point to observe is that in many situations the issue of whether the holder took in good faith for purposes of (a)(2)(ii) will be difficult, if not downright impossible, to distinguish from the "without notice" requirements listed in (a)(2)(iii) through (vi). The issue of good faith rarely, if ever, comes up in a vacuum, and so it naturally tends to overlap or become intertwined with more specific questions of whether the person taking the instrument had notice of a particular reason to question the enforceability of the instrument. Some courts go to great trouble to deal with the two separate criteria set forth in §3-302(a)(2) — good faith and lack of notice — distinctly and independently. Sometimes they seem successful in doing so. You will, however, come across other cases where it seems as if the court has not been able (or has simply not bothered) to keep distinct the two different notions as they apply to the facts at hand. You may wonder if this is because the court failed to keep each part of the puzzle distinctly in view (we are all human, and as we've already noted, the pieces of the puzzle do overlap to a considerable extent, if not totally blur one into the other) or whether the court consciously concluded that the two criteria do not need separate consideration, given the circumstances and given that they both are intended to address the same ultimate concern. A good deal of this, of course, depends on how the good faith requirement of (a)(2)(ii) is to be applied. As we will explore soon enough, this itself is no easy matter.

8b. If Steve had no knowledge or any reason to believe that Roberta had acquired the check from Quincy by selling him a phony antique, then Steve could legitimately claim that he had no notice that Quincy had a defense against his obligation to pay on the instrument. Steve would be a holder in due course of the check.

9a. Yes. The Little Rock bank has taken for value and with no notice of any defenses available to any party or claims of another to the instrument. The note is not overdue, nor does it contain any unauthorized signature or alteration. The remaining question is whether there is any reason to doubt the good faith of the bank in taking the note under the circumstances set out here. I can't see why we would. The bank has taken the note for a discount, but the discount, we are told, is within the range of what this bank or another similarly situated would expect to get for a note on these terms and reflecting this type of venture. Little Rock qualifies as a holder in due course.

9b. The issue here is whether Little Rock has acted in good faith in taking the note for this more deeply discounted price. Were this question to be addressed under the historical subjective test of good faith discussed in the introduction, would the Little Rock bank be found lacking in good faith? Remember that the note it purchased was "regular on its face" and the only other fact it knew was that Horace Underwater was willing to sell the bank the note at a very appreciable discount. Couldn't the bank honestly take advantage of the situation without being in bad faith? Would these facts and nothing more allow the purity of its heart to be called into question?

Given that the note in question was created in 2005 and negotiated to the bank soon after its issuance, however, we confront the issue of good faith not under the prerevision Article 3 and the subjective standard, but as dealt with under the 1990 revisions and the objective standard of good faith. With this standard now applying to Little Rock Bank and Trust's conduct in taking the note for $22,000, how would you answer the question of whether it had acted in good faith? At least we are given some guidance by the *Maine Family Federal Credit Union* case (discussed in the introduction) on where to start looking. What can we determine about what industry standards are with regard to such transactions? What would other, similarly situated banks be expected to do when confronted with a note of this kind offered to them on these terms? Would they as a matter of course inquire further into the background of Horace Underwater and into the details of the Underwater Estates real estate venture? Even if they would not make a full investigation into all aspects of the Underwater Estates plan, wouldn't they ask some fairly pointed questions, given the otherwise inexplicably low price at which they are being offered the note?

You have to consider as well the second prong of the test as the Maine court enunciated it. If other banks would as a matter of industry practice make further inquiries of the type that Little Rock did not, it does not seem difficult to conclude that this customary commercial behavior could be considered to constitute "reasonable standards intended to result in fair dealing." True, these other banks would not be making the further inquiry because they feel themselves obligated to police every deal with which they become even tangentially involved; the Maine court did not mean to suggest that any bank that purchases a note from someone like Horace Underwater must necessarily ensure the "fairness" of its transferor's conduct in every particular and with respect to every other party with whom he may have dealt. If other banks in Little Rock's position would make such further investigation, however, it must be traceable in some degree to their concern about not getting caught in the middle of a fraudulent or unduly risky scheme. This would be enough, I think, to conclude that their standard of conduct would qualify as what the court referred to as "reasonable standards intended to result in fair dealing."

A more interesting question comes up if we conclude, upon investigation, that other banks would *not* have acted differently from Little Rock had the same opportunity been presented to them by Horace. They would, just as eagerly, have bought up the note obligating Thomas to pay $50,000 five years hence for the remarkably low price of $22,000, with no questions asked. In other words, what if Little Rock could show that its actions had in fact "comported with industry or 'commercial' standards applicable to the transaction" at hand? Under the two-step analysis supplied by the Maine court, we would still be allowed to conclude that Little Rock had not acted in good faith, because, even if it acted in accordance with industry standards, those standards were so lax that they could not be considered "reasonably intended to result in fair dealing." If an entire industry were to adopt practices of dealing that fail to take into account some reasonable measure of "fair dealing" however exactly (or vaguely) this phrase comes to be understood, no one member of the industry could show itself to have been acting in good faith merely because it acted according to this industry's practices — if the industry-wide practices don't measure up.

10a. No. IEC could never qualify as a holder in due course. Even though it gave value and (we may assume) acted in good faith, at the time it took transfer of the note it had notice that a party, here Thomas the maker, had a defense to payment on the instrument. That defense is, as we have postulated, one of those "described in Section 3-305(a)." IEC fails to meet requirement (vi) of §3-302(a) and is not a holder in due course.

10b. Although IEC cannot itself claim to be a holder in due course, it took the instrument from a party who was, the Little Rock Bank and Trust. (Recall that at the time Little Rock took the instrument, it had no notice that Thomas had any defense on the instrument.) This being so, IEC can assert the rights of a holder in due course under the so-called *shelter doctrine* of §3-203(b):

> Transfer of an instrument, whether or not the transfer is a negotiation, vests in the transferee any right of the transferor to enforce the instrument, *including any right of a holder in due course. . . .*

So, although IEC is not a holder in due course, at the time of transfer it acquired the rights of a holder in due course from its transferor, the Little Rock Bank. Whatever the rights of a holder in due course are — and it is this we will get into in more detail in Chapter 8 — IEC has them, even if IEC itself does not qualify to be considered a holder in due course because of the circumstances known to IEC at the time it took the note.

At first this result, and the whole shelter doctrine principle, may seem like little more than a play on words. IEC is not a holder in due course, but it does have all the rights of a holder in due course. The concept is an important one, however, and one you should be sure to appreciate. It serves an important function in the actual practice of dealing with negotiable instruments. Look at the beginning of the second paragraph of Comment 2 to §3-203.

> Under subsection (b) a holder in due course that transfers an instrument transfers those rights as a holder in due course to the purchaser. The policy is to assure the holder in due course a free market for the instrument.

To appreciate the policy justification for the doctrine to which this comment refers, consider the situation from the point of view of Little Rock Bank and Trust. In 2005, it purchases a note from Underwater due in five year's time. In doing so it becomes a holder in due course. Some time later it becomes apparent that Underwater may well have engaged in fraud in procuring the note from the investor Thomas. This does not change Little Rock's position. It is still a holder in due course of the note, and if it held onto the note until the due date in 2010 would be entitled to payment of the full $50,000 from Thomas. Any defense to payment of the note that Thomas might hope to use would turn out to be unavailing against Little Rock, because that bank would still qualify as a holder in due course. Whatever Underwater may have done to procure the investment, and whatever trouble he may be in from other quarters because of what he's done, Thomas's note remains due for the full amount to the Little Rock bank when the due date comes up in 2010.

So Little Rock is holding a valuable asset, a note of Thomas's payable to it for $50,000 in 2010. But what if the bank, for one reason or another, wants to sell that asset? It stands to reason that it should be able to get in return cash or its equivalent, in an amount reasonably related to the value of the note as it now stands in the bank's posses-sion. The value of the note to the bank, even after all the details about Underwater's disgraceful behavior become generally known, is its value as a note enforceable by a holder in due course. Any party to whom the bank now tries to sell the note could not, as we have seen, itself qualify to be a holder in due course. If any potential buyer were to consider taking the note, knowing it would then hold the note without the rights of a holder in due course, that buyer would justifiably figure the note to be far less valuable to it than the bank's appraisal of the note's worth. The bank would be holding an asset that it rightfully considers to be worth so much to it, but as a practical matter it would not be able to find a buyer for the asset who would be willing to pay anything like the value the asset has in the hands of the bank. The bank would be stuck having to hold onto the note until 2010, for it would be the only holder that could get the maximum amount due on the note when the due date arrives.

There is no good reason to prevent the bank from transferring the note into the hands of another party. Thomas, when he signed a note on these terms in 2005, had to be aware that the note could come into the hands of a holder in due course, as indeed it has, and that he would have to pay the $50,000 due in 2010 to whomever is holding the note at the time, whatever he may later discover about the Underwater Estates venture. Remember that he signed the note payable to Underwater Estates. He did not have anything to do with picking out the party, in this case Little Rock Bank and Trust, to whom it was then negotiated. Nor could he assert any reason to suppose that it might not then be negotiated one or several more times. When you issue a negotiable instrument and send it out into the world, you have to expect that it may pass from hand to hand any number of times; the issuer's consent to, or even his awareness of, all subsequent transfers is most definitely not required. And so it can't really be said that Thomas has anything to complain about if the party to whom he is obligated to make the $50,000 payment in 2010 is the Little Rock Bank or some other party entirely, as long as that party is one legitimately "entitled to enforce" the instrument at the time it becomes due.

Therefore, if Little Rock Bank and Trust is going to be able to sell off the note to some other party (such as IEC) in exchange for the value that the Little Rock Bank reasonably puts on the note, the bank has to be allowed to sell the note *along with* the bank's rights to enforce the note as a holder in due course would be able to do. Otherwise it just wouldn't be able to find a buyer willing to pay the appropriate price. The shelter doctrine of §3-203(b) is what allows such a transaction to take place. In the words of the comment, it "assures the holder in due course [Little Rock in our example] a free market for the instrument.",

Let me give you one other example of how the shelter doctrine could work in practice. Imagine that A makes a note payable to B in one year. B immediately negotiates the note over to one C, who takes it as a holder in due course. Suppose that when the year is up, A fails to make payment to C. C could of course go through the process of trying to collect from A what is due on the note, up to and including bringing suit on it. But it may be that C is not in the best position, for one reason or another, to go through all that this entails. Or perhaps it simply doesn't find it worthwhile to act as its own collection agent in this way. After a few modest attempts to get payment out of A, C would like to sell the note to D, a firm that is more than willing to take on the collection responsibilities. D, however, cannot by acquiring the note become a holder in due course, as the note is already overdue (§3-302(a)(2)(iii)). D can, however, under the shelter principle of §3-203(b), take the note and in so doing acquire from its transferor C any rights to enforce it as a holder in due course. The sale of the overdue note from C to D can take place and at an appropriate price.

For two recent examples of the shelter doctrine in operation, see *Tiffin v. Cigna Insurance Co.*, 297 N.J.Super. 199, 687 A.2d 1045, 31 U.C.C.2d 1040 (1997), and *Tiffin v. Somerset Valley Bank*, 343 N.J.Super. 73, 777 A.2d 993, 44 U.C.C.2d 1200 (2001), even if the court in the later case makes the mistake of phrasing its conclusion — as by now you would know not to do — as a finding that the plaintiff had "the status" of a holder in due course. What it meant to say, undoubtedly, was that the plaintiff, while not having such status had "the rights" of a holder in due course nevertheless. The Tiffin in both cases is the same person, as you might have guessed — one Robert Tiffin who is in the business of purchasing, presumably in the New Jersey area if nowhere else, negotiable instruments that have been dishonored. He certainly appears to know his business. He argued both of the cited cases pro se and won them both.

Finally, note that the drafters of §3-203(b) were careful to close one potential loophole that the shelter doctrine would otherwise make possible, and that would only lead to mischief or worse. Reread this subsection, but now focus on the concluding language:

> . . . but the transferee cannot acquire rights of a holder in due course by a transfer, directly or indirectly, from a holder in due course if the transferee engaged in fraud or illegality affecting the instrument.

Take the hypothetical we have been working with. Imagine that Underwater had engaged in fraud to procure the note from Thomas. He takes the note and negotiates it to the Little Rock Bank, which takes the note as a holder in due course. Suppose that Underwater were then to repurchase the note from Little Rock. Could he then claim to have obtained, through this transfer, the rights of a holder in due course, despite his own fraudulent behavior, thanks to the shelter doctrine and the fact that its transferor was a holder in due course? Of course not! As Comment 2 to §3-203 remarks:

> There is one exception to [the shelter doctrine] rule stated in the concluding clause of subsection (b). A person who is party to fraud or illegality affecting an instrument is not permitted to wash the instrument clean by passing it into the hands of a holder in due course and then repurchasing it.

The shelter doctrine is an important tool enhancing the free transferability of negotiable instruments, but it is a tool that cannot be allowed to fall into the wrong hands.

See Revision Alert on the following page.

Revision Alert

The crucial definition of the term *good faith* may be found in the revised version of Article 3 at R§3-103(a)(6). But then again it may not. If on looking at R§3-103(a)(6) you find that subpart with no definition but simply marked "Reserved," it is because the particular jurisdiction has adopted the Revised Version of Article 1 promulgated in 2001 and this, the so-called objective, definition of good faith can now be found in its R§1-201(b)(20). The definition thus automatically applies to any use of the term in Article 3, and a separate definition of it in the article would be redundant.

8

Defenses, Claims of Others, and the Holder in Due Course

Introduction

We have already considered, in Chapter 3, how any party signing an instrument takes on the obligation to pay the instrument under certain well-defined circumstances. The obligation of a maker to pay on a note is set forth in §3-412, the obligation of an acceptor to pay on a draft in §3-413, and so forth. In each instance, as we know, the obligation is owed to a "person entitled to enforce the instrument" as defined in §3-301. Should a person entitled to enforce find himself or herself in the unenviable position of having to bring (or at least threaten) suit in order to compel performance of the obligation of a maker, a drawer, an acceptor, or an indorser, the defendant may raise as a defense any argument that the plaintiff is not in fact a person entitled to enforce the instrument. The defendant may also question whether all the elements of the plaintiff's prima facie case asserting obligation have been met; that is, whether the facts bring the case within the rules laid out in §§3-412 through 3-415, whichever the plaintiff is relying upon to advance his or her claim of the defendant's obligation to pay on the instrument.

In addition to any efforts the defendant will make to undercut the plaintiff's prima facie case, he or she may also wish to assert certain affirmative defenses arising out of the circumstances under which his or her signature on the instrument was obtained. In this chapter we explore the nature of these affirmative defenses, as well as the related concept of what Article 3 refers to a "claim in recoupment," which the defendant may use to lessen, if not totally do away with, its obligation to pay what is due on the instrument. We will also consider instances when the person holding an instrument has to contend with someone else's claim that the instrument is rightfully that other person's property and should be returned to him or her.

In examining such situations — the assertion of affirmative defenses and the related claims in recoupment by a party whose obligation to pay on an obligation is the matter in dispute, or the claim of a property interest in an instrument presently held by another — the full import of the question of who is a holder in due course comes to the fore. By the very nature of negotiable instruments, the answer to when and whether a particular defense will be available against a holder claiming the right to be paid on the instrument, or the right to consider the instrument his or hers free from the claims of others, frequently depends on whether the holder has acquired the status of a holder in due course. The concepts and rules with which we will be dealing in this chapter predate the Uniform Commercial Code by a century or more. We find them carried through to the present day for our use in a couple of crucial sections of the present version of Article 3, §§3-305 and 3-306.

Look first at §3-305(a). It says that, "except as stated in subsection (b) [an exception of no small importance, which we'll visit in a moment], the right to enforce the obligation of a party to pay an instrument is subject to" three distinct types of defensive claims. The first set of defenses, those listed in subsection (a)(1), are what have traditionally been referred to as the *real defenses*. Although the list may seem long, as a practical matter the instances in which one of the real defenses is available to a defendant turn out to be relative few. Each of the real defenses, as we will see in the examples to follow, is very limited in scope.

Subsection (a)(2) defines what are conventionally referred to as the *personal defenses*. Under this part, the right to enforce the obligation of a party to pay an instrument is subject to

> a defense of the obligor stated in another section of this Article or a defense of the obligor that would be available if the person entitled to enforce the instrument were enforcing a right to payment under a simple contract.

Though stated in relatively simple terms, the personal defenses cover a lot of territory. The type of standard, common law contract defenses that will constitute personal defenses for the purposes of negotiable instruments law include such old favorites (from your study of contracts) as failure or want of consideration, mistake, and knowing misrepresentation rising to the level of fraud that induced a party to enter into a contract from which he or she might otherwise have steered clear.

Subsection (a)(3) deals with what the current version of Article 3 has dubbed *claims in recoupment*. A claim in recoupment is not, strictly speaking, a defense; even if available to the defendant, it does not totally do away with his or her obligation to pay what is due on the instrument. What is meant by a claim in recoupment is a legally recognized argument that the amount owed by the obligor should be reduced by some amount because of an offsetting claim the obligor can assert "if the claim [of the obligor for a reduction] arose from the transaction that gave rise to the instrument." Some illustrations of what will or what will not constitute a claim in recoupment appear in Examples 4 and 5.

We now turn to the all-important subsection 3-305(b):

> The right of a holder in due course to enforce the obligation of a party to pay the instrument is subject to the defenses of the obligor stated in subsection (a)(1), *but is not subject to* defenses of the obligor stated in subsection (a)(2) or claims in recoupment stated in subsection (a)(3) against a person other than the holder.

The emphasis has, of course, been added by me, but I could not resist. A party that qualifies as a holder in due course (or that can rely on the rights of a holder in due course thanks to the shelter doctrine of §3-203(b)) when enforcing the instrument is subject to the real defenses. The holder in due course, however, is immune from any personal defense that the defendant would otherwise have available and from any claims in recoupment that the obligor would have against a party other than the plaintiff himself or herself.

If you had been wondering about why we spent as much effort as we did in Chapter 7 looking at the question of how a party can establish its status not merely as a holder or a person entitled to enforce, but as a holder in due course, your curiosity should now be more than satisfied. Once a negotiable instrument has come into the hands of someone who qualifies as a holder in due course, the personal defenses and most claims in recoupment are cut off once and for all; anyone who has taken on the obligation to pay the instrument by signing it in one capacity or another is forevermore barred from asserting any personal defense to avoid payment or claim in recoupment to offset what he or she will be made to pay on the instrument.

To conclude this introduction, I ask that you turn to §3-306.

> A person taking an instrument, other than a person having rights of a holder in due course, is subject to a claim of a property or possessory right in the instrument or its proceeds, including the right to rescind a negotiation and to recover the instrument or its proceeds. *A person having rights of a holder in due course takes free of the claim to the instrument.*

Again the emphasis is mine. The claims that are the subject of this section are to be distinguished from any possible claims in recoupment. What the section lumps together as *claims to an instrument* are claims by some party that he or she has a "property or possessory right in the instrument" that gives him or her greater right to the instrument than that of the present holder. The simplest example is the situation in which a thief has made off with a piece of bearer paper. Recall that the thief does qualify as a holder. He or she would not, however, be the legitimate owner of the instrument. The person from whom the instrument was stolen clearly has a argument for its return, based on a property right, and should be able to assert such a claim against whatever party is currently in possession of the instrument. Whether such a claim will be successful depends, as we will examine in Example 10, on whether the party now holding the instrument can successfully claim holder in due course status. Holder in due course status not only cuts off the personal defenses and claims in recoupment, but also protects the holder from such property-based claims of others.

EXAMPLES

1. Ms. Boss, who runs a small business, decides to give a Christmas bonus to each of her employees. She writes up a set of checks, including one payable "to the order of Louie Lacky." When Lacky comes into Boss's office to pick up his check, the two of them get into an argument and Boss decides not to give Lackey his bonus. The check written out to him remains on her desk. When Boss then leaves the room, Lacky spies the check and quietly slips it into his pocket. By the time Lacky deposits the check in his own checking account, Boss has become aware of its absence and has put a stop-payment order on the check. The check, having been dishonored, is returned to Lacky by his bank.

   (a) If Lacky brings an action against Boss, based on her obligation under §3-414(b) to pay on the dishonored check of which she is the drawer, should Lacky's suit succeed? Recall §3-105.

   (b) What if, instead of directly depositing the check, Lacky had taken it to the Midtown Liquor store where he cashed the check for its full amount? Assume that there is no reason why Midtown, in taking the check, would not become a holder in due course. Midtown deposits the check, which is not paid because of Boss's stop-payment order and is returned to Midtown dishonored. If Midtown brings suit on the check against Boss, will its suit be successful?

2. In 2005 Thomas is invited to make an investment in Underwater Estates, which he is assured by its promoter, Horace Underwater, is going to be a fast-growing and highly profitable real estate venture. Thomas acquires an interest in this company by giving a note payable to Underwater Estates for $50,000, payable five years from the date of signing. By the time 2010 rolls around, it has been discovered that Horace Underwater had been convincing people (including Thomas) to invest in this project by knowingly giving them false information and projections as to its future profitability.

   (a) Assume that in 2010, when the note becomes due, it is still being held by Underwater, who brings suit to enforce it asserting

Thomas's obligation under §3-412 to pay on the note according to its terms. Will Thomas have to pay the $50,000 due on the note?

(b) Assume instead that Underwater had sold the note, soon after obtaining it, to one of the major banks in the community, Little Rock Bank and Trust. The Little Rock Bank qualifies as a holder in due course at the time it takes transfer of the note. In 2010 it is still holding onto the note, and when Thomas does not pay the $50,000 when due, it brings suit against Thomas. Is Little Rock Bank and Trust entitled to collect this amount from Thomas?

3. In March of 2004, Seymour Sellers agrees to sell a quantity of high-quality widgets to Bertha Byers, who uses such widgets in her manufacturing operations, for the price of $12,000, delivery of the widgets to be made no later than April 1. Sellers does not ask for cash payment at the time the contract of sale is signed, but does get from Byers a note payable "to the order of Seymour Sellers" for the amount of $12,000 and due on May 1, 2004. Sellers never delivers the widgets to Byers. Byers never pays on the note.

(a) Assume the note is still being held by Sellers. After May 1 he brings a suit on the note against Byers. Should Sellers's suit succeed in getting him the $12,000?

(b) Assume instead that soon after he took possession of the note, Sellers sold it to the First National Bank for $11,000, and that the bank in taking the note qualifies as a holder in due course. When Byers does not pay the $12,000 due on the note on May 1, the bank brings an action against her for this amount. Will the bank's suit be successful?

4. This example starts out as does the preceding one: Seymour Sellers contracts to sell some widgets to Bertha Byers for the price of $12,000, with delivery of the widgets to be made no later than April 1. Sellers receives in March, at the time of the signing of the contract of sale, a note signed by Byers payable "to the order of Seymour Sellers" for the amount of $12,000 and due on May 1, 2004. This time, however, the widgets are delivered as promised before April 1. Unfortunately, Byers soon discovers some flaws in the widgets. They do not meet the specifications of the contract of sale entered into between Sellers and Byers. Byers determines that she will not return the widgets. She is able to fix the flaws so that the widgets end up meeting the contract specifications, but to do so she has to spend $1,400 of her own money.

(a) Assume the note is still held by Sellers. Under the circumstances, is Byers still obligated to pay Sellers the full $12,000 on the note by May 1?

(b) Assume instead that soon after he took possession of the note, Sellers sold it to the First National Bank for $11,000, and that the bank in taking the note qualifies as a holder in due course. When Byers does not pay the $12,000 due on the note on May 1, the bank brings an action against her for this amount. Will the bank's suit be successful and for what amount?

5.   Now assume that Sellers and Byers enter into two separate contracts of purchase and sale. Under the first, Sellers will deliver the widgets by April 1. Sellers takes a note from Byers for $12,000, payable on May 1, in payment for the widgets. Under a second contract, Sellers agrees to supply Byers with a quantity of gaskets for $5,000, which Byers pays up front and in cash. Both the widgets and gaskets arrive on time. The widgets are as ordered; there is nothing wrong with them. The gaskets are, however, a different story. Byers is forced to spend $740 of her own money to repair the many that arrived broken or bent. When the note becomes due on May 1, it is still in Sellers's possession. Sellers insists on being paid the full $12,000 promised in the instrument. Byers argues that she has the right to deduct the $740 that she had to spend to bring the gaskets up to the quality promised her by Sellers from the amount due on the note. Which party has the better argument?

6.   To expand his fledgling Internet company, Younger buys an assortment of computer equipment from Carl's Computer City. In exchange for the merchandise, he gives Carl a note calling for Younger to make monthly payments of a stated amount over the next three years. Carl immediately sells this note to Merchants Credit Association, which takes the instrument as a holder in due course. Soon thereafter, Younger comes back to Carl's. He wishes to return everything he purchased and "cancel" the note that he signed. It turns out that Younger is 17 years old. Carl tells him that even if he wanted to do as Younger asks, he no longer holds the note, as he has transferred it to Merchants Credit. Younger stops making his monthly payments on the note. Can Merchants Credit successfully bring suit against Younger on the note?

7.   Mrs. Hodge entered into an agreement with Fred Fentress under which Fentress would do certain plumbing work for Hodge. Hodge gave Fentress a check for $500, and Fentress promised to return the next day with the necessary equipment to do the work. Fentress never returned. He did, however, cash the check at the Kedzie & 103rd Street Currency Exchange, which in taking the check qualified as a holder in due course. By the time the Currency Exchange itself tried to obtain payment on the check, Hodge had placed a stop-payment order on it. The check was returned unpaid to the Currency Exchange, which then sued Hodge on her obligation as the drawer of a dishonored check. Hodge asserted as a defense the fact that Fentress was not a licensed plumber. The state's plumbing licensing law requires that all plumbing, including just the type of work that Fentress initially contracted to do for Hodge, be performed only by plumbers licensed under the licens-

ing law. Hodge argues that because Fentress was in violation of this law, the transaction giving rise to the check was illegal. Does this give her an effective defense to the collection suit brought by the Currency Exchange?

8.   To get the capital he needs to expand a small business he operates, Cosmo Graphics arranges to borrow $80,000 from the firm of Ventura Capital. In exchange for the money, he gives a note the text of which reads that "the undersigned Borrower(s) agree to pay to the order of Ventura Capital" interest and principal on a schedule set out within the note. Graphics signs on the bottom on a line marked for "Borrower." Graphics has been told by Ventura Capital that he will need a co-signer on the note. He goes up to Dimmer, one of his senior employees, and asks if Dimmer would just please sign this piece of paper (the note) on the bottom next to his signature. "It's just a formality," he assures her, "and nothing for you to worry about." Dimmer signs as requested.

(a) Is Dimmer obligated on the note?

(b) Would it make any difference to your answer if Ventura Capital had transferred the note over to another firm, Centura Capital, which in taking the note would qualify as a holder in due course?

9.   On February 1, 2005, Annie Able borrows $12,000 from Bennie Baker. She gives Baker a note payable to his order for $12,000 plus interest payable on December 1, 2005.

(a) On November 24, Able pays Baker the amount due on the note, which is still held by Baker. Does Able have any further obligation on the note? See §§3-601 and 3-602(a).

(b) Suppose that when Able makes her payment to Baker, he is no longer holding the note. He transferred it in March to Carla Charles. What is the result?

(c) Finally, suppose that Baker was still holding the note when Able made her payment in November. Baker, however, does not return the note to Able, nor does he cancel the note by doing anything like ripping it in half or stamping it with a "Paid" stamp. (See §3-604.) On November 28, Baker negotiates the note to one Helen Chang, who qualifies as a holder in due course and has no knowledge or reason to know that Able made payment to Baker earlier in the month. Chang is expecting payment from Able of the full amount due on the note on December 1. When she doesn't receive this payment, she brings suit against Able for the amount of the note that she now holds. Is Chang entitled to payment?

10. Ms. Boss makes out and delivers a paycheck to one of her employees, Terry Toady. Toady immediately signs the back of the check with his name and puts the check in his jacket pocket, intending to deposit it in his bank on his way home. Before he leaves work for the day, however, another employee, Sally

Sly, takes the check from Toady's pocket. Fortunately for Toady, someone sees Sly taking the check and the next day informs Toady of what has happened.

    (a) Assuming the check is still in Sly's possession, does Toady have the legal right to get it back from her?

    (b) Assume instead that by the time Toady catches up with the check, Sly has cashed it at a local grocery store, Ralph's Market. Assume further that Ralph's Market qualifies as a holder in due course of the check, which now sits in Ralph's cash register waiting to be deposited by Ralph along with other checks he has taken during the week. Does Toady have the right to regain possession of his check from Ralph?

EXPLANATIONS

1a. Lacky's suit to enforce Boss's obligation on the check should fail. Under §3-105(a), this check was never issued, and subsection (b) of this same section states that "nonissuance is a defense." For the sake of completeness, we should note that this defense would come under §3-305(a)(2) as "a defense of the obligor stated in another section of this Article." Boss has an effective defense against Lacky, who stands as holder of the instrument but not a holder in due course.

1b. If, as we are assuming, Midtown qualifies as a holder in due course, then Boss's defense of nonissuance could not be successfully invoked against Midtown. Under §3-305(b), the rights of a holder in due course are not subject to the defenses of the obligor, here Boss, stated in subsection (a)(2). For confirmation, look at Comment 2 to §3-105:

> Subsection (b) [of §3-105] continues the rule that nonissuance . . . is a defense of the maker or drawer of an instrument. Thus, the defense can be asserted against a person other than a holder in due course.

2a. When Thomas is sued on the note by Underwater, he will have available the personal defense of good old garden-variety fraudulent inducement. Thomas's agreement to take on the obligation represented by the note was induced by Underwater's fraudulent representations made to Thomas at the time of his signing concerning the underlying transaction. This is just the kind of conventional contract defense covered by subsection (a)(2) of §3-305.

2b. If Little Rock Bank and Trust qualifies as a holder in due course of the note, then it is entitled to collect the full amount of Thomas's obligation on the note when due, and it is not subject to the defense of fraudulent inducement that Thomas would want to interpose. Fraud of this type is a personal defense and will be of no avail against a holder in due course.

    You might have been tempted, in answering this question, to try on Thomas's behalf to squeeze the defense upon which he seeks to rely into the real defenses of §3-305(a)(1)(iii), and thereby make it a defense that is not cut off even if the party enforcing the instrument is a holder in due course. As we will see in Example 8, however, the type of fraud to which (a)(1)(iii) refers is a very different situation from what we have here. Fraudulent statements relating to the underlying transaction made to induce another to sign an instrument, such as Underwater has at least allegedly engaged in, clearly fall within the scope of the personal and not the real defenses. Hence, even if Underwater's fraud of this type could be easily proved by Thomas, it would not relieve Thomas of the obligation to pay the instrument now that it is in the hands of a holder in due course.

3a.   Byers should be able to defend herself successfully by invoking the standard contract defense traditionally referred to as *failure of consideration.* (In more modern contract lingo, we might speak of this as being the absence of a condition precedent, the delivery of the goods, to the existence of Byers's obligation to pay for them. But it amounts to the same thing.) Byers gave her promise to pay the money in the future in exchange for a promise on Sellers's part to deliver some high-quality widgets, and Sellers has totally failed to live up to his part of the bargain. As a matter of fact, this particular defense is incorporated directly into Article 3 in §3-303(b): "If an instrument is issued for a promise of performance, the issuer has a defense to the extent the performance of the promise is due and the promise has not been performed." Either way of looking at it, this is a personal defense under §3-305(a)(2) and as such is available to Byers when she is being sued on the note by a person who does not qualify as a holder in due course.

3b.   The bank, being a holder in due course, will be able to enforce the note and collect the $12,000 from Byers. As a holder in due course, it is not subject to the personal defenses such as she would try to assert here. Where does that leave Byers? Well, she will have to pay First National on the note and then pursue Sellers by other means. She can bring an action against him under Article 2 (see §§2-712 and 2-713) for any damage caused to her by his failure to deliver the goods contracted for. This remains a matter between Byers and Sellers, however. As far as the bank is concerned, being as it is a holder in due course of the note, it can enforce the note against Byers free and clear of any personal defenses she would have at her disposal if she were being sued by Sellers himself or any other holder that could not prove itself to have taken as a holder in due course.

4a.   No. Under §3-305(a)(3), Byers would be able to assert a claim in recoupment for $1,400 against Sellers in his suit against her. Sellers would be entitled to payment of $10,600 ($12,00 minus $1,400) on the note, but no more. This is what Article 3 considers a claim in recoupment, because it is a claim — in this case for breach of warranty (see §2-714) — that arises from the same transaction that gave rise to the instrument.

4b. Because First National Bank stands as a holder in due course, it will be able to enforce the instrument without being subject to any claim in recoupment that Byers may have. Notice that §3-305(b) states that the holder in due course is not subject to "claims in recoupment stated in subsection (a)(3) against a person other than the holder." Whatever claim in recoupment Byers may have is a claim against Sellers, not against First National Bank, which is now the holder. Sellers's failure to make widgets that were up to par may not be used to reduce the amount owed to First National on the note that it holds as a holder in due course.

5.   Sellers wins this argument. He is owed the full $12,000 due on the note exchanged for the widgets. Byers does have a claim for breach of warranty, because of the broken and bent gaskets, amounting to some $740, but this does not qualify as a claim in recoupment that can be asserted against Sellers to diminish the right he has to receive the $12,000 due on the note. A claim in recoupment under §3-305(a)(3) must be a claim arising "from the same transaction that gave rise to the instrument." See *Zener v. Velde*, 132 Idaho 352, 17 P.3d 296, 42 U.C.C.2d 1073 (Id. App. 2000). Byers's claim for breach of warranty arose from a different transaction than the one that gave rise to the $12,000 note. Hence, Sellers's right to enforce Byers's obligation as the maker of the note is not "subject to" her breach of warranty claim arising under this other transaction. Byers does, of course, have the right to collect $740 from Sellers for the damages he has caused her by his failure to deliver the gaskets as warranted, but she will have to pursue him separately for this amount. She cannot simply offset it against the amount due on the note. Observe that this result does not depend on whether the person holding the instrument and to whom obligation is due is a holder in due course. Rather, it is the result of what "claim in recoupment" means in the Article 3 context.

6.   When Merchants Credit attempts to collect from Younger on the note, Younger may try to use as a defense the fact that he signed the note when he was still a minor. Among the real defenses of §3-305(a)(1) to which even a holder in due course is subject is "infancy of the obligor to the extent it is a defense to a simple contract." As Comment 1 states,

> No attempt is made [in this section] to state when infancy is available as a defense or the conditions under which it may be asserted. In some jurisdictions it is held that an infant cannot rescind the transaction or set up the defense unless the holder is restored to the position held before the instrument was taken which, in the case of a holder in due course, is normally impossible. In other states an infant who has misrepresented age may be estopped to assert infancy. Such questions are left to other law, as an integral part of the policy of each state as to the protection of infants.

So the answer to this question will depend on exactly how the common law of contracts in the jurisdiction in which this story is being played out treats the defense of infancy.

7.   This example is based on the case *Kedzie & 103rd Currency Exchange v. Hodge*, 156 Ill. 2d 112, 619 N.E.2d 732, 21 U.C.C.2d 682 (1993). The question is whether Mrs. Hodge can assert, against the holder in due course, the defense of illegality under §3-305(a)(ii). Again, as in the case of the infancy defense, the question has to be answered by reference to the common law of the jurisdiction, but the test of whether the defense is available is different. The defense of "illegality of the transaction" is, under (a)(ii), available against a holder in due course only if, under the law of the jurisdiction, it "nullifies the obligation of the obligor." This test — which applies as well to the defenses of duress and lack of legal capacity — requires a showing that, under the applicable law of the jurisdiction, the defense renders the obligation not merely voidable at the election of the obligor, but entirely null and void from the outset.

No single test has been adopted by all the states to determine when illegality of a transaction renders all obligations under that transaction null and void, as opposed to merely voidable at the election of one of the parties. In the *Hodge* case, the Illinois Supreme Court held that the defense was not available against the check-cashing agency suing as a holder in due course. The defense of illegality nullifies the transaction under Illinois law only when "the instrument arising from the contract or transaction is, itself, made void by statute." The Illinois plumbing license law made it illegal to do plumbing without a license; it did not specifically make it illegal to issue an instrument in payment for plumbing to be done by someone without the requisite license.

Although the *Hodge* case was decided under the prerevision version of Article 3, there is no reason to think it would come out any differently today. In both versions, the test of whether illegality of the transaction rises to the level of a real defense, available even against a holder in due course, depends on the "other law" of the jurisdiction, and there is no reason to think that the law of Illinois as to when illegality renders a transaction void rather than merely voidable would have changed with the adoption of the new Article 3. For a similar case decided under the revised Article 3, which comes to basically the same conclusion applying Pennsylvania law, *see State Street Bank & Trust Co. v. Strawser*, 908 F. Supp. 249, 30 U.C.C.2d 477 (M.D. Pa. 1995).

Not all states draw the line exactly where Illinois does, requiring a specific declaration by the state's legislature that any instrument issued under the circumstances is void as a matter of law. Some would find illegality in the underlying transaction (at least if it were not a mere technical violation of law but a particular heinous encroachment on what is deemed to be a particularly significant state interest) enough to render void any instrument issued as part of the transaction, even if the state legislature had not addressed the matter directly. In any event, the defense of illegality as it stands in (a)(1)(ii) has to be thought of as a narrow one. As a matter of fact, the illegality defense seems to arise most often not in the situation of unlicensed plumbing and the like, but when the instrument in question was issued to pay a gambling debt or to borrow money with which to gamble. Some states, even those that allow legalized gambling, have specific statutes rendering void any instrument issued to pay a gambling debt or to obtain funds on credit with which to gamble, in which case even the holder in due course of such an instrument would be unable to enforce it. Other states, though not having statutory pronouncements directly on point, may reach the same result. On this defense, as well as the defenses of incapacity and duress, which are grouped in (a)(1)(ii) with illegality as defenses available only when the result is to "nullify" the obligation of the defendant, see the third and fourth paragraphs of Comment 1 to §3-305.

8a. Dimmer will almost assuredly be held obligated on the note as a co-maker. She may try to assert the defense, provided for in §3-305(a)(1)(iii), of "fraud that induced the obligor to sign the instrument with neither knowledge nor reasonable opportunity to learn of its character or its essential terms," but she would have a hard time making the case that this applies to her situation. First, note that fraud of the type being talked about here is not of the same type as we dealt with in Example 2. That was the essentially different — and doubtless far more common — fraudulent inducement, and it fell within the grab bag of personal defenses of (a)(2). The subject of (a)(1)(iii) is what has historically been referred to as *fraud in the factum*. It consists of fraudulent behavior designed to get someone's signature on a document without the signer's knowing or having a reasonable opportunity to discover just what the paper he or she is signing is all about. As the fifth paragraph to Comment 1 explains,

> The common illustration is that of the maker who is tricked into signing a note in the belief that it is merely a receipt or some other document. The theory of the defense is that the signature on the instrument is ineffective because the signer did not intend to sign such an instrument at all.

Fraud of this type is, as you might expect, exceptionally difficult to prove. As the comment continues,

> The test of the defense is that of an excusable ignorance of the contents of the writing signed. The party must not have only been in ignorance, but also must have had no reasonable opportunity to obtain knowledge. In determining what is a reasonable opportunity all relevant factors are to be taken into account, including the intelligence, education, business experience, and ability to read or understand English of the signer. Also relevant is the nature of the representations that were made, whether the signer had good reason to rely on the representations or to have confidence in the person making them, the presence or absence of any third person who might read or explain the instrument to the signer, or any other possibility of independent information, and the apparent necessity, or lack of it, for acting without delay.

Applying this test to Dimmer's case, it is hard to imagine that she will be able to prove the kind of excusable ignorance of what she was signing that would allow her to rely on this defense. Dimmer may have acted pretty dimly in signing this note as she did, but there is no indication, at least from the information I've given you, that she is generally lacking in intelligence, education, or the like, nor that she had, in the words of the section, no "reasonable opportunity to learn of [the note's] character or its essential terms." As you may imagine, the defense of fraud in the factum is available in only a very limited number of situations. For a recent example of a failed attempt to show fraud in the factum, see *Ruane v. Jancsics,* 2001 Mass. App. Div. 103, 45 U.C.C. 2d 1122. The circumstances under which Dimmer signed don't seem to fit within this defense.

8b. If (and as we have just seen it is a very big *if*) Dimmer were successfully to assert the fraud in the factum defense, then she would be able to use it against Centura Capital, even if that firm did qualify as a holder in due course. The defense arising from this species of fraud, limited as it is in practice, is a real defense. As such, once proven it would be available against a holder in due course.

9a. No. Able's paying Baker has discharged her from any further obligation on the note. Under §3-601(a), "The obligation of a party to pay the instrument is discharged as stated in this Article," and according to §3-602(a), subject to some exceptions none of which are relevant here,

> an instrument is paid to the extent payment is made (i) by or on behalf of the person obliged to pay the instrument, and (ii) to a person entitled to enforce the instrument. To the extent of the payment, the obligation of the party obliged to pay the instrument is discharged. . . .

In this instance, Able was the person obliged to pay on the note and Baker was a person entitled to enforce the instrument. The payment by Able to Baker discharged Able from any further obligation to pay on the note.

Discharge of this type is not, as you can check, listed among the defenses to obligation in §3-305. That section recites the affirmative defenses that a person charged with an obligation on an instrument may seek to assert. Discharge by payment is not an affirmative defense. If you are discharged from an obligation, for whatever reason, your defense is simply that you are no longer subject to the obligation being asserted against you. Anyone trying to enforce the instrument will fail to make out a prima facie case against you. You don't need to bring up any affirmative defenses. The effect of payment and potential discharge is, however, sufficiently important that we cannot let it go unaccounted for, and the present chapter seemed as good a place as any to deal with it.

9b. Able is not discharged by her payment to Baker if he no longer holds the instrument. Under §3-602(a), an instrument is paid to the extent that payment is made to a person entitled to enforce the instrument. As of the moment Able pays Baker in this hypothetical, Baker is no longer a person entitled to enforce the note. That would now be Charles. Charles can, and we have to assume will, insist that Able make full payment to her as and when the note becomes due, and Able will not be able to argue against Charles that the note has been paid off. It has not.

So, the first rule of thumb in paying off an instrument is to be sure that the person to whom you are making payment is at the time truly in possession of the instrument and entitled to enforce it. Don't just assume. Ask to see the instrument and accept no substitutes.

9c. Chang is entitled to payment from Able even though Able paid off the note when it was still in the hands of Baker. See §3-601(b): "Discharge of an obligation of a party is not effective against a person acquiring rights of a holder in due course without notice of this discharge." Chang, we are assuming, is not only a holder in due course but also had no notice of the discharge. Thus, she could sue Able for the full amount of the note without having to recognize any previous discharge that occurred when Able paid Baker.

So, the second rule of thumb in paying off an instrument is to make sure that you take back physical possession of the instrument (if it is being fully paid off) or see it destroyed or fully canceled before your eyes. This assures that it can never later fall into the hands of someone qualifying as a holder in due course. If you are paying off only a portion of what is due on the instrument, make sure that this partial payment is duly noted *on the instrument itself*. That way no one later taking the instrument, even if he or she qualifies as a holder in due course, can claim lack of notice of the discharge.

10a. Yes. Notice that Sly is in fact a holder of the check. She has possession of a bearer instrument. Sly is not, however, a holder in due course. Among other things, she didn't give value for it — not to mention her lack of good faith. In any event, under §3-306, "[a] person taking an instrument other than a person having rights of a holder in due course, is subject to a claim of a property or possessory right in the instrument or its proceeds including a claim . . . to recover the instrument or its proceeds." Toady has such a claim to the check as his property and will be able to enforce this claim against Sly.

10b. No. Section 3-306 concludes with the statement that "[a] person having rights of a holder in due course takes free of the claim to the instrument." Ralph is, we are assuming, a holder in due course of the check, and took it free from any claim to the check that Toady would have. Once again, and for the last time (at least in this chapter), we see the awesome power that holder in due course status confers upon a party. The holder in due course takes the instrument free of all but the limited "real" defenses and free from the claims of others to the instrument itself. Holder in due course status is far from being just a matter of prestige or bragging rights. It figures mightily into the bottom line.

Revision Alert

The 2002 Revision of Article 3 adds some language to §3-602 that may be some help to parties in the position of our friend Able confronted in Example 9b. Recall that he made payment to the original payee of a note of which he was the maker, but that the payee had previously transferred the note to another party. His obligation on the note was not discharged under current §3-602(a). How could he have made such a bush-league error? The same outcome might still be true under R§3-602(a), but note the following that has been added to a new subsection (b):

> . . . [A] note is paid to the extent payment is made . . . to a person that was formerly entitled to enforce the note only if at the time of the payment the party obliged to pay has not received adequate notification that the note has been transferred and that payment has been made to the transferee.

The subsection goes on to prescribe what is required for adequate notice of the transfer, and further states:

> Upon request, a transferee shall seasonably furnish reasonable proof that the note has been transferred. Unless the transferee complies with the request, a payment made to the person that formerly was entitled to enforce the note is effective [for purposes of discharge] even if the party obliged to pay the note has received a notification under this paragraph.

The reason given in an accompanying comment by the revision drafters for this amendment is that, "Unlike the earlier version of Section 3-602, this rule is consistent with Section 9-406(a), Restatement of Mortgages §5.5, and Restatement of Contracts §338(1)."

So, in our Example 9b, under this revision, Able *might* be discharged of any obligation on the note upon his payment to Baker *if* either Baker failed to give him adequate notice of the transfer to Charles or if Charles fails to comply with Able's perfectly reasonable request that he, Charles, prove that he still holds the note transferred to him. The rule of thumb stated in the second paragraph of my explanation to that Example in the text — it hardly need be stated — still goes.

The Consumer Context

Introduction

Traditionally, the holder in due course doctrine has been thought of as one of the most significant features — indeed, probably the principal feature — distinguishing the negotiable instrument from the nonnegotiable contractual promise to pay, even when that promise to pay is memorialized in a writing of some detail and sophistication. Negotiability makes a big difference. It is, of course, perfectly possible for people to buy and sell rights arising under a contract. Your study of the common law of contracts presumably included at least an introduction to the law governing the assignment of contract rights. As a practical matter, however, the assignment of a contract right in exchange for cash or anything else of present value carries a great deal of risk for the buyer, which consequently severely limits the market for such rights. The purchaser of a nonnegotiable contract right will, under the fundamental principles of contract law, take the right subject to all defenses the obligor would have against the initial obligee. In contrast, the purchaser of a negotiable instrument who can assert the rights of a holder in due course will, as we have seen, take the instrument and the promise of payment it represents free of the most common defenses that the obligor may later try to interpose. The holder in due course doctrine cuts off these defenses and thus greatly reduces the risk that the purchaser of the instrument takes in giving present value in exchange for the instrument and its promise of payment in the future. In so doing, the holder in due course doctrine greatly facilitates the marketability of negotiable instruments.

A party signing a negotiable instrument should be aware that in doing so, he or she faces the very real possibility that the instrument will end up in the hands of someone who qualifies as a holder in due course, and that consequently the defenses available when the obligation on the instrument comes due will be greatly limited. There is nothing inherently unfair or unreasonable about this result. A signature on a negotiable instrument in connection with a loan, the sale of goods or services, or any other transaction, should result in the signer's being able to obtain credit at a lower rate of interest than if he or she were attempting to obtain credit without being willing to assume obligation on an instrument. The creditor can extend these more favorable terms to the borrower precisely because it has the possibility of selling off the instrument to another, who could thereby qualify as a holder in due course. The party purchasing the instrument as a holder in due course is willing to pay more for it because that holder in due course status cuts off the most common defenses to later enforcement of the instrument, thus reducing the note purchaser's risk. Holder in due course status allows the purchaser to value the instrument without having to take into account any of the personal defenses the obligor might later try to assert based on irregularities, or even outright fraud, in the original transaction giving rise to the instrument.

The holder in due course doctrine as a core feature of negotiable instrument law has a long history, and as we have seen it carries through to the most recent version of Article 3. By the middle of the last century, however, attention was increasingly being drawn to the argument that the doctrine could and did work a particular hardship on consumer borrowers. Sophisticated businesspersons who signed instruments could be expected to know and appreciate (even if sometimes we wonder whether they really did) the consequences of taking on obligation by signing a negotiable instrument. In contrast, it is feared that all too often the consumer creditor will sign just about any paper put in front of him or her without question and without a full understanding of all the consequences that may flow from that signature.

The basic problem as it relates to the consumer transaction can be related fairly easily. Consider the following transaction:

The consumer buys some expensive item, say a car, from the retailer. The buyer may pay some of the price as a cash down payment, but the bulk of the buyer's obligation to pay for the car will be evidenced by a note that he or she signs, calling for monthly installment payments over a period of a few years. The seller then sells off the note for cash to a local bank or other financial institution. There is, of course, nothing wrong with or suspicious about this. Most consumer purchasers are not in a position to buy big-ticket items such as automobiles other than on credit. The seller will insist on the buyer's signing a note, rather than just contractually obligating itself to pay over time under a simple common law contract, so that the seller can sell off (or, as we sometimes say "discount") the note. The bank is willing to buy the note because it is in negotiable form and the bank can take it as a holder in due course.

The trouble — at least from the buyer's point of view — comes when something goes wrong with the car or if the buyer later becomes aware that he or she was induced into purchasing the car on the basis of fraudulent misrepresentations by the seller. Under such circumstances the buyer may legitimately argue that he or she has the right, under the basic law relating to the purchase and sale of goods, to return the car and get his or her money back. Or perhaps he or she will want to keep the car but subtract from what he or she owes on it the amount of damages caused by the car's failure to be as warranted by the seller. The problem is that any such arguments, although they will be good against the seller, will have no effect on the consumer's obligation to keep paying the monthly installments on the note, which is now in the hands of the bank. The bank, if it can properly claim holder in due course status, has every right to insist that the consumer continue to meet its obligation as maker of the note. Any personal defenses or claims in recoupment that the injured buyer might want to assert are cut off and not available to him or her now that the note has found its way into the possession of a holder in due course. The car buyer is relegated to seeking whatever remedy he or she can against the breaching or defrauding seller; what he or she *cannot* do is stop paying the bank on the note. The monthly car payments, as the buyer will naturally think of them, are still due regardless of the car's condition or what the buyer has later learned about the seller's tactics that led to the sale. The bank's position, simply put, will be, "Keep paying us on the note. We had nothing to do with the sale of the car. Whatever problems you have with it, you will have to take up with the dealer." What we may well think of as a particular unfairness to the consumer in such a situation can be compounded if we consider that whatever rights the buyer may retain against the seller may be of little value if, by the time the buyer becomes aware of what has happened, the seller has become insolvent or is otherwise unavailable for suit.

A Common Law Response

Should the law concerning negotiable instruments do away with the holder in due course rule, either entirely or at least in the case of consumer transactions? Around the 1960s this question became a subject of considerable debate by academics and other commentators. On one side were those who argued that the fundamental inequity imposed upon consumers in such situations — where they typically had no way of being aware, at the time of signing a note, of all the implications of the obligation they were undertaking — called for some type of relief. Those who argued against either doing away with or significantly cutting into the holder in due course doctrine, even in the consumer context, argued that to do so would only make it that much harder for consumers to obtain credit with which to make large purchases, or would greatly increase the cost of whatever forms of credit remained available to them.

Meanwhile, as the academic debate raged, consumer advocates began to find some success in the states, through both court decisions and legislative enactments. For one thing, the courts began to recognize that the party claiming holder in due course status was not in all instances a truly independent third party that had purchased the note from the seller in an arm's-length transaction. Certainly, if the bank had with any regularity been purchasing notes taken by the retailer in exchange for its wares, and had some reason to be aware that the retailer was selling shoddy merchandise or engaging in deceptive practices, it could be held not to be a holder in due course because of its failure to act in good faith in taking the instrument, even if it had no notice of a defect in the particular goods sold. Beyond this, several decisions looked beyond the paperwork of the transaction and determined that the party presenting itself as a holder in due course was not in fact as divorced or isolated from the initial transaction giving rise to the note as we would commonly expect a true holder in due course to be. In some instances the seller and the financial institution taking the note, supposedly as holder in due course, were in actuality just two parts of the same business enterprise, organized to appear as distinct entities but in fact operated and controlled by the same people. Even if the seller and the institution to which it sold the note were not really just two divisions of the same operation, there might be such a regular and mutually beneficial relationship between the two (say, between a car dealership and the one major bank in town to which it steered all customers interested in obtaining car loans) that the court might find it inappropriate for the bank later to claim holder in due course status. This led, in many jurisdictions, to judicial adoption of the so-called *close-connectedness doctrine*, under which the court would refuse to recognize the right of a holder in due course to avoid the personal defenses or claims in recoupment that would have been available against the "closely connected" entity from which it purchased the note had the note still been in that party's possession. In the oft-cited case of *Unico v. Owen*, 50 N.J. 101, 232 A.2d 405 (1967), the Supreme Court of New Jersey reasoned:

> The basic philosophy of the holder in due course status is to encourage the free negotiability of commercial paper by removing certain anxieties of one who takes the paper as an innocent purchaser knowing no reason why the paper is not as sound as its face would indicate. It would seem to follow, therefore, that the more the holder knows about the underlying transaction, and the more it controls or participates or becomes involved in it, the less he fits the role of the good faith purchaser for value; the closer his relationship to the underlying agreement which is the source of the note, the less need there is for giving him the tension-free rights considered necessary in a fast-moving, credit-extending commercial world.

The court concluded by articulating a test that other courts were later to follow for determining when and whether the relationship between the retailer and the financial institution to which it sells its consumer paper is sufficiently close to conclude that the institution's right to enforce the instrument is not freed of the personal defenses or claims in recoupment.

> [W]hen it appears from the totality of the arrangements between the [retailer] and financier that the financier has had a substantial voice in setting standards for the underlying transaction, or has approved the standards established by the [retailer], and has agreed to take all or a predetermined or substantial quantity of the negotiable paper which is backed by such standards, the financier should be considered a participant in the original transaction and therefore not entitled to holder in due course status.

Over the ensuing years, the close-connectedness doctrine has been applied almost exclusively in cases in which the maker of a note has been a consumer buying for his or her own personal use. Nevertheless, a handful of cases extend the notion to the protection of the small business borrower. See, for instance, *Saint James v. Diversified Commercial Finance Corp.*, 102 Nev. 23, 714 P.2d 179 (1986).

Legislative and Regulatory Responses

While the courts in many states were adopting and refining the close-connectedness doctrine to give the consumer purchaser a measure of relief, a number of state legislatures were enacting statutes intended to confront the same problem. Such legislation was not adopted in all states, nor is the legislation necessarily the same from state to state in the jurisdictions where the legislature did take action. Although such state statutes operate in various ways, the principal intent of each is to provide that if a party takes a note from a consumer in violation of whatever provisions are set forth in the statute (such as having to put the legend "Consumer Note" on the paper itself), and then sells the note to a third party, that third party will not be able to take advantage of holder in due course status. This result is often limited by the requirement that the third party must have been aware of the violation.

The state responses to the problem of consumer protection, as it arises in connection with the law of negotiable instruments and the time-honored holder in due course doctrine, have tended to fade into the background in more recent years, due to the promulgation in the mid-1970s of the Federal Trade Commission Holder-In-Due-Course Regulations (16 C.F.R. Part 433).* We will explore in more detail exactly how these regulations work in

---

* I assume, if you are studying this topic in your course, that the full text of these regulations will be available to you as part of whatever hefty volume of "Selected

the examples and explanations of this chapter, but the basic idea is simple enough. The regulations make it an *unfair or deceptive act or practice* under Section 5 of the Federal Trade Commission Act (15 U.S.C. §45) for any seller to take from a consumer a note that does not bear, in at least 10-point bold type, a legend reading:

NOTICE

ANY HOLDER OF THIS CONSUMER CREDIT CONTRACT IS SUBJECT TO ALL CLAIMS AND DEFENSES WHICH THE DEBTOR COULD ASSERT AGAINST THE SELLER OF GOODS OR SERVICES OBTAINED PURSUANT HERETO OR WITH THE PROCEEDS HEREOF. RECOVERY BY THE DEBTOR HEREUNDER SHALL NOT EXCEED AMOUNTS PAID BY THE DEBTOR HEREUNDER.

The following examples explore when such a legend is required to be placed on a consumer note, what its effect is when it does appear, and what consequences follow should it not. As we will see, not every note, and indeed not every note signed by a consumer, has to bear such a legend. The legend quoted here is required in some instances when the note signed by a consumer is issued to the seller, either directly or indirectly. In other instances, credit will be obtained not from the seller directly but from some other lender, and a slightly different legend *may* be required. See 16 C.F.R. §433.2(b). Key to determining whether a note issued to a lender other than the seller requires this legend is the concept of the *purchase money loan* as defined in 16 C.F.R. §433.1(d) to be:

A cash advance which is received by a consumer in return for a "Finance Charge" within the meaning of the Truth in Lending Act and Regulation Z [which you need not worry about here], which is applied, in whole or substantial part, to a purchase of goods or services from a seller who (1) refers customers to the creditor or (2) is affiliated with the creditor by common control, contract, or business arrangement.

EXAMPLES

1.   Stan and Dan are neighbors. Stan agrees to buy a used car from Dan (who happens to be a podiatrist), in return for which he gives Dan a note for the purchase price, made payable to Dan one year hence. The note contains no special legend of the type called for by the FTC Holder-In-Due-Course Regulations. Is Dan as seller in violation of §433.2 of those regulations? See 16 C.F.R. §433.1(b) and (j).

Commercial Statutes and Other Materials" you have obtained to furnish you with your own personal copy of the Uniform Commercial Code. If for some reason you don't have the FTC regulations in your course materials, you could, needless to say, find them yourself in the Code of Federal Regulations under the cite given.

2.   Sarah Student arranges to borrow $10,000 from Hometown National Bank. She intends to and does use the borrowed money to help pay for her legal education. The bank makes Sarah sign a note in connection with this loan. Does this note have to bear any special legend under the FTC regulations?

3.   Stewart Student decides to buy a house. He arranges with Hometown National Bank to borrow the money to buy the house, signing a so-called mortgage note indicating that the note is secured by a mortgage that the bank will hold on the property. Does this note have to carry an FTC holder in due course legend?

4.   Able, of Able's World of Wheels, is an authorized dealer in automobiles manufactured by the Zephyr Motors Manufacturing Corporation. He sells one such vehicle to Christine, who plans to use the car for her everyday personal use. Christine gives Able a down payment representing 10 percent of the price and also signs a note promising to pay Able the rest of the price in monthly installments (reflecting, of course, an agreed rate of interest) over the next four years.

   (a) Is the note that Christine signs required to carry, in the appropriate size bold type, the legend found in §433.2(a) of the FTC regulations?

   (b) Does the inclusion of this provision in the note prevent the note from being a negotiable instrument under Article 3? See §3-106(d) and Comment 3 to that section.

   (c) Assume that the note signed by Christine does bear the required FTC legend. Soon after acquiring the note, Able sells it off to Downtown Federal Bank. Can Downtown Federal qualify as a holder in due course of the note? See §3-302(g) and Comment 7 to that section.

5.   Beatrice owns and operates another authorized Zephyr dealership. When Ralph decides to buy a car from her on credit, she does not extend the credit to him directly. What she does do is suggest that he speak to a particular loan officer at Uptown Bank and Trust, who should be able to arrange for that bank to give Ralph an auto purchase loan, the proceeds of which he can then use to pay Beatrice for the car. Ralph does obtain a loan from Uptown. In connection with the loan agreement, Ralph is asked to sign a note under which he is to make monthly payments to repay the bank for what it loaned. Uptown forwards the loan proceeds to Beatrice who then completes the sale of the car to Ralph.

   (a) If the parties involved want to be sure that the FTC Holder-In-Due-Course Regulations are not violated, what must be true of the note signed by Ralph and made payable to Uptown Bank and Trust? See 16 C.F.R. §433.2(b).

   (b) Suppose that, instead of sending potential credit buyers like Ralph to Uptown Bank and Trust, Beatrice has an arrangement with Zephyr Motors Acceptance Corporation (ZMAC), a subdivision of the Zephyr Corporation (a separate subdivision of which is Zephyr

Motors Manufacturing). ZMAC specializes in making auto loans to people interested in buying autos from Zephyr dealerships. Beatrice gives Ralph all the appropriate papers to sign to apply for a loan from ZMAC and forwards these to a special agent at ZMAC who is accustomed to working with Beatrice and her customers. ZMAC approves the loan. When he picks up his new car, Ralph is required to sign a note made payable to ZMAC. What must be true of this note if Beatrice is to steer clear of any violation of the FTC regulations?

6.   Charlie operates yet another Zephyr dealership. He sells a car to one Lenni for a price of $20,000. Lenni gives Charlie a $2,000 down payment and also signs a note payable to him, under which the remainder of the price will be paid off in monthly installments of $480. The note that Lenni signs bears, in the correct form, the legend called for in the FTC regulations. Charlie immediately sells this note off to the Midtown Bank for Savings. After Lenni has made the first two monthly installment payments, a significant defect in the car's emergency brake (which you may assume was present at the time of the sale by Charlie but had not previously been discovered or discoverable by Lenni) allows the car, while parked on a steep incline, to roll backward and off a cliff. Fortunately, no one is injured, but the car is a total loss. Also lost in the accident is more than $4,000 worth of computer equipment that Lenni had stored in the trunk at the time of the accident.
    (a) Can Lenni stop making payments on the note, which is now in the hands of the Midtown Bank?
    (b) Is Lenni entitled to recover from the Midtown Bank the $2,960 she has already paid on the car, as well as the $4,000 in consequential damages she suffered because of the car's defective condition?

7.   Dexter, of Dexter's Auto and Truck Emporium, is the last of the Zephyr dealers whom it is our destiny to meet. He sells a used Zephyr auto to one Johanna, who plans to use the car for purely personal purposes, for only $500 down. For the remainder of the price he takes an installment note made out to his firm. This note does not bear any legend as called for by the FTC regulations. Dexter sells this note to the Eastside Bank. Soon after the sale, Johanna becomes aware that the odometer of the car has been tampered with and that the car has been driven many more miles than she had been led to believe by Dexter at the time she bought it. Johanna drives the car back to Dexter's dealership, fully intent on returning the car and demanding her money back. It turns out that Dexter has closed up shop. The building that housed the dealership is boarded up and deserted. Dexter is nowhere to be found. Meanwhile, Johanna has been given notice by the Eastside Bank that it holds the note signed by her and that it fully expects her to make the monthly payments called for by the note. Is she under an obligation to do so?

EXPLANATIONS

1. No. The operative language of 16 C.F.R. §433.2 makes it an unfair or deceptive trade practice for a seller to take either a note or the proceeds of a note in exchange for goods or services if the note in question fails to bear an appropriate legend whenever a sale is made to a consumer. Unless Stan is buying the used car for some business purpose of which we are not aware, he comes within the definition of a *consumer* under 16 C.F.R. §433.1(b): "A natural person who seeks or acquires goods or services for personal, family or household use." Dan, however, does not fall within the restricted definition of *seller* in 16 C.F.R. §433.1(j): "A person who, in the ordinary course of business, sells or leases goods or services to consumers." This transaction does not fall within the scope of the FTC regulations.

2. No. The regulations apply only when the underlying transaction is a "sale or lease of goods or services" to a consumer. Here there is a direct loan of money that Sarah is going to use for other (if perfectly praiseworthy) purposes. Such notes issued in connection with student loans do not require the FTC legend and are, in fact, often transferred to parties who may qualify as holders in due course.

3. No. The note was signed to obtain money not to acquire goods or services but to purchase real estate. Again, as in Example 2, such mortgage notes are very often sold off by the bank that originally took them and can easily fall into the hands of a holder in due course.

4a. Yes. Able is a seller of the type to whom the FTC regulations are directed per 16 C.F.R. §433.1(j) and Christine is a consumer buyer under §433.1(b). Under §433.2(a), it would be an "unfair or deceptive act or practice within the meaning of Section 5 of [the Federal Trade Commission Act]" for Able as a seller, directly or indirectly, to "take or receive a consumer credit contract" that fails to carry, in the appropriate size and bold type, the notice set out in §433.2(a). The term *consumer credit contract* is defined in §433.1(i) and includes a "financed sale" as defined in §433.1(e), which is what we have here between Christine as the buyer and Able as the financing seller. Able would be in violation of the Federal Trade Commission Act if the note that he gets Christine to sign did not include the required notice.

4b. No. Section 3-106(d) was included in the revision to Article 3 to address just this point. The inclusion of the FTC notice does not make the promise embodied in the note conditional for the purposes of §3-104(a) and hence the note is still a negotiable instrument within the meaning and covered by the terms of Article 3 of the Uniform Commercial Code.

4c. No. As you will have noticed in the concluding language to §3-106(d), there cannot be a holder in due course of an instrument bearing a notice of the type required by the FTC regulations. Subsection §3-302(g) repeats this message: "This section [defining the holder in due course] is subject to any law limiting status as a holder in due course in particular classes of transactions."

5a. The transaction here comes within the definition of *purchase money loan* under 16 C.F.R. §433.1(d). Ralph has received a cash advance (which we can assume was received by him in return for a *finance charge* as that term is defined in another set of FTC regulations), which he applies to the purchase of the car from Beatrice as seller. Furthermore, she refers customers to this particular bank, the creditor. This being true, under §433.2(b) Beatrice would be in violation of the FTC regulation if she were to take, as full or partial payment for the sale to Ralph, the proceeds of the purchase money loan unless the note signed by Ralph at the bank bore the form of notice set forth in part (b) of §433.2.

Note that although I asked the question in terms of what "the parties involved" would have to do to ensure that the FTC regulations were complied with, it is really only the seller, Beatrice in this case, who has anything to fear if the FTC legend is either intentionally or inadvertently left off the note Ralph signs at the bank. As you will have noticed by now, the FTC Holder-In-Due-Course Regulations speak only to the *seller's* behavior and how it may be in violation of the Federal Trade Commission Act if the seller should fail to act as those regulations require. Neither the consumer buyer nor any third-party financer, which either takes up a note originally written to the seller as payee or makes a purchase money loan with which the consumer buyer can make cash payment to the seller, can be in violation of the FTC regulations. So, in this case, it is for Beatrice to be concerned that the note Ralph signs payable to Uptown Bank and Trust bears the correct legend. Otherwise, her taking the proceeds of the loan as partial payment for the car subjects *her* — not Ralph or the bank — to proceedings for violation of the FTC Act. Therefore, Beatrice has to make sure that the form of note the bank asks Ralph to sign carries the correct notice, even though she is not even a party to the note. Beatrice should not, as a practical matter, have trouble making sure that the note is as it should be. Remember, the reason the FTC regulations apply to this particular purchase and sale transaction, to which Beatrice is most definitely a party, is because the loan by the bank qualifies as a purchase money loan under §433.1(d) as a result of Beatrice's practice of "refer[ring] customers to the creditor" Uptown Bank and Trust.

5b. This note must also bear the notice required under 16 C.F.R. §433.2(b). This is a purchase money loan as defined in §433.1(d) because the seller, Beatrice, "is affiliated with the creditor [ZMAC] by common control, contract, or business arrangement." This final term, *business arrangement*, may seem fairly open-ended, and a reading of §433.1(g) where it is defined will only confirm this impression. Clearly, however, the intent is to cover the kind of relationship that Beatrice, a Zephyr auto dealer, has with Zephyr Motors Acceptance Corporation.

6a.   Yes. Because the note that Midtown holds bears a correct FTC notice, that bank cannot qualify as and does not have the rights of a holder in due course. Under the law of sales, Lenni should be able to revoke her acceptance of the automobile under §2-608 of the Uniform Commercial Code. Under §2-711, the justifiably revoking buyer may then "cancel," which would allow her to stop making payments to the seller. Midtown's entitlement to enforce the instrument is subject to any personal defenses or claims in recoupment that Lenni would have against Charlie (the seller and original payee of the note), so Lenni would be within her rights to stop making payments to Midtown.

6b.   Under U.C.C. §2-711, the revoking buyer is entitled to "recover so much of the price as has been paid." Lenni should also be able to recover consequential damages to the tune of $4,000, under §2-715(b). All of this would amount to a claim in recoupment, which she would have against Charlie, her seller, and hence against Midtown Bank for Savings, which has taken the note but which does not qualify as a holder in due course. Lenni will not, however, be entitled to recover all of this from Midtown Bank for Savings. Look to the last sentence of either version of the FTC notice: "Recovery hereunder by the Debtor shall not exceed amounts paid by the Debtor hereunder." Lenni may recover from Midtown only up to what she has paid that bank on the note, which in this case is $960. For return of the down payment of $2,000 and payment of the consequential damages of $4,000, she will have to look to Charlie directly.

7.   Whether or not Johanna has to keep paying Eastside Bank on the note is not clear. Dexter as seller was clearly in violation of the FTC regulations and hence guilty of an "unfair or deceptive act or practice" as defined in Section 5 of the Federal Trade Commission Act. Should he ever be found, he will be subject to the type of civil proceedings that the FTC Act empowers the FTC to bring in such cases. He could be subject to a cease-and-desist order issued by that agency or to civil penalties.

The problem for Johanna is that the neither the FTC Act nor the Holder-In-Due-Course Regulations provide any private right of action on the part of the individual consumer who has been subjected to the unfair or deceptive act or practice that constitutes the violation of the FTC Act. Dexter's failure to include the proper notice on the note puts him in the wrong, but the absence of the notice may make it possible for Eastside Bank to argue that, whatever wrong Dexter may have done, it still can and does qualify as a holder in due course. Eastside has done no wrong, at least as far as the FTC regulations are concerned, and it has taken a note that bears no forbidding notice or other indication that would bar the bank from claiming holder in due course status. See, for example, *Pratt v. North Dixie Mfgd. Homes*, 2003 Ohio 2363, 2003 Ohio App. Lexis 2195.

All hope is not lost for Johanna on this issue, however. Many states have adopted separate consumer protection legislation which, either explicitly or by judicial interpretation, provides that when a note is issued and fails to carry the FTC notice when that notice is called for by the federal regulations, no subsequent holder may assert the rights of a holder in due course. In other states, courts have held to the same effect despite the lack of legislation directly on point. This result is not, however, a foregone conclusion. See *Crisomia v. Parkway Mortgage, Inc.*, 2001 Bankr. Lexis 1469 (E.D. Pa. 2001), and *Morales v. Walker Motor Sales, Inc.*, 162 F.Supp.2d 786 (S.D. Ohio 2000). So Johanna will have to do some digging into her state's legislative and common law to see if she can find any relief there.

Another argument Johanna may advance is that under Article 3 of the U.C.C., as adopted in all of the states, a sophisticated lender such as Eastside Bank cannot qualify as a holder in due course under §3-302(a), as it could not have been acting in "good faith" in purchasing a consumer note that failed to display the expected FTC notice. After all, the bank would know of the FTC regulations and should realize that any note signed by a consumer made payable to an auto dealership should, in order to comply with those regulations, bear the required legend. This note did not. Especially now, in light of the new expanded definition of *good faith* in §3-103(a)(4) introduced by the 1990 revision of Article 3, this argument has a lot going for it.

See Revision Alert on the following page.

Revision Alert

A significant consumer protection part of the 2002
Amendments to Article 3 comes into play in situations such as
the one Johanna of our last example found herself confronting.
Recall that she signed a note that was supposed to have the FTC
Notice printed on it but did not, and the note came into the
hands of a party that would like to take advantage of holder-in-
due-course status. Under the current version of Article 3 there
is no obvious relief for her. The revised version, first of all,
would add a definition of *consumer transaction* in R§3-
301(a)(3). Secondly, language would be tacked on to §3-305,
in R§3-305(d), providing that in a consumer transaction if an
instrument is issued that under other law *ought* to contain a
statement such as the FTC Notice but *does not* contain the statement, then the instrument is in effect treated — now under
Article 3 authority — as if it bid bear the statement anyway.
That is, "the instrument has the same effect as if the instrument
included such a statement," and in particular no one can assert
the special rights of a holder in due course of the instrument.
Another addition, R§3-305(f), states explicitly that, "This
section is subject to law other than this article that establishes a
different rule for consumer transactions."

PART THREE

The Check Collection System

10

The Basic Scheme of Check Collection

Introduction to Check Collection

It all starts when someone writes a check. It is perfectly possible, of course, for any of us to write a check on any bank. All it takes, according to Article 3, is a pen, a piece of paper, and the minimal effort it takes to write on the paper something that qualifies as a check under the definition of §3-104(f). The whole exercise doesn't make much sense, however, unless the drawer has an active checking account with the bank in question. As background to the writing of any check of significance, we have to posit that the drawer has opened a checking account with the bank named as drawee on the check and that the account is still active. We will look at the relationship between the bank and its checking account customer in more detail in Part Four, but a brief introduction at this point will set the stage for the topic on which we now embark, the check collection process.

The relationship between a bank and its checking account customer is that of debtor and creditor. The customer deposits some funds in an account with the bank. The bank, by accepting the funds pursuant to the agreement setting up the account, takes on an obligation to the customer equal in amount to what the customer has available in his or her account. The bank owes this amount back to the individual customer and hence stands as a debtor. The customer is owed this amount by the bank and takes on the role of creditor. The customer has advanced funds to the bank, which he or she has the right to get back or use as he or she sees fit.

The customer can take advantage of the fact that the bank owes it this amount of money in a number of ways. The customer can always withdraw funds directly from the account. The customer may also direct the bank to use some of his or her funds on deposit to pay another. The customer can *order* the bank to pay a certain amount of money to another, and the

169

bank is obligated (assuming various conditions are met, of the type we will be meeting in this and chapters to follow) to comply with the customer's order. The interesting aspect of all this is that the customer does not directly order the bank to pay someone else with funds available from the customer's account. With the typical checking account, the customer cannot just call up the bank and tell it to dispense some amount to any particular person. The order to the bank is made in a very indirect fashion. That, of course, is where the check comes in. The customer initiates the order by issuing a check naming the bank as drawee. The check may then be transferred any number of times, physically passing from hand to hand. Eventually, if the check is to turn into actual funds for someone in possession of it, the check must be presented to the drawee bank. The bank, having received an order to pay in this roundabout fashion, will in the normal course of things (again assuming that a variety of conditions are met) respond to its customer's order by releasing funds equal in amount to what is written on the check to whatever party presented the check to the bank. The bank obeys the orders of its checking account customer, which come to it in the form of pieces of paper — checks — presented to it. Our concern in this chapter is how the check written by the customer eventually makes its way to the drawee bank.

With this general background in mind, we return to where we began: It all starts when someone who has established a checking account with a bank writes a check on that account. The check is then issued and presumably finds its way into the hands of the named payee.* So we begin with a situation that can be diagrammed like this:

---

* It is, of course possible, that a check can be issued and never even get to the named payee. It may be given to someone else, somebody X, who is instructed to deliver it to the payee but who decides that he or she would rather keep it for himself or herself. What happens then? We deal with the knotty and intriguing problems created by the thieves and forgers who unfortunately do inhabit this world in Part Five. For the most part, in this chapter and those immediately following, we will take a rosier view of the world, assuming that no thievery or forgery intrudes into the life stories of the checks with which we are concerned. As a matter of fact, in the overwhelming majority of cases this is not just a rosy view of the world but an accurate one. The system of check collection that we are about to explore could not really function as it does if this were not so. Theft, forgery, or any other kind of irregularity in the check collection process is the exception, the very rare exception, rather than the rule. Even though we will later spend a good deal of energy examining what happens when theft or forgery rears its ugly head, you should appreciate that by and large the typical check goes through the collection process quite mechanically and with little or no fuss. The vast majority of checks are collected upon simply as a matter of course, with no questions asked or needing to be asked — as I hope you've personally found true with the checks you yourself have written or received.

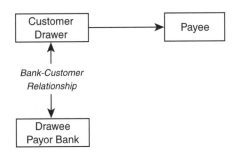

You will have noticed that I chose in the diagram to refer to the drawee bank as the *Payor Bank*. This term, which we will be using more and more in what is to come, is not of my invention. See §4-105(3). The payee who is now in possession of the check may choose to collect on it himself or herself, but as we know he or she may instead transfer the check to another, either by negotiation or otherwise.

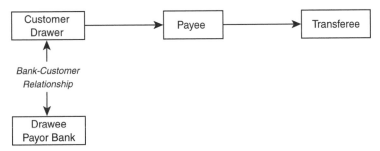

There may in fact be several transfers of the check before it eventually comes into the hands of someone who wants to do more with it than just pass it on to another. This party wants to collect the funds that the check represents. If each of the transfers has been a valid negotiation (and, as we are assuming in this chapter, no nasty business such as theft or forgery has been involved), then this person should qualify as a "person entitled to enforce" the instrument under §3-301. We know that the holder of a draft such as a check must first try to enforce the instrument and get the money that it represents by presenting it to the drawer. In this case, that means presenting the check to the bank on which it is written, the *payor bank*.

If the person attempting to collect on the check is in a hurry, or if he or she just happens to be in the neighborhood where the payor bank is located,

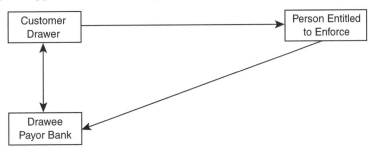

he or she can make a direct presentment by going to the bank and handing the check to a teller there, *over the counter* as we say. The rule governing presentment over the counter is found in §3-502(b)(2). Recall that upon presentment of any draft — and that includes a check — to the drawee, the drawee will be confronted with the decision of whether to accept the draft as written. If the drawee does not accept the draft, declining to comply with the order given it by the drawer, it will have dishonored the instrument. *Dishonor* of a check presented over the counter occurs when "presentment for payment is duly made to the drawee [the payor bank] and the [check] is not paid on the day of presentment." It is important to note that the payor bank is given some time, until the end of the day on which direct over-the-counter presentment is made, to determine whether to honor the check that it has just been handed. It does not dishonor the check by refusing to pay it immediately. The bank is given this time because it has to be able to determine a number of things in order to decide whether it is obligated to pay this check: such as that the drawer does in fact have an account at the bank, that the account is still active, that the bank has not received a stop-payment order from its customer telling it not to pay the check in question, and of course the all-important consideration of whether the customer's account has sufficient funds available to cover the check.*

You will also want to remember, from our past work, that if the bank does not honor the check, in this or in one of the more complicated settings to which we will soon turn, and even if this is what we will later term a *wrongful dishonor* (meaning that under the circumstances the bank should have, under its agreement with its customer, honored the check), the wrong committed by the payor bank is committed against the customer, not against the person entitled to enforce the check. (We will deal with the problem of wrongful dishonor in Chapter 13.) The person attempting to enforce a draft never has a right to the drawee's acceptance. If the check is dishonored and returned unpaid, the person left holding the unpaid draft must then proceed against the drawer under §3-414(b) to obtain relief. The person entitled to enforce the check has no right to insist that the bank pay it even if, under the circumstances, there is nothing fishy about the check and the bank should,

---

*Note as well that the bank will not be found to have dishonored a check presented over the counter unless the check was properly presented, and that in particular the person seeking payment in this fashion must not just "exhibit the instrument" but "give reasonable identification" of him or herself. See §3-501(b)(2). The Court of Appeals of Maryland has recently ruled that a bank's requirement that a noncustomer presenting a check over the counter place an "inkless" thumbprint or fingerprint on the check itself was a reasonable part of the identification process. *Messing v. Bank of America, N.A.*, 373 Md. 672, 821 A.2d 22, 50 U.C.C.2d 1 (Md. App. 2003). The procedure is, in fact, part of the Thumbprint Signature Program created by the American Bankers Association, working with a number of federal agencies, in response to a rising number of check frauds.

according to the terms of its agreement with its customer, have paid the item when presented.

Depositing for Collection

In many instances, of course, people or institutions holding checks will not want to take the trouble or be in a position to present the checks they have received directly to the payor bank. What they will do instead is deposit the checks in a bank with which they have established their own bank-customer relationship. Their bank will not itself pay the check. What it will do for its customer is itself present, or take steps intended to lead to the eventual presentment of the check, in one way or another, to the payor bank. As we will see in this chapter, the bank, by taking deposit of a check, obligates itself to act in a way reasonably calculated to effect collection of the funds that the check represents. The money, if it is forthcoming, is still to be paid by the payor bank.

By depositing a check for the purpose of collection, the customer has entered it into a complex and highly sophisticated system by which collection is made through banking channels. It has also plunged us directly into the world of Article 4 of the Uniform Commercial Code. Look at §4-101 and the comments to that section. As the first comment indicates, by 1990 something like 50 billion checks made their way through the check collection system each year in the United States. By the end of the 1990s, the number was something more in the range of 68 billion a year. Section 4-102(a) deals with the scope of Article 4 in a somewhat cryptic fashion:

> To the extent that items within this Article are also within Articles 3 and 8, they are subject to those Articles. If there is a conflict, this Article governs Article 3, but Article 8 governs this Article.

Fortunately, we don't have to worry about Article 8 at all. For that matter, we don't really have to worry about conflicts between Articles 3 and 4, as we just don't see any popping up.* As far as what *items* are within the scope of Article 4, look at the definition of that term in §4-104(a)(9). An *item* is "any instrument or a promise or order to pay money handled by a bank for collection or payment." This includes some types of items with which we will not bother ourselves, but it certainly includes the simple check deposited for collection.

Having deposited a check in its account for the purposes of collection, the customer has singled out this bank as what we can now, using the definition of

---

* In 1990, many changes were made to Article 4 to conform it to the major overhaul being done on Article 3. The drafters chose to refer to their efforts as promulgation of amendments to and not an entirely revised version of Article 4. In any event, we will be working with the 1990 version of Article 4, just as we have been doing with Article 3.

§4-105(2), refer to as the *depositary bank* with respect to this item. The situation stands like this:

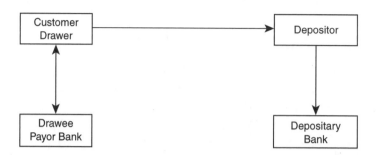

Before it proceeds any further with its handling of the check, the depositary bank will do two things. First of all, it will record the amount of the check as a credit to the depositor's account, but this will of necessity be a *provisional* credit only. Until the check has been presented to the payor bank and honored, the depositary bank will not consider this an unconditional addition to the amount in the depositor's account. The check represents a potential for money to come into that account, but until the check is honored and funds are received, directly or indirectly, from the payor bank, the depositary bank will consider it only a provisional addition to the account. As you have no doubt experienced in your own life, the depositary bank will not consider the amount of the check as immediately accessible for withdrawal by the depositor out of his or her account as cash or as funds available to cover any checks the depositor himself or herself has written. As we proceed with the story of check collection, we will see what happens to this *provisional* credit to the depositor's account in the depositary bank: whether it firms up and turns into a *final* credit, to add to the funds in the depositor's account actually and without question, or whether it ends up being withdrawn, leaving the depositor with none of the money in his or her account and holding a dishonored check.

The second thing the depositary bank will do upon receipt of the check is encode its amount onto the check itself. If you look along the bottom of any preprinted check form, you will see a series of oddly shaped but still perfectly readable numbers encoded on the check. This is the so-called MICR (for *Magnetic Ink Character Recognition*) line. On the check form as it is made available to the bank's customer, the first set of numbers represents the routing number of the particular bank on which the check is to be drawn (a unique number assigned by the American Bankers Association). The next series of numbers represents the customer's account number at that bank. These in turn are followed by the check number of that particular one of the customer's preprinted checks. Once the check is issued by the drawer and deposited into someone else's account, the depositary bank adds to the end of the line, in MICR characters, the amount of the check. After the check is encoded with its amount by the depositary bank, this is probably the last time it will be individually handled or even looked at by a real live human being. From this time forward, the check can be and is (with only rare exceptions) sorted, handled, moved around, and evaluated by high-speed reading and sorting machines, which are able not only to read but also to react to the information as carried on the MICR line. As Comment 2 to §4-101 makes clear, only because the huge number of checks that run through the check collection system each day can be dealt with through this automated system can the system operate as efficiently and as cheaply as it does.

Forwarding for Collection

The depositary bank is now in possession of a fully encoded check and has given a provisional credit to the depositor. What next? As part of its agreement with its customer (the depositor), the depositary bank as the first of the *collecting banks* (per §4-105(5)) is now charged with acting as an agent for the customer in seeing that the check gets sent on its way to the payor bank for presentment. See §4-201(a). In carrying out its role as agent for collection, the depositary bank, as well as any other collecting bank encountered along the way, is charged with exercising reasonable care on behalf of the depositor. See §§4-202(a) and 4-204(a). What constitutes reasonable care, and the exact route the check will take on its way to the payor bank, will necessarily vary depending on the circumstances. The depositary bank will first cull out, through its automated sorting machines, any checks written on itself, so-called *on-us* items. When the depositary bank also happens to be the payor bank, the bank then takes on the responsibility of acting as the payor bank upon presentment; it must examine the item and determine whether to honor it. If it does honor, the provisional credit in the depositor's account is stripped of its provisional status and the amount in the depositor's account is increased by the amount of the check. As a result of the check having been honored, the balance in the drawer's account is decreased by the same amount.

At the same time that the depositary bank is sorting out the checks written on itself, its sorting machines are also separating out other checks, on the basis of where the payor bank is located and other factors that the depositary bank has determined will control how it deals with each of the many checks it has received that day for the purposes of collection. For instance, the depositary bank may have a policy of directly presenting checks to all local banks, or at least certain banks that it can anticipate will regularly account for a large number of the checks it receives for deposit. On such items the depositary bank then takes on the role of the *presenting bank*, as defined in §4-105(6). It is perfectly possible for the depositary bank in such a situation to present a single item by properly delivering it to the payor bank, but this would happen only rarely. More likely is that the depositary bank will bundle together all the items it has received that day written on the payor bank in question. It delivers this packet of items, along with a computer printout that lists the items individually and gives the total of all items in the bundle, directly to the payor bank. It would not be unusual for the payor bank itself to have received, during the same period, a large number of checks written on the depositary bank. The roles now switch, and when Bank A directly presents to Bank B a bundle of checks written on the latter bank, Bank B will take the opportunity (or rather, follow the agreement or practice that the two banks have entered into for dealing with items written on each other) to hand over and hence present any checks deposited at Bank B that are written on Bank A. The two banks have directly presented those items deposited at one and written on the other.

In many metropolitan areas where there are a number of larger banks, any one of which can expect to receive for deposit a significant number of checks written on each of the others, this process of reciprocal direct presentment has been more formally organized by the establishment of local clearing houses. These are voluntary organizations that have as members the major banks in the locality. Suppose that Bank A is a member of the local clearing house in its area, along with five other banks, B through F. Each day Bank A will sort out and bundle the checks it has received for deposit written on each of Banks B through F. At a given time and place, all as specified in rules promulgated by the clearing house, someone from Bank A will bring each of these bundles of checks to the floor of the clearing house. There he or she will deliver to a representative of each of these other member banks the items that Bank A has received made payable on those other banks. Bank A's representative will at the same time receive from each of Bank B, Bank C, and so on, any items written on Bank A that each of those banks has received. The clearing house mechanism results in a large number of local checks being directly presented by the depositary bank to the payor banks on which they are written, in a particularly efficient fashion.

Any given bank on any given day may of course receive hundreds, thousands, or tens of thousands of checks written on any number of banks spread wide across the country. For checks that are not on-us items, or for which the depositary bank does not have an established mechanism for making direct presentment to the payor bank, the depositary bank will fulfill its obligation to the depositor by forwarding the check to another bank that stands in a better position to present the check or at least to forward the check to a bank closer geographically and in a better position to act as the presenting bank. This bank may then present the item to the payor bank or, if it is not set up to do so itself, forward the check one more time to another bank that may be able to do so. And so it goes. The check continues to be forwarded through a series of what are termed *intermediary banks* (§4-105(4)) until eventually it comes into the possession of a bank that is in a position to act as the presenting bank, which will then present the check to the payor bank.

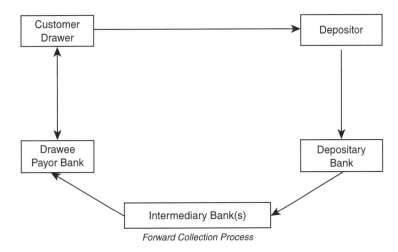

Forward Collection Process

For any given check, there is no way of telling with any certainty in advance exactly how many intermediary banks, if any, will be involved in the collection process before the check makes it way to its final destination, the payor bank. In some instances, as we have seen, no intermediary banks are involved at all, as when the depositary bank takes a check written on itself or on a bank to which it can directly present. In other instances, the check may have to go through a number of intermediary banks before it reaches one that can and will act as the presenting bank. Nor is it possible to say that there is only one correct way for any given item to make its way through the maze of banks throughout the country on its way to the payor bank. A given check could make its way from the depositary bank to a distant payor bank through a variety or routes, each of which consists of a series of steps that would be deemed reasonable under the circumstances.

Nevertheless, any bank involved in the process is not allowed to spend as much time as it likes to take the action required of it, nor can it just forward the check to any old bank it wishes. Under §4-105(5), the term *collecting bank* is used to refer to any bank in the collection process other than the payor bank, which therefore includes the depositary bank as well as any intermediary bank or banks involved. This will become important when we later look at the affirmative obligations of a collecting bank as set forth in Article 4, which are designed to make sure that the process of check collection goes forward in a reasonable manner intended to get the check to the payor bank in a timely fashion, if not necessarily by the absolutely quickest means theoretically available.

In considering the use of intermediary banks, special note must be taken of the system of Federal Reserve Banks spread across the country. The country is divided into 12 distinct Federal Reserve Regions, some of which have further subdivided themselves into more than one territory. Any bank in the United States will lie within the defined territory of a single Federal Reserve Bank. The system of Federal Reserve Banks provides to all banks operating in this country a nicely integrated and convenient network of check-clearing centers. Although there is no requirement that these Federal Reserve banks be used as intermediary banks to facilitate the collection process, they often are. A bank in one of the Federal Reserve's check collection regions, in which has been deposited a check written on a bank in another region, may as a matter of course forward that check to the Federal Reserve Bank in its own region, knowing that the check will then be forward to the Federal Reserve collection center servicing the area in which the payor bank is located. A depositary bank that receives a large number of checks written on banks across the country may choose to sort the checks it has taken for deposit by the Federal Reserve collection center covering the area in which the drawee bank is located. It can then send these bundles of checks directly to the various remote Federal Reserve collection centers, bypassing its local Federal Reserve. (Remember that this is all possible because the MICR line conveniently carries, in coded form, information about the exact bank on which the check is written. The first four digits of the MICR line, in fact, just happen to denote which Federal Reserve processing center covers the area in which the payor bank is located.) A given depositary bank will determine how to deal with checks written on distant banks based on what is most efficient and most cost-effective given its own individual circumstances.

The influence of the Federal Reserve Banks, and of the numerous local clearing houses, in the overall process of check collection is considerable. Section 4-103(a) allows the provisions of Article 4 to be varied by agreement of the parties involved. Subsection (b) then provides:

> Federal Reserve regulations and operating circulars [issued by the individual Federal Reserve Banks], clearing-house rules, and the like have the effect of agreements under subsection (a), whether or not specifically assented to by all parties interested in the items handled.

Although Comment 3 to this section is somewhat heavy going, and I would not advise you to worry over every detail, it is worth looking over at this point. It reminds us that even though the rules governing check collection (with which we will concern ourselves in the examples to follow) are laid down by Article 4, any bank must be concerned as well with the other regulatory requirements of the Federal Reserve system operating as a whole, the rules of individual Federal Reserve Banks with which it may deal, and the requirements of any clearing house of which it is a member, if it is to do a proper job of check collection and avoid liability for failure to do so.*

---

* The two principal regulations of the Federal Reserve System that most directly affect the check collection process, and in doing so may supersede the rules as laid down in Article 4, are known as Regulation J and Regulation CC. Regulation J applies to all banks dealing with any Federal Reserve Bank in the check collection process, and as a practical matter does not differ from the standards set forth in Article 4 in any significant (for us) detail. Regulation CC, promulgated to effectuate

As the check is passed from bank to bank in the forward collection process, each transferor bank will expect to receive from its transferee *settlement* for the item at the time of transfer. Under §4-104(a)(11):

> "Settle" means to pay in cash, by clearing-house settlement, in a charge or credit or by remittance, or as otherwise agreed. A settlement may be either provisional or final.

As Comment 10 acknowledges in its final paragraphs, this definition is purposefully broad, to take into account the wide variety of means that banks use to settle for items they receive through the collection process. For our purposes, it is sufficient to know that each bank that takes a check for collection, as well as the payor bank to which the check is eventually presented, will at the time it receives the item "pay" for it by settling for the item in one way or another, making immediately available to its transferor funds equivalent in value to the amount of the check. Such settlements are in almost all cases provisional. Just as the depositary bank has, upon receipt of the check from its customer, *provisionally* credited his or her account with the amount of the check, each bank through whose hands the check then passes will *provisionally settle* with the prior bank in the chain. As we will see in the next section, these provisional settlements will firm up and become final settlements automatically upon final payment of the check by the payor bank. In the unlikely event that the payor bank dishonors the check and does not finally pay it, all provisional settlements are then reversed or charged back by the parties who made them, in effect undoing them and wiping them off the books. Look at Comment 1 to §4-214.

The Check Reaches the Payor Bank

Eventually, if the collection process has gone forward as intended, the payor bank will be presented with the individual check that started off this whole affair. Unless the payor bank is itself also the depositary bank, the payor bank is required to settle for the item with the presenting bank by midnight of the banking day on which it was presented with the item (§4-302(a)(1)). Such settlement is, in almost all instances, provisional only. The payor bank then has one additional day until its *midnight deadline*, as defined in

---

the federal Expedited Funds Availability Act and applicable to every bank in the country, worked some very major changes in the check collection process. Chapters 12 and 15 deal with the changes wrought by Regulation CC both in the basic workings of the check collection process and in the fundamental bank-depositor relationship. For the purposes of this chapter, however, we will concentrate on the law as laid down by Article 4, even if parts of what we see here have been superseded by the later issuance of Regulation CC. It turns out that the best way to appreciate the significance of the changes brought on by Regulation CC is first to appreciate what the situation was like before its introduction.

§4-104(a)(10) — "midnight on its next banking day following the banking day on which it receives the relevant item" — to decide whether to accept the check or dishonor it (again, §4-302(a)(1)). It is given this additional time to determine whether the account on which the check is drawn is an active account, whether there are any outstanding stop-payment orders on the particular check, and of course whether the drawer has sufficient funds in his or her account to cover the item. If the payor bank decides to honor the check (or, as we will see in more detail in Chapter 11, it fails to dishonor and return the check by the passing of its midnight deadline), we speak of the check as having been *finally paid*. We will leave all the intricacies of final payment for Chapter 11. For the moment, it is sufficient to note that if a check is finally paid by the payor bank — and more than 99 percent of all checks are — then the check has found, at least for a time, its final resting place. The payor bank will hold onto the check, at least unless and until it returns it as a canceled check to the drawer along with that customer's monthly statement, if that is what it is required to do by its agreement with the customer. Also, at the moment of final payment, all the provisional settlements that have been created in the various intermediary banks the check passed through on its route to the payor bank automatically firm up, as does the previously provisional credit allocated to the depositor's account by the depositary bank (§4-215(c) and (d)). See, *Kimberly A. Allen Trust v. Firstbank of Lakewood, N.A.*, 989 P.2d 203, 40 U.C.C.2d 1048 (Colo. App. 1999).

As we have already noted, the vast majority of checks are honored once received by the payor bank. Given the huge number of checks working their way through the system at any given time, however, even if the percentage of checks that are not finally paid by the payor bank is small, the absolute number of them is hardly insignificant. Many checks do bounce, and the system has to provide for what happens in any such instance. Once the payor bank decides, prior to its midnight deadline, not to honor a check, that bank's obligation then is to return the item to the presenting bank (§4-301(a)). That bank will in turn have to transmit the item back to the bank from which it, the presenting bank, received the check. And so it goes. The check is bounced back, retracing the route it originally took on making its way to the payor bank, but now as a so-called *return item*, until it eventually arrives back at the depositary bank.*

As the dishonored check makes its way through the return process, all provisional settlements given by each transferee bank to its transferor are revoked or charged back (§4-214). Notice that any of the collecting banks is subject to the duty of ordinary care while playing its part in this return process, just as it was earlier in forwarding the check for collection (§4-202(a)(2)).

---

* This description does not take into account the changes introduced into the return process by Regulation CC of the Federal Reserve. We will take a special look at those changes in Chapter 12.

The depositary bank will, when it receives the unpaid item, withdraw the provisional credit to the depositor's account and notify the depositor of what has happened. The depositary bank has carried out its role as an agent in attempting to collect on the check, but now it has the sad duty to inform its customer that the collection attempt was unsuccessful.

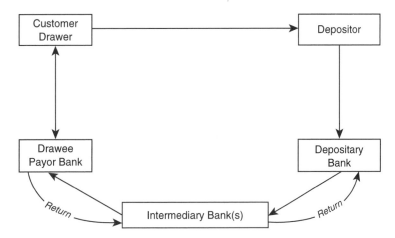

An extremely important aspect of the process we are examining is that if and when a check is finally paid by the payor bank, none of the banks that have been involved in the collection process — and this includes the depositary bank — will ever expect to receive affirmative notice of the happy event. The payor bank that finally pays an item is not required to, nor does it in the regular course of events, send any message back up the chain of banks through which presentation was made. It does not notify anyone that, yes, the check is good. It simply accepts the check, deducts its amount from its depositor's account, and that is that. Under the system as it operates, a collecting bank is just left to assume that any check that has passed through its hands has in fact been finally paid, from the fact that the bank never hears to the contrary. No news, as far as the intermediary and depositary banks are concerned, is good news. If these banks do not receive any negative information about the check in question within some period of time, they should rightly be able to conclude that the check has been honored, all provisional settlements have become final, and the depositor has this amount of money in his or her account to do with as he or she sees fit. A problem, particularly for the depositary bank, which we now have to acknowledge and about which we will have much more to say in what follows, is that by the nature of the system there is no exact amount of time or number of days, either dictated by statute or regulation or necessarily following from the process of collection, that it will take for bad news to reach the depositary bank. The forward collection process may involve only a single transfer of the instrument or quite a few. If the payor bank dishonors a check, it is required to return that check within a certain amount of time, and the returned item will work its way back along the route it originally took in the forward collection process. Thus, it can take quite some time, the exact extent of which cannot be stated with any certainty, for a dishonored check to make its way back to the depositary bank. No news is good news in the check collection process, but there is no way for the depositary bank to know with certainty by what date bad news would arrive if any were on its way.

EXAMPLES

1.   Annie writes a check payable to Patrick on her account with the North Street branch of the First National Bank of Springfield. On Monday morning, Patrick deposits this check in his own checking account, which coincidentally also happens to be with the North Street branch of First National.

    (a) What are the obligations of the folks at the North Street branch with respect to this check?

    (b) What if Patrick's account with First National is held at the South Street branch of the bank? He deposits the check on Monday morning at this South Street location. What must happen here? See §4-107.

2.   Annie writes another check, to one Pauline. Pauline deposits this check in her account with the Second National Bank of Shelbyville on a Wednesday at 2:45 in the afternoon. That bank does nothing with the check on Wednesday, but groups it with the items it receives on Thursday morning for the purpose of processing. Is the bank within its rights to do so? See §4-108.

3.   The Barker Company, which operates a manufacturing plant in Bakersfield, California, arranges to buy some supplies from the Stanley Corporation, which is located in Salem, Massachusetts. Stanley agrees to sell the supplies to Barker on credit. Once Barker has received the supplies, it draws a check for the price on its checking account with Bakersfield Bank and sends this check to Stanley. When Stanley receives the check, it promptly deposits it, along with others it has received that day, in its account with the Salem State Bank. It makes this deposit on Monday morning. By late on Monday afternoon, the Salem bank has encoded the check and forwarded it, along with a large number of other checks it has received payable by nonlocal banks, to the Federal Reserve Bank of Boston.

    (a) Has the Salem bank taken appropriate action with respect to this check? Consult §§4-202 and 4-204(a).

    (b) What if the Salem bank had not sent the bank to the Boston Fed until Tuesday?

    (c) What if it had waited until Wednesday? See §4-103(e).

4.   Assume that the check from Example 3 is in fact sent to the Federal Reserve Bank of Boston on Monday and is received by that bank on Tuesday. The Boston Fed then forwards the check to the Los Angeles Federal Reserve Bank check processing center on Wednesday morning. Assuming that

Bakersfield is within the territory covered by the L.A. Federal Reserve check-processing center for collection purposes, has the Boston Fed met its obligations with respect to the item?

5.   We continue with the story of this particular check. Assume that it was sent by the Boston Fed to the Los Angeles Fed, which receives it on Thursday morning. What must the Los Angles Fed do then?

6.   The Los Angles Fed presents this check to Bakersfield Bank, the bank on which it has been drawn. That bank honors the check. What are the consequences of this final payment by Bakersfield Bank?

7.   Suppose that by the time Bakersfield Bank receives the check from the Los Angeles Fed, it has already received a stop-payment order from its customer, the Barker Company, which on inspection determined that the supplies sent to it by Stanley were substandard and will have to be returned. Bakersfield Bank dishonors the check by returning it to the Los Angeles Fed on the next day.

    (a) What is the Los Angeles Fed now supposed to do with the check?

    (b) Complete the story of this dishonored check. What route will it take now and where should it end up?

8.   Leno Electronics, a firm located in Burbank, California, also arranges to buy some supplies from the Stanley Corporation of Salem, Massachusetts. Leno's contract with Stanley is unlike that which Barker entered into, in that Stanley refuses to sell to Leno on credit. Stanley agrees to send the merchandise to Leno only after receiving payment for it. Leno writes out a check drawn on its account with the Burbank Bank of Commerce and mails this check to Stanley. Stanley deposits this check into its account with Salem State Bank. This check is properly forwarded for collection via the Boston Fed and the Los Angeles Fed. The Los Angeles Fed presents the check to the Burbank bank, which dishonors it, because Leno Electronics does not have sufficient funds in its account to cover the amount of the check. The Burbank bank promptly returns the check to the Los Angeles Fed, which in turn promptly returns it to the Boston Fed. The Boston Fed then promptly returns the check to the Salem State Bank. This dishonored check arrives at the offices of the Salem State Bank on a Tuesday morning. There it lies for more than a week, until an officer of the bank calls the Stanley Corporation to inform it that the check it has deposited has bounced and that the amount of the check, previously credited to Stanley's account, is being withdrawn. It turns out that just the day before, Stanley shipped out the supplies it had contracted to sell to Leno. Does the Burbank bank have any liability to its customer Leno?

EXPLANATIONS

1a. In this instance, the depositary bank, First National Bank of Springfield, happens also to be the payor bank, so there is no need for any forwarding of the item or any provisional settlements between banks. The people at the

North Street branch will give Patrick a provisional credit for the amount of the check and then must treat the check as one presented for payment to it as the payor bank on Monday. The bank will be deemed to have finally paid the item if it does not return the item to Patrick by its midnight deadline, which would in this case be midnight on Tuesday. See §4-301(b) and Comment 4 to that section.

1b. Section 4-107 provides that:

> A branch or separate office of a bank is a separate bank for the purpose of computing the time within which and determining the place at or to which action may be taken or notices or orders shall be given under this Article and under Article 3.

As Comment 1 notes, exactly how the situation should be dealt with will depend on the facts of the case. If we assume that the North Street branch and the South Street branch of First National have not so integrated all of their check-handling and payment procedures as to in effect operate as a single entity for check-collection purposes, then the North Street branch, after giving a provisional credit to Patrick, will have to forward the check for collection to the South Street branch, within the time limits and exercising the degree of care as it would be required to observe with respect to any other bank. Once the item is received at the South Street branch, that branch will deal with it as with any other item it receives for payment. Notice that §4-107 does not say that the two branches are to be considered separate banks for all purposes. So, for instance, there will be no need for the South Street branch to give a provisional settlement to the North Street branch upon receipt of the item. In this respect the depository bank and the payor bank should be considered one and the same, the First National Bank of Springfield, and there is no need for a bank to settle with itself.

2.   Under §4-108, the Shelbyville bank will be within its rights to consider this as a check received on Thursday *if* it has previously "fixed an afternoon hour of 2 p.m. or later as a cutoff hour for the handling of money and items and the making of entries on its books." If the Shelbyville bank has set such a cutoff hour, and that time is no earlier than 2 p.m. but no later than the 2:45 when Pauline deposited her check, under §4-108(b) the check "may be treated as being received at the opening of the next business day."

3a.   First we note that under §4-202(a) a collecting bank, which by definition (§4-105(5)) includes the depositary bank (Salem State Bank in our case), must exercise ordinary care in its handling of the item, including "presenting an item or sending it for presentment." Under the following subsection (b),

> A collecting bank exercises ordinary care under subsection (a) by taking proper action before its midnight deadline following receipt of an item, notice, or settlement. Taking proper action within a reasonably longer time may constitute the exercise of ordinary care, but the bank has the burden of establishing timeliness.

The Salem bank does not present the item directly, but does send it for presentment to the Federal Reserve Bank of Boston, and it does so on the afternoon of the day on which it received the item. The bank has acted with ordinary care with respect to the timing of its actions.

As Comment 2 to §4-202 states, if the collecting bank does not itself present the item but does forward it to be presented, subsection (a) "requires ordinary care with respect to routing (Section 4-204), and also in the selection of intermediary banks or other agents." So we look to §4-204. Under subsection (a) of that section,

> A collecting bank shall send items in a reasonably prompt method, taking into consideration relevant instructions, the nature of the item, the number of those items on hand, the cost of collection involved, and the method generally used by it or others to present those items.

Given the circumstances here, and assuming that the Stanley Corporation has not issued contrary instructions to the Salem bank (which would be very unlikely), the Salem bank would undoubtedly be found to have sent the item for eventual presentment via a "reasonably prompt method" by forwarding it to the Federal Reserve Bank of Boston. The Salem bank was not required to send it to the Boston Fed and the Boston Fed only. It was entitled to use any "reasonably prompt method" given the circumstances. For the Salem bank to send a check written on a bank in a distant part of the country to the local Federal Reserve bank for collection through the network of Federal Reserve Banks would be considered, barring some very unusual circumstances, just the kind of thing that a bank in Salem's position would do. Being a "method generally used by it or others to present those items," this should constitute a "reasonably prompt method" of doing what the bank is required to do, following its obligation to its depositor to send the check on for collection while exercising ordinary care. Notice that at this point the Salem bank should have received a provisional settlement for the amount of the check from the Boston Fed.

3b. The Salem bank's actions will still be deemed to have been taken with "reasonable care" for the purposes of §4-202(a). Under subsection (b), the bank had until its midnight deadline, which was midnight on Tuesday, to take proper action.

3c. The Salem bank here would probably be found to have failed to use the requisite reasonable care in sending the check on for presentment. By sending the check to the Boston Fed, the bank still chose a "reasonably prompt method" under §4-204(a) for making collection, but it will be argued that Salem bank failed to take this action with the ordinary care required by §4-202(a), because the bank didn't act until after the midnight deadline had passed. Under §4-202(b), it would still be possible, of course, for Salem State Bank to argue that its taking the proper action — sending the check on to the Boston Fed — within a "reasonably longer time" than its midnight deadline still constituted the exercise of ordinary care, but it would have the burden of establishing timeliness and this is usually a hard burden for a bank to meet. If the bank had a particularly compelling argument that, although it was aware of its delay in sending the item for collection, the delay was justified by some extraordinary conditions, it might also find some relief in §4-109(b). Barring a serious breakdown in its computer facilities, war, or other emergency conditions, however, it looks like the Salem bank has failed to use the ordinary care required of it by §4-202 in sending the check on for presentment.

The consequences of a bank's failure to use ordinary care in the handling of an item are laid out in §4-103(e).

> The measure of damages for failure to exercise ordinary care in handling an item is the amount of the item reduced by an amount that could not have been realized by the exercise of ordinary care. If there is bad faith it includes any other damages the party suffered as a proximate consequence.

This language, at least as far as I am concerned, takes a bit of explaining. Note first of all the important caveat of the final sentence of Comment 6 to §4-103:

> Of course, it continues to be necessary under subsection (e) as it has been under common law principles that, before the damage rule of the subsection becomes operative, liability of the bank and some loss to the customer or owner must be established.

So, even if Salem State Bank failed to meet its obligation of ordinary care by taking too long to forward the check for collection, there will be no damages to pay if, as would presumably be true in most cases, the check is paid as a matter of course when it does eventually reach the payor Bakersfield bank. True, the provisional credit to Stanley's account in the Salem bank will firm up somewhat later than it should have, but the money will be there and eventually become a firm credit nevertheless. Under the normal workings of the check collection system, the exact moment when the provisional credit in Stanley's account loses its provisional status is usually not even known either to Salem as the depositary bank or to Stanley as the customer. It just happens at some point when the check is finally paid in California. Also, the time when the funds represented by the check become available to Stanley in its account, for withdrawal or to cover checks that it may write, is (as we will see in Chapter 15) not controlled by when the check is finally paid. In the large majority of cases, then, even if a collecting bank fails to act with ordinary care in forwarding a check for collection, if the only consequence of this failure is a delay in presentation of the check to the payor bank, no harm will be done to the depositor and no damages will be due at all.

Suppose, however, that when the check (which has not been forwarded by the depositary bank in a timely fashion) reaches the payor bank, the account on which the check was written does not include enough to cover the check. The payor bank therefore does not pay the check but returns it for insufficient funds. The provisional credit that was added to the depositor's account balance when he or she deposited the check is charged back, so the amount of the check is never finally added to the balance in the depositor's account. Now §4-103(e) kicks in. The depositor will argue that the damage caused by the depositary bank's failure to use ordinary care is equal to the amount of the check. Had the depositary bank not dawdled, so the argument goes, the check would have arrived at the payor bank earlier, when there was still money in the drawer's account to cover it, and it would have been paid. The depositor's argument relies on the factual assertion that had the depositary bank acted with ordinary care, the check would have been finally paid by the payor bank and the amount of the check would have ended up as funds available to the depositor in its account. If in fact it is true that the full amount of the check could have been realized by the exercise of ordinary care on the bank's part, then the "amount that could not have been realized by the exercise of ordinary care" is zero. The depositor *could* have realized the full amount of the check had its bank acted with ordinary care in handling the item. The depositor is therefore owed damages by the depositary bank, which failed to exercise ordinary care in forwarding the item — damages equal to the full amount of the check without any reduction.

Now assume instead that the depositary bank could show that even if it *had* exercised ordinary care and forwarded the check for collection in a timely fashion, the check *still* would have been returned unpaid due to insufficient funds in the drawer's account. Then the depositor has not really been hurt by the depositary bank's failure to use ordinary care. Had the bank used ordinary care, the depositor would have ended up with nothing but a bounced check in its hands. As it was, with the depositary bank not having used ordinary care, the result was the same. The damages due to the depositor under §4-103(e) for the depositary bank's failure to exercise ordinary care in this instance is the amount of the check reduced by "an amount that could not have been realized by the exercise of ordinary care" — which in this case turns out to be the full amount of the check. The depositor is owed no damages.

4.   Yes. The Boston Fed, as a collecting bank, is under the same obligations of ordinary care set forth in §§4-202 and 4-204 as is any other collecting bank. Here it seems clearly to have met those obligations. It received the check on Tuesday and forwarded it for collection on Wednesday. It has exercised ordinary care, at least as far as the timing of its actions under §4-202(b), by acting before its midnight deadline, which would have been midnight on Thursday. Its forwarding of the item to the Los Angeles Fed would seem, in the absence of instructions to the contrary or other unusual circumstances, to be a "reasonably prompt method" of dealing with the check for the purposes of sending it on for eventual presentment to a bank located in the Los Angeles Fed's territory.

5. First of all, the Los Angeles Fed will have to settle with the Boston Fed for the amount of the item. This will be a provisional settlement. The Los Angeles Fed then has until its own midnight deadline, midnight on Friday, to forward the check either directly to Bakersfield Bank for presentment or to another bank to which it might customarily and reasonably forward any checks payable on Bakersfield Bank. The Federal Reserve bank in a given territory is not absolutely required to present directly any checks it receives payable on banks within its territory. In many instances it might well do so, especially if the bank in question is a large one for which the Fed on any given day can expect to receive a large number of items. If the bank is a smaller one, however, the Fed may direct the check to one of the larger local banks that it knows has entered into an agreement to directly present checks to the bank in question. A Federal Reserve Bank is, like any collecting bank in the process, required by §4-204(a) only to use a "reasonably prompt method, taking into consideration relevant instructions, the nature of the item, the number of those items on hand, the cost of collection involved, and the method generally used by it or others to present those items."

6.   As it turns out, the Los Angles Fed decides to take on the role of presenting bank and thus forwards the check directly to Bakersfield Bank, the payor bank. Bakersfield will, upon receipt, settle provisionally for the amount of the item with the Los Angeles Fed. Then, as the payor bank, it must decide whether to pay the item. We will deal with the situation confronting the payor bank upon presentment of the check, and particularly when that bank will be held to have "finally paid" the item, in more detail in Chapter 16. We assume that final payment has occurred here, as the payor bank has honored the check. What are the consequences? For one thing, Bakersfield Bank will charge against the Barker Company's account the amount of the check. (Whether it has the right to do so is another topic, covered in Chapter 13.) As far as the check collection process is concerned, the important thing to note is that Bakersfield Bank will now just hold onto the check. Depending upon the agreement it has with its customer, the Barker Company, the bank may later send the *canceled check*, as we call it, to Barker along with its monthly statement, or it may record a digital image of the check that will later accompany the monthly statement. In any event, the important thing to note is that the check comes, at least temporarily, to rest once it reaches the payor bank and that bank finally pays on the item.

As of the moment of final payment by the payor bank, all provisional credits generated in the forward collection process between banks are said to "firm up" and become final. See §4-214(c). The provisional credit that Salem State Bank gave to its depositor, the Stanley Corporation, also transmogrifies from a provisional to a nonprovisional addition to Stanley's account. The interesting and important thing to acknowledge about all this is that none of the collecting banks (including the depositary bank) and the depositing customer himself or herself, has any way of actually knowing exactly when the provisional settlements or credits each has received during the course of the forward collection process firmed up and became final. It all depends on when final payment is deemed to have occurred at the payor bank. None of the prior parties in this process will know the precise moment when this final payment occurs. Nor is the payor bank required to send any notice back up the stream of collection to the effect that final payment has been made. The vast majority of checks are finally paid by the payor bank, and the exact moment when this happens is really irrelevant to the prior banks in the process and to the depositor himself or herself. What is important when a check is honored by the payor bank is that all provisional settlements do eventually (even if we don't know precisely when) become final, and the provisional credit that the depositary bank has made to the depositor's account does the same.

7a.   Bakersfield Bank is obligated to follow the stop-payment instruction of its customer and to dishonor the check. To do so it needs to and has returned the item within the proper amount of time to the presenting bank, the Los Angles Fed. At this point it will have revoked, or as the term is used, *charged back* the provisional settlement it made in favor of the Los Angeles Fed on the previous day. The Los Angeles Fed is obliged to continue the return process by sending the check to the bank from which the Fed originally received it, in this case the Boston Fed. Note that in doing so the Los Angeles Fed is obligated, as will be all banks now involved in the return process, to use ordinary care in "sending a notice of dishonor or nonpayment or returning an item . . . to the bank's transferor after learning that the item has not been paid" under §4-202(a)(2). The operative rule now becomes that of §4-214(a): The Los Angeles Fed is entitled to charge back the amount it gave its transferor, the Boston Fed, in provisional settlement for the item, "if by its midnight deadline or within a longer reasonable time after it learns the facts it returns the item."

7b.   Once it is received by the Boston Fed, the check will then be sent by that bank in return to the Salem State Bank. The Boston Fed will charge back the provisional settlement it made earlier on the Salem bank in exchange for the item. The Salem bank will then be obligated to return the check or give notice of its dishonor within a timely fashion to its customer, the Stanley Corporation. The Salem bank will, at the same time, withdraw the amount of the check that it had provisionally credited to Stanley's account from that account. The dishonored check should eventually end up in the hands of the Stanley Corporation, which is going to have to decide what to do about the situation of having been paid for some supplies with what turns out to be a bum check.

8.   The Salem State Bank received the facts regarding the dishonor of this check, through return of the check itself, on Tuesday. It is then entitled,

under §4-214(a), to "charge back the amount of any credit given for the item to the customer's account, or obtain refund from its customer . . . , if by its midnight deadline or within a longer reasonable time after it learns the facts it returns the item or sends notification of the facts." Unfortunately for the Salem State Bank, it allowed its midnight deadline to pass without either returning the item to Stanley or sending notice of the check's dishonor to that firm. What are the consequences for a depositary bank that fails to inform its depositor of the return of a check within the time limit provided? Stanley would want to argue that once the depositary bank fails to give notice within the time provided for, it is thereafter foreclosed from revoking the provisional credit recorded in the customer's account, but this is not the rule. Subsection 4-214(a) continues: "If the return or notice is delayed beyond the bank's midnight deadline or a longer reasonable time after it learns the facts, the bank *may* revoke the settlement, charge back the credit, or obtain refund from its customer, *but it is liable for* any loss resulting from the delay." See Comment 3 as well as *Essex Construction Corp. v. Industrial Bank*, 913 F. Supp. 416, 29 U.C.C.2d 281 (D. Md. 1995), and *Liberty Bank & Trust Co. v. Bachrach*, 1996 Okla. 143, 916 P.2d 1377, 30 U.C.C.2d 612 (1996).

In a majority of cases, it is probably fair to say that the bank's depositor will not be able to show that it suffered any actual loss due to the depositary bank's failure to give timely notice of the check's dishonor. Getting a bit of bad news some days later than one is entitled to doesn't usually amount to an actual loss and mere speculation is not enough to make the case. See *U.S. Bank Nat. Ass'n. v. First Security Bank*, *N.A.*, 2001 U.S. Dist. Lexis 16714, 44 U.C.C. 2d 1088 (D. Utah 2001). The Stanley Corporation has been sent a check by Leno Electronics, which check bounces. Becoming aware of this fact a few days later than it should have, especially considering that there is no definite amount of time knowable in advance within which a returned check will necessarily be received by the depositary bank, would normally not impose any distinct loss on Stanley. In the particular facts as I have posited them, however, there may be liability on the Salem bank's part for failure to give notice of dishonor in a timely fashion. Recall that Stanley as seller set up its transaction with Leno as buyer so that Stanley would not send the merchandise contracted for until it had received payment. Stanley receives a check from Leno, which it duly deposits. It then waits for some period of time to see if the check is good. Not having heard that the check has bounced, it sends off the stuff. As it turns out, had the Salem bank given it notice within the proper time, Stanley would have known that Leno Electronics' check was no good and it would not have shipped out the goods. To the extent that Stanley may now be unable to get payment for what it has delivered, or that it will have to spend a good deal on lawyers' fees and the like eventually to get payment from Leno, this would seem to be a case in which the Salem State Bank's failure to give notice of nonpayment within the proper amount of time could in fact make it "liable for any loss resulting from the delay."

11

Final Payment

Introduction

In Chapter 10 we saw how a check drawn on a particular payor bank makes its way to that bank for the purposes of collection. Upon being presented with the individual check, the decision the payor bank must make is no different from that of the drawee of any draft: Is the draft with which it has been presented, a written order directed to it to pay a sum of money, to be accepted or not? Once we are dealing with a check, we tend to use the terminology of the payor bank's decision to *honor* or *dishonor* the item, but the fundamental question with which the payor bank, as drawee of a negotiable instrument, is faced upon presentment of the instrument is in essence that confronted by any drawee of a draft. The payor bank, of course, is not free to make the decision about honoring the check on whim alone. If the drawer has opened a checking account with that bank — which is something the bank should surely be able to establish quickly enough — then the bank's obligations to its customer come into play. We will deal with the full scope of a bank's obligations to its checking account customer in a later part of this book. For the moment, it is enough to point out that central to the bank's responsibilities will be its obligation to honor any check that it receives drawn on the customer's account that is what Article 4 terms a *properly payable* item. If the payor bank fails to honor a properly payable item, it will be liable for any harm done to its customer. In contrast, if the bank pays an item that is *not* properly payable, it will not be able to charge the amount against the customer's account and can itself be left holding the bag for the loss that ensues.

We will postpone for a while any further discussion of exactly what makes a check properly payable and what will make it a "not properly payable" item. What is important here is to recognize that the payor bank's decision to honor or dishonor an item is not free from consequence, not by a long shot. At the same time, we will see that the payor bank is not given an unlimited amount of time to make the decision. Under the rules of Article 4 governing check collection, the presentment of an item to a payor bank starts the clock ticking on some very precise and unforgiving deadlines. Look at §4-302(a). It provides that a payor bank will be accountable for any item presented to it in either of two situations: either because it "retains the item beyond midnight of the banking day of receipt without settling for it" (what is sometimes referred to as the *midnight rule*); or because it "does not pay or return the item or send notice of dishonor until after its *midnight deadline*" (for a definition of which see §4-104(a)(10)). If the bank does not take appropriate action with respect to the item before the passage of either of these deadlines, it will be held as a matter of law to have accepted the check and the responsibility of an acceptor of a draft to pay it, whether or not the check was indeed properly payable and whether or not the payor bank will be able to charge its customer's account for the amount of the item.*

On Final Payment

Crucial to all that follows is the notion of *final payment* as set out in Article 4. Under §4-215(a),

> An item is finally paid by a payor bank when the bank has first done any of the following:
> (1) paid the item in cash;
> (2) settled for the item without having a right to revoke the settlement made under statute, clearing-house rule, or agreement; or
> (3) made a provisional settlement for the item and failed to revoke the settlement in the time and manner permitted by statute, clearing-house rule, or agreement.

The possibility allowed for in the second part — the payor bank's having irrevocably settled for an item — is exceptionally rare and not something that we will give any significant time to. The other two possibilities — payment in cash and failure to revoke in a timely fashion a *provisional* settlement given for an item upon presentment — cover the vast majority of cases and must be explored more fully, as they will be in the following examples.

As we have already seen in Chapter 10, checks written on any single payor bank are deposited at various depositary banks around the country. Each then eventually makes its way to a bank that is in a position to act as a presenting bank with respect to the particular item. That bank will present to the payor bank, which will then *provisionally* settle for the item by the end of the day with the presenting bank. The key questions then become: What must the payor bank do, and how soon must it do it if it wishes to avoid final payment of the particular item under §4-215(a)(3)? Subject to different

---

* This chapter deals with the payor bank's responsibilities and potential liability under the rules of Article 4. The provisions of Article 4 have now been supplemented and in some limited cases superseded by the promulgation of Regulation CC by the Federal Reserve. We will look at the consequences of Regulation CC in Chapter 12.

deadlines or procedures supplied by any clearing-house rules governing present-ment of the particular item or to an "other agreement" between the presenting and payor banks, the answers to these questions are to be found in the payor bank's right to revoke a provisional settlement as set forth in §4-301.

Final payment of an item is a watershed event in the check collection process. In the words of Comment 1 to §4-215, final payment is "the 'end of the line' in the collection process and the 'turn around' point commenc-ing the return flow of proceeds." If presentment has been made to the bank through a series of collecting banks, each of which has received provisional settlement for the item, upon final payment all provisional settlements firm up and become final settlements (§4-215(c)). Any provisional credit that the depositary bank allocated to the depositor's account becomes, as of the moment of final payment by the payor bank, a final credit (§4-215(d)). If the payor bank does not make any initial settlement or later final payment by the time it is obligated to do so, but tries to avoid the consequences by later returning the check, it will be considered *accountable for* the amount of the item under §4-302(a). For the payor bank to be accountable under this section means that the person entitled to enforce the check will be able to hold the payor bank strictly liable for the amount of the check.* If you look at the very end of Comment 3 to §4-302, you'll see the following language:

> If a payor bank is accountable for an item it is liable to pay it. If it has made final payment for an item, it is no longer accountable for it.

That is to say, once a payor bank has made final payment, it *has already* paid the item and thus is no longer accountable for it. If it failed to finally pay the item when it should have, it is then accountable for that item and can be made to pay as it should have.

Among the most significant consequences of final payment of a check is that once final payment has occurred, it cannot be undone. Final payment really is meant to be final. Under normal circumstances, the payor bank cannot revoke a settlement that has become final, nor does it have any right under Article 4 to get back any final payment that it made in cash. Under certain limited circumstances, however, a payor bank that has paid an item by mistake may look for relief to §3-418 and the possibility of *restitution* of the amount paid mistakenly. We will look at the operation of §3-418 in the final examples of this chapter.

---

* For the purposes of this chapter, we will continue to assume that the person attempting to collect on the check, either by presentment to the payor bank for payment over the counter or by depositing the check in his or her own account, does qualify as a person entitled to enforce the check. A whole separate set of concerns arises, as you can imagine, when the person attempting to collect on the check has no right to do so, as when there has been theft or forgery. We will give such problems all the attention they deserve in Part Five.

EXAMPLES

1.   David Drake has a checking account at the North Side branch of Payson State Bank. He draws a check for $2,000 on this account payable to Paula Paley. Paley takes this check to the North Side branch of Payson and presents it to a teller, asking for immediate payment of the check in cash. The teller looks at the status of Drake's account and determines that it is within the bank's guidelines for him to accept the item. He hands over $2,000 in cash to Paley.

  (a) Has this check been finally paid?

  (b) Suppose instead that Paley had asked that she be issued a cashier's check by Payson for $2,000 in exchange for the check she has received from Drake. The teller does issue her such a cashier's check. Has the check issued by Drake to Paley been finally paid by the Payson bank?

  (c) Suppose that Paley herself has an account with the same branch of Payson. She deposits Drake's check in her account by indorsing it and handing it over to a teller, along with a deposit slip indicating a deposit of a single check for $2,000. Has this check been finally paid as of this moment?

  (d) Finally, suppose that the situation is as in part (c), except that when Paley presents Drake's check to the teller, she says she would like to "deposit it as cash" in her own account. Paley signs the back of the check and hands it over to the teller, along with a deposit slip indicating that she is depositing $2,000 in cash. What is the result?

2.   David Drake draws a second check on his account for $1,500, made payable to Patricia Parsons. Parsons has an account with the Payson bank, but her account is held at the South Side branch of that bank. Parsons deposits this check in her account on Monday morning.

  (a) Has this check been finally paid?

  (b) What is the obligation of the South Side bank with respect to this check?

  (c) The South Side branch forwards this check to the North Side branch, which receives it on Tuesday morning. What are the North Side branch's obligations with respect to the check? What must it do if it wishes to avoid final payment of the check or becoming accountable for the amount of the check?

3.   Drake draws a third check to pay his Vista credit card bill. He sends this check to the address in a distant city indicated on the bill. Vista deposits this check (along with a load of others it has received) into its account with Depot Bank for Commerce, a bank in the city in which the Vista headquarters are located. The Depot Bank forwards Drake's check for collection through normal banking channels. Eventually the check ends up in the possession of one Prestige Bank, a major bank located in the same city as the smaller Payson State Bank and to which checks written on Payson are

routinely routed. On a Tuesday morning, Prestige Bank presents this check for payment to the Payson bank. The Payson bank never makes a settlement, provisional or otherwise, with the Prestige Bank but does, upon finding that Drake's account doesn't include sufficient funds to cover the check, return the check to Prestige by special messenger on Wednesday afternoon.

   (a) Has Payson made final payment on this check?
   (b) Can Payson be held accountable for the amount of the check to Vista? If so, why?

4.   Drake draws yet a fourth check, this one to pay his Mastercharge bill, and sends the check off to Mastercharge. That company deposits the check in its account with Downtown Federal Bank, which forwards the check for collection through customary banking channels. This check is eventually forwarded to Prestige Bank, which presents it for payment to the Payson bank on a Wednesday morning. Payson does settle with Prestige for this check by the end of Wednesday. On Thursday, having determined that Drake does not have sufficient funds in his account to cover the check, Payson decides not to honor it. The check is put in an envelope and mailed off to Prestige Bank on Thursday afternoon. It is received by Prestige Bank on the following Monday.

   (a) Has Payson successfully avoided making final payment on this check?
   (b) Suppose instead that Payson does not mail the check to Prestige until Friday morning, but that the returned check still is received by Prestige on the following Monday. Under this set of facts, can Payson claim that it has avoided making final payment on the check? Does Payson have any argument that the result in this situation should be no different from that in part (a), because its failure to act until Friday did not cause any additional delay in the return of the item (in each case it was received by the presenting bank on the following Monday) and its lateness in returning the item could have caused no damage to Mastercharge?

5.   The DotCom Corporation is another customer of the Payson State Bank. DotCom writes a check for $15,000 to Paul Perkins, a consultant who has completed a project for the company. Perkins deposits this check to his account with the New Economy Bank and Trust. This check is forwarded for collection to the Payson bank, which receives it on a Monday morning. By the time Payson gets the check, DotCom has issued a proper stop-payment order covering the check, and this stop-payment order has been received by Payson. Through a foul-up at that bank, though, the fact that payment on the check has been stopped is not recognized by the Payson bank's computer system, and the check is not returned to the presenting bank by the end of Tuesday.

   (a) Has Payson made final payment of this check?
   (b) Will Payson be able to charge the amount of the check against the amount in DotCom's account?

(c) When Payson becomes aware of what has happened, will it be able to recover the $15,000 from Perkins under the theory of restitution? Look to §3-418.

(d) Assume instead that the check written out and delivered to Perkins was not for work already done for DotCom. Perkins, as a consultant, has a policy of demanding payment in advance for any project he agrees to take on. The bank mistakenly pays the check over a valid stop-payment order it has received from DotCom. By the time Payson contacts Perkins to explain what has happened and demand restitution of the $15,000 now under the control of Perkins, the consultant has not yet begun to do any work on the DotCom project. Under this assumption, can Payson get restitution from Perkins?

6. DotCom writes a second check out of its account with Payson State Bank, this one to Star Microsystems for $23,500 to pay for some computer equipment that DotCom bought and received from Star. At the time the check is presented to the Payson bank, DotCom does not have sufficient funds in its account to cover the check. In this situation, Payson would as a matter of course dishonor and return the check, but through a mistake it does not. It holds onto the check beyond its midnight deadline. Will Payson be able to get restitution of the $23,500 from Star Microsystems?

7. Dexter Moneybucks, the wealthy financier, also has an account with Payson State Bank. He draws a check for $45,000 payable to the Uptown Art Gallery to pay for a painting he is adding to his extensive collection of modern art. The check is presented to Payson on Tuesday morning, and that bank settles for the $45,000 with the presenting bank by the end of that day. On Wednesday morning, it is brought to the attention of the account manager responsible for the Moneybucks account that there are not sufficient funds in the account to cover the check. Not wanting to offend an important customer of the bank, she telephones Moneybucks and informs him of the situation. She tells him she will be forced to dishonor the $45,000 check that has just been presented unless that amount is in his account by the end of the day. Moneybucks assures her that this is just a temporary problem and that the bank should soon be receiving a deposit of funds for his account that will more than cover the check to the Uptown Art Gallery. Later in the day, the account manager again investigates the situation and discovers that no new funds have come into Moneybucks's account. She elects to give this valued customer a bit more time before bouncing one of his checks and then leaves for the day without having taken any action with respect to the check. On Thursday morning she once again inquires into the status of the Moneybucks account, and things are no better. No new deposits have been made by him. Is it too late for the Payson bank to avoid making final payment on this $45,000 check? Does the bank have any argument, based on the theory of restitution, that it should be able to recover the $45,000 paid to the art gallery under the circumstances?

EXPLANATIONS

1a.   Yes. This is the simplest case going. Under §4-215(a)(1), the payor bank has finally paid an item when it has "paid the item in cash."

1b.   The prevailing opinion seems to be, yes. Once the payor bank has issued a cashier's or teller's check in exchange for a check that was presented directly over the counter, the presented check has indeed been finally paid. This follows from the general notion that a cashier's or teller's check is, for all practical purposes, if not literally cash, then at least should be considered a "cash equivalent" for the amount of the check. Hence, final payment has been made by virtue of §4-215(a)(1). Some might want to analyze the situation instead as one in which, under §4-215(a)(2), the payor bank has "settled for the item without having a right to revoke the settlement," but the result remains unchanged. The check written by Drake to Paley has been finally paid by Payson State Bank's giving a cashier's check to Paley in exchange for the item.

A distinct question, and one that we do not get into here (wait for Chapter 14), is whether Payson State Bank will ever have the right to refuse payment on the cashier's check it has just given to Paley, and if so under what circumstances. Even in the very rare case when Payson may have a right to withhold payment on its cashier's check, this doesn't really affect the answer to the question with which we are at present concerned. The check in question — the one drawn by Drake on his account with Payson State Bank and made payable to Paley — has been finally paid by Payson's acceptance of that check and payment for it by way of a cashier's check of its own.

1c.   No. As of this moment, Payson has been presented with the check in question but has not finally paid it. It will be required, by the end of the day, to provisionally credit the amount of the check to Paley's account, but it will then have an additional day to determine whether it wishes to revoke the provisional credit and return the check to the depositor Paley. If it does revoke and return before its midnight deadline, it will avoid final payment of the check and any accountability for that check.

1d.   Paley will want to argue that this check has been finally paid by, in effect, the payment of $2,000 to her in cash (making the case like that in Example 1a) which she then deposited in her own account just as she might deposit any other cash she had in her possession. The bank will want to argue that what really occurred is that it took the check for deposit (as in Example 1c), with the understanding that anything later paid on the check would be automatically deposited into Paley's account just as if it were cash. The bank may be able to take advantage of some language that it carefully included in the agreement signed by Paley upon her opening the account, to the effect that any cash given for an on-us item deposited at the bank is to be considered merely an advance of cash to the depositor and may be recovered if the check is not finally paid. Barring such language, and a court's being willing to enforce it under the circumstances, Paley probably has the better argument. For a case on point — although not every commentator is particularly keen on the outcome — that supports Paley's position here, *see Kirby v. First & Merchants National Bank*, 210 Va. 88, 168 S.E.2d 273, 6 U.C.C. 694 (1969).

2a. No. It has not been paid in cash and any credit that the South Side branch may add to Parsons's account will be provisional only. Final payment has not been made.

2b. Under §4-107, the answer to this question will depend on how the North Side and the South Side branches of the Payson bank have set up their check collection and check clearing operations. If the two branches use a common facility for handling checks (located somewhere in the middle of town, presumably), then the situation is to be dealt with just as if Parsons had deposited directly in the payor bank. The check will be finally paid if it is not returned to her by the midnight deadline following a Monday-morning presentment. If instead the North Side branch and the South Side branch work through independent check collection centers, each located at the branch in question, then the South Side branch's obligation with respect to this check is that of a collecting bank. It must forward the check to the North Side branch, thereby presenting it, by its midnight deadline. The South Side branch acts as the depositary bank but is not the payor bank. It is not in a position to finally pay on the item.

2c. The North Side branch is under no obligation to settle for the check by the end of Tuesday with the South Side branch. For this purpose at least, the two branches are not considered separate banks between which settlement must be made. The North Side branch must, however, determine whether to honor or dishonor (by return) the check, and it must do so by its midnight deadline — midnight on Wednesday, in this case. To avoid finally paying the check or becoming accountable on it, the North Side branch must under §4-301(a) and (b) "return the item" or "send written notice of dishonor or nonpayment [in the unlikely event] the item is unavailable for return" prior to the passing of its midnight deadline. For what constitutes effective return for the purposes of Article 4, see §4-301(c). Other than cases in which a check has been presented through a clearing house and special clearing-house rules apply, an item is deemed returned "when it is sent or delivered to the bank's customer or [as in this case] transferor or pursuant to instructions." Therefore, to avoid final payment on this particular check, the North Side branch of Payson must send the check back to the South Side branch before midnight on Wednesday.

3a. No. Payson has not taken any action that would constitute final payment under any part of §4-215(a).

3b. Yes, Payson can be held accountable to Vista for the amount of the check because of its failure to settle with Prestige Bank, the presenting bank, by midnight on the day on which it was presented with the item for collection. Reread carefully §4-302(a). In this case Payson has failed to meet its obligation under the midnight rule, which governs the payor bank's obligation initially to settle for any item with which it is presented; hence, it is accountable for the item. This example is based on the noted case of *Hannah v. First National Bank*, 87 N.Y.2d 107, 661 N.E.2d 683, 637 N.Y.S.2d 953, 28 U.C.C.2d 417 (1995), which held that the payor bank was not absolved from its violation of the midnight rule for settlement even though it returned the presented item prior to the expiration of its midnight deadline. The New York Court of Appeals declared:

> The statutory requirement that the payor bank settle for the item on the day of receipt is the first step toward effectuating the overarching purposes of article 4 of the Uniform Commercial Code, to make the transactions it regulates swift and certain. Although timely dishonor may minimize the pecuniary harm to the particular parties involved, forgiveness of the payor bank's untimely conduct would do a significant disservice to the integrity of the complex, ordered, and predictable operation of article 4's rules governing banks.

The *Hannah* case was decided under the prerevision version of Article 4 (the state of New York had not at the time — and as a matter of fact has still not, as of this writing — adopted the 1990 revisions to Articles 3 and 4), but there is no reason to believe that the result would have been any different had the revised version been in effect.

4a. Yes. The Payson bank provisionally settled with the presenting bank on the day of the check's presentment, so it can then avoid making final payment, under §4-215(a)(3), by revoking the settlement "in the time and manner permitted by statute, clearing-house rule, or agreement." The statutory right to revoke the provisional settlement is found in §4-301(a):

> If a payor bank settles for a demand item . . . presented otherwise than for immediate payment over the counter before midnight of the banking day of receipt, the payor bank may revoke the settlement and recover the settlement if, before it has made final payment and before its midnight deadline, it
> (1) returns the item; or
> (2) sends written notice of dishonor or nonpayment if the item is unavailable for return.

Subsection 4-301(d)(2) provides that an item other than one presented through a clearing house is returned "when it is sent or delivered to the banks' customer or [as in this case] transferor or pursuant to instructions." As Comment 6 to this section helpfully informs us, the definition of *sent*, as that term is used in this section, is to be found in Article 1, at O§1-201(38) or R§1-201(b)(36). Quoting from the original Article 1:

> "Send" in connection with any writing or notice means to deposit in the mail or deliver for transmission by any other usual means of

communication with postage or cost of transmission provided for and properly addressed and in the case of an instrument to any address specified thereon or otherwise agreed, or if there be none to any address reasonable under the circumstances.

So, if Payson deposited the envelope containing the dishonored check in the mail before its midnight deadline, it has effectively returned the check prior to its midnight deadline and has not finally paid on the item. This all assumes, of course, that the envelope bore the proper address and sufficient postage.

In *First Bank v. Farm Worker's Check Cashing, Inc.*, 745 So. 2d 994, 39 U.C.C.2d 663 (Fla. Dist. Ct. App. 1999), the payor bank did mail out the checks it sought to dishonor prior to its midnight deadline, but they were sent to the wrong address. The customer check cashing service had notified the bank of a prospective move of its business office and had filed a change of address notice with the bank, but that notice specified that the change of address was not to be effective until March 31, 1995. The bank sent the returned checks to this new address prior to the specified effective date. As a result, it was held that the bank had not sent the items in return in a proper fashion and that final payment had occurred.

4b. If Payson does not return the check until Friday morning, after its midnight deadline has passed at the end of the day on Thursday, then it has finally paid the item. It has no right to revoke on an item that it has finally paid. Even if the check does work its way back through the return process and what should be now regarded as nonprovisional settlements are somehow revoked, this is of no help to Payson, because under §4-302(a)(1) it would still be accountable for the item for its failure to "pay or return the item or send notice of dishonor until after its midnight deadline." For the payor bank to be "accountable" for an item means that it must pay the full amount of the check to the person entitled to enforce. One way or another, Mastercharge is entitled to the amount of the check. If the check was properly payable, of which there seems to be no doubt in this example, then Drake's account at Payson will be overdrawn due to payment of the check. Payson has the right to expect that Drake will eventually cover the negative balance in his account by the deposit of additional funds, but that is a matter between Payson and Drake, its customer. It need not concern Mastercharge.

It is very important to appreciate that Payson does not have any defense here based on the fact that its failure to act by its midnight deadline does not seem, in this particular instance, to have actually delayed eventual return of the check to the depositary bank at all. The payor bank's obligation to return the check prior to its midnight deadline (as well as its obligation to settle for the check prior to midnight on the day of receipt, as we saw in the previous example) does not depend on the showing of any harm brought about by the delay. Nor does this accountability on the instrument require any showing that the payor bank's failure to meet the specified deadlines set for it in Article 4 was the result of lack of ordinary care or anything like that. Compare this result to the example in Chapter 10, in which a collecting bank failed to act within a timely fashion as a participant in the collection process. For a collecting bank, liability for failure to act as required under Article 4 is determined by the actual damage resulting from its failure to follow the rules. This is not the case for the payor bank; liability after final payment, and accountability should it fail to make available to the depositor the amount of the check as it is obligated to do upon final payment, is not limited to any harm that can be shown to have been caused by the payor bank's delay. Accountability under §4-302 is treated as strict liability. See the discussion in *First Nat. Bank in Harvey v. Colonial Bank*, 898 F. Supp. 1220, 28 U.C.C.2d 290 (N.D. Ill. 1995) and *Bank of America, NT & SA v. David W. Hubert, P.C.*, 115 Wash. App. 368, 62 P.2d 904, 49 U.C.C.2d 899 (2003).

5a. Yes. Payson, by retaining the check beyond its midnight deadline, has finally paid on the check.

5b. No. Payson is allowed to deduct from its customer's account only the amount of those checks that are properly payable. A check on which the bank has received a valid stop-payment order will not be considered properly payable. Payson cannot charge the amount of this check to DotCom's account.

5c. Under §3-418(a), the payor bank is given a statutory right to restitution if a check was finally paid by mistake in two distinct situations.

> Except as provided in subsection (c), if the drawee of a draft pays . . . the draft and the drawee acted on the mistaken belief that (i) payment had not been stopped pursuant to Section 4-403 or (ii) the signature of the drawer on the draft was authorized, the drawee may recover the amount of the draft from the person to whom or for whose benefit payment was made. . . . Rights of the drawee under this subsection are not affected by the failure of the drawee to exercise ordinary care in paying . . . the draft.

Here Payson as drawee paid under the mistaken belief that there was no stop-payment order covering the check. The catch here, as least as far as Payson is concerned, is in the all-important introductory words to this subsection, "Except as provided in subsection (c)." That subsection states that the remedy provided for in subsection (a), upon which Payson would be hoping to recover, "may not be asserted against a person who took the instrument in good faith and for value or who in good faith changed position in reliance on the payment." Payson should not be able to get restitution from Perkins of the $15,000 mistakenly paid by it. Recall the definition of *value* found in §3-303(a). Perkins will have taken the check "for value" if he took it in exchange for a promise of performance on his part, to the extent the promise has been performed. If we assume, as we have no reason not to, that Perkins acted in good faith in taking the instrument for the work he did, then he has taken the instrument "in good faith and for value" and hence is not vulnerable to any action for restitution that Payson State Bank may attempt to bring under §3-418(a).

5d. Payson will assert its right to restitution under §3-418(a). The question is whether Perkins can establish that he is insulated from Payson's claim based on subsection (c). Based on the facts as we are now assuming them to be, Perkins cannot claim to be a person who took the instrument for value. Recall that under §3-303(a), a promise of performance not yet performed does not constitute value for Article 3 purposes. Perkins may still be able to defeat the restitution claim, but only if he can establish that he "in good faith changed position in reliance" on the mistaken payment of the check. Let us continue to assume that Perkins has been acting in good faith. Perhaps he can demonstrate that once he obtained payment on the check from DotCom, he turned down other jobs, because he can take on only so many consulting projects at one time. This could constitute a change in position in reliance on the payment of the check, which would bar restitutionary recovery by Payson.

Even if he acted in good faith, if Perkins cannot prove that he either gave value for the instrument or acted on reliance on its being paid, then Payson would be entitled to restitution under §3-418(a). Note that even after making restitution Perkins will not be out of pocket any money. He will only be in the same position he would have been in had the Payson bank not made the mistake and observed the stop-payment order it had received from DotCom. Perkins may, of course, have a contractual cause of action against DotCom for a possible repudiation of whatever consulting agreement it entered into with Perkins, but that is between the consultant and the company. Payson has made a mistake, but in this particular situation it can escape from the consequences through the route of restitution. It's a fair guess, however, that this type of situation will be the exception rather than the rule. As Comment 1 to §3-418 concludes,

> The result in the two cases covered by subsection (a) is that the drawee in most cases will not have a remedy against the person paid because there is usually a person who took the check in good faith and for value or who in good faith changed position in reliance on the payment or acceptance.

Just to get to the circumstances posited in this part of the example, we had to assume that Perkins was able to get prospective clients to pay up front for the consulting work he proposes to do for them. In all likelihood, even the most sought-after consultant (even in the red-hot world of Internet commerce, where we have to admit that just about anything seems possible) would not be able to insist on payment on terms such as this.

6.   Payson has made final payment on this check by holding onto it past Payson's midnight deadline. Payson can find no support for recovery in restitution in subsection (a) of §3-418, because the mistake that it made is

not of either variety covered there. The bank will have to look instead at subsection (b):

> Except as provided in subsection (c), if an instrument has been paid . . . by mistake and the case is not covered by subsection (a), the person paying . . . may, to the extent permitted by the law governing mistake and restitution . . . recover the payment from the person to whom or for whose benefit payment was made. . . .

As Comment 3 to this section makes clear, this subsection, by directing courts to deal with cases not governed by subsection (a) under "the law governing mistake and restitution," is referring the issue in such instances to the common law of restitution, as the courts of the jurisdiction in which the problem is being addressed understand that law to be. In the particular example we have before us — and in most actual instances, as Comment 3 is quick to point out — there is no need to delve into the intricacies of the general common law remedy of restitution. Any right to recover under §3-418(b) is explicitly made subject to subsection (c), just as we earlier saw any cause of action under subsection (a) to be. Here Star Microsystems took the check for $23,500 "in good faith and for value," and hence it is immune from any action in restitution that Payson might be tempted to bring.

7. It is too late for the bank to avoid making final payment on the check. It has already done so by failing to return the check to the presenting bank prior to the passing of its midnight deadline on Wednesday midnight. Nor should Payson be able to assert any kind of right of restitution under the circumstances. Any possibility of restitution, founded as here it would have to be on §3-418(b), takes as its starting point a finding that the check in question had been paid "by mistake." However much the account manager at Payson bank will later regret making the decision she did — not to arrange for return of the check on Wednesday afternoon even if she would have been within her (and her employer's) rights to do so — this was not a mistaken payment in the sense that word is used in the law of restitution. The bank, through its agent, made a conscious decision to act as it did, paying an item by retention beyond the midnight deadline even if it was under no contractual obligation to its customer Moneybucks so to do. It did not "mistakenly" pay the check. It knowingly and willingly allowed the check to be paid even though this created an overdraft in Moneybucks's account. In effect, the bank advanced the money to cover the check to Moneybucks on unsecured credit, and Payson will have to go after Moneybucks if he doesn't quickly bring his account balance into the black. The case of *First National Bank v. Colonial Bank*, cited earlier, though dealing with a much more complex situation than the rather simple one presented here by Moneybucks's efforts to add yet one more expensive artwork to his collection, addresses itself to this issue and concludes (as we have) that no "mistaken payment" is involved when a bank knowingly holds onto a check beyond its midnight deadline on the assurance that the customer will soon be coming up with the funds necessary to cover the check.

Revision Alert

The 2002 Revision makes two important amendments to §4-301, both of which are intended, as an additional Comment 8 informs us, to facilitate "electronic check-processing." Recall that in the present version of §4-301(a) a payor bank can avoid being accountable for an item by either physically returning the item or by sending to the presenting bank a "written notice of dishonor or nonpayment if the item is unavailable for return." Revised §4-301(a) gives the payor bank three possibilities; it avoids accountability if it

(1) returns the item;

(2) returns an image of the item, if the party to which the return is made has entered into an agreement to accept an image as return of the item and the image is returned in accordance with that agreement; or

(3) sends a record providing notice of dishonor or nonpayment if the item is unavailable for return.

Notice that in part (2) electronic return of an *image* of the check is not made conditional on the check's not being available for physical return.

Note as well that part (3) refers to the sending of a "record" and not a "written" notice. What's a *record*? This is a new concept that has been making its way into the modern Uniform Commercial Code as various articles have been revised in this new age of electronic communication. You'll find the word defined either in R§1-201(b)(31), if you are working with the 2001 Revision of Article 1, or in R§3-103(a)(14) if you are not. It is "information that is inscribed on a tangible medium or that is stored in an electronic medium and is retrievable in perceivable form." So a writing, as that continues to be defined in Article 1, would be a record, but a record would not necessarily be a writing. For example, consider an e-mail message, here one sent by the payor bank to the presenting bank making clear that it is dishonoring a given check. The message is received by the presenting bank and stored as a "file" on its e-mail system but never printed out to be held in an old fashioned file cabinet. (In fact it would most likely be forwarded to the bank that had transferred the check to the presenting bank, and so on until it arrives as an e-mail to the depositary bank.) This message is a record even if it is never printed out on paper by anyone. It is enough that it is "retrievable in perceivable form," that it has been preserved and should the need arise *could be* later printed out or simply pulled up on a computer screen for the eye to see. As you should also be able to convince yourself, a phone message, *if* it is recorded *and* the recording is saved in some form from which the message can later be heard, also qualifies as a record even if it is never reduced to writing.

12

Expedited Return Under Regulation CC

The Expedited Funds Availability Act

As we have seen in Chapters 10 and 11, and as you are most likely aware from your own experience, when a customer deposits a check into his or her account, the money that the check represents is not immediately "available" to the customer. There will be some number of days before the depositary bank will allow the customer to withdraw the amount as cash or consider it as funds in the account to be used to cover checks that the customer himself or herself has written and that are presented for payment. This follows from what we know of the check collection process as we have looked at it so far: The deposited check results in only a *provisional* credit to the customer's account. When a check is deposited, it must then be sent on for collection. Eventually it reaches the payor bank. In the large majority of cases, that bank honors the check, in which case and at which time the provisional credit in the depositor's account is said to "firm up" and does indeed become the depositing customer's money in the bank. A small percentage (but still a significant number) of checks presented for payment, however, are not honored by the payor bank. Once dishonored, they are expected to make their way back to the depositary bank, which will, upon receipt of the dishonored item, remove the provisional credit from the customer's account balance. The check never turns into available funds at the depositor's disposal.

So, the deposited check creates only a provisional credit in the customer's account, and this provisional credit will either firm up to become available funds *or* be withdrawn entirely if the check in question is dishonored by the payor bank. The real problem here has always been not just that some checks will be returned unpaid, but that there is obviously no way for either the customer or the depositary institution to know, at the time of deposit, which checks those will be. Nor could there be any way to fore-cast with confidence how many days it will take for a dishonored check to make its way back to the depositary bank and for the sad fact of dishonor to become known. The forward collection process is, thanks to its mechanical and automated nature, fairly quick and efficient. Still, it may take several transfers of any single item, passing from the hands of one bank to another, for a check sent for collection to reach the bank on which it was written, especially if that bank is in a distant part of the country. Each of the collecting banks is then obligated to send the check off to its next destination, so there will be further time in transit. Once the check reaches the payor bank, we know that bank must act by its midnight deadline if it wants to dishonor the item, but even then its only obligation to avoid final payment under Article 4 is that it return the check by sending the item back to the presenting bank. That bank in turn will have a couple of days to figure out how and from whom it received the check and then send the item back to that transferor. And so it goes. The returned check is sent back to the depositary institution retracing in reverse the path it took on forward collection. This return process, historically, has always been slow, as there was no automated procedure for return of dishonored checks. It had to be done on a item-by-item basis and by real live individuals looking over each check and determining what to do with it next. Slow going indeed.

Because of this predicament, it became customary for depositary banks to create their own internal rules for when they would consider the amount represented by any deposited check as fully available funds in the customer's account. Each bank would adopt a policy of placing "blanket holds" of a certain number of days on all deposited checks, usually distinguishing between local and nonlocal checks.* In response to rising consumer ire and critical commentary directed at the lengths of the blanket holds of individual banks and the banking industry in general, the federal government passed the Expedited Funds Availability Act in 1987. The general purposes and detailed provisions of the Act have been effectuated through the promulgation of an administrative regulation by the Board of Governors of the Federal Reserve System — Regulation CC: Availability of Funds and Collection of Checks (12 C.F.R. Part 229).

---

* A case from 1978 in which the availability schedule of a particular savings bank in New York City was challenged — unsuccessfully — as "illegal" on a number of grounds gives the following information: The typical commercial bank in New York would at the time restrict withdrawals against local checks to 3 business days and imposed longer holds, generally from 5 to 10 days, on nonlocal checks. Savings banks, which by their nature were not able to present directly to the Federal Reserve or through the New York Clearing House Association, imposed even longer holds, typically from 5 to 8 days on a local check and from 8 to 21 (with an average of 15) days on a nonlocal one. *Rapp v. Dime Savings Bank*, 64 A.D.2d 964, 408 N.Y.S.2d 540, 24 U.C.C. 1220 (1978).

Introducing Regulation CC

Regulation CC is lengthy, wordy, and complex. It is, after all, a federal regulation.* It applies to all banks (as that term is defined in loving detail in 12 C.F.R. §229.2(e)) in the United States. In broad outline, its effect is two-fold. One part of Regulation CC (Subpart B, which we will explore in Chapter 15) dictates for all banks a mandatory schedule for when funds reflecting any deposited check must be made available to the depositor and how the depositor is to made aware of his or her rights under the system. Individual banks are no longer free to impose whatever hold policies they wish. Regulation CC sets forth the maximum time during which a bank may restrict use of funds represented by any deposit. Not surprisingly, considering that the regulation is meant to carry out what Congress chose to entitle the *Expedited* Funds Availability Act, the availability schedule now mandated by Regulation CC generally allows for quicker use by the customer of funds than was true prior the adoption of the Act and promulgation of the regulation.

Regulation CC and Check Collection

By effectively requiring that depositary banks make funds based on deposited items available to their customers on a accelerated basis, the Act was necessarily increasing the risk to the depositary institution that it would part with funds on the basis of what would later turn out to be uncollectible items. In particular, the expedited availability schedules of Subpart B made even easier a not terribly sophisticated, but nevertheless often quite effective, type of check fraud. A customer could deposit a check that he or she knew for a fact or had every reason to believe would not be honored by the bank on which it was drawn. The check would typically be drawn on a distant institution, such that even under the best of circumstances the forward collection, the anticipated dishonor, and then consequent return of the item would take a fairly long time. The customer could then wait out the relatively brief (at least for his or her purposes) time that Subpart B of Regulation CC gave the depositary bank to restrict availability on the item. As soon as that time had run, the customer would withdraw in cash all of the money in his or her account, and then vanish into thin air. By the time the depositary bank got return of the item unpaid, it was too late to do anything and that bank would usually simply have to bear the loss.

---

* Being a federal regulation, it is also subject to change from time to time. For the record, I am working with the version of the regulation as it stands current as June 2003. I am also assuming that you have available to you a copy of Regulation CC in the selected commercial statutes volume you are using to consult the various parts of the Uniform Commercial Code.

In a rough attempt to counterbalance this consequence of what it was doing to benefit the individual customer (most of whom were, of course, not involved in any kind of fraud, and most of whose checks would clear with no difficulty) by shortening the time for availability of funds, Regulation CC also took on a second task. It set forth a new set of rules, again applicable to all banks, designed to get notice of a check's dishonor more quickly to the depositary bank. This aspect of Regulation CC is found in the provisions of its Subpart C, and it is the subject to be covered in this chapter.

The first thing to note is that the rules of Article 4 on check collection and return, as we have seen them in Chapters 10 and 11, are not done away with or preempted by Regulation CC. A payor bank will have to make sure that it meets the standards of *both* Article 4 and Regulation CC in handling any return of items. See *Farm Credit Services v. American State Bank,* 212 F. Supp. 2d 1034 (W.D. Iowa 2002). It is true that, to the extent the rules of Article 4 are inconsistent with those in Regulation CC, it is the regulation that governs. See, for example, Comment 4 to U.C.C. §4-214. Recall that the basic requirement under Article 4 of a payor bank that determines not to make final payment on a check is that the bank return the check to the presenting bank by the payor bank's midnight deadline. The presenting bank is then required to return the check to the bank from which it received it, and so on. Under the traditional way that returned checks were handled and under Article 4 as it is still written, return of an unpaid check anticipates that the check will physically retrace the steps of forward collection, only in reverse. In some, perhaps a majority, of instances, return by this means will also comply with the requirements of Regulation CC. If so, all to the good. But to the extent that this means of return does not satisfy the requirements of expeditious return and notice of dishonor of Regulation CC, the federal regulation governs and the payor bank is under an obligation to comply with its more stringent requirements.

The changes this aspect of Regulation CC have brought to the business of returning unpaid checks are quite significant. For one thing, Regulation

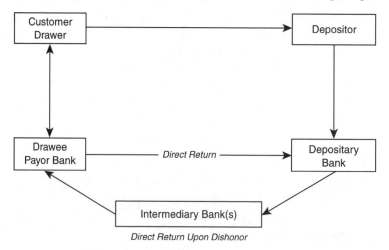

Direct Return Upon Dishonor

CC allows for, although it does not necessarily require, *direct return* of a dishonored item, with the payor bank returning any check that it determines not to honor directly to the depositary institution, with no intermediate stops along the way.

Regulation CC also contemplates that in some situations, the payor bank will return the dishonored check to the depositary bank not directly, but via a route of go-between banks, so-called *returning banks*, different from those through which the check initially passed during the forward collection process.

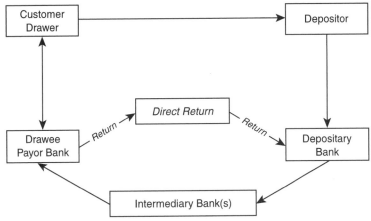

Return Upon Dishonor Through Returning Banks

The mechanism that the payor bank will employ to make return in this fashion is what Regulation CC refers to as the *qualified return check*. Under §229.2(bb) of Regulation CC, a qualified return check is

> a returned check that is prepared for automated return to the depositary bank by placing the check in a carrier envelope or placing a strip on the check and encoding the strip or envelope in magnetic ink.

You can find more detail on what is required for a check to be converted into a qualified return check as part of §299.30(a)(2)(iii). Once a check is converted into a qualified return check, with a new MICR line on the bottom or on a carrier envelope into which the check has been placed, it can be processed automatically through the machinery that banks already have on hand to handle the forward collection process. The return process can be accomplished with the speed and efficiency of the forward collection of checks.

Checking Out the Back of a Check

Before looking into the various obligations that Regulation CC imposes on a payor bank that decides to dishonor a check, it is interesting to look at one change Regulation CC forced in the way checks are handled; a simple enough matter, but one that makes all that follows possible. Prior to the introduction of Regulation CC, each bank in the collection chain would usually put some stamp, notation, or set of numbers on the back of any check that passed through its system. After the depositor had indorsed the back of the check, the depositary bank would then itself stamp or mark the back in some fashion, as would each succeeding collecting bank in turn. The result was that the back of any individual check, by the time it reached the payor bank, bore a mess — and I mean this quite literally — of colorful, overlapping, smeared-together, and difficult-if-not-impossible-to-read markings. Good perhaps as modern art, but not for administration of the check collection process. Even if at this stage the payor bank had for its own reasons *wanted* to get in touch with the depositary bank, there was no way the people at the payor bank could have told with any certainty just by looking at the check exactly *where* and at which bank it had been deposited. Any marking the depositary bank may have put on the back was by this time more than likely to have been rendered indecipherable by all the markings that had been piled on top of it. Below I reproduce for your consideration the back of one of my returned checks from the pre-Regulation CC era.

Given such a display, all the payor bank could be sure of, and this only by looking at its own records, was from which bank it had received the item. Thus, the best it could do by way of return was to send it back to the presenting bank from whence it had come. That bank, once it received the returned item, would have its own difficulty in trying to determine what bank had transferred the check to it. It was certainly not something that could be handled by machine or on other than an item-by-item basis. The back of the check could be consulted, but again it was unlikely that much could be gleaned from that source. Any collecting bank would have to do some digging into other records it had on hand (and now we see why it was given two days for processing by Article 4) to determine to what bank the check should next be returned.

Under §229.35(a) of Regulation CC, each bank that handles a check during forward collection "shall legibly indorse the check in accordance with the indorsement standard set forth in Appendix D to this part." It is doubtful that you will have the said Appendix D easily available to you, and I am not suggesting that you run out and find yourself a copy (unless you just happen to have a thing for the minutiae of the Code of Federal Regulations). What I can relate, however, is that Appendix D sets forth with precision the standards for who should stamp where on the back of any check. A certain portion of the back of the check, roughly the middle third, is intended for the use of the depositary bank and the depositary bank only. The space above is meant for the depositing customer to make his or her indorsement. The space below is where any intermediary bank is allowed to place its mark. In the middle, however, the depositary bank is directed to make its indorsement, which must contain that bank's unique nine-digit routing number set off by arrows pointing toward the number at each end, the bank's name and location, and the indorsement date. All this information is to be placed on the check by the depositary bank in the prescribed location and in dark purple or black ink. Many preprinted checks now come to the customer with the prescribed areas marked off on the back of the check. I know that mine do, even invoking in small print the Federal Reserve Board of Governors Reg. CC, as you can see by looking at the "Before" picture of the back of a check which I have more recently written as it appears on one of my more recent checks. Look at the example on the following page.

You can see for yourself what happened to this particular check, which I mailed off, presumably in some preaddressed envelope, to pay for my subscription to the *Wall Street Journal*. The *Journal* has in its very personal way indorsed the check for deposit, as you see on the far right. In the middle you can make out that it was deposited at a bank that goes by the name, or at least the initials, of FNBB located at 2 Morrissey Boulevard in Boston. Equally, if not more, important, that bank's routing number is given as ▶011000390◀. The other markings are relevant only in that they do not cover up or render illegible the information that allows us to identify the depositary bank. Had my bank decided to dishonor this check (say, because I had insufficient funds in my account, though I must assure you that it did not have to), my bank would have had available *from the check itself* all the information it needed about the identity and whereabouts of the depositary bank, which would have made it possible for it to follow the various dictates of Regulation CC, Subpart C, to which we now turn.*

---

* Notice that "a paying bank that is unable to identify the depositary bank with respect to a given item" will be given a special dispensation, under 12 C.F.R. §229.30(b), from the obligation of expeditious return. For a case in which the depositary bank was held partially responsible for a loss that ensued based on its failure to make its mark legibly in the designated place on the back of the check, see *USAA Investment Management Co. v. Federal Reserve Bank*, 906 F. Supp. 770, 28 U.C.C.2d 959 (D. Conn. 1995).

Expeditious Return

Regulation CC made three major changes to the check collection process. The first, the requirement of *expeditious return*, is found in 12 C.F.R. §229.30(a): "If a paying bank [the term used in Regulation CC for what Article 4 terms the *payor bank*] determines not to pay a check, it shall return the check in an expeditious manner as provided in either paragraphs (a)(1) or (a)(2) of this section." As we will see in the following examples, the paying bank will be able to establish that it has met its obligation of expeditious return by demonstrating that its handling of the check for return satisfies either the *two-day/four-day test* of §229.30(a)(1) or the *forward collection test* of §229.30(a)(2).

BEFORE

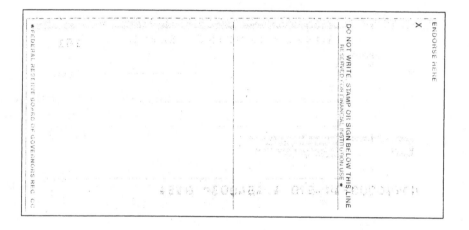

AFTER

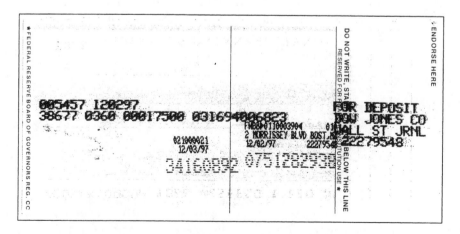

In many instances, a payor bank's return of a check in a manner that would avoid accountability for the amount of the item under Article 4 will, without anything more, also meet that bank's Regulation CC obligation of expeditious return. This will not always be true, however, and so the payor bank must make sure that it does what it must to meet *both* its Article 4 and its Regulation CC responsibilities. It is important to remember that the rules of Regulation CC supplement, rather than preempt, what we have already learned about how the payor bank must handle a check under Article 4. The significant difference in approach, which you will discern by reading the relevant portions of Regulation CC, is that the rules of Article 4 are written in terms of when the payor bank must *send* the check for return — that is, get the check off the bank's hands and route it on its way so that it will eventually arrive back at the depositary bank; Regulation CC is written in terms of what the payor bank must do to enable the depositary bank actually to *receive* the returned check in as expeditious a manner as possible. When the depositary bank receives the check in return, and is then on notice to withdraw any provisional credit it added to the depositor's account, is of course what really matters as far as that bank is concerned. Regulation CC is written to address this concern directly.

Notice of Dishonor

The second significant change wrought by Regulation CC on the process of check collection is found in 12 C.F.R. §229.33(a). If a payor bank determines to dishonor a check in the amount of $2,500 or greater, it must not only return the check in compliance with both Article 4's and Regulation CC's obligations of expeditious return, but must also send *notice of nonpayment* directly to the depositary bank, by a means and within a timeframe laid out in that subsection. If the payor bank decides to dishonor a larger item, it is under the obligation not only to return it in an expeditious manner but in addition to send the depositary bank advance notice that the check has been dishonored and is on its way back to the depositary bank. Again, Regulation CC is written with the needs of the depositary bank in mind; the quicker it learns that a deposited check is not going to convert to collected funds, the better position it is in to withdraw any provisional credit it has given and prevent the depositor from withdrawing or making use of what will turn out to be uncollectible funds.

Possible Extension of the Midnight Deadline

The third way in which Regulation CC alters the rules of check collection and return is found in 12 C.F.R. §229.30(c). In this one respect, Regulation CC does not merely supplement or give an alternate route for a payor bank that decides to dishonor a check to meet its obligations under Article 4; it may actually override what is perhaps the most basic requirement of Article 4 in some limited situations. Under §229.30(c), the crucial midnight deadline by which the payor bank need act if it is to avoid accountability on an item under Article 4 may be *extended* if the bank uses means of expeditious return that fit the bill under this subsection of Regulation CC. The regulation even provides that the midnight deadline may be "extended further if a paying bank uses a *highly expeditious* means of transportation." What exactly this means in practice is just the kind of thing we will explore in the examples.

Two final points before we turn to the examples. First of all, I want to make clear that it is not my purpose here to explore every possible nook and cranny of Regulation CC, Part C. Each and every detail is more than we need, and probably more than we could bear at this juncture. You should be aware, however, that if a particular term within those parts of the Regulation that we do need is unclear to you, or if you are just plain curious about how exactly it is to be read, §229.2 of Subpart A of Regulation CC provides us with the definitions of key terms — some 43 of them — as those terms as used in the Regulation. Finally, it is important to note the nature of the liability a bank may face if it fails to meet the requirements placed upon it by Subpart C of Regulation CC. Look at 12 C.F.R. §229.38(a). A bank can be held liable for its failure to exercise ordinary care or act in good faith in carrying out the dictates of Subpart B. The measure of damages for failure to exercise ordinary care is not the full amount of the item, but rather "the amount of the loss incurred, up to the amount of the check, reduced by the amount of the loss that party would have incurred even if the bank had exercised ordinary care." A bank cannot be held accountable for the full amount of a check simply because it failed to use ordinary care in carrying out its obligations under Subpart B of Regulation CC; it will be held responsible only for the amount of actual loss a party has suffered as a result of that failure.

EXAMPLES

1.   Able writes a check to Barker for $45,000, payable on Able's account with Big Apple Bank of New York City. This check is deposited by Barker in an account she has at a Manhattan branch of Gotham Bank on Monday. Both banks are members of the New York Clearing House Association. Gotham presents the check to Big Apple at a clearing held on Tuesday morning. On Tuesday afternoon, Big Apple determines not to pay the check, because Able has insufficient funds in his account. It returns the check to Gotham, following the clearing-house's rules, at a clearing held on Wednesday morning.

   (a) Has Big Apple avoided making final payment on the item under Article 4?

   (b) Has Big Apple complied with its obligation of expeditious return under §229.30(a) of Regulation CC?

(c) Has Big Apple met its notice obligation under §229.33(a) of Regulation CC?

2.   Able writes a second check to Charters for $15,000, payable on his account with Big Apple Bank of New York City. This check is deposited by Charters in an account he has at Greenlawn Bank, a bank located in the suburbs of New York. Greenlawn presents this check directly (along with others it has received written on Big Apple) by courier to Big Apple on a Tuesday morning. On Wednesday, Big Apple determines not to pay the check, again because of insufficient funds in Able's account. By Wednesday evening, Big Apple has put the check in an envelope correctly addressed to the Greenlawn bank and has deposited this envelope in the mail with correct postage.

(a) Has Big Apple avoided making final payment on the item under Article 4?

(b) Has Big Apple complied with its obligation of expeditious return under §229.30(a) of Regulation CC?

(c) What if, instead, Big Apple had on Wednesday sent this check directly to Greenlawn via an overnight courier service, paying for next-day morning delivery?

(d) Would your answer to part (c) of this example be any different if it turned out that the courier service, through some mix-up on its part, did not actually deliver the check to Greenlawn until Friday, rather than on Thursday morning as it had promised to do?

3.   The third check Able writes on his account with Big Apple is for $12,500. It is made payable to Drennan, who deposits it in the Bakersfield Bank of Bakersfield, California. The check is eventually presented to Big Apple Bank on a Wednesday. Big Apple determines not to honor the check.

(a) Would Big Apple be in compliance with Regulation CC if it simply mailed this check on Thursday evening to the Bakersfield Bank via first-class mail?

(b) What if it sent the check on Thursday evening to Bakersfield via a private delivery service that promised not next-day delivery, but delivery within two days of receipt?

4.   Able's fourth check is written on Big Apple Bank to Earl for $500. Earl deposits this check in the Burbank Bank of Burbank, California. This check is forwarded through customary banking channels and eventually comes into the possession of Gotham Bank of New York City, which presents it for payment to Big Apple on a Monday morning. By the time of its arrival at Big Apple, Able has issued a stop-payment order on the check, so Big Apple decides to dishonor the check. On Tuesday it delivers the check to the New York Fed with instructions that it be returned to the depositary bank in California.

(a) Has Big Apple complied with its obligation of expeditious return under Regulation CC by acting as it has? You may assume that Big

Apple would normally handle any check deposited with it and made payable on a California bank such as Burbank by forwarding such a check to the New York Fed for collection.

(b) Suppose that, prior to delivering the check over to the New York Fed for return, Big Apple had converted the check in question into a qualified return check. How would this affect your answer to the previous question?

5. Able keeps writing checks on his Big Apple account. This one is for $28,000 made payable to Friendly, who deposits it in her bank account at First National Bank of Fresno, in California. The check is presented to Big Apple on a Monday. By Tuesday Big Apple has decided, for whatever reason, not to pay the check. It converts the check into a qualified return check and delivers the check in this form to the New York Fed by Tuesday evening. Has Big Apple done all that is required of it to avoid potential liability for violation of Regulation CC? What more must it do?

6. Able writes one final check (at least as far as we need be concerned). It is made payable to Garber and is for $53,600. Garber deposits this check in an account he has at a Manhattan branch of Gotham Bank on a Monday morning. Gotham presents the check in question (as part of a parcel containing a large number of checks) directly to Able's branch of Big Apple on Tuesday. Big Apple does nothing with the check on Wednesday, but on Thursday morning discovers that Able's account is woefully overdrawn. A vice president of Big Apple hops in a taxi and makes her way to Garber's branch of Gotham Bank. There, at 3:58 p.m., she hands the check over to that branch's Director of Check Processing.

(a) Has Big Apple done all that is required of it to avoid any violation of Regulation CC?

(b) Gotham argues that Big Apple can be held accountable for the full amount of the check for failing to dishonor the check prior to its midnight deadline under Article 4. What response does Big Apple have to this assertion? See §229.30(c)(1) of Regulation CC. Is Big Apple's position hurt by the facts that this is the first time it has ever done anything like this (that is, having a vice president return a check directly to the depositary bank by means of a taxicab) and that it ordinarily uses much more conventional methods for return?

EXPLANATIONS

1a. Yes. Big Apple was presented with the check on Tuesday. Under U.C.C. §4-301(a), it had until its midnight deadline, in this case midnight on Wednesday, to return the item and revoke the provisional settlement it would have given to Gotham on the day of presentment. It returned the check on Wednesday morning. See §4-301(d)(1).

1b. Yes. Big Apple is required by 12 C.F.R. §229.30(a) to "return the check in an expeditious manner as provided in either paragraphs (a)(1) or (a)(2) of this section." Big Apple could demonstrate that it met this responsibility by invoking either of the two tests. Under the two-day/four-day test of (a)(1), it would have to show that it "sen[t] the return check in a manner such that [the check] would normally be received by the depositary bank not later than 4:00 p.m. (local time of the depositary bank) of . . . the second business day following the banking day on which the check was presented for payment," as this check was deposited in a local bank. (As to what constitutes a *local* bank, see the definition in §229.2(s), followed up by §229.2(m).) In the case before us, because both banks are members of the New York Clearing House, it would seem no problem for Big Apple to assert that having received the check from Gotham on a Tuesday and returning the check to that bank on the following day would "normally" assure that Gotham received it back prior to 4:00 on Thursday. In fact, if the clearing-house rules allowed, Big Apple could have returned the check on a clearing on Thursday and still have met this test, if the clearing were held prior to 4:00 in the afternoon.

1c. This check is for an amount of $2,500 or more. Big Apple, as a payor bank that has determined not to pay the check, is thus obligated to provide notice of its nonpayment such that the notice is received by 4:00 p.m. (local time) of the second business day following the banking day on which the check was presented. (As to the distinction between a *banking day* and a *business day*, as those terms are used in Regulations CC, consult 12 C.F.R. §229.2(f) and (g).) So Big Apple had to give notice of its nonpayment to Gotham prior to 4:00 p.m. on Thursday.

You will have noticed two differences in the payor bank's notice obligation as opposed to its obligation of expeditious return. First of all, there is no difference in the time limit imposed on the payor bank for giving the requisite notice depending on whether the bank is a local or a nonlocal bank. Notice of the type that Regulation CC requires when larger checks are returned can as easily be made across the country as across town, so the deadline for notice is 4:00 p.m. on the second business day following presentment regardless of where the depositary bank is situated. Secondly, the two different tests relating to the payor bank's actual return of a check it has determined not to pay are written in terms of actions that would result in the returned check's "normally being received" by the depositary bank by such-and-such a time (in the two-day/four-day test), or a manner in which a similarly situated bank would "normally handle" such an item for forward collection (in the forward collection test). The obligation to provide notice of return of a larger check is not set out in terms of what a bank must do that would "normally" get the notice to the depositary bank in a timely fashion. It is an absolute obligation to provide the notice in a timely fashion. Look over §229.33(b) and (c) on what information the notice must contain and on the *depositary bank's* obligation to accept such notice.

The question remains: Has Big Apple given the requisite notice in the situation we have before us? Look to the concluding language of §229.33(a):

> Notice may be provided by any reasonable means, including the returned check, a writing (including a copy of the returned check), telephone, Fedwire [a telecommunications system run by the Federal Reserve System], telex, or other form of telegraph.

Big Apple actually physically returned the check to Gotham prior to 4:00 p.m. on Thursday, so the return also functioned as the proper notice, assuming that the returned check was accompanied by all the information required by §229.33(b).

2a. Yes. Big Apple was presented with the check on Tuesday morning. Under §4-301(d)(2), it returned the check for Article 4 purposes when it "sent" the check back to Greenlawn on Wednesday evening. Because this action was taken prior to its midnight deadline, Big Apple has avoided final payment and any accountability on the item under Article 4.

2b. It is doubtful that Big Apple has accomplished expeditious return by mailing off the check by first-class mail. Big Apple will want to claim that its actions comply with the two-day/four-day test of 12 C.F.R. §229.31(a)(1), but do you think that an envelope deposited in the mail in New York City on a Wednesday night would "normally be received" by an addressee in the suburbs by 4:00 p.m. on Thursday? (I am assuming, of course, that Greenlawn would be a local bank with respect to Big Apple.) I don't want to seem unduly cynical, but I don't think so myself. At least, that has not been my experience with the postal system, whatever other fine things I may have to say about the institution.

Big Apple would also have the opportunity to show that it met its obligation of expeditious return by compliance with the forward collection test of §229.31(a)(2), but again I think it would have difficulty. Would a "similarly situated bank" in New York City *normally* handle a single check for this amount, drawn on a suburban bank, by sending it off by mail to that bank? I don't see that as likely. The forward collection test, as we will see in Example 4b, is meant to and does come into play more when the check is converted into that interesting item, the "qualified return check" and thereafter sent back to the depositary bank through normal banking channels.

By acting as it has, Big Apple does not stand in a good position to successfully claim, should it later become necessary, that it met its obligation of expeditious return under Regulation CC. Remember, however, that this failure will not normally make it liable for the full amount of the check, but only for any actual loss caused by the tardiness of the return. It may well be that no damage was done by the fact that this check was not returned in an expeditious manner. At least Big Apple can hope that this is the case.

2c. Had Big Apple sent the check off on Wednesday evening in this manner, it would have fulfilled its obligation of expeditious return by meeting the two-day/four-day test. The overnight courier service would normally be expected to get the check to Greenlawn by 4 p.m. on Thursday. Use by Big Apple of this (admittedly more expensive) method of return has saved the day.

2d. The answer should not change just because in this unusual instance the overnight delivery service didn't function as it is expected to and usually does. Note once again that the language of the two-day/four-day test speaks in terms of the returning bank's use of a means of return such that the check would "normally" be received by the local bank by 4 p.m. of the second business day following the banking day on which the check was presented to the payor bank. The fact that in a particular instance the means selected, which would normally suffice, fails in that one instance to get the returned check to the depositary bank by this deadline, does not prevent the returning bank from relying upon its compliance with the two-day/four-day test to establish expeditious return.

3a. First we look at the duty of expeditious return. Now we apply the four-day part of the two-day/four-day test of 12 C.F.R. §229.31(a)(1). Would a first-class letter deposited in the post in New York City on a Thursday evening normally be received by an addressee in Bakersfield, California, no later than 4:00 p.m. on the following Tuesday? (This is assuming that we haven't run into any of the holidays not counted as a business day under §229.2(g).) There is obviously no bright-line answer to this question. My tendency is to say that Big Apple would have met the test, or am I now giving the post office more credit than it is due?

We also have to look at Big Apple's obligation under the notice requirement of §229.33. Unless that bank has taken some action of which we are not aware, it has apparently *not* lived up to the standards imposed upon it by that part of Regulation CC. Because this check is for more than $2,500, Big Apple is required to give the Bakersfield Bank, as the depositary institution, notice of the fact that the check is being dishonored by 4:00 p.m. California time on Friday, the second business day after which Big Apple was presented with the check. So Big Apple appears to be vulnerable on this score.

3b. Big Apple's handing the returned check over on Thursday to the delivery service for two-day delivery would fulfill its obligation of expeditious return, as this would normally result in the check being returned to the depositary bank in California no later than Monday. This would still not, however, put the bank in compliance with the notice requirement of 12 C.F.R. §229.33(a). Big Apple cannot count on return of the check to fulfill the notice requirement, as return would not come by Friday at 4:00 p.m. Big Apple, because of the size of the check, will have to use some other means — such as a telephone call, a telex, or a fax — to give the requisite notice to Bakersfield by 4:00 p.m. on Friday California time.

4a. No. Big Apple will not be able to rely on the two-day/four-day test of 12 C.F.R. §229.31(a)(1) to build a case for expeditious return. It was presented with the check on a Monday morning. It puts this check into the hands of the New York Fed on Tuesday. Would this normally result in the check coming into possession of the California bank by Thursday at 4:00 p.m.? The answer really has to be no. It is going to take the New York Fed at least a day and perhaps two to turn this item around, and then send it across the country. There is no reason to believe that it will then send the check directly to the Bakersfield Bank. More likely, the New York Fed would send it on to the Los Angeles Fed. That bank will in turn then have to take a day or two to determine where the check should go next, and even if the Los Angeles Fed is in a position to deliver it directly to Bakersfield, by this time the week is almost surely drawing to a close.

The problem here is not that Big Apple Bank started the return by delivering the check to the New York Federal Reserve Bank rather than the exact bank by which it had been presented the check, the Gotham Bank. The real cause of the delay, beyond what might otherwise be accomplished through ordinary banking channels, is that on each step of the return process the check must be handled, sorted, and sent on its way again on an item-by-item basis and with the aid of human intervention rather than by purely automated means. Recall that any check deposited in a bank and then sent on its way in the forward collection process can be sped along from bank to bank because of the MICR line on the bottom of the check, which makes possible the automated reading, sorting, and handling of the item. The ability to handle the item through this technology allows the turnaround time at any of the collecting banks along the way to be kept relatively brief. The MICR line on any check, however, does not — indeed it cannot — contain any information about the bank into which the check is ultimately deposited. Thus, any check that is returned usually has to be dealt with at any given returning bank by real live people, who individually examine the back of the check and the bank's own records to figure out where the check has come from and where it should next be sent so that it will eventually arrive at its proper destination, the depositary bank. This traditional means of return is by all accounts a tedious, expensive (relative to automated handling), and sluggish process. Therefore, a check that is returned in this manner with the goal of getting it across the country and into the hands of the depositary bank is almost assuredly going to take more than four days to make its way to its intended destination.

Can Big Apple rely instead on its compliance with the forward collection test of §229.31? No, not if all it did was send the check to the New York Fed with instructions that it eventually be returned to a particular bank in Bakersfield, California. Although Big Apple or a similarly situated New York City bank might normally handle a check for an amount such as this by delivering it over to the New York Fed for forward collection, there is a big difference here. As we've just noted, any check that it would deliver for forward collection would be encoded with the routing number of the payor bank on the MICR line, and therefore would be presented to the New York Fed all ripe and ready for automated processing. The check that Big Apple delivered to the New York Fed for return in this part of the example is still in its "raw" state. There is no way it can be handled in an automated fashion to get it to the Bakersfield Bank in as little time as possible. It will be much slower going than any check Big Apple sent for forward collection along this route. Big Apple has not met its duty of expeditious return as judged by either the two-day/four-day test or the forward collection test.

4b. Because the check in question has been converted into a qualified return check, it now bears a new MICR line, one that points the check directly to the *depositary* institution. Big Apple can now introduce that check into customary banking channels as it would a check destined for forward collection, here by sending the check to Big Apple's local Federal Reserve Bank. The check will be handled and sorted automatically and will make its way to the Bakersfield Bank efficiently and quickly. Thus, Big Apple would probably be found to have met its duty of expeditious return.

The concept of the qualified return check was first added to the system by the introduction of Regulation CC in the late 1980s. Prior to that, all returns were done by hand and the extra time that this process entailed was one of the principal justifications given by banks for placing those long blanket holds on all deposits. With the new possibility of converting checks destined for return into qualified return checks, and thus avoiding the laborious and time-consuming hand return procedures, the process of return was dramatically altered. Initially, not all banks had the technology required to do the actual conversion of a check into a qualified return check. Today, most large banks, and probably most banks in general, have the necessary machinery. What if, we can still ask, the payor bank does not have the means available to transform a check it wants to dishonor into a qualified return check? That bank is allowed to deliver the check to another bank that *does* have the necessary technology, on the agreement that the transferee bank will make the conversion and then send the check on its way. Note the language toward the end of §229.31(a), following the description of the qualified return check:

> The time for expeditious return under the forward collection test, and the deadline for return under the UCC and Regulation J [with which you need not be concerned], are extended by one business day if the returning bank converts a returned check to a qualified returned check. This extension does not apply to the two-day/four-day test specified in paragraph (a)(1) of this section or when a returning bank is returning a check directly to the depositary bank.

5. Big Apple has met its obligation of expeditious return, but it still has to be concerned about its duty to give notice of nonpayment under 12 C.F.R.

§229.33(b), as this is a check for an amount greater than $2,500. It must provide that notice to the First National Bank of Fresno such that the notice is received by that bank no later than 4:00 p.m. (Fresno time) on Wednesday. The qualified return check may be speeding its way through a series of returning banks, but it still seems highly unlikely that the check itself will arrive in Fresno in time to satisfy the notice requirement. Big Apple will have to make a phone call, or send off a fax or a telex, to the Fresno bank, with all the information required by §229.33(b).

6a. It seems so. It has made expeditious return of a local check by satisfying the two-day test. True, it doesn't usually return checks by taxi, but that is not the test. Use of the cab on the second day following the day of presentment, at least if the vice president took the cab early enough in the afternoon, certainly seems to be a manner of return "such that the check would normally be received" by 4:00 p.m. on that day. Even in New York City traffic. As this is a check for a large amount, Big Apple also has to worry about whether it has satisfied its obligation of notice for nonpayment. Because it was able to return the actual check to the depositary bank prior to 4:00 p.m. on Thursday — if just barely — it has complied with this aspect of Regulation CC as well.

6b. Gotham's argument is that even if Big Apple has complied with Regulation CC, it is obligated for the full amount of the check for its failure to dishonor the check prior to its midnight deadline, which would have passed at the end of the day on Wednesday. Regulation CC, however, provides in §229.30(c) for an *extension of the midnight deadline* in certain circumstances.

> The deadline for return . . . under the U.C.C. . . . is extended to the time of dispatch of such return . . . where a paying bank uses a means of delivery that would ordinarily result in receipt by the bank to which it is sent (1) On or before the receiving bank's next banking day following the otherwise applicable deadline. . . .

Were it not for this portion of Regulation CC, Big Apple's deadline for return would indeed have been midnight on Wednesday. But all it would have had to do to satisfy that deadline would have been to *dispatch* the check back to Gotham by that time. Under the just-quoted portion of Regulation CC, this deadline is extended to the time of dispatch, whenever that may be, because Big Apple used "a means of delivery that would ordinarily result" in *receipt* by Gotham no later than the end of the "next banking day following the otherwise applicable deadline"; that is, by the end of Wednesday. Again, whatever may be true of New York City traffic, Big Apple's use of this atypical but effective and expeditious method of getting the returned check actually into the hands of the depositary bank fits within the criteria of 12 C.F.R. §229.30(c)(1). That being so, Regulation CC supersedes or alters the strict midnight deadline rule of Article 4. Big Apple has met its extended midnight deadline obligation and cannot be held accountable for the amount of the item.

Gotham may want argue that the extension given to a returning bank under §229.30(c)(1) should be available only to a bank that *ordinarily or normally* uses the particular means of expeditious return involved, and not when the extraordinary means are relied upon in only one particular instance. (After all, Big Apple does not usually return local checks via taxi; it did so in this case only to avoid a potential large liability.) This argument was tried and found wanting in *First National Bank v. Standard Bank & Trust*, 172 F.3d 472, 38 U.C.C.2d 1 (7th Cir. 1999), the case on which this example is loosely based. On a Friday, First National presented checks, totaling just shy of $4 million, to the bank on which they were drawn, Standard. Standard was still holding the checks on Tuesday morning. That afternoon it attempted to dishonor the checks, following what would otherwise have been the passage of its midnight deadline at the end of Monday. Three of its bank officers "dashed off" to First National's Operations Processing Center and were able to deliver the checks there at 3:58 p.m. First National argued that Standard was accountable for the amount of the checks under Article 4 because it failed to return them by its midnight deadline. Standard claimed that it was entitled to rely on the extension of the Article 4 midnight deadline created by §229.30(c)(1) of Regulation CC. First National argued that the extension did not cover Standard's actions, as the extension was intended by the writers of Regulation CC to apply only to banks that "regularly" use courier services or other exceptionally fast means of delivery to return checks. The Seventh Circuit rejected this argument, holding that a reading of §229.30(c)(1) on its face demonstrates that the extension provided "may apply to one-time single check transactions." For another interesting case Seventh Circuit involving the applicability of §229.30(c)(1), the result of which ended up resting on the correct reading of the term "banking day" as used in that provision, see *Oak Brook Bank v. Northern Trust Company*, 256 F.3d 638, 44 U.C.C.2d 1082 (7th Cir. 2001).

In our example and in the *First National Bank* case, the payor bank was saved from liability under Article 4 by extension of its midnight deadline by only a single day, thanks to the initial language of §233.30(c)(1). If you read further into this paragraph you find that:

> [T]his deadline is extended *further* if a paying bank uses a *highly* expeditious means of transportation, even if this means of transportation would ordinarily result in delivery after the receiving bank's next banking day.

This particular bit of Regulation CC is indeed unclear. Apparently a payor bank could invoke it to avoid accountability under Article 4 even if its attempt to return the check was more than just one day past its midnight deadline. How much "further" could or should the otherwise applicable deadline be extended? What would constitute a "highly expeditious" and not merely an "expeditious" means of transportation for getting the check back into the hands of the depositary bank? As far as I am aware, no court has yet been called upon to tackle these questions.

PART FOUR

The Bank-Customer Relationship

13

The Duty to Pay and Wrongful Dishonor

Introduction

The relationship between a bank and its checking account customer is that of contract. By the customer's applying to open an account and the bank's accepting the customer's application, the two parties have entered into an agreement. What are the terms of that agreement? They are found in whatever documents passed between the parties at the time of agreement: in this case, the application form, any informational literature the bank gave to the customer, the signature card that the bank asked the customer to sign, and so forth. For most consumer customers, the terms of the contract are usually offered on pretty much a take-it-or-leave-it basis. Larger commercial entities may be in a position actually to negotiate some of the terms of the contract. Section 4-103(a) specifically provides that, subject to certain limitations, "[t]he effect of the provisions of this Article may be varied by agreement."

This agreement between the customer and the bank is governed by the basic principles of contract law. In addition, of course, the rules laid down by Article 4, as well as those arising from clearing-house rules and federal regulations such as Regulation CC (see §4-103(b)), govern the relationship. In this chapter we examine the provisions of Article 4 regarding the bank's obligation to its customer to handle any check written on the account (or at least purportedly written on the account), upon presentment in accordance with the bank's contractual obligations. Look first at §4-401(a):

> A bank may charge against the account of a customer an item that is properly payable from the account even though the charge creates an overdraft. An item is properly payable if it is authorized by the customer and is in accordance with any agreement between the customer and the bank.

227

The key here is obviously the term *properly payable*. When a properly payable check is presented to the payor bank, §4-401(a) provides that the bank "may" pay the check. The bank will then be entitled to deduct the amount of the check from the balance in the customer's account. On first reading, this might suggest that it is within the payor bank's discretion whether to pay a check, even when that check is properly payable. Look, however, at §4-402(a):

> Except as otherwise provided in this Article, a payor bank wrongfully dishonors an item if it dishonors an item that is properly payable, but a bank may dishonor an item that would create an overdraft unless it has agreed to pay the overdraft.

So, if an item is properly payable the bank is *required* to honor it. If a bank wrongfully dishonors an item, it can be held liable, under §4-402(b), which we will explore more fully in the examples, for damages proximately caused by the wrongful dishonor.

What if a payor bank is presented with a check that is, for one reason or another, *not* properly payable? Although §4-401(a) does not lay out the consequences as clearly as we might wish, the rule is clear: The bank will then have no right to charge such a payment against the customer's account. Section 4-401(a) gives the bank the right to charge against an account *only* properly payable items. If the bank does pay the check and deducts its amount from the customer's account, it can be made to recredit the account when the fact of its payment of the not-properly-payable item has been established. The payor bank will then be left to bear the loss of its payment on an item that was not properly payable. Whether it will be able to pass that loss on to another party, and if so how, are matters that we will consider in Part Five. In this chapter we focus on a set of preliminary questions: When *must* a bank pay a customer's check? In what instances *may* it pay the check and charge the customer's account even if it is not obligated to do so? When is the bank *precluded* from charging against a customer's account a check that it has paid?

EXAMPLES

1.   Andrew has a regular checking account with the Paley National Bank. He writes a check for $400 payable to one Bette. Bette signs the back of the check and deposits it in her own bank account. The check is presented to Paley. At the time of presentment, Andrew has more than $1,000 in his account. He has not issued any stop-payment order on the check.
   (a) May Paley honor this check? Must it do so?
   (b) How would you answer the preceding questions if, at the time Paley is presented with the check, Andrew's account contained only $156 in available funds?

2.   Andrew hires one Thad to do some redecorating in his apartment. When he is left alone in Andrew's den, Thad (who turns out to be not just a decorator but also a thief) finds Andrew's checkbook in a desk drawer. Thad takes one of the checks from the book. He writes out a check to a confederate, Theo, forging Andrew's signature on the drawer line. Theo signs his own name on the back of the check and deposits it in his bank. The check is presented to Paley National Bank. May Paley pay this check and deduct its amount from Andrew's account?

3.   Andrew himself writes a check payable to the order of Clara and delivers it to her. Thelma (another thief) steals Clara's wallet, which contains the check. Thelma forges Clara's signature to the back of the check and deposits the check in Thelma's own bank account. When this check is presented to Paley National Bank, may that bank pay it and deduct its amount from Andrew's account?

4.   The DotCom Corporation also has a checking account with Paley National Bank. As part of its contract with that bank, Paley has agreed that it will not honor any check written on the DotCom account for more than $50,000 unless the check bears the signatures of both the president and the treasurer of the corporation. The president writes out and signs a check for $74,510. She does not get the signature of the company's treasurer on the check, but delivers it directly to the payee. When this check is presented to Paley, may the bank honor it and deduct its amount from the DotCom account?

5.   For many years the married couple of Xavier and Yolanda Zendel have had a joint checking account with Paley National Bank. Either is authorized to sign a check payable from the account on his or her own without the signature of the other. Unfortunately, in the early part of 2004, the couple come to the conclusion that they have irreconcilable differences, and they separate. In March of that year, Yolanda writes a check from the account for $12,000 to pay for a used car for herself. When this check is presented to Paley, the Zendels' account has only $10,500 in it. A decision is made at the bank, given the couple's long history of good relations with the bank, to pay the check even though it will result in an overdraft of $1,500 with respect to the account.

   (a) Was Paley within its rights to honor the check?
   (b) Is Xavier liable to pay toward reducing and eventually eliminating the overdraft? See §4-401(b).

6.   Darla is another of Paley's checking account customers. On March 13, 2004, she writes a check payable to Ethan for $3,500. The date she writes on the check is "September 1, 2004." She hands the check over to Ethan with the understanding that he will not attempt to cash or collect on the check until the September date. Ethan immediately deposits the check in his own account, and it is presented to Paley on March 17, 2004. Paley pays the check and deducts the $3,500 from Darla's account. Was it within its rights to do so? See §4-401(c) and Comment 3 to that section.

7.   Frederick, another of Paley's customers, writes a check out of his account for $2,435. The check is presented to Paley on Monday morning. On Monday evening, Paley determines that Frederick's account contains only $1,500 in available funds, and that hence it will dishonor the check. It returns the check to the presenting bank on Tuesday morning. As it turns out, by Tuesday afternoon Frederick has deposited another $1,000 in cash into his account. He argues that had the bank waited until later on Tuesday, there would have been no need for it to dishonor this check and that in addition, had the new funds not come into his account, the bank would still have been able to return the check prior to its midnight deadline at the end of Tuesday. Did Paley wrongfully dishonor the check by returning it on Tuesday morning? See §4-402(c) and Comment 4 to that section.

8.   Frederick writes several other checks on his account with Paley. On a Thursday morning, three checks, in the amounts of $1,000, $500, and $400, are simultaneously presented to the bank. Frederick has $1,234 in his account. Paley determines to honor the $1,000 check and then to dishonor both the $500 and the $400 checks. It returns these two checks with an indication that they have been dishonored because of insufficient funds in the drawer's account. It also charges Frederick a fee (as set forth in the agreement he signed to open his account) of $25 for each of the two checks returned. Frederick argues that it was much more important to him that the two smaller checks be honored than that the $1,000 one be paid. In addition, he points out, by dealing with the three checks as it has, Paley has been able to extract from him $50 in fees for having to return two checks. Had it paid those two checks and dishonored the one larger one, he could have been charged only one $25 fee. Was Paley wrong to deal with the checks as it did? See §4-303(b) and Comment 7 to that section.

9.   Geraldine writes a check to Hal out of her account with Paley National Bank on February 1, 2004, writing that date on the check in the space provided. She immediately mails this check to Hal, who receives it on February 5. This check gets lost among all of the papers, news clippings, photographs, and other junk piled high on Hal's exceptionally messy desk. He comes upon it again around Thanksgiving of that year. He signs the back of the check and deposits it in his own account. The check is presented to Paley on December 1, 2004.

   (a) If Paley dishonors the check, would it be guilty of a wrongful dishonor? See §4-404.

   (b) If Paley does honor the check, will Geraldine have any argument that it was not a properly payable item and that its amount cannot be charged to her account?

10.   On May 11, Paley National Bank is presented with a check written by one of its customers, Isaac, on his account with the bank. Paley pays the check. As it turns out, Isaac (after a long and fruitful life) has died (peacefully

in his sleep) on May 9. When it paid the check in question, Paley had not yet been informed of Isaac's death.

    (a) Was Paley within its rights in paying the check? See §4-405(a).

    (b) Suppose instead that Paley had become aware of Isaac's death on May 10. Would it then have been under an absolute obligation to dishonor the check? See §4-405(b) and Comment 2 to this section.

11. Cosmo Graphics runs a small business enterprise that he has incorporated (with himself as president, naturally) under the name of Graphics Surprise, Incorporated. He opens a checking account in the name of the corporation with Paley National Bank. He also signs a lease in the name of the corporation for office space in a building owned and operated by Cubicle Realty Associates. A monthly rental check, which Cosmo writes out of the corporate account, is sent to Cubicle Realty, which deposits the check in its own bank account. The check is presented to Paley, but Paley, because of a computer error at the branch that handles the Graphics Surprise account, dishonors the check even though there is more than enough money in the corporation's account to cover it.

    (a) Would Cubicle Realty, as payee of the check, have any cause of action for wrongful dishonor of the check under §4-402(b)?

    (b) Would Cosmo Graphics personally have such a cause of action?

12. Graphics writes a second check on the corporate account, this one to Woodchip Industries, a major supplier of high-quality paper and other products to the graphics industry. Woodchip has for several years been willing to sell to Graphics Surprise on a credit basis, delivering goods as ordered on the understanding that they would be paid for within 60 days of delivery. The check that Graphics sends to Woodchip is intended to pay for some supplies delivered in the prior month. Again, due to a mix-up at Paley National Bank, this check is wrongfully dishonored and is returned to Woodchip unpaid. A representative of Woodchip calls up Graphics and complains to him about what has happened. She explains that it is her company's policy, once it has received "a bum check" from any of its customers, not to make any further deliveries except in exchange for a certified or cashier's check for the full price of any supplies delivered. An order that Woodchip has just received from Graphics Surprise will not be processed except on that basis. Graphics says that he doesn't know what has gone wrong, but he will look into it. In the meantime, he is under time pressure to get the needed supplies so as to fulfill commitments to his own customers, but he does not have the cash available to pay up-front for all that is needed. He is able to buy on credit from another supplier what he needs, but only at a significantly higher price than he would have had to pay Woodchip for the same stuff.

    (a) When it eventually becomes clear what has happened, can Graphics Surprise, Inc. hold the Paley bank liable for the increased cost of supplies due to the bank's wrongful dishonor of the check?

(b) Assume further that, because of the delay caused by the mix-up, Graphics Surprise is slightly late in delivering its own work to a number of its own customers. In an effort to placate these customers and to safeguard good customer relations, Graphics agrees to a 10 percent reduction in what is owed on each of these jobs. Is the amount that Graphics Surprise loses because of this decision also recoverable from Paley?

13. Arnold Moneybucks is a prominent businessperson in the community. He has a checking account with Paley National Bank. Because of a mix-up at the bank, a number of checks that Arnold wrote in connection with a variety of business matters are all dishonored, even though he has more than enough in his account to cover every one of them. Arnold starts getting a series of phone calls asking him what has happened and suggesting that perhaps his business empire, which has seemed so impressive up to this point, is beginning to collapse. Arnold makes an angry call to his personal account manager at Paley. She quickly discovers the bank's error and apologizes profusely. She offers to and does contact individually each of the persons who have received return of a check written by Arnold and explains the situation to them. She assures each that Arnold's financial situation has never been stronger and that the return of the checks was due solely to a mistake on the bank's part. Each of the checks is redeposited by its recipient and is paid by Paley with no trouble. Arnold contacts you (a licensed lawyer) for advice. He would like to sue Paley for its several instances of wrongful dishonor of his checks. He argues that the whole incident has caused him great mental anguish and that in addition it has been very embarrassing to him, casting doubt within the local business community on his creditworthiness and reputation. He even thinks that punitive damages may be in order. How do you advise Arnold?

EXPLANATIONS

1a. *May* Paley honor this check? Yes, under §4-401(a). There is absolutely nothing here to suggest that this is other than a properly payable item. *Must* it do so? Yes again, now under §4-402(a). Were it not to honor the check, Paley would be responsible for its wrongful dishonor. I grant you that the situation given and the questions presented here are about as easy as they come. What is significant — other than the pleasure of getting a real easy question every now and then — is that checks just like this one account for more than 99 percent of all checks presented to any given payor bank. The bank's computerized processing machines read all the necessary information from the MICR line, verify that there are sufficient funds in the account, and make sure that no stop-payment order or other special instruction has been received by the bank with respect to either the account or this particular check. If nothing rings a warning bell, which will be true for the overwhelming majority of checks presented, the check is paid and the customer's account charged its amount without any human intervention. The check collection system (which, remember, processes something like 65 billion or more checks a year in this country) would not be able to operate, or at least not as efficiently and without greatly increased cost to the customer, if this were not so.

1b. Under §4-401(a), Paley may if it so chooses pay the check and charge it to Andrew's account "even though the charge creates an overdraft." So Paley *may* honor the check. See, for example, *McGuire v. Bank One, Louisiana, N.A.*, 744 S.2d 714, 42 U.C.C.2d 804 (Fla. App. 1999), where the payor bank was held to have done no wrong by paying a properly payable check for $20,000 (and charging a $22 overdraft fee) when its payment created an overdraft of $188,198.79 in Ms. Lottie M. McGuire's personal account. Ms. McGuire had written the check to one Timothy P. Looney who, representing himself as an investment broker, promised he would arrange for the proceeds of the check to be used to purchase a large amount of bonds on McGuire's behalf. McGuire then arranged for the $200,000 to be transferred into her checking account from a second investment account she had with the Bank One. When Looney, who unfortunately turned out to be a con man, presented the check to the bank the transfer had not yet been made and there was nowhere near this amount available in the checking account on which it was drawn. Still, the bank paid the check even though it created this large overdraft. Looney, needless to say, absconded with the money. For the record, he was later caught and sentenced to serve time in a federal penitentiary, but McGuire was still out all this money. She tried to recover it from Bank One on the theory that it should not have honored this check when doing so created an overdraft, or at least one this large. As the court concluded, "It is unfortunate that McGuire was the victim of fraud. However, her loss is not one for which Bank One can be found liable under the circumstances of the case."

On the second question of our example, whether the Paley Bank is obligated to pay Andrew's check if doing so would create an overdraft, the answer is clearly no, unless part of its contract with Andrew provides him with overdraft privileges. See the concluding language to §4-402(a).

2. No. This is not a properly payable item under §4-401(a). It has not been "authorized by the customer." Note the statement in Comment 1 to this section that "[a]n item containing a forged drawer's signature or forged indorsement is not properly payable." In this case we have a forged drawer's signature, and the check therefore is not properly payable.

3. No. Here we have a forged indorsement, which means that the item is not properly payable. Andrew, in writing out this check, authorized its payment only to Clara or to some other party who later qualifies as a "person entitled to enforce" the check, as defined in §3-301. Because of the forged indorsement, Thelma is not a person entitled to enforce the check, and so the check is not properly payable to her.

For our present purposes, it is sufficient to see that in both this example and in Example 2, the Paley bank will be required to recredit Andrew's account for the amount of any check it charged to the account that turns out, because of forgery, to be a not-properly-payable item. This leaves Paley bearing the loss unless it can assert a right on its own account against another party, claiming that the other party should pay Paley all or part of the loss it has suffered. In Part Five, we will pick up the story of how losses resulting from forgery and other mischief with respect to checks may be shifted from one party to another under various theories of liability. The conclusion here is only the beginning of the analysis: A check that bears a forged drawer's signature or a forged indorsement is not properly payable and cannot be charged to the customer's account.

4.   No. This check is not properly payable, not because of any forgery but because it is not, in the words of §4-401(a), "in accordance with any agreement between the customer and the bank." Paley's computers should have been programmed to screen for any check written against the DotCom account for an amount in excess of $50,000 (again, something that can be read from the MICR line and hence dealt with on an automated basis) and to pull that check out of the stream of checks being dealt with in the customary automated fashion. The check would have to be examined by a real live human, who could then make sure that the two signatures required were present on the check. If the bank had done what it committed itself to do, this check would not have been paid. The check is not properly payable and its amount cannot be charged against the DotCom account.

Not all special agreements as to what is and what is not a properly payable item necessarily work in the customer's favor. In *Spears Insurance Co., Ltd. v. Bank of America, N.A.I.*, 2000 U.S. Dist. LEXIS 961, 40 U.C.C.2d 807 (N.D. Ill. 2000), the corporate customer authorized the bank to pay out of its account in accordance with a resolution passed by the corporation's board, a certified copy of which was delivered to the bank. The resolution provided in relevant part:

> [T]he bank is authorized and directed to honor checks, drafts or other orders for the payment of money drawn in this Organization's name . . . when bearing or purporting to bear the facsimile signature(s) of any 1 of the following persons and for amounts over $100,000 require 2 signatures one of which must be manual and of the following: [listing the titles of corporate officers entitled to sign] regardless of by whom or by what means the facsimile signature(s) may have been affixed to such checks, drafts or other orders, if such facsimile signature(s) resemble(s) the facsimile specimens duly filed with the Bank by the Secretary or other officer, agent or partner of this Organization.

The bank had been furnished with the information that Ronald N. Woodward was the Chief Financial Officer and Treasurer of the corporation — one of the officers whose facsimile signature could authorize a check — and with a specimen of his facsimile signature. For reasons that are unclear Woodward was ousted from office, but the bank was never officially informed of that fact. A series of checks, all well under $100,000 and bearing what was undisputedly a facsimile of Woodward's signature closely resembling that on file at the bank, were presented to and paid by the bank. The corporation claimed that the checks in question were counterfeit and hence not properly payable. The court concluded that the bank was within its rights to consider the checks properly payable under the terms of the agreement between the corporate customer and the bank. The resolution was held to be a valid variation of the terms of Article 4 under §4-103(a), because the standard to which it held the bank was not "manifestly unreasonable." Such "facsimile signature agreements" are in fact not uncommon for larger corporate clients, whose smaller checks are signed not manually but through the use of a check writing machine, and (as the court pointed out) such agreements have been accepted as reasonable and enforceable in a number of prior cases. Another recent case that came to the same conclusion is *Arkwright Mutual Ins. Co. v. Nationsbank, N.A. (South)*, 212 F.3d 1224, 41 U.C.C.2d (11th Cir. 2000).

5a. Yes. Yolanda may, by her signature alone, authorize the bank to pay on a check. Under §4-401(a), as we know, the bank is allowed to accept the check and charge the account on which it is drawn even if the charge results in an overdraft.

5b. Under §4-401(b), Xavier would not be liable for the amount of the overdraft if he "neither signed the item [which he did not] nor benefited from the proceeds of the item." If the proceeds of the check were used by Yolanda to buy a car that Xavier is not going to be able to use, and if Xavier was under no obligation (under a separation agreement, for example) to provide Yolanda with transportation, he should be able to establish that he did not "benefit" from the proceeds of this check. There will, of course, be more complicated cases in which it is debatable whether a customer who has not signed a check issued from a joint account has or has not "benefited" from the proceeds of the check. This just doesn't seem to be one of them. The example does point out how careful a payor bank must be in deciding when to honor a check that will result in an overdraft of the account, other than when it has contractually committed itself to extend overdraft privileges to the particular customers. If Yolanda cannot be made to come up with the $1,500, Paley will have to bear the loss arising from its decision not to reject the check when it had the right to do so.

6. Paley was within its rights to honor the postdated check and to charge its amount against Darla's account unless Darla had given the bank the form of notice called for in §4-401(c), which alerts the bank that a postdated check has been issued and that it is not to pay the item until the date written on the check. The notice that Darla is entitled to give under this subsection is, as you can see, treated as a kind of before-the-fact stop-payment order.

The underlying reason for Article 4's treatment of postdated checks in this fashion, which was introduced in the 1990 revisions, is (as you may have guessed) the simple fact that the date of any check is not something encoded on the MICR line. A payor bank's automated system will have no way of discerning when a postdated check has been presented and is making its way through the system. If, however, the customer gives the bank the type of notice provided for in §4-401(c), "describing the check with reasonable certainty" (a concept we will confront in greater detail in Chapter 14 as it applies to the stop-payment order), the bank will be able to enter into its computer the information necessary to ensure that the check is not paid but is instead culled out for individual treatment from the steady stream of items being automatically processed.

The bank may, of course, charge a fee for dealing with any such check on this basis, just as it will be entitled to charge a fee for a stop-payment order. As you can see from Comment 3, Article 4 makes no attempt to regulate the fees that banks may charge their customers for this and other types of special services — in fact, the drafters most deliberately avoided doing so, much to the dismay of consumers' rights advocates. The fees banks charge, at least to their consumer customers, have been and continue to be regularly challenged on a variety of different theories. Such challenges have been, almost without exception, unsuccessful. The courts usually defer either to federal authorities that have the power to oversee banking and the structure of the fees banks may charge their customers, at least if the applicable fees are properly disclosed to the customer at the time the account is opened; or to the general power of the marketplace to provide the consumer what he or she needs at a "reasonable" market price. The long and the short of it is that should you as a consumer be unhappy with the service provided by your bank or the fees it charges, go and shop around for another bank which will treat you better. Individual consumers and consumers' rights advocates are, needless to say, not pleased with this answer, but by and large that's the way it is.

7.   Paley did no wrong in dishonoring the check based on its initial determination of what funds were available in Frederick's account. Subsection 4-402(c) and the accompanying comment are perfectly clear on this point.

8.   Paley, which has apparently adopted an internal procedure for dealing with items presented at the same time in descending order of their amount, paying the largest check first, has done no wrong. It is allowed under Article 4 to establish its own rules for the priority it gives to multiple items presented on the same account.

This practice of dealing with multiple items in descending order of amount, which admittedly may, in situations such as we have here, result in the bank's having to return (and collect fees for) a greater number of checks than would another practice, has been criticized by consumer advocates as just another way for banks to increase the fees they can levy against their hapless customers. *Smith v. First Union National Bank*, 958 S.W.2d 113, 35 U.C.C.2d 1309 (Tenn. Ct. App. 1997), involved an attempt to bring a class action suit against a bank that had adopted this practice for processing items, claiming it to be "unfair, deceptive and unlawful." A motion to dismiss was sustained by the trial court, and the dismissal was affirmed by the Court of Appeals of Tennessee. More recently, in *Daniels v. PNC Bank, N.A.*,137 Ohio App. 3d 247, 738 N.E.2d 447 (2000), a similar attempt at a class action was brought, the plaintiff alleging that the defendant bank had engaged in a "check sorting and posting scheme specifically for the purposes of generating additional revenue at the expense of its own 'valued' customers." The plaintiff argued, among other things, that the bank's practice breached a duty of good faith and fair dealing, constituted unconscionable conduct, and was tantamount to the collection of liquidated damages. The trial court had dismissed the complaint, and this dismissal was affirmed by the Court of Appeals of Ohio. It should be pointed out that the bank's justification for dealing with multiple items in this way — other than that the law gives them the right to do so if they wish — is that it is a reasonable assumption that a customer would want a larger check, which presumably reflects a more significant transaction and for which dishonor could have particularly serious repercussions for the customer, to be honored if at all possible, even if it means having to dishonor some greater number of smaller items to do so.

9a. No. Under §4-404, "[a] bank is under no obligation to a customer having a checking account to pay a check, other than a certified check, which is presented more than six months after its date." Paley is not obligated to pay this "stale" check.

9b. No, unless Geraldine could show that Paley's acts of paying the check and charging her account were in some way lacking in good faith. For the operative definition of that term, see §3-103(a)(4). Given what facts we have here, there doesn't seem to be anything that would constitute bad faith on Paley's part. Remember that the date of a check is not information carried on the MICR line, and so the automated systems at Paley would not normally have any way of even recognizing a stale check. Such a check registers on the bank's computers as just another check drawn on Geraldine's account, which has been presented for payment.

A tale worth telling in this regard is that of *IBP, Inc. v. Mercantile Bank*, 6 F. Supp. 2d 1258, 36 U.C.C.2d 270 (D. Kan. 1998), where a check for $135,234.18 was presented to and paid by the payor bank *nine years* after it was written. On July 15, 1986, the plaintiff, IBP, Inc., issued and delivered to Meyer Land & Cattle Company a check for this amount, written on its account with the Mercantile Bank of Topeka, for the purchase of some cattle. "Incredible as it may seem," in the words of the court, "officials at the closely-held family-run Meyer business apparently misplaced the check." It was found in the fall of 1995 by Tim Meyer, the president of the Meyer

Company, behind a desk drawer in his home. The check was then deposited for collection. The Mercantile Bank, its computers showing no outstanding stop-payment order covering the check, withdrew the amount from IBP's account and paid the check. As the court noted,

> IBP issues thousands of checks on its Mercantile account every month. In the period of July 1995 through December 1995, IBP drew 73,769 checks on the account. In September 1995 alone, the month in which Mercantile processed the 1986 check to Meyer, IBP drew 14,852 checks. For IBP, a $135,234.18 check is not extraordinary as the company issues numerous checks each month for amounts well in excess of $100,000.

Mercantile had pointed out that if it were to be responsible for recognizing stale checks, it could not rely on automated processing and the MICR line, and would have to conduct manual examinations of each and every check written by its customer, "an extraordinarily expensive and inefficient way of transacting business." The court concluded,

> it is undisputed that Mercantile had no knowledge that the IBP check it honored in 1995 was more than nine years old. It is similarly uncontested that IBP frequently drafted checks of equal or greater value on its account. Furthermore, IBP was cognizant of Mercantile's procedures for seeking a stop-payment order, yet it chose not to secure (or at least update) such an order.

The court granted summary judgment to the bank, finding that it was not lacking in good faith in paying the item.

10a. Yes. According to §4-405(a): "Neither death nor incompetence of a customer revokes the authority to accept, pay, collect [an item], or account [for its proceeds] until the bank knows of the fact of death or of an adjudication of incompetence and has reasonable opportunity to act on it."

10b. No. Under §4-405(b), even with knowledge (as of May 10) of the death on May 9, Paley could have rightfully paid any check presented to it through May 19 written by Isaac before his death, as long as it was not "ordered to stop payment by a person claiming an interest in the account." The rationale for this rule, allowing "holders of checks drawn and issued shortly before death to cash them without the necessity of filing a claim in probate," is given in Comment 2. Notice that if "a person claiming an interest in the account" does order the bank to stop paying on such checks, the bank is obligated to obey. It is not authorized or required to make a determination, and to take on the risk of making what may later turn out to be a mistaken conclusion, of whether the person making such an order does actually have a legitimate interest in the account and is entitled to give such an instruction regarding how it is to be dealt with. As Comment 3 states: "The bank has no responsibility to determine the validity of the claim or even whether it is 'colorable.'"

11a. No. Subsection 4-402(b) makes a payor bank that wrongfully dishonors a check liable only to "its customer." The term *customer* is defined in §4-104(a)(5). In this case the customer is clearly the corporation, Graphics Surprise, Incorporated. Cubicle Realty is not the bank's customer and can assert no statutory liability on the part of Paley for the fact that the check was wrongfully dishonored. Cubicle's relief, if any there be, will be against its tenant, Graphics Surprise, Incorporated.

11b. No. Cosmo Graphics personally is not the customer of the bank; the corporation, a separate legal entity, is. As you can see from Comment 5, the courts in some instances have been willing to blur the line between the business entity that has an account with the bank and the individuals who are running the entity, but this Official Comment at least, and most other commentators as well, look unfavorably on such results.

12a. Yes. Graphics Surprise, Inc., is the customer here and can under §4-402(b) hold Paley liable for "damages proximately caused by the wrongful dishonor" of its check to Woodchip Industries. It should easily be able to prove that those damages include the additional cost the corporation incurred to obtain the needed supplies, which cost it would not have had to bear save for the bank's wrongful dishonor of the check.

12b. I would say yes, although it is less clear-cut than the previous part of this example. Subsection 4-402(b) states:

> Liability is limited to actual damages proved and may include damages for an arrest and prosecution of the customer or other consequential damages. Whether any consequential damages are proximately caused by the wrongful dishonor is a question of fact to be determined in each case.

Fortunately, this wrongful dishonor has not resulted in any arrest or prosecution of Graphics for the passing of bad checks, but it has, he will argue, resulted in another form of consequential damages for which the corporation should be compensated. Graphics may not have been contractually bound to give its own customers discounts for late delivery, but it doesn't seem an unreasonable thing for Graphics to have done, and the company should be able to establish the exact dollar figure of the loss and that it followed directly and "proximately" from the bank's wrongful dishonor. As the passage quoted from §4-402(c) indicates, this type of claim for damages has to be evaluated on a case-by-case basis. My own response is that Graphics Surprise, Inc., has a good argument here for the award of this amount as actual and proximately caused consequential damages.

13. I think you would have to advise Arnold, as tactfully as possible, that he would not be able to recover any damages from the bank under this scenario and that his only recourse would be to take his business elsewhere if he thought he could get better service from some other bank. As far as Arnold's mental anguish goes, there is no reason to question how truly disturbing the entire

episode may have been for him, but §4-402(b) allows only for the recovery of "actual damages" caused to the customer. Although courts have in some instances awarded an amount for mental anguish for wrongful dishonor, these cases are few and far between and usually involve some particularly egregious behavior on the part of the bank, such as failing to admit that it has wrongfully dishonored or failing to respond to the customer's complaints in a reasonable and timely fashion, resulting only in its clumsily adding insult to injury. Here Paley seems to have been more than willing to admit its mistake and make amends and did what it could to right the situation as soon as possible.

What of Arnold's protest that the incident has in some general, if not necessarily quantifiable, way done harm to his reputation within the business community in which he works? Comment 1 makes clear that the drafters don't believe damages should be awarded on this basis alone, although it has to go into a bit of history to explain why. Prior to promulgation of the Code, there was authority in many states for what was known as the "trader rule," to the effect that someone in business, a "merchant or trader," could recover damages for wrongful dishonor even when no direct actual damages had resulted. The idea was that such a party should be able to recover for the injury to his, her, or its reputation and good name that was assumed to flow from a wrongful dishonor of just the type Arnold is arguing he suffered here. The original version of Article 4 was intended by its drafters to do away with the trader rule, but through some problems with its wording (or perhaps because of resistance on the part of some courts to believe that the adoption of Article 4 could really have changed a rule with which they were all familiar and perfectly satisfied), not all courts came to this conclusion. Thus, the revision drafters tried to be even more explicit. As Comment 1 explains, the 1990 revision of this section "precludes any inference that Section 4-402 retains the 'trader' rule."

As to punitive damages, it seems exceptionally unlikely that Arnold will have any chance of collecting here. Comment 1 concludes with the statement that "[w]hether a bank is liable for noncompensatory damages, such as punitive damages, must be decided by Section 1-103 and Section 1-106 ('by other rule of law')." The standards by which the various states adjudge whether punitive damages can rightfully be awarded to a plaintiff may vary to some degree, but I think it almost universally true that punitive damages are normally not even considered unless some compensatory damages have arisen from the wrong committed. In this situation, Arnold won't be able to show any "actual" damages, so I can't see how he could possibly be able to collect any punitives. Paley National Bank has apparently angered one of its valued customers by its wrongful dishonor of a number of his checks. Its customer relations department may have to put in a bit of overtime undoing the harm that's been done. The bank, however, will not have any monetary liability to Arnold under §4-402(b).

In a recent South Dakota case, much more sympathetic I assure you than Arnold's, the Supreme Court of that state upheld a jury's reward of $250,000 for a livestock dealer's lost income and a separate $200,000 for the "lost value of his business" caused by a wrongful dishonor. It reversed, however, an additional award of $150,000 for "emotional distress" suffered by the plaintiff. It also held that the trial judge had been correct in not even submitting the question of punitive damages to the jury. *Maryott v. First National Bank of Eden*, 2001 S.D. 43, 624 N.W.2d 96, 44 U.C.C.2d 240.

14

Stopping Payment

Introduction

The first seven examples in this chapter deal with the right of a customer who has written a check on his or her account to stop payment of that check. Article 4 covers the topic in §4-403, which you should read through as preparation for those examples. As Comment 1 to that section states:

> The position taken by this section is that stopping payment . . . is a service which depositors expect and are entitled to receive from banks notwithstanding its difficulty, inconvenience and expense.

Whether the customer has the right to issue a stop-payment order is not in doubt. Still, questions remain that call for our attention: Who may issue a stop-payment order? What information must the order include to be effective? When will an order be too late to be effective? If a stop-payment order is given to the bank, how long does it remain in effect? If a bank mistakenly pays a check on which a valid stop-payment order has been received, what is its liability? All this and more in the examples to follow.

The later examples (8, 9, and 10) deal with a related but distinct set of issues concerning cashier's checks, teller's checks, and certified checks — or, as they are often collectively referred to, *bank checks*. The fundamental distinction between such checks and the typical personal check is that the party taking a bank check is relying on the fact that such checks carry with them the assurance of a bank that they will be paid. Creditors will insist on being paid with a bank check just so they don't have to worry about the customer's not having enough money in his or her account to cover the item. But again questions remain. Can the customer who has arranged for the issuance of a bank check ever effectively order the bank to stop payment on it? Can the bank that issued the check itself decide that the check is not to be paid? If so, under what circumstances? If a bank wrongfully refuses to pay on a cashier's check that it has issued, stops payment of a teller's check that it has drawn on its own account with another

243

bank, or dishonors a personal check that it has certified, what are the consequences? When you get to these later examples, you will want to look over §3-411 for guidance.

EXAMPLES

1.   Angela has a regular checking account with the Paley National Bank. She writes a check for $350 payable to one Bertie. Bertie signs the back of the check and places it in his wallet. Or at least he thinks he does. Later, when he plans to go to his own bank and deposit the check, he cannot find it. He does remember that it was written on the Paley bank. Can Bertie, by notifying that bank and giving it all the pertinent information, effectively stop payment on this check?

2.   For many years, the married couple of Xavier and Yolanda Zendel have had a joint checking account with Paley National Bank, on which either is authorized to sign a check payable from the account on his or her own without the signature of the other. On January 3, 2004, Xavier (having made a New Year's resolution to get in shape) writes a check on this account to pay for a family membership in a local health club. When he informs Yolanda of what he's done, she finds the idea ridiculous. She immediately goes to Paley National and fills out and signs a stop-payment order form covering the check. Is the bank obligated to dishonor the check written to the health club by Xavier?

3.   Angela from Example 1, who has a checking account with Paley National Bank, writes a check to one David Driller, a contractor who has done some household remodeling for her. Immediately after she mails the check off to him, she becomes aware of some problems with the work he has done. She contacts the Paley bank by phone and says that she wants to stop payment of the check. She gives the bank representative with whom she speaks her name and account number and tells him that the check was "written recently to David Driller." The bank representative asks her for the number of the check and for its exact amount, but Angela is unable to recall either. All she can say is that "the check was written recently and was for something like $4,500 or $4,600."

   (a) Has Angela made a valid stop-payment order on this check, so that the bank is under an obligation to dishonor it upon presentment?

   (b) What if instead Angela, though she had not been able to give the exact number of the check, had told the bank that the check was for $4,515.27? As it turns out, the check was actually written to David Driller in the amount of $4,515.72. Should Angela's attempt to stop payment be deemed effective?

4.   Angela writes a check from her Paley National Bank account to Earl. The check is dated February 12, 2004, and she hand-delivers it to Earl on that day.

The next day she telephones the bank and says she wants to stop payment of the check. She accurately gives the bank her account number, the number of the check, and its amount.

(a) Is Paley obligated to dishonor the check based on this oral notice? If so, for how long will this stop-payment order be effective?

(b) Assume that Angela stops by the bank on February 14, 2004, and fills out a form provided by the bank for written stop-payment of checks. She fills in all the information requested by the form and the information she gives is accurate in every detail. For how long will her stop-payment order on this check now be effective?

(c) Assume that Angela does no more regarding this check. Earl deposits it in his bank in November of 2004 and it is duly presented to Paley. If Paley pays the check, will it have the right to charge against Angela's account the amount of the item?

5. Paley National Bank normally opens for business at 9:00 in the morning. It has established a cutoff time of 11:00 a.m. for receipt of stop-payment orders, the fact of which is made known to its customers as part of the initial agreement opening any account. Marty, another of Paley's checking account customers, writes a check on March 3. On March 6, at around 3:00 in the afternoon, he comes into the bank and fills out a stop-payment order giving all the essential information about the particular check he wants to have stopped. As it turns out, the check in question was presented to Paley on March 5, and Paley made provisional settlement for the check with the presenting bank on that day. If Paley does not return the check and revoke this provisional settlement by midnight on March 6, thus making final payment of the check, will it be able to charge its amount against Marty's account? See §4-303(a).

6. Arnold Moneybucks, one of the community's most prominent (and flamboyant) businesspersons, also has a checking account with Paley National Bank. After treating several of his friends to an expensive dinner at the city's newest fashionable restaurant, La Pretense, Arnold pays for the feast with a personal check. The next day Arnold decides that the meal did not live up to his expectations and, in addition, that several of the restaurant staff were insufficiently attentive to him and his guests. He contacts the Paley bank and issues a stop-payment order on the check he wrote the evening before.

(a) Assuming that this stop-payment order is received by the bank well before the bank is presented with the check, is the bank obligated to follow the order and dishonor the check?

(b) A review question: Assume that when the check is presented to Paley, that bank does not pay it, but returns the item with a notice that it has been dishonored due to a stop-payment order given by the drawer. The unpaid check eventually makes its way back into the hands of the owner of the restaurant, Chef Maurice. Does Maurice have any cause of action against Paley National Bank for its refusal to pay the check? Does he have any cause or causes of action against Arnold?

(c) Now suppose that even though the stop-payment order was received by Paley in plenty of time before the check was presented, that bank by mistake pays the check over the valid stop-payment order. It deducts the amount of the check from Arnold's account. When Arnold hears about this, he flies off the handle. He also threatens suit against the Paley bank. If he does sue the bank for its failure to comply with his stop-payment order, what damages would he be entitled to collect? See §4-403(c) and §4-407, paragraph (2).

7.   Cosmo Graphics, president and sole shareholder of Graphic Surprise, Incorporated, contracts to buy on behalf of the corporation some high-quality paper from one of its suppliers, Woodchip Industries. The contract calls for Graphic Surprise to buy 10 crates of a certain kind of paper at a price of $500 per crate. Immediately upon receiving the shipment from Woodchip, Graphics sends that company a check written on the corporation's account with Paley National Bank for $5,000. The next day, as he is moving the crates of paper into his supply room, Cosmo becomes aware that the shipment he has received contained only nine crates. Cosmo issues a stop-payment order on behalf of the corporation to the Paley bank covering the $5,000 check written to Woodchip. Due to a foul-up at the bank, the check is paid over the valid stop-payment order and the $5,000 is charged to the Graphic Surprise account. Cosmo, when he becomes aware that the check has been paid over its stop-payment order, insists that the bank recredit the corporate account with the $5,000. The bank refuses to do so.

(a) If Graphic Surprise is forced to bring an action against Paley, to what amount will it be entitled?

(b) Suppose instead that the Paley bank, upon becoming aware of its mistake and in order to maintain good relations with its customer, does immediately recredit the Graphic Surprise account with the full $5,000. Paley is now out $5,000. Graphic Surprise is in possession of nine crates of high-quality paper for which it has, as of this point, paid not a penny. And Woodchip has been paid $5,000 for 10 crates of paper when it only delivered 9. What can Paley do to deal with its loss? Consult §4-407, paragraphs (2) and (3).

8.   Johanna has been looking to buy a cabin in the mountains that she can use as a summer retreat. When she finally finds one that seems to be just what she is searching for, Caleb, the current owner, tells her that many people have shown an interest in the property. If she wants to make sure that she gets it, he tells her, she should bring him a bank check for $10,000 (10 percent of the asking price) as soon as possible. Johanna writes a check for this amount out of her account at Paley National Bank and goes to the bank, where she has

the check certified. Immediately after delivering this check to Caleb, she begins to regret her decision to buy this particular cabin.

(a) Can Johanna issue a stop-payment order covering this check that the bank is obligated to obey? See §4-303(a).

(b) Suppose instead that Johanna had obtained from Paley a cashier's check in the amount of $10,000 payable to Caleb. Would she have the right to stop payment on this check?

(c) Finally, suppose that the check Johanna gave to Caleb was a teller's check made payable to him, which Paley National Bank had drawn on its own account with State Street Bank. Does Johanna have the right to stop payment of this check?

9. The DotCom Corporation also has a checking account with Paley National Bank. The treasurer of DotCom, who is authorized to act in all banking matters for the corporation, requests that Paley issue a cashier's check for $45,000 payable to one Edwin Commerce, deducting the cost of the check from DotCom's account. DotCom exchanges the cashier's check for a sealed envelope, which Commerce has promised contains the details of a new computer program that will be of considerable value to DotCom's operations. As soon as the people at DotCom receive this envelope, they go to work testing the new program. By the end of the day it becomes apparent that the "new" program is in fact nothing special, but rather just a clumsy compilation of some well-known programs that are in the public domain. Edwin Commerce, they conclude, has tried to pull a fast one on them. DotCom's treasurer immediately contacts its account manager at Paley, who determines that the cashier's check has not yet been presented to or paid by the bank. The treasurer wishes to stop payment on this check, but she is informed by the account manager that this is not possible. DotCom has no authority to stop payment on the cashier's check. The manager does suggest that, given the importance of keeping up its "valuable relationship" with the ever-growing DotCom Corporation, he will arrange for the bank to refuse payment on the cashier's check upon its presentment to the bank. If the bank does refuse to pay on the cashier's check, what will be the consequences? See §3-411 and Comment 1 to that section.

10. In December of 2004, a teller at Paley National Bank is presented over the counter with a check for $12,000 payable to "Sally Kahn Valley," purportedly drawn on the account of the DotCom Corporation. The person presenting is able to give the teller several pieces of personal identification showing that she is indeed Ms. Valley and furthermore that she is an employee of DotCom. She explains that the check represents a year-end bonus that she just received from her employer. She asks that the teller accept the check and issue her in return a cashier's check for the same amount. The teller makes inquiries of the bank's computer system and determines that DotCom has more than enough in its account to cover the check, and also that the bank

has not received any stop-payment order with respect to it. The signature of DotCom's treasurer on the check looks close enough to the official signature that the bank has on record. The teller accepts the check being presented by Valley and issues her a cashier's check for $12,000. About an hour later, the Paley bank is contacted by DotCom's treasurer. He has just been made aware that one blank check is missing from the company's checkbook. When he gives the bank the number of the missing check, he is informed that a check bearing that number, made out for $12,000, has already been paid. The treasurer assures the bank manager that he never signed any such check and that any signature on the check that appeared to be hers is certainly a forgery. Valley is nowhere to be found. The certified check that was issued to her is presented to Paley several days later, after Valley apparently used it to open an account at a bank in a distant part of the country.

(a) Would Paley be within its rights in refusing to pay the cashier's check?

(b) What if Valley had taken the check to a local auto dealership and indorsed it over to that dealership in exchange for a used car in which she fled the scene? The dealership, which you may assume took the cashier's check as a holder in due course, then deposits the check for collection. Could Paley refuse to pay the cashier's check under this set of facts?

EXPLANATIONS

1. No. Under §4-403(a), only "a customer or a person authorized to draw on the account if there is more than one person" may stop payment. Bertie is the payee of the check, not its drawer. Note the language in Comment 2: "Subsection (a) follows the decisions holding that a payee or indorsee has no right to stop payment." What is Bertie to do now? He can request of Angela that *she* stop payment of the check and issue him another one for the same amount, but recall (from Comment 4 to §3-310) that Angela is not legally obliged to stop payment or to issue a new check. Bertie may just have to live with the fact that he has either lost or had stolen a bearer instrument worth $350, which can end up being no different than if the same had happened to $350 of cash that he remembers placing in his wallet.

2. Yolanda is not the customer who wrote the particular check in question, but she is a "person authorized to draw on the account." In this case, there is more than one person so authorized. So under §4-303(a), Yolanda may stop payment of the item. The Zendels are going to have to work things out between themselves, but the bank is unquestionably under an obligation to follow Yolanda's stop-payment order.

3a. This would not be, at least according to most authorities, a valid stop-payment order. A stop-payment order may be oral (see subsection (b)), so that is not the problem. Any stop-payment order, however, must, according to subsection (a), "describ[e] the item or account with reasonable certainty." The Code itself does not give any further guidance about what is required to meet this measure, but consider the language that concludes Comment 5:

> In describing the item, the customer, in the absence of a contrary agreement, must meet the standard of what information allows the bank under the technology then existing to identify the item with reasonable certainty.

Think what this means. Most commentators conclude that the bank has to be given the kind of information that could be entered into the bank's computerized system for examining checks and determining whether they are properly payable. This means that, in addition to the number of the account on which the check was written, the customer would have to give the bank either the *exact* amount of the check or the *exact* number of the check and preferably both. Each of these two pieces of information is, as we know, carried on the MICR line and can be read by the bank's automated equipment. The bank should be able to program its system so that when a check written on the particular account is presented for this amount or with this check number, the automated processing procedures will "spit out" the check so that it doesn't get paid in the ordinary course of things. The payee's name, however, is never encoded on the MICR line. If the bank were obligated to stop payment on a check based solely on account number and the payee's name, the only way it could do so would be to have its system initially reject any check written on the account for individualized sight examination of each check. Someone at the bank would have to look at the payee's name on each and every check in order to catch the one check on which the customer has requested that payment be stopped. This would be a timely and expensive procedure. It seems sensible to insist that, if this is all the information the customer can remember about a check he or she has written, the customer can't really expect such costly service from the bank — unless, that is, he or she is willing to enter into a special arrangement and pay an additional fee for the service. As the Seventh Circuit Court of Appeals remarked,

> [The customer] knew that the information she provided [her account representative] for the stop-payment order was incomplete at best, lacking a vital piece of identifying information — the exact check number. One does not need to be a banker or versed in banking law to know that this is a vital piece of information for locating or stopping a check. It is, as the courts below noted, a matter of common sense.

Rovell v. American National Bank, 194 F.3d 867, 39 U.C.C.2d 1147 (7th Cir. 1999).

It is interesting to speculate on what would happen in our example if Paley National Bank's technology allowed an automated search for, say, any item written on an account for between $4,500 and $4,600. Computers certainly can be programmed to do such things. If that were the case, then the bank would presumably have the obligation to enter a stop-payment order based on this information and could be expected to comply with the order. The fact is, however, that the "technology now existing" (to use the language of Comment 5) at all banks of which I am aware, allows searching for checks based only on the precise check number or the exact amount of the check as encoded on the MICR line. Banks have not seen fit to invest the money it would take to upgrade or reinvent their computerized systems to allow for more flexible or intricate searches. Apparently no need has been felt by the average bank to offer more sophisticated service of the type that new technology could provide. The present system, inflexible as it may be, seems to work well enough for the typical bank's and the typical customer's purposes.

3b. If the technology used by the bank to identify a check on which a stop-payment order has been placed is as rigid as it presently is, the fact that the order identifies the check by amount incorrectly — even if that error would seem obvious or trivial to any human looking at it — would be enough to render the stop-payment order ineffective. To a computer, $4,515.27 and $4,515.72 are as unequal as any two unequal numbers can be, and a search for any item that is supposedly written for the first amount would not pick up an item written for the second.

Some courts, faced with the type of "minor" error that Angela has made here, have bent over backward to find that the bank was obligated to stop payment. For example, in the well-known case of *Staff Service Associates, Inc. v. Midlantic National Bank*, 207 N.J. Super. 327, 504 A.2d 148, 42 U.C.C. 986 (1985), the customer issued a stop-payment order giving the amount of the check as $4,117.72, intending to cover a check that was actually for $4,117.12. As a result of this incorrect information being programmed into Midlantic's computers, the check when presented was paid and the amount was charged to Staff Service's account. Staff Service sued the bank for wrongful payment of the check, and the New Jersey Superior Court was asked by the bank to grant summary judgment in its favor. This the court declined to do. After reviewing prior cases, which had gone both ways on the issue, the New Jersey court declined to take a hard-line approach.

> Staff Service's representative did not know that Midlantic utilized a computer to effect stop payment of a check. In addition, Midlantic never informed Staff Services that the exact amount of the check is necessary for the computer to pull the check. It chose a computerized system which searches for stopped checks by amount alone. By electing this system Midlantic assumed the risk that it would not be able to stop payment of a check despite the customer's accurate description of the account number, the payee's name, the number and date of the check and a de minimis error in the check amount. . . . Midlantic should not be permitted to relieve itself of this risk unless it calls attention to its computerized system and the necessity for the exact check amount to meet computer requirements.

The court held that Midlantic had not met the burden imposed upon it for "relieving itself of this risk," even though the stop-payment form that Staff Service's representative signed included the following statement at the bottom:

> IMPORTANT: The information on this Stop Payment Order must be correct, including the exact amount of the check to the penny, or the Bank will not be able to stop payment and this Stop Payment Order will be void.

Staff Service's representative acknowledged that he had read this language. Assuming that the analysis of the situation and the test given by the court in this case are a good way of handling the problem presented — and I assure you not everyone would be willing to agree on even this — was the court's application of its own test to the facts of the case correct?

4a. Yes. Under §4-403(b), a stop-payment order need not be in writing to be effective. This oral order will, however, lapse and cease to be effective 14 days after it is given to the bank unless it is confirmed in writing within the 14-day period.

4b. Angela has confirmed the stop-payment order in writing only one day after having initially given the order. Her stop-payment order is now effective for six months from February 13, 2004, the date on which the order was originally given.

4c. Yes. By the time the check is presented to Paley, Angela's stop-payment order will have lapsed, and the bank will be within its rights to pay the check and charge it against Angela's account. Recall that, according to §4-404, although a payor bank is not *obligated* to pay a so-called stale check (one that is outstanding more than six months after its date) it *may* do so if it acts in good faith. See the concluding language of Comment 6 to §4-403:

> When a stop-payment order expires it is as though the order had never been given, and the payor bank may pay the item in good faith under §4-404 even though a stop-payment order had once been given.

Consider the story of Mr. Scott D. Liebling, attorney at law. Mr. Liebling represented one Fredy Winda Ramos in a personal injury action. When a settlement was concluded, he issued a check out of his account with Mellon bank (#1031) in the amount of $8,483.06 to Ramos, representing her proceeds from the settlement. About five days later, he mistakenly issued a second check (#1043) to Ramos for the same amount. Six days later, when he became aware of his mistake, Liebling called Ramos and advised her that the second check had been issued in error. He instructed her to destroy this second check. He called the bank and gave an oral stop-payment order on check #1043. Some 19 months later, Ramos deposited this check in her account and the Mellon bank paid it. Ramos was not easily available for suit, so Liebling brought an action against Mellon arguing that it should not have honored the check. He could not argue that the bank had wrongfully paid over a valid stop-payment order, because the order had long since lapsed. The court found no lack of good faith on the part of the bank in paying the check, even though it carried a date more than a year old, recognizing that the bank's computerized system for processing checks would have had no means of identifying a stale check or one on which a stop-payment order had once been placed after that order ceased to be effective. *Scott D. Liebling, P.C. v. Mellon PSFS (NJ) National Ass'n*, 311 N.J. Super. 651, 710 A.2d 1067, 35 U.C.C.2d 590 (1998).

What could attorney Liebling have done to avoid this result? Under §4-403(b), "[a] stop-payment order may be renewed for additional six-month periods by a writing given to the bank within a period during which a stop-payment order is effective." So Liebling could have repeatedly renewed the stop-payment order every six months to assure himself that check #1043 would never be paid. Doing so would eventually become not just boring but also costly, as each renewal would presumably result in an additional fee. If Ramos were willing to outwait Liebling on this score, she would presumably be able to get paid on the second check eventually. Other than continually renewing his stop-payment order, the only things Liebling could have done to make sure that this second check was never paid and charged to his account would have been to get the check physically returned to him or to close the account altogether. Note that §4-403(a) provides not just for the issuance of stop-payment orders but for a customer or any person authorized to draw on an account to "close the account" by a proper order to the bank. Of course, what Liebling should have done in the first place to avoid this whole problem was be careful enough with his business to avoid issuing two checks to cover the same debt.

5.   Yes. Subsection 4-303(a)(5) provides that a stop-payment order received by the payor bank comes too late to "terminate, suspend, or modify the bank's duty or right to pay an item or to charge its customer's account for the item" if the stop-payment order comes after "a cutoff hour no earlier than one hour after the opening of the next banking day after the banking day on which the bank received the check and no later than the close of that business day." Paley received the check on March 5. It had established a cutoff hour of 11:00 a.m., which would fit within the timeframe of this provision. Marty's stop-payment order was received by the bank after the cutoff hour on March 6, the day following receipt of the item by Paley, so it comes too late to be effective.

6a.   Yes. The bank is obligated to obey an effective stop-payment order. It is not required to determine — indeed, it is not given any right to rule on — whether the customer has a good or a bad reason for wanting to stop payment, nor whether its customer has any right as against the payee to stop payment. The bank's role is to serve its customer and to obey the customer's order.

6b.   Maurice has no cause of action against the bank for its refusal to pay the check. This goes back to §3-408 and the elemental proposition that the drawee of an instrument, in this case the bank on which a check has been written, is not liable on the instrument until the drawee accepts it. Arnold has ordered his bank not to accept the item, and the bank has followed through on this order.

Maurice does, of course, have rights against Arnold. Once the check is dishonored, he can hold Arnold, as its drawer, liable on the check under §3-414(b). Or he could assert his rights on the underlying contract that Arnold entered into with the restaurant to pay for the meal. Recall §3-310(b)(1) and Comment 3 to that section. Arnold does have to pay for his meal, and those of his friends, one way or another.

6c. Under §4-403(c),

> The burden of establishing the fact and amount of loss resulting from payment of an item contrary to a stop-payment order . . . is on the customer. The loss from payment of an item may include damages for dishonor of subsequent items under §4-402.

It is hard to see how Arnold will be able to establish any loss resulting from Paley's mistaken payment of this particular check over a valid stop-payment order. As we saw in the prior part of this example, one way or another it seems fairly clear that Arnold would eventually have to pay Maurice the amount of the check, so Arnold has apparently suffered no loss by the payment of the check, the result of which has been to discharge his obligation to pay Maurice for the fancy meal. Perhaps Arnold can meet the burden of proving that, had the check been stopped, he would have been able to negotiate with Maurice and end up paying some lesser amount for the meal. Payment of the check will in effect have denied Arnold the opportunity to enter into this negotiation; after all, once Maurice has been paid for the meal, Arnold has little leverage to exert against the chef. If Arnold can prove actual loss on this basis — which I have to admit does strike me as very unlikely — then he would be able to collect this measure of damages from Paley for its mistaken payment of the check.

Note also that Arnold may have suffered loss if, assuming (as he had every right to do) that the check to Maurice would be stopped on his order, he wrote additional checks out of the account that wound up being dishonored because the amount available in Arnold's account had been mistakenly decreased by the amount of the check to the restaurant, leaving too little in the account to cover these other checks. If the account would have been able to cover these other checks had Paley not mistakenly failed to observe the stop-payment order on the check to Maurice, then these other checks have been wrongfully dishonored, and Arnold is entitled to whatever damages he can show resulting from the wrongful dishonor as specified in §4-402(b).

Another way to reach the same result is via §4-407. Suppose that Arnold sues the bank for the amount of the check, relying upon §4-401 and the fact that the bank had deducted from his account the amount of a not-properly-payable item. Under §4-407, paragraph (c), "to prevent unjust enrichment" (of the type we would find if Arnold were allowed to have eaten his meal and never been made to pay for it), Paley would be "subrogated to the rights of the payee or any other holder of the item [here Chef Maurice] against the drawer [Arnold] . . . either on the item or under the transaction out of which the item arose [the fabulous feast]." Arnold would sue the bank for the amount of the check. Paley would be able to assert on its behalf the right of Maurice to be paid the amount of the check for the meal itself. The two claims would most likely cancel one another out, with the consequence that Paley owes Arnold nothing for its mistaken payment of the check. Maurice, because he has been paid on the check and may not even be aware that Arnold attempted to stop payment on it, has nothing to complain or to worry about. Arnold may, of course, still want to bring to Maurice's attention his displeasure with the meal and the service he received at La Pretense, and that is something that may (or may not) be of concern to Maurice. But this could have happened even if Arnold had not paid by check but had instead just pulled out a large wad of big bills at the end of the meal and paid by cash.

You may find it interesting (and morally instructive) to look at the recent case of *Seigel v. Merrill Lynch, Pierce, Fenner & Smith*, 745 A.2d 301, 40 U.C.C.2d 819 (D.C. Ct. App. 2000). The plaintiff, Walter Seigel, wrote several checks from a Merrill Lynch account — Merrill Lynch for these purposes serving as a drawee bank — to various Atlantic City casinos. The checks were exchanged for chips that he then proceeded to gamble away. Upon his return from Atlantic City, Seigel stopped payment on the checks. Many of the checks (we are not told for how much) were subsequently dishonored by Merrill Lynch, but the firm accidently paid some others totaling $143,000 even though they were covered by the stop-payment orders. Seigel then brought an action against Merrill Lynch for its failure to observe the valid stop-payment orders. He argued that had these checks not been paid he would have been able to defeat efforts by the casinos to collect on them, claiming among other things that the casinos would have had no right to enforce the checks as he was a "compulsive gambler" protected under New Jersey law. The court concluded that Seigel was not covered by a New Jersey statute designed to protect compulsive gamblers under a specific procedure not applicable to Seigel's case, and that compulsive gambling in and of itself is not a defense to a contract action on a check such as this under the common law of New Jersey. Seigel also claimed that the checks were unenforceable under the District of Columbia's version of the historical Statute of Anne, which makes it illegal to make a loan to another when the proceeds of the loan are to be used for gambling. The District of Columbia court reasoned that even if this were true — and it had its doubts — the casinos could have pursued Seigel in the courts of New Jersey or his home state of Maryland and eventually obtained a judgment against him. That being so, the court concluded the Seigel had failed to establish that Merrill Lynch's mistaken payment of the checks over stop-payment orders caused him to suffer any actual loss. The trial court's summary judgment in favor of Merrill Lynch was therefore affirmed.

7a. If we assume that the only loss to Graphics is the $500 it paid for a crate of paper that it never received, then under §4-403(c) it would be entitled to only this amount from Paley.

7b. As of this point, both Graphic and Woodchip stand "unjustly enriched," Graphic because it has nine crates of paper for which it has paid nothing, and Woodchip because it has collected on a $5,000 check when it was entitled to only $4,500. Paley can bring an action under §4-407(2) against Graphic, using the fact that it is subrogated to the rights of the payee of the check, Woodchip, either on the item or under the purchase and sale transaction out of which the item arose. Had the check been properly dishonored, Woodchip would have been put to the task of either suing on the check for $5,000, in which case it would have been subject to a claim in recoupment for $500 and ended up receiving only $4,500. If Woodchip had sued on the original contract of sale, it would presumably have been able to collect only $4,500 for the 9 crates that were delivered. Either way you look at it, §4-407(2) allows Paley in this circumstance to take up any rights that Woodchip would have had to collect $4,500 from Graphic.

In addition, under §4-407(3), Paley could bring an action against Woodchip, arguing that it was subrogated to the rights of the drawer of the check, Graphic Surprise, against the payee, Woodchip, "with respect to the transaction out of which the item arose." Had Graphic not been able to stop the check in time, it would have ended up paying $5,000 for only 9 crates of paper, $500 more than it should have had to. So Graphic would have had a claim, based on the law of sales, for $500 against Woodchip. Via paragraph (3) of §4-407, Paley, which has mistakenly paid the check over the stop-payment order, is under the circumstances subrogated to Graphic's rights to payment of this amount from Woodchip.

If all goes well for Paley in these two causes of action, it should end up whole. Paley's decision to immediately recredit Graphic's account for the full $5,000 that Paley paid out mistakenly may well have been a sensible move, considering that it had indeed made a mistake and that it wants to protect its reputation for good customer service. This assumes, of course, that the cost of each of the two lawsuits is zero — which is quite an assumption when you think about it. Paley also runs the risk that when it does try to collect what is rightfully owed by each of the two parties, Graphic and Woodchip, it will find itself right in the middle of a dispute between the two where the facts are muddled. (Is it really undisputed that Graphics received only 9 crates of paper? Woodchip may well claim that it had sent out all 10. To which Graphics may respond, upon closer examination, that it was really only 8, and that the paper wasn't of the quality ordered in any event.) The possibility of coming to some dispassionate and amicable settlement of the whole sordid affair may be far from a first priority on either Graphic's or Woodchip's part. Notice how much better off Paley would have been if it could have gotten Graphic's agreement in the first place to recredit its account only with the $500 that its customer then claimed to be in dispute. Paley would then only have had to pursue Woodchip for the $500 that Paley would have been out of pocket. Of course, the best by far would have been for Paley not to have made such a mistake in the first place and to have observed and acted upon Graphic Surprise's stop-payment order. Then the whole controversy would have been left to the actual parties initially involved, the buyer and the seller, and the bank could have stayed out of it entirely. Recall Examples 6a and 6b, and the case of Arnold Moneybucks's disappointing dinner.

8a.   No. Johanna has no right to stop payment on a check once it has been certified. Under §4-303(a)(1), a stop-payment order "comes too late" once "the bank accepts or certifies the item."

8b.   No. Under §4-403(a), the right to stop payment is available only to "[a] customer or a person authorized to draw on the account." As this is a cashier's check, the drawer of the check is Paley National Bank, not Johanna. She is not in a position to issue a stop-payment order on the check.

8c.   Once again the answer is no. Paley has drawn this check on its own account with State Street Bank. Johanna is not a customer of that bank nor herself authorized to draw on that account, so she is not in a position to issue a stop-payment order to State Street, the drawee bank.

This example just makes official what Caleb apparently knew from the start (and which is confirmed by Comment 4 to §4-403). By insisting on a bank check in payment rather than a personal check, he protects himself from the check being stopped by Johanna should she later have a change of heart or find a mountain retreat more to her liking.

9.   Under §3-411(b), if the bank "wrongfully" refuses to pay the cashier's check when the check is presented,

> the person asserting the right to enforce the check is entitled to compensation for expenses and loss of interest resulting from the nonpayment and may recover consequential damages if the obligated bank refuses to pay after receiving notice of particular circumstances giving rise to the damages.

This section, which was added to Article 3 as part of the 1990 revision, does not specifically lay out when a bank that has issued a cashier's check acts "wrongfully" in refusing to pay, but it seems clear from other parts of this section and from the comments that the bank has no right to deny the holder of a cashier's check his or her money based solely on some argument that *the customer*, the purchaser of the bank check, may have against the party to whom the check was initially issued. In the case before us, this translates into the statement that Paley National Bank, having issued a cashier's check payable to Mr. E. Commerce at the request of DotCom, would have no right to refuse payment on this check based on any defense, argument, or claim that DotCom may have against Commerce. Note the following language from Comment 1:

> [A cashier's check or teller's check] is taken by the creditor as a cash equivalent on the assumption that the bank will pay the check. Sometimes, the debtor wants to retract payment by inducing the obligated bank not to pay. The typical case involves a dispute between the parties to the transaction in which the check is given in payment. . . . A debtor using any of these types of checks has no right to stop payment [as we saw in the previous example]. Nevertheless, some banks will refuse payment as an accommodation to a customer. Section 3-411 is designed to discourage this practice.

The Paley bank is in no position to determine whether the computer program that Commerce handed over to DotCom is, as the company seems to believe, nothing like what was promised. Perhaps the people at DotCom are just too dense to appreciate the impressive new functionality of what Commerce has delivered to them. In any event, the message of §3-411 to Paley is that it need not, and indeed that it *should not*, get involved in this controversy. Its only role has been to issue a cashier's check at the request of a customer, for which it presumably got fully paid by deducting available funds out of DotCom's account. The bank should pay the check when presented, and leave DotCom to pursue Commerce by other means if the company feels it has been cheated in the underlying transaction. Permitting a bank that has issued a cashier's or a teller's check at the request of a customer, or that has already certified a customer's personal check, later to refuse payment on that check as a favor to its customer is seen as seriously undermining the functionality of bank checks in the commercial world. *See*, for example, *DPR, Inc. v. Burgess*, 730 So. 2d 474, 41 U.C.C.2d 165 (La. Ct. App. 1999).

10a. This example differs dramatically from the previous one, in that here the bank wants to deny payment on the cashier's check not as an accommodation to its customer but to *itself* avoid loss. If it has to pay the $12,000 on the cashier's check it has issued to Ms. Valley, it will not be able to charge this amount to DotCom's account, because the check it took from Valley was not properly payable. The question is when, if ever, a bank that has issued a cashier's or teller's check, or that has certified a personal check, can use a defense *of its own* to justify refusing payment on such a check.

Look first to §3-411(c). The expenses or consequential damages for which a bank refusing to pay on such a bank check may be liable under subsection (b) are not recoverable "if the obligated bank asserts a claim or defense *of the bank* that it has reasonable grounds to believe is available against the person entitled to enforce the instrument." So if Paley refuses to pay the check when Valley is the person attempting to enforce the instrument, it should not have to worry about being made to pay any expenses or consequential damages, under §3-411, that Valley might claim she has suffered.

This still leaves the more important question unanswered: If Paley does refuse to pay on the certified check, even if it will not be held responsible for any expenses, interest, or consequential damages, should it be held liable for the $12,000, the actual amount of the check? This is an issue on which courts and commentators have differed and will presumably continue to differ, because Articles 3 and 4, even in their revised state, fail to address the question directly or impose a set answer.

Under the prerevision version of the Code, the majority of courts took what became referred to as the "cash equivalent" approach to questions involving bank checks. Under this approach to the problem, a bank's issuance of a bank check was considered to be the functional equivalent of its having paid out cash in the amount of the check. Just as there was no way for a bank to "stop" the recipient of cash from using it as he or she saw fit, considering the issuance of a bank check as equivalent to a cash payment meant that the issuing bank would never be in a position to rightfully refuse payment on a cashier's, teller's, or certified check. This would be so even if the bank reasonably believed itself to have, and in fact did have, a defense of its own (such as fraud, lack of consideration, or mistake) that it could assert against the person seeking payment on the check. A passage from an earlier case is often cited to explain the rationale behind this cash-equivalence approach:

> A cashier's check circulates in the commercial world as the equivalent of cash. People accept a cashier's check as a substitute for cash because the bank stands behind it, rather than an individual. In effect, the bank becomes a guarantor of the value of the check and pledges its resources to the payment of the amount represented upon presentation. To allow the bank to stop payment on such an instrument would be inconsistent with the representation it makes in issuing the check. Such a rule would undermine the public confidence in the bank and its checks and thereby deprive the cashier's check of the essential incident that makes it useful.

National Newark & Essex Bank v. Giordano, 111 N.J. Super. 347, 268 A.2d 327, 7 U.C.C. 1153 (1970).

A second, minority approach to the problem has been to consider the bank check as equivalent to a note issued by the bank. If this is the view taken, then the bank, in refusing to pay on a bank check it has issued, would be permitted to introduce any and all defenses of its own that it could muster against payment of the obligation, if it were later sued for the amount of the check. Some cases take a middle ground and hold that the bank can rely upon a defense that it was defrauded into issuing the check, but not on simple lack of consideration for the check or mistake on the bank's part in issuing it.

As the 1990 revisions were being prepared, arguments were made on both sides that either one or the other of these approaches should be formally recognized by the revision, but the revision drafters chose not to incorporate either view into the Code. Thus, the debate will continue. Whether Paley would be within its rights to refuse payment on the cashier's check it issued to

Valley will depend on the rule of the jurisdiction, or, if the jurisdiction has yet to address the issue, on which approach it decides to adopt and on how it understands that approach to operate in any particular situation. Two postrevision cases each provide a good summary discussion of this problem, and both ultimately adopt the "cash equivalent" approach to bank checks. *Gentner & Co. v. Wells Fargo Bank*, 76 Cal. App. 4th 1165, 90 Cal. Rptr. 904, 40 U.C.C.2d 38 (1999), considers the problem under each of the approaches and concludes that, "[f]ortunately, the . . . revisions to the Commercial Code allow us to resolve the issue before us without resort to a blanket rule or a rule under which the nature of a cashier's check fluctuates from case to case." The court's holding, given the facts before it, was that:

> [A]s between the bank and a payee who acts in good faith, the Commercial Code clearly requires the bank to suffer the loss occasioned by its error in accepting or paying a check covered by a stop payment order, and that the result is the same whether the check is paid in cash or exchanged for a cashier's check.

See also *Flatiron Linen, Inc. v. First American State Bank*, 23 P.3d 1209, 44 U.C.C. 673 (Colo. 2001).

10b. No. Everyone seems to agree, without question, that once a bank check is in the hands of a holder in due course who seeks to collect upon it, the bank has no option but to pay. If you look at this under the cash-equivalent approach, then it doesn't matter who is seeking to enforce the cashier's check. It must be paid. Under the "note approach," the bank would be allowed to assert it own defenses against the person seeking to enforce the check, but because the note has come into the possession of a holder in due course, those defenses the bank might have had against Valley, all being personal defenses, would not be available against the car dealership. If Paley refuses to pay the cashier's check, it will be sued by the dealership and have no legitimate defenses to the claim that it should pay the full amount of the check. Note also that it could be held liable to the dealership, in addition to the $12,000, for expenses, loss of interest, and possibly consequential damages under §3-411. Subsection (c) of that section absolves the bank of any such additional liability only when it can assert a claim or defense of its own "that it has reasonable grounds to believe is available against the person entitled to enforce the instrument." Unless Paley has "reasonable grounds to believe" that the dealership is not a holder in due course, it would have no defense to payment of the cashier's check that it could reasonably believe would be good against that party. Paley had better pay on the cashier's check when the dealership comes calling.

Revision Alert

Under the 2002 Amendments to Article 4, what would be necessary to extend a stop-payment order beyond 14 days to six months and for additional six-months periods after that would be a "record" and not a "writing." See R§4-303. What's the difference? See the last part of the Revision Alert at the end of Chapter 11. Have you been communicating with your bank, either about stopping payment or other matter, by sending it unwritten records lately?

15

Funds Availability Under Regulation CC

Introduction

Prior to the passage in 1987 by the federal government of the Expedited Funds Availability Act and the promulgation by the Federal Reserve System of its Regulation CC (designed to implement the Act), individual banks had a great deal of latitude to decide for themselves how long a customer who deposited a check would have to wait until the amount of the check would be available for his or her use.* We have already dealt with one aspect of Regulation CC — Subpart C, calling for expedited return and notice of nonpayment by a payor bank that determines to dishonor an item — in Chapter 12. In this chapter we consider a second major consequence of Regulation CC; indeed, that which is the primary explanation for its existence (as you can see from the title of the Act that it implements, the Expedited Funds Availability Act). Subpart B of Regulation CC makes mandatory, for all banks in the United States, an availability schedule under which the depositing customer will have as a matter of law the right to withdraw in cash or have applied against checks that he or she has written the funds represented by any given deposit. A bank may, if it wishes to do so, make funds available on a shorter timetable than that called for in Regulation CC, Subpart B, either in an individual case or as a matter of general policy designed to attract and hold either all or some particular favored customers. It cannot, however, deny availability beyond the times established in the regulation.†

---

* If, because of the order in which you are studying the various payment systems topics, you have not yet looked at Chapter 12, which first introduced the Expedited Funds Availability Act and Regulation CC, you should at this point read the first section of introductory text to that chapter.
† The Regulation also requires that any bank properly disclose its availability policy to the account holder. See C.F.R. §§229.15 and 229.17.

The funds availability schedule dictated by Regulation CC is set forth in three sections, at which we will be looking in the examples. Section 229.10 (12 C.F.R. §219.10) calls for *next-day availability* of certain types of deposits. The general *availability schedule*, for items that do not deserve next-day availability treatment, is found in §229.12. This section basically provides for what we can term *second-day availability* for local checks and *fifth-day availability* for nonlocal checks. It is obviously important for compliance with the mandated availability schedule that a bank be able to distinguish a *local* check from a *nonlocal* one. See the definitions in 12 C.F.R. §229.2(m), (r), and (s). Note furthermore that the check processing region of the payor bank of any check deposited into an account is information that the bank should be able to determine directly through its automated systems, from the MICR line on that check.

It will also become important for you to pay attention to Regulation CC's carefully wrought distinction between a *business day* and a *banking day*. See the definitions in §229.2(f) and (g). What counts as a business day is defined without reference to any particular bank's activities; any weekday other than one of a set of predetermined holidays will be a business day for the purposes of Regulation CC. What is and what is not a banking day, in contrast, can differ from bank to bank. For any particular bank,

> "Banking day" means that part of any business day on which an office of a bank is open to the public for carrying on substantially all of its banking functions.

A set of exceptions to the next-day and general availability schedules is set forth in 12 C.F.R. §229.13. I will not attempt, in the following examples, to place before you every twist and turn of these sections, which are, as you can see, not lacking for detail. We can, however, make a quick tour of the highlights.

EXAMPLES

In all of the following examples, you should assume that the Depot National Bank has adopted an availability schedule that conforms to the requirements of Regulation CC and has not agreed to give any customer availability of funds on a speedier basis.

1.   Chuck has an account with the Depot National Bank. As of the beginning of business on Monday morning, this account contains only $15. At 10:00 in the morning, Chuck goes into the bank and deposits with a teller $300 in cash. As soon as he walks out of the bank, he spies in the window of a nearby store a small, hand-held computerized personal digital assistant, which he realizes he would very much like to have. The owner of the store tells Chuck that the regular price for the gadget is $375, but he would be willing to let Chuck have it for $300 if Chuck can pay in cash by the end of

the day. Chuck immediately returns to Depot National and fills out a withdrawal slip requesting that he be given $300 in cash. He presents this withdrawal slip to the teller. Is the bank obligated to hand over to Chuck $300 in cash? See §229.10(a)(1).

2. Marisa, another customer of Depot National Bank, has arranged with her employer for her weekly paycheck to be automatically deposited into her account at the bank by electronic means. On Friday, the employer electronically deposits into Marisa's account $875.60, representing her week's salary (net, of course, of a whole host of deductions for taxes and the like). Prior to this deposit, the available balance in Marisa's account was down to $100. Also on Friday, Depot is presented with a check that Marisa has issued to her dentist, in the amount of $135. On Friday evening, Depot dishonors this check and returns it to the presenting bank. Assuming that Depot has not agreed to give Marisa any overdraft privileges, did Depot wrongfully dishonor by not accepting this check? See §229.10(b).

3. Emily deposits a cashier's check for $2,500, issued by Paley National Bank, into her account with Depot National Bank on a Tuesday morning by personally handing it over to a teller at the bank. As of when will this $2,500 be available in Emily's account as a matter of right? See §229.10(c)(1)(v).

4. Joel has an account with the North Street branch of the Depot National Bank. On Wednesday he deposits a check that he received from Lenore, which check was written by Lenore out of her account with the Southern Avenue branch of Depot National Bank. As of when will the amount of this check be available to Joel in his account? See §229.10(c)(1)(vi).

5. On Monday Susan deposits three personal checks — in the amounts of $125, $75, and $240 — totaling $440 into her account with Depot National Bank, all three of which are written on other banks.

   (a) As of Tuesday, does Susan have available in her account any money represented by these three checks? If so, how much? See §229.10(c)(1)(vii).

   (b) What if the three checks Susan deposits on Monday are for only $12, $7.50, and $20, for a total of $39.50? When would Depot have to make this amount available to her?

6. Richard deposits a single check for $350, drawn on a local bank, into his account with Depot National Bank on Monday morning.

   (a) As of when must the full amount of this check be regarded as fully available to him so that he could withdraw this amount in cash? Must it be treated as part of the amount in his account available to cover any check he himself may have drawn? See §229.12(b)(1).

   (b) What would be your answer to the previous question if instead the $350 check deposited by Richard was a nonlocal check (as defined in §229.2(v))? See §229.12(c)(1).

7.   Andrea deposits a single check for $1,000, written on a nonlocal bank, into her account at Depot National Bank on a Thursday. The following Thursday she goes to the bank and requests that it issue to her a cashier's check for $900, authorizing the deduction of this amount from her checking account to pay for the cashier's check.

   (a) Assuming that Andrea has no money in her account other than that from this deposit, is the bank obligated to issue the cashier's check as she requests? See §229.12(d).

   (b) What if her request had been for a cashier's check in the amount of $300?

   (c) What if her request for the $900 cashier's check had come on the following day, that is, the Friday of the week following her Thursday deposit?

8.   Julia has just moved into a new city and wants to open a checking account there. She comes into Depot National Bank on a Monday to open an account with that bank. As an initial deposit, she gives the bank a personal check for $12,000, which she has written to herself out of an account she already has with another bank in the distant part of the country that she has just moved from. When will funds be available in her new Depot account as a result of this initial deposit? See §229.13(a).

9.   Amanda deposits a personal check for $50,000 into her existing account with Depot National Bank.

   (a) As of when must the bank make this amount available to her? See §229.13(b) and §229.13(h)(2) and (4).

   (b) If Depot does decide to apply the large-deposits exception of §229.13(b) to this deposit, what other obligation does it have under Regulation CC? See §229.13(g)(1).

EXPLANATIONS

1.   No. Under 12 C.F.R. §229.10(a)(1), a cash deposit made in person to an employee of the depositary bank must be available as of right "not later than the business day *after* the banking day on which the cash is deposited."

So Chuck may withdraw the $15 that has been sitting in his account for some time, but he does not have the right to withdraw the $300 in cash he just deposited earlier in the day. At first this may strike you as strange or inherently unfair to the depositor. The fact is, however, that under Regulation CC there are *no* circumstances under which the depositor is entitled to availability on the actual day of deposit. The earliest that a deposit must be made available to the customer is next-day availability in those instances covered by §229.10. The rationale for this is that the depositary bank has to be given at least one day to deal with the deposit and to take a look (by automated means in the normal course of things) at the status of the customer's account. Later in the day on Monday, Depot National Bank may find that Chuck's account is overdrawn, in which case it would be within its rights to apply the $300 to that overdraft. Or a check drawn by Chuck on his account, say for $240, may have been presented to Depot during the course of the day. Depot would be within its rights to pay this check, leaving only $75 in Chuck's account as of the opening of business on Tuesday. By making next-day availability the earliest that a deposit must, as a matter of law, be afforded to the customer, the regulation allows the depositary bank one processing cycle, at the end of the day of deposit, to assess the status of the depositor's account in light of the deposit and all other factors.

2. No. The amount deposited into Marisa's account by electronic means will qualify for next-day availability under 12 C.F.R. §229.10(b), so that it will be available to cover any checks written by Marisa on her account as of the opening of business on the following Monday (provided that Monday is a business day under §229.2(g), of course). As of Friday, when Depot determined to bounce the check written to her dentist, Marisa still had only $100, less than the amount of the check, available in her account, so this was not a wrongful dishonor.

Recall that under §4-401 of the Code, Depot was not *required* to dishonor the check. It could have decided to honor it even though this would have resulted in a temporary overdraft. The bank's computers could be programmed to account for funds that have been deposited which are not yet technically available in the customer's account, but which should become so in due time. Or the bank's systems could determine to hold onto the $135 check presented to it until the following Monday. When Marisa's pay becomes available in the account — and provided that no other checks are presented by that time not all of which could be covered by her then-available funds and that Marisa has not withdrawn too much in cash from her account — Depot could then determine whether to honor the item prior to midnight on Monday, which would still be within its midnight deadline. Any of these possibilities will, needless to say, add significantly to Depot's cost and potential risk in dealing with Marisa's account. If Depot were willing to do this for a relatively small-time customer like Marisa, the easier route would probably be for it just to extend to her some measure of overdraft privilege once she has proven herself to be a responsible customer. This privilege limit could easily be programmed into its computer system once and for all.

3. Under 12 C.F.R. §229.10(c), "certain check deposits" are entitled to next-day availability. We will not look at each of the types of checks that so qualify, but as you can see just by glancing through paragraphs (i) through (iv), this favored treatment is reserved for checks that figure almost certainly to be paid because they are drawn on the credit of the government or a governmental agency. Similarly, under (v), with which we deal here, the credit behind the check is that of a bank, and there should be no doubt that such a check will be paid without question.

Emily's deposit of the cashier's check on Tuesday will result in its amount being available in her account as of the next business day, Wednesday, if her deposit meets the criteria of §229.10(c)(v). We know that she deposited it into an account in her own name and that her deposit was directly in person to an employee of the bank. The only questions remaining are whether her bank calls for such a deposit to be made using a special deposit slip or deposit envelope, as may be required by the bank under §229.10(c), and if so whether she actually did use the special deposit slip or envelope to make the deposit. The rationale for this special method of deposit, which is also found in §229.10(c)(iv) governing checks drawn by a state or unit of local government, is that the depositary bank would not be able to determine simply from reading information off the MICR line whether the type of check deposited was such as would qualify for next-day availability. The bank is authorized to institute a system for such deposits that will call to the teller's attention the nature of the check. Note that if Emily's deposit of a certified check does not, for some reason, qualify for next-day availability under §229.10(c)(v) — if, for example, she had not deposited in person to an employee of the bank or if she had failed to use the special deposit slip or envelope required by the bank in such situations — the availability of the funds represented by the check is governed by the general availability schedule of §229.12. That is, the Depot bank will only be required to determine, as it easily can do from the MICR line, whether the bank on which the check is drawn makes this a local check (in which case second-day availability will apply) or nonlocal check (which would be entitled to fifth-day availability). See §229.12(b)(4) and (c)(1)(ii).

4.   This check qualifies for next-day availability under the cited part of 12 C.F.R. §229.10, so the amount of the check must be added to the available funds in Joel's account as of Thursday.

5a.   None of the three checks that Susan deposited on Monday is individually entitled to next-day availability. Under §229.10(c)(vii), however, Susan is entitled to next-day availability of *the lesser of* $100 or "the aggregate amount [which in this case would be $440] deposited on any one banking day . . . by check or checks not subject to next-day availability." So Susan is entitled to have $100 added to her available funds on Tuesday. The remaining $340 represented by these checks, which was not made available under this provision, will be available in her account on either Wednesday or the following Monday, depending on whether the individual checks are local or nonlocal items.

5b.   Under 12 C.F.R. §229.10(c)(1)(vii), the full $39.50, being less than $100, would be subject to next-day availability and hence available to Susan on Tuesday.

6a.   The entire amount of this local check must be considered as funds available in Richard's account "not later than the *second* business day following the banking day on which" the check was deposited. So the full $350 will be available in his account on Wednesday, under the requirement of second-day availability for local checks. Note that, depending on what other checks Richard may have deposited on Monday, it is possible that up to $100 of this check was made available to him on Tuesday, under the rule of §220.10(c)(1)(vii), which we looked at in Example 5b. In any event, whatever was not made available to him on Tuesday must be made available on Wednesday, the second business day following deposit.

6b. The funds represented by this nonlocal check (see 12 C.F.R. §229.2(v)) must be made available for withdrawal "no later than the *fifth* business day following the banking day" of deposit. That would mean — assuming that we haven't run into any of the holidays that are not treated as business days under §229.2(g) — that the full $350 would be available in Richard's account on the Monday following the Monday of deposit. This is, not surprisingly, referred to as fifth-day availability for nonlocal checks.

It will not have escaped your attention that the amount of time a customer must wait, under Regulation CC, for availability of funds from any particular deposit will depend on a number of factors. The overall pattern, however, is not that difficult to appreciate. Those deposits made in a form least likely to encounter any difficulty in the collection process — deposits of cash, electronic deposits, government and bank checks, and on-us items — are given the special treatment of the next-day availability rule. Personal checks written on banks other than the depositary bank have to go through a more complicated collection process and are generally thought to carry a greater risk of nonpayment. Dishonor of a local check will usually, if not invariably, be known to the depositary bank within a couple of days. The time it will take for a depositary bank to receive notice of dishonor of a nonlocal check will typically be longer. The scheme of availability set out in Regulation CC is a rough attempt to reflect the realities facing the depositary bank; the greater the risk that any particular item will not eventually end up as collected funds, the greater the amount of time the bank is given before it must make available the amount of the item to its customer.

7a. Under 12 C.F.R. §229.12(d), a depositary bank may extend by one business day the normal second-day or fifth-day availability provided for in subsections (b) and (c), setting the time that funds are available "for withdrawal by cash or similar means." Such similar means include the issuance of a cashier's check. So, although Andrea would have available, as of the Thursday following her Thursday deposit of a nonlocal check, the full $1,000 for use in covering checks she has written that have been presented to the bank, she will have to wait one more day to withdraw this amount in cash or to use it to purchase a cashier's check. She does not, as of Thursday, have the right to purchase a $900 cashier's check based on her deposit exactly five business days earlier of the $1,000 nonlocal check.

7b.   Notice the last two sentences of 12 C.F.R. §229.12(d):

> A depositary bank shall, however, make $400 of these funds available for withdrawal by cash or similar means not later than 5:00 p.m. on the business day on which the funds are available under paragraphs (b), (c) or (f) of this section. This $400 is in addition to the $100 available under §229.10(c)(1)(vii).

So, if Andrea is willing to wait until 5:00 p.m. to pick up the cashier's check she has requested, she would then have the right to a cashier's check in this amount and would not have to wait until the following day. In fact, because $100 in automatic next-day availability under §229.10(c)(vii) will have been allocated to this particular check, she would be entitled to withdraw in cash or purchase a cashier's check for up to $500 as a matter of right by 5:00 p.m. on Thursday. The remaining amount of the check will have to become available on the next business day.

7c.   By this day all of the $1,000 represented by the check deposited six business days earlier must be available to Andrea, either to cover checks written on her account or for "withdrawal by cash or similar means." Even taking into account the one-day extension of 12 C.F.R. §229.12(d), she is entitled to purchase a cashier's check with these funds on this Friday.

8.   Since Julia's deposit into this new account does not fall within either §229.13(a)(1)(i) or (ii), Regulation CC does not impose any mandatory availability schedule on Depot National. Julia is going to have to ask the bank what schedule it uses to make a deposit such as hers into a new account and live with those conditions. Or, of course, she can shop around for another bank in the same locality that has a more favorable availability schedule for deposits made into new accounts by personal checks. She's probably going to have to wait some time. What might she have done in opening her new account to speed things along, or at least to get some help from Regulation CC in seeing that the bank is obligated to *some* mandatory schedule of availability? For one thing she could have brought in a check for $12,000 that was either certified or a cashier's or a teller's check. Had she done this, then under §229.13(a)(1)(ii), she would have been entitled to $5,000 of next-day availability, with the remaining $7,000 available to her no later than nine business days after her deposit, that being Friday of the week following her opening of the account. What could she have done to speed things up even more? For one thing, she could have carried $12,000 in cash into the offices of Depot National Bank, but carrying that amount of cash across the country or even across town is not something that we should be quick to recommend. A safer way would have been for her to have arranged for an electronic transfer of funds from her distant bank directly into her new Depot account, either beforehand or with the aid of the person at Depot who helps her open the new account. In either instance — cash or electronic payment — she would have been entitled to next-day availability under 12 C.F.R. §229.13(a)(1)(i).

9a.   Under 12 C.F.R. §229.13(b)(1), the general availability rules regarding checks of any kind do not apply "to the aggregate amount of deposits by one or more checks to the extent that the aggregate amount is in excess of $5,000 on any one banking day." Under §229.13(h)(2), if this exception applies, the depositary bank may extend the time of availability to "a reasonable period after the day the funds would have been required to be made available had the check been subject to . . . §229.12." Paragraph (h)(4) tells us that,

> For the purposes of this section, a "reasonable period" is an extension of up to one business day for checks described in §229.10(c)(1)(vi), five business days for checks described in §229.12(b)(1) through (4) and six business days for checks described in §229.12(c)(1) and (2) or §229.12(f). A longer extension may be reasonable, but the bank has the burden of so establishing.

So, unless Depot decides to impose an even longer extension and bear the burden of establishing reasonableness, it must make the $50,000 represented by this check available to Amanda no later than seven business days after deposit (two days extended by five) if the check is a local check and eleven business day (five days extended by six) if it is a nonlocal check.

Many banks do not take full advantage of the extensions allowed by this provision, especially when the customer is a business entity that makes deposits of checks for large amounts on a fairly regular basis, but do impose some shorter extensions or allow for availability of at least some portion of the funds at an earlier date.

9b.   Depot is required by the cited paragraph to give Amanda written notice informing her of (among other things) the amount of the deposit that is being delayed; the reason for the exception to its normal availability rules, of which she presumably has knowledge and on which she might otherwise believe she could rely; and "the time period within which the funds will be available for withdrawal."

In these examples we have dealt with only two of the exceptions, provided in 12 C.F.R. §229.13, that may extend the time that the depositary bank has to make the funds deposited available to the customer: the new account and the large deposit exceptions. You can see that there are others of which you should be aware, even if it is not necessary to go into them in detail. Extension of the availability schedule is also allowed when the check is a redeposited check (one that has already been deposited once and returned dishonored); when the customer has "repeatedly overdrawn" his, her, or its account in the recent past; when there is other "reasonable cause to doubt collectibility"; and under certain defined emergency conditions.

PART FIVE

Problems of Theft, Forgery, and Alteration

16

Who Bears the Risk of Theft, Forgery, and Alteration?

The Ways of the Thief

Recall the route that the typical check takes on its way from the customer, who as drawer of a draft is expressing an order, to the payor bank, which as drawee is obligated to carry out that order.

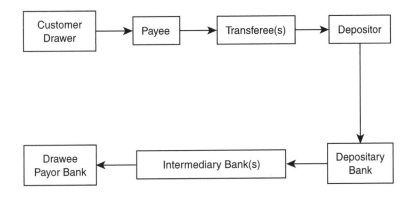

The road can be a long one. The customer first issues the check to the payee. The payee may immediately deposit the check himself or herself, but he or she need not necessarily do so. The check may first be transferred to one or a series of holders before it comes into the hands of a party who decides to deposit it into the depositary bank. At that point, the item enters the check collection system, which we have already looked at in the earlier chapters of Part Three. We know that the depositary bank may, depending on the circumstances, itself present the check directly to the payor bank, or it may instead forward the check for collection through one or a series of intermediary banks. The last of the intermediary banks takes on the special role of being the presenting bank, which forwards the check without intermediary to the payor bank. One way or another, the check is eventually presented to the payor bank.

It will be important to remember for what follows that every time the check is passed from one party to another as it makes its way around the circuit, other than the initial *issuance* by the drawer and the culminating *presentment* to the payor bank, the event can and should be characterized as a *transfer* of the check. Equally important is to recognize that neither issuance nor presentment of a check is an incident of transfer. Issuance is issuance. Presentment is presentment. Any movement in between is a transfer.

This travel of any individual check — from issuance, through anywhere from none to a large number of transfers, to eventual presentment — is referred to in the jargon of the trade as the *downstream flow* of the instrument. As we saw in Chapter 13, at the end of its flow downstream, when the check is presented to the payor bank, that bank will be under a duty (set forth in §4-401(a)) to its customer to honor the check and release funds in the amount of the check for the benefit of the depositor if and when the check is "properly payable." You will also recall from Comment 1 to that section that a check is *not* properly payable if it contains a forged drawer's signature or a forged indorsement. In the preceding chapters we dealt for the most part only with examples in which there was no forgery of any signature, theft of the instrument from its rightful owner, or alteration of any of the instrument's terms. In this chapter, along with Chapters 17 and 18, we abandon this restriction and deal instead with just those situations where some such skullduggery has taken place. A thief has entered the picture. He or she, by nefariously monkeying with or redirecting the intended downstream flow of a check — by busting into the nice, neat diagram with which we began this chapter — is able to divert the flow of funds away from the rightful claimant and into his or her own pocket.

One thing should be made clear from the outset: If the thief of funds is found out and caught, he or she will be made to pay the price. There should be nothing surprising in this. Theft is theft, and there are laws against that kind of thing. Quite apart from whatever criminal sanctions may apply, the thief will be legally liable to whoever has been wrongfully deprived of funds and must turn over the ill-gotten gains. As a matter of fact, part of what we will see in this chapter is just how, section by section, Articles 3 and 4 of the Uniform Commercial Code give the wronged party the statutory authority to recover the stolen amount from the thief. The more interesting, and troubling, problems we have to explore, however, each go one step beyond this. It will probably not shock you to learn that often the thief of funds, just like any other garden-variety thief, disappears with his or her ill-gotten gains before the fact of the theft is uncovered. Even if the thief does stick around and is caught, he or she often enough does not have the funds still on hand to repay the wronged party. What, we then have to ask, should the result be in such a case? Who among all the various parties, individuals and banks, involved in the scenario should end up bearing the loss when the thief cannot be found or, even if found, is not in a position to make full recompense for what he or she has taken? The thief is not around or is not able to put money back in the pot to ensure that everyone else comes out whole. The government may impose criminal sanctions against the malefactor, but it certainly isn't going to cough up the funds to undo the harm the criminal has done. It is inevitable in such a situation that some *innocent party* is going to be left to suffer the loss and have nowhere to turn for relief.*

Thieves are very ingenious types; let's give them that much. There are any number of stratagems that a person intent on getting his or her hands on funds intended for someone else may use to suit the sinister purpose. Almost all instances of theft by check, however, sort themselves out into one of four paradigm cases, each of which occurs with stunning and saddening regularity:

1. The thief forges the signature of the customer-drawer to create a check purportedly authorized by the account holder, or what is sometimes referred to as a "forged check."
2. The thief makes away with a check written to another and then forges that person's indorsement to collect the funds himself or herself.
3. The thief steals a check that is a bearer instrument and collects on it.
4. The thief alters a check either to make it appear to be payable to someone other than the true payee or to inflate the amount for which the check appears to be written.

In the examples of this chapter, we will work our way through each of these paradigm situations in detail.

---

* It might have struck you at this point that whichever party we eventually find is going to have to bear the loss occasioned by the theft should insure against this type of loss. This, of course, just begs the question. Once we have determined the legal rule as to who must bear the loss in a given situation, then it may make sense for that party to pay for insurance covering the type of loss in question. An appropriate form of insurance may indeed be available. Many homeowner's insurance policies, for instance, provide coverage for losses due to stolen or forged checks, and businesses can purchase similar insurance. In some situations it may turn out that the ultimate risk-bearer will reasonably decide to "self-insure" against such losses; that is, to consider them over time as just another inevitable, recurring, and to some degree predictable cost of doing business. But it makes no sense for a party to insure against a loss that it will not be made to bear. So the answer to the question of who may even have to consider the insurance option depends on what we will conclude, upon investigation, about who will be made to bear the risk of loss as a matter of legal principle.

The tools we will need to grapple with the problems arising from this type of misbehavior are several. We already have available to us the all-important "properly payable" rule of §4-401(a).* Beyond this we will have to make use of warranty theory as it is made part of the law governing negotiable instruments — both the warranties of transfer and the warranties of presentment — and the doctrine of conversion as it applies to checks.

The Transfer Warranties

The transfer warranties allow those who have taken transfer of a check under certain conditions to sue back "upstream" those through whose hands the check previously passed if the earlier party transferred the check in breach of one of the warranties. The Code provisions creating and governing these warranties are §3-416 in Article 3 and §4-207 in Article 4. Section 3-416 states the general rules in terms applicable to all negotiable instruments. Once a check has been deposited and entered into the check collection process, it is §4-207 that technically applies to the transfers that take place within that system. Fortunately for us, the two sections are virtually identical, both in language and certainly in intended effect. As the short Official Comment to §4-207 states:

> Except for subsection (b) [a matter with which we are not going to concern ourselves], this section conforms to Section 3-416 and extends its coverage to items [which include checks once they've entered the check collection system]. The substance of this section is discussed in the Comment to Section 3-416.

Because Section 3-416 is accompanied by such a rich load of comments, it seems a better place to look to pick out the details of the transfer warranties in general. By way of introduction, I suggest we break the topic down into a series of questions, most of which we can easily answer from the language of §3-416, primarily subsection (a), itself.

Who gives the transfer warranties?

> "A person who transfers an instrument for consideration." Note from Comment 1 that "[a]ny consideration sufficient to support a simple contract will support these warranties."

Who receives the transfer warranties?

> "[T]he transferee and, if the transfer is by indorsement, . . . any subsequent transferee."

---

* When you get to the examples involving alterations made to a check, you will want to consult §4-401(d)(1), which gives the variant of the properly payable rule as it applies to altered items.

What does the transferor warrant to be true?

(1) That "the warrantor is a person entitled to enforce the instrument." The end of Comment (2) states that this is "in effect a warranty that there are no unauthorized or missing indorsements that prevent the transferor from making the transferee a person entitled to enforce the instrument."

(2) That "all signatures on the instrument are authentic and authorized."

(3) That "the instrument has not been altered."

(4) That "the instrument is not subject to a defense or claim in recoupment of any party that can be asserted against the warrantor."

(5) That the warrantor has no knowledge of any insolvency proceedings commenced against the drawer of the check.

What are the rights of a transferee against a transferor who has breached one of these warranties?

> Look now to subsection (b): Any transferee who took the instrument in good faith "may recover from the warrantor as damages for any breach of warranty an amount equal to the loss suffered as a result of the breach, but not more than the amount of the instrument plus expenses and loss of interest as a result of breach."

May the transfer warranties be disclaimed with respect to checks?

> No. See the first sentence of subsection (c).

The Presentment Warranties

The presentment warranties allow a payor bank that has paid on a check under certain conditions to sue back "upstream" those through whose hands the check previously passed if the earlier party transferred or presented the check in breach of one of the warranties. The presentment warranties are found, in substantially similar form, in §§3-417 and 4-208. Again, for reasons of practicality I suggest we look to the Article 3 section to pick up the details, at least as they relate to checks, and that we do so by breaking the topic down into a series of questions, most of which we can easily answer from the language of §3-417, primarily subsection (a), itself.

Who gives the presentment warranties?

> A person obtaining payment on a check or a previous transferor of the check.

Who receives the presentment warranties?

> The drawee-payor bank that pays on a check.

What does the presenter or prior transferor warrant to be true?

(1) That "the warrantor is, or was, at the time the warrantor transferred the [check], a person entitled to . . . obtain payment . . . of the [check] or authorized to obtain payment . . . of the [check] on behalf of a person entitled to enforce it." Comment 2 states that this is "in effect a warranty that there are no unauthorized or missing indorsements."

(2) That the check has not been altered.

(3) That the warrantor "has no knowledge that the signature of the drawer of the [check] is unauthorized."

What are the rights of a bank that pays a check against a presenter or prior transferor who has breached one of these warranties?

> See subsection (b).

May the presentment warranties be disclaimed with respect to checks?

> No. See the first sentence of subsection (e) as well as the first two sentences of Comment 7, which give the justification for this rule.

Conversion of an Instrument

Conversion is a concept deriving from the basic principles of property law. A person converts the property of another when he or she wrongfully deprives the other of that property or its value. The converter has stolen the property of another and, not surprisingly, is expected to give it back. The application of the conversion notion to negotiable instruments, including checks, goes beyond this elementary example, however, as you can see by a careful reading of §3-420(a).

Who may bring an action in conversion?

> Section 3-420 never states, in so many words, who may qualify to assert a claim in conversion. We generally tend to think of the plaintiff in any conversion action as the "rightful owner" of the instrument, which will usually translate into the "person entitled to enforce" the instrument under §3-301 at the time the conversion took place. Notice that the last sentence of §3-420(a) gives some explicit directives about who may *not* bring an action in conversion (as we will examine more fully in Examples 2b and 5).

Against whom may an action in conversion be brought?

> The introductory sentence to §3-420(a) states that "[t]he law applicable to conversion of personal property applies to instruments." So any thief who steals a negotiable instrument will be liable in conversion no differently than if he or she had stolen a piece of jewelry, a book, or an amount of cash. Subsection (a) goes on, however, to provide: "An instrument is *also* converted if it is taken by transfer, other than negotiation, from a person not entitled to enforce the instrument *or* a bank makes or obtains payment with respect to the instrument for a person not entitled to enforce the instrument or receive payment." This latter type of conversion — which may be the result of actions by a totally innocent and decent party — will play a large part in many of the following examples. Note for the moment the statement in Comment 1 that "[t]his [sentence] covers cases in which a depositary bank or a payor bank takes an instrument bearing a forged indorsement."

What amount may a wronged party collect from the converter?

> See §3-420(b).

Putting It Together

We now have at least an introduction to all of the pieces the puzzle that we will need to sort out the mess the thief has left in his or her wake. The examples in this chapter give us the chance to work out how these pieces come together in a variety of scenarios to give us the legal analysis on which will turn the thorny question of which party must ultimately bear the burden of the loss to the thief — assuming, of course, that the thief is not available to pay up and come clean. In the Code we are given an array of distinct and highly precise legal concepts, each of which we have to be ready to apply when the time is right: the properly payable rule, the transfer warranties, the presentment warranties, and conversion. These, together with the large number of parties who may be involved in even the simplest of situations, can make the questions of who *can* and who *should* sue whom and *on what grounds* at first (and I stress, only at first) seem fairly daunting, if not downright mystifying. That said, let me suggest a general approach to problems of this type to help you to sort them out and work them through.

First and foremost, I cannot urge too strongly that you first draw out at least a rudimentary diagram that helps you keep track of exactly who each of the parties is, what role each has played, and exactly what has happened to the particular check whose misadventure we are tracking. Feel free to use the format of diagram I have been using so far in this book (I'll be relying on it myself in the explanations of this and succeeding chapters.) — but the exact form of your diagram is, of course, not the important thing. First get the facts straight, and do this by whatever visual means work best for you.

Next thing to do is to stare at your diagram. If, as we will assume, the thief has made off with some money that is not rightfully his or hers, then some other party is as of this moment left holding the bag, so to speak. That party, which could be a private party, a consumer or a business, or one of the banks that figures in your diagram, is *out of pocket* a sum of money equal to the amount that has been stolen. There's no way around it: The sums must always equal out. If the thief has successfully made off with some money, somebody else is, when we first enter the scene to do our analysis, short by the same amount. So the key fact on which we now focus is exactly which party now stands aggrieved by the loss of funds.

Now the fun begins. Though I do not want to minimize how serious this is to the actual parties involved, from our perspective it may not be unsporting to think of the situation as analogous to one extended game of "hot potato." Someone must ultimately bear the loss and be left holding the bag, but who will it be? Initially we look at the problem from the point of view of the party we have just identified as being the one left out of pocket the amount of the theft when we first take a look at the scene. That party takes a look around him, her, or it (as on behalf of that party we take a good long look at our diagram). Is there anyone else upstream or downstream of the presently aggrieved party on the route the check has traveled to whom that party can *shift* the loss by one means or another? Recall the tools at hand: a customer can make its bank recredit its account for any amount paid on a not properly payable item; a transferee can, in the appropriate instances, enforce the transfer warranties against upstream parties; the payor bank can assert the presentment warranties; the rightful owner of a check can bring an action for conversion against parties downstream who have done him, her, or it wrong if the facts fit within the confines of §3-420. One way or another, the initially aggrieved party will try to shift the burden of the loss from its shoulders onto those of someone else.

If the initially aggrieved party is able to shift the loss onto another in some way, that is of course not the end of the story. We now have to ask whether *that* party, who is now out of pocket the amount of the theft, can itself shift the loss once again, either upstream or downstream, to get out from under the burden of loss. And so it goes. Our complete analysis may conclude that there is from the very start no chance of the initially aggrieved party shifting the loss to anyone else; that party may be stuck with the loss and have nowhere else to turn. In other situations, we may determine that the loss can legitimately be shifted from one party to another several times until it eventually comes to rest with some party who will have to be the ulti- mate loss-bearer. The game of hot potato cannot and does not go on forever. Eventually things come to an end, and we will have discovered what party is the ultimate loss-bearer in the situation.

What you will begin to see as you work through the examples is that, although each scenario has its own peculiarities and calls for distinct analysis, the actual events can and will be grouped into a limited number of archetypes or patterns, reflecting those four paradigmatic categories of thievery mentioned early in the first part of this introduction; for each pattern, a general rule will appear. Your task now is to work through each of the examples carefully, so that you can discern those patterns as they emerge and the general rules or results that apply to each of them.

EXAMPLES

1.   Andrew, who has a checking account with Payson State Bank, hires one Thad to do some redecorating in Andrew's apartment. When he is left alone in Andrew's den, Thad (who turns out to be not just a decorator but also a thief) finds Andrew's checkbook in a desk drawer. Thad rips out one of the checks from the middle of the book. Later that night, Thad uses the stolen check form to write out a check to himself for $700, forging Andrew's signature on the drawer line. Thad signs his own name on the back of the check and deposits it in his bank, the Depot National Bank. The check is forwarded by Depot National for collection to Payson State via two intermediary banks, First Intermediate and Second Intermediate. Second Intermediate presents the check to Payson, which pays the check out of Andrew's account. The $700 makes its way into Thad's account with Depot. Thad quickly withdraws all his available funds from his Depot account and disappears from the scene. When Andrew gets his next monthly statement from Payson, he carefully looks it over and quickly discovers that this one check for $700 has been paid out of his account based on a check that he never signed or authorized. No wonder the balance in his account is $700 less than he expected it to be!

(a) Does Andrew have a right to insist that Payson recredit his account with the $700?

(b) Assume that Payson does recredit the account as Andrew insists. Now *it* is out that amount of money. May Payson assert a breach of a transfer warranty against any party to make itself whole? Why not?

(c) May Payson assert a breach of a presentment warranty against any party to make itself whole?

(d) How does this particular scenario play itself out? That is, which party ends up "losing" the $700 that Thad the thief has made off with?

(e) The basic pattern of thievery set out in this single, humble example repeats itself all too often in everyday life, with only the details changed. The one consistent element is that the theft is accomplished by the creation of a so-called *forged check* — that is, one on which the signature of the drawer has been forged — that is presented to and paid by the payor bank. Who do you conclude will ultimately be made to bear the loss to the thief in any general case of this type? Does this result depend on any showing that the party bearing the loss acted in bad faith or with a lack of ordinary care in its handling of the particular item? In this regard, take a look at the definitions given in §3-103(a)(4) and (7).

2.   Before his unfortunate disappearance, Thad the decorator was also finishing up a job at the home of one Cara. While doing his last bit of "cleaning up," he comes across a check resting in the top drawer of Cara's bureau. The check, for $1,200, has been written "to the order of Cara" by one Bernie out of his account with the Payson State Bank. Bernie sent this check to Cara to repay a loan she had made to him a few months earlier. Thad puts this check in his pocket on the way out of Cara's home. Thad signs the name "Cara" on the back of the check. Under this he signs his own name and deposits the check in his bank, the Depot National Bank. The check is forwarded by Depot National for collection to Payson State via two intermediary banks, First Intermediate and Second Intermediate. Second Intermediate presents the check to Payson, which pays the check out of Bernie's account. The $1,200 makes its way into Thad's account with Depot. Thad quickly withdraws all his available funds from his Depot account and disappears from the scene. When Cara returns to her home, she is pleased with how the redecorating work has come out and how clean Thad has left the place, but quickly discovers that the check she had received from Bernie is missing. She contacts Bernie, who calls his bank, only to be told that the check has already been paid out of his account.

  (a) Cara tells Bernie that he should send her another check for $1,200 so that she can consider the loan repaid. Is Bernie obligated to do as she says? Recall §3-310(b)(1) and consult Comment 4 to that section.

  (b) Bernie does write Cara a second check for $1,200, which she quickly deposits in her own bank and which is paid by Payson State. Bernie has now had $2,400 deducted from his account and has the benefit of only satisfying a single debt for $1,200. He quite understandably looks for a means of recovering what he has lost on account of the first, stolen check. Can Bernie bring a conversion action against any of the other players in this story? See the last sentence in §3-420.

  (c) Does Bernie have the right to insist that Payson State recredit his account with the $1,200 paid on this first check?

  (d) Assume that Payson State does recredit Bernie's account for the $1,200 represented by the first check. Under this set of facts, may Payson assert a breach of a transfer warranty against any party to make itself whole?

  (e) May Payson assert a breach of a presentment warranty against any party to make itself whole?

  (f) Assume that Payson successfully asserts a breach of a presentment warranty against Second Intermediate Bank. That bank pays Payson

$1,200. What route would you now suggest to Second Intermediate to avoid itself having to bear the loss of this amount?

(g) If every party pays careful attention to its rights, which party ends up "losing" and not being able to pass on to any other the $1,200 that Thad the thief made off with when he stole the check belonging to Cara and forged her signature on the back of it?

3. The fact pattern is the same as in Example 2. Cara, however, decides to take another route to recovering the $1,200 represented by the check Thad has stolen from her bureau, a route that need not involve Bernie at all.

(a) May Cara bring an action claiming the conversion of this stolen check? Against whom may she bring such an action? Look at §3-420(c) and Comment 3 to that section.

(b) Suppose Cara successfully brings a conversion action against Payson State Bank and is paid $1,200 by that bank. Is there any other party against which Payson may proceed to itself recover this loss? If so, on what basis?

(c) How does the end result compare with the result in Example 2?

4. We look at this same set of facts one last time. If she had wanted to, could Cara have brought a conversion cause of action against Depot National Bank directly?

5. Danielle owes some money to her friend Edgar. She prepares a check, drawn on her account at Payson State Bank, made out to Edgar for $124. She puts this check in the mail correctly addressed to Edgar, but for some mysterious reason it never arrives. Several weeks later, Edgar calls Danielle asking where his money is. She tells him about the check that she previously mailed to him. He assures her that he never received it. Danielle goes to her bank and is able to find out that the check was cashed (bearing an indorsement of "Edgar" which even Danielle can tell looks nothing at all like Edgar's signature) at some place named The Korner Deli, which had then deposited the check in its account at Depot Bank. The check had been forwarded to Payson, which paid it in the normal course of its operations. Danielle reports all this to Edgar. She says to him, "You are obviously going to have to look into how, if at all, you can get your $124 back." Edgar objects. His position is that he has never been paid the $124 and that Danielle still owes it to him. He insists on immediate payment of this amount, either by another check or in cash. As far as the first check is concerned, he tells Danielle, "That's *your* problem, not mine." The two of them want to remain friends, so they consult you for advice. As of this moment, who bears the loss? How should that party proceed to get the $124 back? Who should eventually bear the loss in this situation if the mysterious stranger who cashed the check while pretending to be Edgar cannot be identified and somehow brought to justice? Be sure, in preparing your explanation to Danielle and Edgar, to consult the last sentence of §3-420(a).

6.   Danielle writes a second check, this one for $300 to Ernesto, out of her Payson account. She mails this check to Ernesto, who receives it. He puts it in his wallet, intending to deposit it in his own account. On his way to the bank, Thelma (a thief) steals his wallet. She finds the check inside. She writes "Pay to Thelma" on the back of the check, under which she signs "Ernesto." Thelma takes this check to Isaac's Liquor Emporium, where she asks Isaac the owner to cash the check for her. After checking Thelma's ID, Isaac asks Thelma to sign the back of the check in her own name, which she does. Isaac takes the check and gives Thelma $100 worth of liquor and $200 cash in return. Isaac deposits this check, along with others that he has taken in during the week, into his account with Depot National Bank. The check is forwarded to Payson State, which pays. By the time Ernesto is able to patch together the story of what has happened to the stolen check, Thelma is, needless to say, nowhere to be found.

(a) Need Ernesto necessarily bear the loss of the $300 represented by the check, along with whatever else of value there might have been in the wallet? How should he proceed to recover at least this $300?

(b) All of the situations, from Example 2 through this one, bear one thing in common: The theft is accomplished by the forgery of an indorsement on the check. Who do you conclude will ultimately be made to bear the theft loss in any general case of this type? Does this result depend on any showing that the party bearing the loss acted in bad faith or with a lack of ordinary care in its handling of the particular item?

7.   Hugo also has a checking account with Payson State Bank. Theo steals a check out of Hugo's checkbook. He makes this check out "to the order of Irving Place," forging Hugo's signature on the drawee line. Irving Place is a real person, a member of the community. In fact, Theo has spent some time preparing a set of fake documents that will allow him to impersonate Irving, if and when the need (for Theo) arises. He uses these documents to cash the check that he has created, bearing as you will recall a forgery of Hugo's signature, at the Main Street Check Cashing Service. Theo signs the back of the check as "Irving Place." The check cashing service deposits this check in its own account. The check is eventually presented to the Payson bank, which pays it. When the facts of what has happened are finally unraveled, Hugo demands that Payson recredit his account with the amount of this bogus check. (Theo is long gone. Or maybe not. As you study the situation, you will note that the identity of Theo as the specific bad actor who pulled this off will not be obvious to any of the other parties to the "transaction." All they will be able to determine is that *someone* has made off with some money that was not his or hers to have. Theo may well still be hanging around town — just being himself, or Mr. Irving Place, as the spirit moves him.) The question then becomes who should bear the loss of the amount of the check. Main Street Check Cashing will argue that the loss should

ultimately be sustained by Payson State Bank, as the check bore a forged drawer's signature. Payson will counter that Main Street itself, as a party who took a check carrying a forged indorsement from the forger himself, should bear the loss. Which argument do you think should prevail?

8.   Lacky receives a paycheck for $1,000 from his employer, Ms. Boss. This check is written on Boss's account with Payson State Bank. Lacky signs the back of the check with his name only and puts it in his wallet. As he is on the way to his bank to deposit this check, a thief comes up from behind, knocks him down, and makes off with his wallet. The check is later deposited in an account held by one Mugsy Boy at the Depot National Bank. Depot forwards the check to Payson, which pays the check out of the Boss account. Mugsy is eventually apprehended, but by the time he is caught he is penniless. He has no money or other valuables on him, and his account at Depot National Bank is running in the red.

  (a) Does Lacky have any legal avenues open to him by which he may recover the loss of the $1,000, which Mugsy stole and apparently has squandered?

  (b) As a general rule, who do you conclude bears the risk of loss of a check that is at the time of the theft in bearer form?

9.   Ms. Boss receives a delivery of supplies needed for her business from Sammy's Supplies Store, along with an invoice requesting that she pay $125 for the supplies within 30 days of delivery. She writes a check out of her Payson State Bank account payable to Sammy's Supplies Store for $125, and mails it to the address given on the invoice. When Sammy receives this check, he is in desperate need of ready cash to keep his business afloat. Using a pen similar in color to that which Boss used to write the check, he is able to insert a comma and a zero between the "1" and the "2" where the amount of the check is given in numbers, so that it now reads "$1,025." He also uses an ink eraser and the pen to change the amount of the check where it is given in words to read "One Thousand Twenty-Five and 00/100 Dollars." He deposits this check in his account with Depot National Bank. The bank forwards the check to Payson which pays it, deducting $1,025 from Boss's account. Because the check is paid, this same amount is soon credited to Sammy's account with Depot. When Boss next receives her monthly bank statement from Payson, she immediately sees what has happened. She complains to Sammy, only to find that by this time he is totally insolvent and not in a position to repay anything to anybody.

  (a) Boss contacts Payson and demands that it immediately recredit her account with the full $1,025. Is it obligated to do so? See §3-407(a) and §4-401(d).

  (b) To the extent that Payson does have to recredit Boss's account, it is then bearing this amount of loss. How should it proceed in an attempt to make itself whole?

10. The firm of Magnetic Resonating Services, Incorporated, which uses as its trade name the shorter "M.R.S., Inc." runs a facility where doctors send patients in need of highly sophisticated (and highly expensive) medical testing. The company insists that all patients pay in full at the time of testing for the services being performed, either in cash, with a credit card, or by check. One morning a patient, Martha Kent, comes in for some testing and as she leaves writes out a check to the order of "MRS" for the $1,200 that she has been told the testing will cost her. This check is written on Martha's checking account with Payson State Bank. It is sitting on top of the reception desk when the next patient, Lois Lane, comes up to the desk to check in. At a moment when the receptionist is distracted by some other business, Lois quietly takes Martha's check and slips it into her purse. She quickly makes up some excuse why she cannot have her medical testing done that morning and leaves the company's facilities. Once home, Lois makes some additions to what is written on the payee line on this check, so that it then reads "MRS. LOIS LANE." Lois deposits this check in her account with the Depot National Bank. The bank forwards the check to Payson, which pays the check out of Martha Kent's account. The $1,200 is added to Lois Lane's account with Depot. By the time the facts of what has happened have been sorted out, Lois has withdrawn everything from her Depot account and is nowhere to be found.

(a) M.R.S., Inc., acknowledges that it was given a check for $1,200 from Martha for the services it provided her, but it has never actually received any of the money represented by the check. How do you suggest it proceed? What party should eventually bear the loss of the $1,200 that Lois Lane has so cleverly made away with?

(b) Looking at this example and the previous one, what do you conclude about who will normally bear the loss occasioned by a thief's alteration of a check?

EXPLANATIONS

1a. First, let's get a good look at the situation:

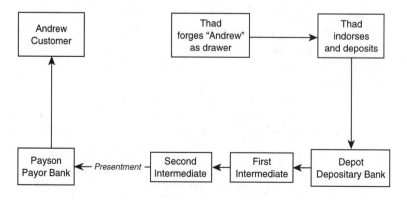

Thad forged Andrew's name as drawer on a check written to himself. Thad indorsed the check and deposited it in Depot Bank. Depot sent the check on for collection to Payson, which paid it out of Andrew's account. Thad has made off with the $700, and Andrew is at this point out that amount of money. This is how things would stand, perhaps indefinitely, except that Andrew becomes aware of the problem — if not all the details, at least that his account has been charged $700 that he did not authorize — and so it is up to him to make the first move to rectify the situation.

Andrew does have the right to insist that Payson recredit his account with the $700. We have already seen that, under §4-401(a), the payor bank may not charge the customer's account for anything other than a properly payable item. An item is not properly payable unless it is "authorized" by the customer, which this check certainly was not. Recall the language in Comment 1 to §4-401 that, "An item containing a forged drawer's signature or a forged indorsement is not properly payable." The check bears a forged drawer's signature, so it was not properly payable. Payson must recredit Andrew's account with the $700.

1b. Payson may not assert the transfer warranties against anyone. The transfer warranties accompany any *transfer*, being given by the transferor to "the transferee and to any subsequent collecting bank" (§4-207(a)). Payson is not a transferee. It was *presented* with the item and, as you'll recall, presentment is not a transfer. Nor is Payson a collecting bank; it is the payor bank, and the payor bank is not a collecting bank (§4-105(5)).

1c. Payson did receive the presentment warranties at the time the check was presented to it and it paid on the item. The problem for Payson will be that, except for Thad himself, no party has breached any of the presentment warranties. Look to §4-208(a) and the analogous §3-417 (where the helpful comments are found). The payor bank can rely upon three warranties of presentment. The first of the warranties, that set forth in subsection (a)(1), may at first seem to apply to the situation, but it does not. As Comment 2 to §3-417 makes clear, "Subsection (a)(1) is in effect a warranty that there are no unauthorized or missing *indorsements*." Thad has indorsed the instrument and in his own name. So there is no breach of that warranty. The check has not been altered in any way, so (a)(2) has not been breached by any party.

This leaves us, and Payson, with the warranty set forth in (a)(3): A warranty that "the warrantor has no knowledge that the signature of the drawer of the draft is unauthorized." The simple fact of the matter is that, other than Thad himself, who certainly is aware that his forgery of Andrew's name as drawer of the check was unauthorized, none of the other parties who subsequently handled the check has breached this warranty to Payson. The banks that handled the check for collection — Depot, First Intermediate, and Second Intermediate — had no knowledge that the signature of Andrew on the drawer line was a forgery.

1d. Payson State Bank, the payor bank that paid on a check with a forged drawer's signature, ultimately ends up bearing the $700 loss. There is no other party — other than, of course, Thad if he could ever be found — onto whom it may shift the burden. The buck (or rather the loss of the 700 bucks) stops at Payson's door.

1e. The general rule is as we see it in this example: The loss of any money to a thief who has created a forged check and by that means made off with the amount of the check, rests on the payor bank that paid the check. It is important to note that this is a rule of strict liability, and does *not* depend on any showing in the particular case, nor on any general assumption, that the payor bank must either have been lacking in good faith or acting negligently in paying the item. There is no reason to think that a payor bank, honoring a check such as this in the ordinary course of its automated operations, is not acting in good faith; that is, with "honesty in fact and the observance of reasonable commercial standards of fair dealing" (§3-103(a)(4)). Nor can it be said to have acted without ordinary care, as defined in §3-103(a)(7), especially when you take into account the second sentence of that definition. The payor bank is an innocent party that must bear the loss resulting from this kind of theft because, when you get down to it, that's the way the rules work. Were it able to make itself whole by shifting the loss to another, that other would itself be an innocent party in no better position to bear the loss.

The result here is not an invention of the drafters of the Uniform Commercial Code. It is generally referred to as the "rule of *Price v. Neal*," after the early English case that first set out the principle. Subsequent renditions of the law of negotiable instruments, up to and including the 1990 revisions to Articles 3 and 4 of the U.C.C., have retained the rule. See Comment 3 to §3-417:

> [S]ubsection (a)(3) retains the rule of Price v. Neal, 3 Burr. 1354 (1762), that the drawee takes the risks that the drawer's signature is unauthorized unless the person presenting the draft has knowledge that the drawer's signature is unauthorized.

At the time of its origination in the mid eighteenth century, the justification for this "rule" would have been that a drawee bank, which would presumably have made a sight inspection and individual determination of whether to pay any check coming to it for payment, would be in the best position to compare the drawer's signature on the check with the sample of the drawer's signature it had on file, and thus to catch the forgery. The rule, as we have seen, has continued unchanged even to this day, when the processing of checks takes place in a very different environment and in very different ways. Whatever rationale there is behind the rule today has to be more than simply persistence of a classic case and a time-honored tradition. It can be argued that the drawee bank, even if it was not lacking in ordinary care in paying this instrument automatically, is still in the best position to determine what level of scrutiny to give to checks presented to it for payment. It cannot and will not sight-examine each and every item; that would simply be too expensive and unwarranted by the level of risk it faces by honoring most checks presented without this kind of special treatment. The drawee bank can, however, set up its computerized systems to sift out for special attention unusually large or otherwise questionable items. Had Thad forged this check to himself for $70,000, let us say, and this is an unusually high amount for a check that passes through Andrew's account, it is unlikely that Payson's computers would have paid it as a matter of course. The bank would have taken more time with the check, comparing the signature on it to the specimen signature of Andrew that it had on file. Even if the forgery was a good one, and the signature looked authentic, someone at Payson might have personally contacted Andrew to inquire whether he had indeed drawn the check in question. Thus the drawee-payor bank is left, by the rule of *Price v. Neal*, to make its own cost-benefit analysis of what level of safeguards it wants to build into its check payment system to reflect the fact that it will have to bear the loss of any forged check it pays.

In this particular example (and in probably the great majority of situations), the thief, having not been overly greedy, the forged check was paid as a matter of course and the loss was left to be borne by the payor bank. Because all banks that carry on this kind of business will end up bearing their share of loss on such forged items, the loss to thieves of Thad's ilk is thought of as roughly balancing out, with each bank taking its share of such losses. The end result is that losses of this type end up being considered as just another cost of doing business for banks like Payson and any other bank that offers checking account services. The cost thus gets spread out among all checking account customers, such as you and I.

2a. My diagram has the situation looking like this:

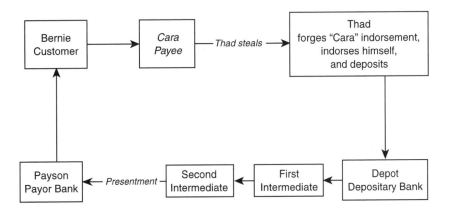

As to the first question presented, no, Bernie is not obligated to send Cara a second check to repay the loan. Upon Cara's receipt and taking of the first check, Bernie's repayment obligation was suspended under §3-310(b)(1). This suspension continues until the check is dishonored "or until it is paid or certified." This check has not been "paid" under the definition of §3-602(a), because payment was not made to a person entitled to enforce the instrument. Thad was not entitled to enforce the instrument because the supposed indorsement of Cara that it bore was forged. Thad is not a holder of the check. The suspension of Bernie's obligation to Cara thus carries on indefinitely, as Comment 4 to §3-310 makes clear. Bernie is not obligated to send Cara a second check, but he may of course do so if he wishes, and if he trusts Cara sufficiently. In this scenario as we first work it through, we will assume that Bernie does.

2b. No, Bernie cannot bring a conversion action against anyone for the wrongful payment of this check. The last sentence of §3-420 explicitly states that a conversion action may not be brought by the issuer of the instrument. This language was added to Article 3's section on conversion (previously numbered §3-419) to clarify an issue that had divided the courts. See the second paragraph of Comment 1 to the current §3-420.

2c. As the comment you just read concludes, "The drawer has an adequate remedy against the payor bank for recredit of the drawer's account for unauthorized payment of the check." The first check that was paid by Payson was not a properly payable item. It bore a forged indorsement. Therefore, Payson does have to recredit Bernie's account for the $1,200 it subtracted from his account balance when it wrongfully paid that check.

2d. No. Once again we rely on the basic principle that the payor bank does not receive the transfer warranties from anyone. There was no transfer of the check to Payson, but rather a presentment.

2e. Yes. Payson as the payor bank may assert, under §4-208, the breach of any presentment warranty against the party that presented the check, which would be Second Intermediate, or against any "previous transferor," which would include First Intermediate, Depot Bank and of course Thad. In this situation, unlike the one we explored in the first example, there has in fact been a breach of a presentment warranty. Recall that the warranty set out in subsection (a)(1) is (in the words of Comment 1 to §3-417) "in effect a warranty that there are no unauthorized or missing indorsements." Here the indorsement purporting to be that of Cara is indeed unauthorized; it is an out-and-out forgery. Payson can assert the breach of this (a)(1) warranty against either of the intermediary banks or against Depot Bank. Payson could also try to bring suit against Thad as well on this theory, but we have to assume that its doing so would only be an exercise in frustration. Thad isn't anywhere to be found, much less served with process.

2f. Payson was not obliged to make its claim for retribution against Second; it could have gone against First or Depot instead. But it certainly was free to do as it has done in going against Second, and so we look at the situation as we then find it. Second Intermediate Bank would not be able to assert any claim of a breach of any presentment warranties that ran to it. Second received no presentment warranties as the check passed through its hands. Second did, however, receive the full panoply of *transfer* warranties of §4-207 from the customer (Thad) and the various collecting banks that were upstream of it as the check flowed (that is, First Intermediate and Depot National). Each of these parties could be held responsible to Second Intermediate for a breach of the warranty set forth in (a)(2), as the signature of Cara on the check was most definitely unauthorized. Second could bring a claim for reimbursement directly against Depot. If instead Second brought its claim against First Intermediate, as it would have every right to do, then First would in turn have the right to proceed against Depot on the transfer warranties that First received, along with the check, during the flow downstream.

2g. One way or another, Depot is going to end up having to bear the loss of this money. It retains the right to go against Thad, of course, but, as we have already concluded, this right is at least in this instance more theoretical than real.

3a. Yes. Cara may bring a conversion action against Thad, under the first sentence of §3-420, but that is not likely to get her anywhere. She may also bring an action, based on the second sentence of that section, against either Payson Bank or Depot Bank. Notice that she may *not* assert liability for conversion against either of the two intermediary collecting banks, First Intermediate or Second Intermediate, because of the special rule laid out in subsection (c) of §3-420. These banks just served as mere conduits, for the paper check and the flow of funds through interbank settlements, in the processing of the check. Were Cara to be extended the opportunity to assert conversion against either of these two banks, all it would mean is that those banks in turn would have to move the loss upstream in a separate action or series of actions. Subsection (c) cuts out the middlemen, so to speak, because there is nothing to be gained in allowing the owner of the check to bring an action based on conversion against them other than in instances (which have to be extremely rare) in which the intermediary bank still retains some of the "proceeds [of the item] that it has not paid out."

3b. Cara has decided to go against Payson in conversion and has been successful. Payson may now assert the breach of a presentment warranty — that found in §4-208(a)(1) — against Depot.

3c. The route we and the parties have taken is different, but the result is, as you would hope, the same. Depot, the depositary bank that took the check bearing a forged indorsement from the forger, ends up bearing the loss. Once again, Depot does have any number of ways to go against Thad, but we have to assume that in all reality they add up to one big fat zero.

4. Yes. Nothing in the text of §3-420 bars Cara from bringing a conversion action against Depot directly. That bank will have to pay up and, as in

the two preceding examples, will be the party that ultimately bears the loss of the $1,200 made off with by Thad the thief.

You might wonder why I set aside a whole example just to ask what turns out to be a particularly easy question. The explanation is that although the question causes no difficulties for us today, with the present revised 1990 version of Article 3, the result would have been otherwise prior to that revision. The section in the prerevision Article 3 dealing with the nature of conversion explicitly extended the defense, which we have already seen in the current §3-420(c), to cover *depositary* banks as well as intermediary banks. The result was that a party in Cara's position would have been forced to bring her conversion action against the drawee-payor bank, which, upon paying up, would have then had to bring a separate action (based on the breach of a presentment warranty) against the depositary bank.

This situation worked an especially great hardship (and for no apparent benefit that anyone could make out) on a party from whom a large number of checks, and not just a single check, had been stolen. Imagine that Thad had stolen from the top drawer of Cara's bureau, say, a dozen checks that had been issued and sent to Cara by a dozen different drawers on a dozen different drawee banks spread all over the country. Thad then takes all these checks, forges Cara's indorsement on the back of each, and then deposits them together (for a total of, say, $4,568) into Depot National Bank. Thad then makes away with all the money before anyone can stop him. If, as was true under the language of the prerevision Article 3, Cara could not bring a conversion action directly against the Depot bank, it would be necessary for her to bring 12 separate conversion actions, one against each of the 12 distinct drawee banks. Each of these 12 banks would in turn have had to bring a distinct action, based on the check it had wrongfully paid, against Depot. If all worked out as it should, the end result would be Cara retrieving (in 12 chunks) her $4,568 and the Depot bank being liable in 12 different actions for a series of judgments totaling that same amount, $4,568. You can understand why commentators and some courts were so critical of the rule, barring as it did someone in Cara's position from bringing one simple action for recovery on the conversion theory against the depositary for all that had been stolen, no matter the number of checks and the multiple jurisdictions in which each of the several drawee banks was located.

The revised version of Article 3 did away with this whole controversy, and the entire problem, by "adjusting" the language that now appears in §3-420(c) so that it does not offer any immunity from a conversion action to the depositary bank. See Comment 3 to this section.

5.   As you will no doubt have already told Danielle and Edgar, the loss of the money represented by this check is as of this moment on Danielle.

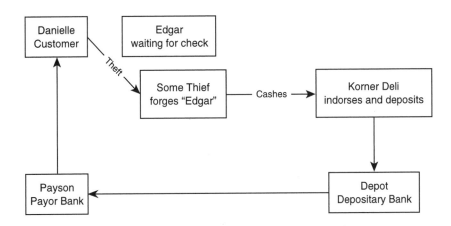

First of all, recall the rule of §3-310(b)(2). Danielle has a preexisting debt to Edgar. She puts a check in the mail to meet that debt, but the check never arrives. Under §3-310(b)(2), her underlying obligation to Edgar, whatever its genesis, would have been suspended only when Edgar "took" the check. Edgar never took this check; he never had a chance to. Therefore, Danielle's underlying obligation to Edgar has not been suspended, much less discharged, by the mailing of the check and its eventual charge against Danielle's account. Danielle must pay Edgar what she owes him and then confront the fact that $124 has been charged against her account by Payson State Bank when it should not have been.

Notice this result also comports with what we find in the last sentence of §3-420. A conversion action may not be brought by "(ii) a payee . . . who did not receive delivery of the instrument either directly or through delivery to an agent or a co-payee." If we were to conclude that, as of this moment, the loss of the $124 is Edgar's to bear, there would be no way for Edgar to move the loss onto anyone else's shoulders. He would end up bearing the loss by the theft of some of his property that he never had possession of in the first place. Placing the loss initially on Danielle may not be a result that particularly delights her, but at least she will have some way of recovering that loss so that she ultimately does not have to bear it.

How should Danielle proceed to make sure she isn't stuck holding the $124 bag? She should contact Payson and convince them that this was not a properly payable item, because it bore a forged indorsement. Payson must then recredit Danielle's account with the amount. Payson can then bring an action based on the breach of a presentment warranty (because the check bore a forged indorsement) against any intermediary bank that passed on the item, against Depot National Bank, against the Korner Deli, or finally against the thief (whatever his or her name may be) — if it can even figure out who that person was. If Payson sues up the chain some party other than the deli, the party onto whom the loss is then temporarily shifted (say, Depot Bank) can then itself sue the Korner Deli on a breach of a warranty of transfer. Ultimately the loss will be borne by the deli unless it can identify, locate, and get its hands on (metaphorically, of course) the thief who cashed the check either pretending to be Edgar or that the signature of "Edgar" on the back of the check was the real thing.

6a. Ernesto, unlike Edgar of the previous example, having actually received the check prior to its being stolen, is in a position to bring a conversion action under §3-420 based on the fact that payment on was made to "a person not entitled to enforce the instrument or receive payment."

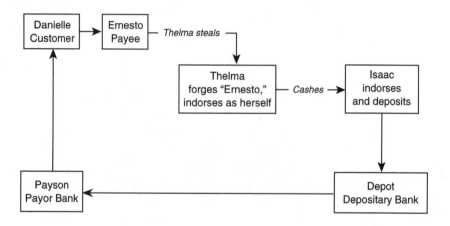

He could bring such an action against Isaac, who has "taken the check by transfer, other than a negotiation, from a person not entitled to enforce the instrument," or against either the Payson or Depot bank. If he does recover his money from either of the banks, that bank would act to recover the loss from Isaac, calling upon either the presentment warranties (in the case of Payson) or the transfer warranties (for Depot). Ultimately, Isaac will bear the loss of the $300.

6b. The general result when a theft of this kind, involving a forged indorsement, has occurred is that the party who took the instrument directly from the forger — the first party downstream of the villain — should end up as the one ultimately bearing the loss. In many cases, such as we saw in Examples 2 through 4, that party will end up being the depositary bank. In others, such as this and the preceding example, it will be a private party who has taken the check from the thief, usually having cashed it or given goods or services in return.

This result, although it doesn't come with a convenient handle as does "the rule of *Price v. Neal*," which we looked at earlier when a different mode of thievery was involved, does share with that rule an important feature: It is a rule of strict liability. The party who has taken an instrument bearing a forged indorsement directly from the forger should end up bearing the loss even if nothing in the particular situation could bring into question that party's good faith or its exercise of ordinary care. Some innocent party has to bear the loss, and the rule has evolved that the loser should be the one who took directly from the thief, even if that party was undoubtedly acting in good faith and can legitimately claim to have done everything within reason considering his, her, or its situation to avoid taking an instrument with a phony indorsement. What justification there is for this result — other than that some innocent party has to bear the loss and no better candidate obviously comes to mind — lies in the fact that the party who takes from the forger, having actually had some sort of direct contact with the malefactor, is in the best position of any of the parties involved to catch the forgery, or, if that is not possible (forgers can be very good at what they do), at least to make a knowing and reasonable, if not necessarily precise and quantifiable, cost-benefit analysis of how much care to take to bring down to a tolerable level the number of instances when it will be made to bear this form of loss.

We cannot reasonably expect that loss due to forged indorsements can be avoided altogether. There is still money to be made in thievery. To the extent that loss of this type is often (probably most often) borne by a depositary bank, the costs end up being spread — as with the rule of *Price v. Neal* — among all checking account customers. When the loss is borne by another private party, such as the Korner Deli in Example 5 or Isaac's Liquor Store in this example, it ends up being factored into the cost of doing business for that enterprise. The Deli or the Liquor Store could, of course, adopt a rigid policy of never cashing so-called third-party checks (such as we saw in this example) or of never cashing any checks, but it may very sensibly determine that such a stance would hurt more than it would help, by alienating long-standing and trusted customers or by driving away new business. In the present example, if Isaac had refused to take the check from Thelma, she would most likely simply have taken her business elsewhere. In the particular instance, this would have been just fine with Isaac, who now knows that Thelma is a thief and passed to him a check on which he will not be able to collect. We have to remember, however, that the great majority of checks are just fine; they do not bear a forged drawer's signature nor any forged indorsement. For Isaac to refuse to take any checks because of the slight, if foreseeable, risk involved in doing so might just cut into his sales significantly if other liquor stores in the area were not so picky.

You should be careful not to fall into the trap of assuming that anyone who takes a check bearing a forged indorsement must have been negligent in some way, or lacking in "ordinary care" as that term is defined in §3-103(a)(7). There is simply no way that a party taking a check can make an in-depth inquiry of each and every indorsement on the instrument. Even if this were possible, we have to acknowledge that any forger who is willing to put in the time and effort should be able to come up with a reasonable likeness of the necessary signature, and with some reasonably convincing (if phony) supporting identification, which always helps. In some situations, of course, it may be appropriate to charge the party taking the instrument with a lack of ordinary care, because of the too-casual or sloppy way it handled the transaction. But that is another story, which we take up in Chapter 17. For the moment, the general rule — that the loss due to a forged indorsement ends up lying at the doorstep of the party who took the instrument from the forger, irrespective of any lack of ordinary care — is what we need to go with.

7.   This example is meant to demonstrate what is usually referred to as the "double forgery problem." As we now know, we have one default rule on who ultimately should bear the loss when a check bears a forged drawer's signature. We have another, different rule when an indorsement has been forged. What happens when both the drawer's signature and an indorsement have been forged, either by one and the same or by two different parties? In our example, Payson State Bank and Main Street Check Cashing might want to keep passing the loss back and forth like a never-ending game of ping-pong, but what good would that do? Eventually, one or the other of the two will have to bear the loss and accept the fact that the loss cannot be shifted to the other party.

The well-known case of *Perini Corp. v. First National Bank*, 553 F.2d 398, 21 U.C.C. 929 (5th Cir. 1977), first took on this issue and concluded that the double-forgery scenario was properly to be dealt with as a forged-check case, one in which the forgery of the drawer's signature causes the loss ultimately to be borne by the drawee-payor bank, rather than as a forged-indorsement case. This does seem to be the better answer. After all, the money that Theo has made away with comes from Hugo's personal store of wealth. Theo's plan of thievery relied upon Hugo's having an account where he did and having at least the amount that Theo planned to make his own in that account. Irving Place, though he might be a real, identifiable person, and though his signature has indeed been forged on the instrument, has not been deprived of anything. Theo has not stolen any money from Irving; Irving is not out of pocket a penny, nor has Theo diverted to himself any money anticipated or due to Irving. Irving may even be unaware of all that has happened regarding this check. So the case does seem in spirit (if that's the kind of word we can use with regard to Theo's enterprise) more like a forged-check case than one where forgery of an indorsement is used to deprive an intended payee of money that is rightfully his or hers. Commentators and later cases have generally cited with approval the result reached in *Perini*, and although that ruling was made under the prerevision version of Article 3, there seems no reason to think that courts would not generally apply it today. *See*, for example, *Gina Chin & Associates, Inc. v. First Union Bank*, 256 Va. 59, 500 S.E.2d 516, 35 U.C.C.2d 1069 (1998).

8a. I'm sorry to say for Lacky, but this one doesn't even seem to rate a diagram. Lacky has no one from whom he will be able to get relief, Mugsy being for all practical purposes out of the picture as far as potential defendants go. Lacky has no cause of action for conversion against anyone downstream from Mugsy. Payment has been made on the check, but to Mugsy, who for all of his faults is still a holder of the instrument and hence a person entitled to enforce it. Remember the general result, which we saw early on, that the thief or finder of bearer paper does indeed become a holder of that paper. Negotiation of bearer paper requires only the transfer of possession, "whether voluntary or involuntary," of that instrument (§3-201(a) and Comment 1 to that section). Nor will Lacky have any more luck trying to get another check in the same amount from Ms. Boss, arguing that he never received the pay due him. His taking of the check suspended Ms. Boss's obligation to pay her employee for his services, and payment of the check resulted in "discharge of the obligation to the extent of the amount of the check" (§3-310(b)(2)). This check was paid, under §3-602(a), because payment was made to a person, Mugsy, who was entitled to enforce the instrument. Lacky has lost and will not be able to retrieve the money represented by the check he was carrying around in bearer form, as surely as he has lost the wallet it was being carried in and any cash or other valuables that might have been tucked away in that wallet as well.

8b. The general rule applicable to the theft of a check in bearer form should be painfully clear. The party who was holding it at the time of the theft bears the loss, with the only hope of recovery being if the thief can be identified and made to pay back what he or she has stolen. There is a lesson here for all of us: Never carry around more bearer paper than you can afford to lose.

9a. We turn at the end to problems of alteration. Payson is obligated to recredit Boss's account with $900, not the full $1,025 it has charged her account. What Sammy has done is clearly an "alteration" under §3-407(a)(i). Under subsection (c) of §3-407, Payson, as the payor bank that paid the fraudulently altered item, "may enforce rights with respect to the instrument . . . according to its original terms." Subsection 4-401(d)(1) tells the same story: "A bank that in good faith makes payment to a holder [and Sammy is that] may charge the indicated account according to . . . the original terms of the altered instrument." So Payson *may* charge Boss's account with the $125 that the check was originally made out for. It may *not* charge her for the $900 that Sammy added on by his alteration.

9b. Payson may assert a breach of the presentment warranty set forth in §4-208(a)(2), resulting in a loss to it of $900, against any bank that handled the check for collection, including Depot National. If Payson were to assert its claim against any intermediary bank, that bank could just pass the loss onto Depot by virtue of the transfer warranty of §4-207(a)(3). So Depot ends up bearing the loss. It can, of course, go against Sammy in an attempt to make itself whole, but we have stipulated that he is penniless, so what good would that do?

Notice that the result we have come to does not depend on any showing that Depot took the check in bad faith or that it failed to take ordinary care. Sammy's alteration might have been clumsy and crude, the kind of work just about anyone with any sense would question, or it might have been done with such skill and artistry that it could have not been caught by even the most careful visual examination. Either way, Depot has to bear the loss of the $900.

10a. M.R.S., Inc., will have to assert a claim of conversion of the instrument. It may assert this claim against either Payson or Depot. Should it go against Payson and receive redress from that bank, then Payson could use the breach of a warranty of presentment against Depot. Thus, Depot ultimately bears the loss occasioned by the alteration. Note also that Martha Kent has the right to have her account fully recredited for the $1,200 that was deducted from her account, because the item was not properly payable. It looks now as if Martha has gotten her medical services from M.R.S., Inc., but has in effect had them paid for by Depot National Bank. Perhaps Depot can recover from Martha on the theory of restitution under §3-418(b) if the common law of restitution of the governing jurisdiction will allow it. Note also the language of §4-208(c):

> If a drawee asserts a claim for breach of warranty under subsection (a) based on an unauthorized indorsement of the draft or an alteration of the draft [which is what Payson will have asserted against Depot to shift the loss to that bank], the warrantor [Depot] may defend by proving that . . . the drawer [Martha] is precluded under Section 3-406 or 4-406 from asserting against the drawee [Payson] the authorized signature or alteration.

The referenced sections, §3-406 and §4-406, are covered in Chapters 17 and 18, after which you will be able to appreciate how they fit into the grand (and admittedly very complex) scheme of things.

I might point out that this example, though of my own devising, was inspired by a problem that comes up each year around April 15 when payment of federal taxes is due. The instructions accompanying the standard tax forms call for any payment made by way of a check to have the check made out to "United States Treasury." Unscrupulous tax preparers have been known to instruct their clients to make out the necessary check simply to "IRS" and to hand it over to the preparer for delivery to the Internal Revenue Service along with the completed tax form. Changing "IRS" to "MRS." is not apparently all that difficult (if you are of a mind to), and the rest of the plot follows the story we have just seen.

10b. The general rule with respect to theft by alteration ends up the same as that when a forged indorsement is involved. The loss to the thief will normally be borne, regardless of good faith or lack of negligence, by the party who took the instrument directly from the alterer.

17

Special Rules for Special Situations

Circumstances Deserving of Special Attention

In Chapter 16 we encountered the basic rules of loss allocation when theft by check has occurred. If the theft was accomplished through forgery of the drawer's signature, the loss will fall on the drawee bank that paid the check bearing the forged signature of its customer. That's the rule of *Price v. Neal*. If the thief makes away with his or her ill-gotten gains by virtue of a forged indorsement or an alteration, the loss ultimately comes to rest on the party who took the check directly from the thief. Those are the general results as they have been handed down to us by history and as they are presently generated by application of the Code's sections on proper payment by the drawee bank, warranties of presentment and transfer, and conversion. Although private parties may get caught up in the proceedings, the losses arising from theft most often end up falling on one bank or another, either the payor bank in the case of a forged drawer's signature or the depositary bank that took a check bearing either a forged indorsement or an alteration. Such losses are usually thought of as most appropriately borne by the banking system — a system that should, at least in theory, be in the best position to develop an appropriate level of safeguards against such misbehavior and that can, in effect, spread the inevitable losses deriving from theft by check among all customers who take advantage of the banks' services by making use of checking accounts.

The history of negotiable instruments law has always recognized, however, that there are some special circumstances in which the application of these general rules should not be the end of the story. For one reason or another, in these instances there is a party who, it seems, should much more appropriately bear the loss. Any attempt to generalize about this set of exceptions or to encapsulate them in a single sentence, other than to say that each will make sense in its own context, is in my experience doomed to failure. I won't

even try. The present version of Article 3 sets them forth in three sections —
§3-404, §3-405, and §3-406 — each of which can cover multiple special
varieties of thievery. We'll begin with a brief, bare-bones look at each of these
sections, and then put the flesh on the bones through the examples and
explanations.

Imposters and Fictitious Payees — Section 3-404

Section 3-404 pulls together three separate instances when the nature of the
theft may justify the loss being borne by the drawer-customer rather than
anyone else who has handled the item.* First of all, in subsection (a), the
section deals with the case in which the drawer writes a check but is
"induced" or duped into handing it over to an impostor, a thief posing as
the payee. Subsection (b) covers two distinct situations. In the first, "the
person whose intent determines to whom an instrument is payable . . . does
not intend the person identified as payee to have an interest in the instrument." In the second, "the person identified as payee of an instrument is a
fictitious person," that is, someone who does not exist except in the mind
and the plans of the thief. If there is anything these three situations have in
common (other than the fact that the drafters of the most recent version of
Article 3 have put them into the same section), it is that in each instance the
drawer has been duped into issuing a check to the wrong party or to a party
who plans to use the check for purposes other than what the drawer
intended. The dupe, as we will see in the examples, is then made to bear the
loss, which at least in theory he or she might have been able to avoid with a
little more care. The loss is best thought of not as a loss to be borne by the
banking system in general, but as one to be borne by the person or enterprise that issued a check under such circumstances.

Fraudulent Indorsement by a "Responsible" Employee — Section 3-405

Subsection 3-405(a) goes to great lengths, as you can see, to define when an
employee can be said to have "responsibility with respect to" a particular

---

* I sometimes find help in thinking of §3-404 as the "duped drawer" section of
Article 3, for reasons that should become obvious. No one likes to be a dupe, and
certainly not in these situations.

instrument. Under subsection (b), if an employer entrusts an employee with responsibility with regard to a particular check, and that employee fraudulently indorses the check, the loss because of the thieving employee will be shifted to the employer. Note that, under §3-305(a)(2), "fraudulent indorsement" comes in two varieties. In the first, the faithless employee indorses the name of the employer on checks that have been issued to the employer and on which the employer is the named payee. The second variety of fraudulent indorsement occurs when the employer has issued a check intended for another named payee and the "responsible" employee forges the indorsement of the named payee. In either situation, Article 3 works to shift the loss onto the employer. This certainly makes sense. If an employee steals from an employer by taking money from the petty cash drawer to which he or she has been given access, or by making off with a valuable piece of office equipment with which he or she has been entrusted, the loss is quite rightly borne by the employer. The same will be true of checks that an employee has been given the responsibility to handle. Losses of this sort are deemed to be part of the cost of doing business and thus should be borne by the employer.

Actual Negligence — Section 3-406

Up to this point, none of the rules we have looked at regarding loss due to theft have depended on any showing that the party who will be made to bear the loss acted with anything less than "ordinary care" (look again at the definition of §3-103(a)(7)) in the particular instance. The general rules of loss attribution that we discovered in the previous chapters, and the special results generated by §§3-404 and 3-405, nowhere call for a showing that the ultimate loss-bearer did not observe, in the case of a person engaged in a business, "reasonable commercial standards, prevailing in the area in which the person is located, with respect to the business in which the person is engaged."* In the situation of wrongful indorsement by a responsible employee, covered by §3-405, for example, there is no need for any other party to show that the employer was negligent in hiring this particular person who turned out to be an embezzler or was negligent in its supervision of the miscreant. The result turns only on the facts that the employee was entrusted with responsibility with respect to the instrument and then took advantage of the situation to make off with some money that did not belong to him or her. Even the best people sometimes go wrong. Even the most intricate monitoring systems that an employer might reasonably think of adopting to keep tabs on the day-to-day functioning of its operations can be circumvented by a

---

* Neither Article 3 or 4 explicitly defines what would constitute "ordinary care" or the lack thereof in the case of a consumer. I think we have to assume that the traditional common law standard for negligence, whatever that may be exactly, is to apply.

determined thief. The risk that something like this will occur with even the most carefully vetted and supervised employee is thought properly to rest with the employer. The employer is made to bear the risk not because it acted negligently in the given case, but because it is thought to be in the best position of any party to evaluate the risk and to take the appropriate level of care, balancing the additional cost of doing even more against the foreseeable risks, to keep losses to a tolerable level.

There are situations, however, when one or another of the parties involved with a check *has* actually failed to exercise the level of care we would expect of someone in that party's position. When this is the case, it makes sense to place at least some of the loss on that party, because of its lack of care that either made the theft possible or at least made it easier for the thief to carry through (and perhaps encouraged the thief to give it a try). Under Subsection 3-406(a):

> A person whose failure to exercise ordinary care substantially contributes to an alteration of an instrument or to the making of a forged signature on an instrument is precluded from asserting the alteration or the forgery against a person who, in good faith, pays the instrument or takes it for value or collection.

We will look at some instances calling for application of this section, which would not be covered by either §3-404 or §3-405, in the examples.

Enter Comparative Negligence

Prior to the revision of Articles 3 and 4, the system of loss allocation dealing with theft by check worked on an all-or-nothing principle. Similar to and no doubt influenced by the doctrine of contributory negligence prevailing in the law of torts prior to the 1960s, earlier versions of Articles 3 and 4 were written so that however the game was played, the loss due to theft would eventually have to be borne in its entirety by one party or the other. There was no mechanism for splitting of the loss even when the situation seemed to suggest that this would be the fair and equitable thing to do. Since the 1960s, as you will recall from your introductory course in torts, the general law of torts has switched to what is referred to as a comparative negligence regime. If two parties were both negligent and the negligence of each contributed to the injury involved, then the two parties will be made to share, on some basis, the monetary damages that ensue.

One of the major changes wrought by the revision of Articles 3 and 4 (effective as of 1990) was incorporation of this comparative negligence principle into the overall scheme for allocation of losses due to theft by check. See, for example, Subsection (b) of §3-406:

> Under subsection (a) [quoted above], if the person asserting the preclusion fails to exercise ordinary care in paying or taking the

instrument and that failure substantially contributes to the loss, the loss is allocated between the person precluded and the person asserting the preclusion according to the extent to which the failure of each to exercise ordinary care contributed to the loss.

See also the beginning of Comment 4 to this section. So, if party X asserts against party Y a failure to exercise ordinary care that substantially contributed to the alteration or forgery of a signature on an instrument, Y is then free to assert against X its own lack of ordinary care that substantially contributed to the loss. If both parties were negligent, the loss will be split, apportioned between the two "according to the extent to which the failure of each to exercise ordinary care contributed to the loss." You will find similar invocations of the comparative negligence principle in the two other U.C.C. sections investigated in this chapter. See Subsection 3-404(d) and the second and last sentence of §3-405(b).

It is important to note that the possibility of actual negligence on the part of any person still does not enter into the picture if we are dealing with the general rules of loss allocation covered in Chapter 16. Those general results are taken as matters of strict liability, and the question of whether there has been actual negligence by anyone in dealing with the particular check involved simply never comes up. However, once a party, in order to get out from under the burden that would normally fall upon it by virtue of those general rules, brings into play any of the special rules of §3-404(a) or (b), §3-405(b), or §3-406(a) to shift the loss onto another, then the party against whom the special loss-shifting rule is being asserted has a right to prove if it can the "lack of ordinary care" of the party invoking that special rule. If it succeeds in its proof, then the concept of comparative negligence comes into play, and the two parties (or maybe more if things have gotten especially complex) end up sharing the loss.

EXAMPLES

1. Arnold Moneybucks has been negotiating over the phone with one Hy Pile, a dealer in oriental rugs, for the purchase of a particular expensive rug that Pile advertised for sale in the local paper. Eventually, Pile offers over the telephone to have the rug in question delivered to Arnold's office, where Arnold can inspect it and make a final determination of whether he wants to pay Pile's asking price of $38,000. The rug is delivered to Arnold, who immediately decides that he loves it and that it is well worth the price. The next day a well-dressed gentleman appears at Arnold's office and introduces himself as Hy Pile. He asks whether Arnold has made a decision on the rug. Arnold tells his visitor that he does indeed want to buy it. He writes a check to the order of Hy Pile for $38,000 payable out of his account at Payson State Bank and hands it over to his visitor. As it turns out, this gentleman is not Hy Pile but is instead one Thad, a drinking buddy of one of Pile's delivery

persons, who has picked up enough information to figure out basically what is going on between Arnold and Pile. Thad takes the check, forges Hy Pile's signature on the back of it, and then deposits it in his own account with Depot National Bank.

(a) By the time the ruse is discovered a few days later, when the real Hy Pile calls Arnold to ask whether he has made a decision about the rug, Thad has vanished, taking with him the $38,000, which he has withdrawn from his account. Arnold immediately notifies Payson and demands that his account be recredited with this amount because the check that was paid bore a forged indorsement. Does Payson have to accede to Arnold's demand? See §3-404(a).

(b) Suppose instead that Arnold receives a call from someone purporting to be Pile, requesting that if Arnold wants to keep the rug he send a check made out to "Hy Pile" to a particular address. The caller is (of course) Thad and the address that of Thad himself. Thad gets the check, forges Pile's name, and again makes away with the money. What is the result here?

(c) Now suppose that Thad does not intrude himself into the situation. When Pile calls Arnold to inquire about the rug, Arnold tells Pile that he definitely wants it. Pile tells Arnold that his assistant, Ms. Knapp, will soon be coming around to Arnold's to pick up a check for the price. Sure enough, later in the day someone introducing herself as Ms. Knapp comes by and asks for the check. Arnold hands over to her the $38,000 check. It turns out that the woman in question is not Ms. Knapp, but one Thelma, a customer in Pile's store who happened to overhear the conversation between Arnold and Pile. Thelma takes the check, forges Pile's signature on it, and deposits it in her account with Downtown National Bank. She later withdraws all the money from this account and makes off for parts unknown. Who bears the loss of the $38,000 that Thelma has taken with her?

(d) Finally, suppose the following: Pile calls Arnold and, upon being informed that Arnold wants the rug, tells Arnold that he will come around within a few days to pick up a check for the price. Later in the day, the real Ms. Knapp comes to Arnold's office. She explains to Arnold that she is Mr. Pile's personal assistant (as indeed she is) and that Mr. Pile has instructed her to come to Arnold's office to pick up a check due him. Arnold gives Ms. Knapp a check made out to Hy Pile for $38,000. Ms. Knapp then forges Pile's signature on the back of the check and deposits it into her own account with Deep River Bank and Trust. Several days later, she withdraws all of her funds from this account, which now includes the $38,000, and goes to the racetrack, where she proceeds to lose everything. When Pile eventually discovers what has happened, he comes to Arnold's office to demand another check for the price of the rug. He tells Arnold, truthfully, that he never authorized Ms. Knapp to pick up the check on his behalf or to deal with it in any way. His voice rising, he asks, "What made you give it to her in the first place? I told you *I* would pick it up!" Assuming that Ms. Knapp is in no position to pay anybody the $38,000 she has made off with and lost on the horses, who must bear the loss of this amount?

2.   Hamilton is the treasurer of the DotCom Corporation. As such, he is authorized to sign, without the co-signature of any other officer, checks for up to $50,000 drawn on the company's account with the Payson State Bank. Hamilton draws a check payable to HAL Systems, a supplier from which DotCom has often bought needed computer components in the past, for $36,724. At present, however, DotCom does not owe any money to HAL. Hamilton takes the check that he has written to HAL and himself indorses it with a signature purporting to be that of HAL. He deposits the check in an account he has himself opened up with Decoy National Bank under the name "HAL Systems, Incorporated." The check is forwarded to Payson, which pays it in the ordinary course of its operations. By the time the theft is discovered, Hamilton is long gone, having moved on to some other Internet start-up.

(a) Who ends up bearing the loss of the $36,724?

(b) How would you analyze the situation if there were no such company as HAL Systems? Hamilton just made up the name, having come up with something that sounds like the kind of entity to which DotCom might owe money. Once again Hamilton signs the name "HAL Systems" on the back of the check and, after depositing it in Decoy to the HAL account he has opened up, makes off with the money.

3.   Jackson, as treasurer of the NewEco Corporation, is authorized to write checks on that company's account with Payson State Bank. One of her primary duties is to authorize the issuance of the weekly paychecks of each of the company's employees. She does so on the basis of information provided to her by one Lincoln, who is head of the payroll department. Lincoln gives Jackson a listing of each employee along with how much is due him or her. Jackson has the checks issued and returns them to Lincoln for distribution to the employees. Beginning in June, Lincoln begins adding to the list that he gives to Jackson the name of one "Mary Todd," assigning to her a salary in line with that of other newly hired employees of the firm. In fact, no Mary Todd exists. When the payroll checks are handed over to Lincoln, he himself takes the one made out to Mary Todd. He indorses it on the back in the name of the fictitious Ms. Todd, and then deposits it in his own account with Depot National Bank. This continues on a weekly basis until it is discovered — soon after Lincoln has quit, cleaned out his account with Depot, and

left the area — that there is in fact no such person working at NewEco by the name of Mary Todd. Who bears the loss generated by Lincoln's scam?

4.   Dr. Tooth runs a thriving dental practice. He employs one Ernie who, in addition to scheduling appointments for patients, is in charge of handling patient accounts, sending out bills as needed, and depositing the checks that Tooth receives for his services into Tooth's business account with Depot National Bank after having presented these incoming checks to Tooth for his indorsement on each. At some point, Ernie begins to set aside for himself some of the checks that come into the office made out to Dr. Tooth. He forges the signature of Tooth on the back of each of these checks and deposits them into his own account at Downtown Bank and Trust. This goes on for some time, until Tooth begins to wonder why his income seems to have dipped in recent months. He confronts Ernie, who admits to the wrongdoing, but informs Tooth that he has by now spent all the money that he siphoned off from the dental practice and is in fact broke. Tooth immediately fires Ernie, but he is now more concerned with getting back the money that was stolen from him. Will Tooth be able to do so?

5.   Dr. Tooth, of the preceding example, replaces Ernie with one Bert, who seems a more trustworthy character. Among the duties Bert takes on is preparing checks for Tooth's signature, so that Tooth can pay the bills that have come into his office for his rent, supplies that he purchased, and other obligations of the dental practice. Among the checks signed by Tooth as drawer are ones written to Oscar's Cleaning Service, a firm that cleans Tooth's office once a week. Bert does not send these checks to Oscar, but instead forges the name of Oscar's Cleaning Service on the back of each and deposits them into Bert's own account with Downtown Bank and Trust. Oscar calls Tooth's office to complain that he has not been getting his checks, but Bert, who initially receives the calls, tells Oscar that there has obviously been some mistake and not to worry. "The check is in the mail." Only after several months of this is Oscar able to get through to Tooth himself and tell him what has been going on. Tooth checks the records while Bert is out to lunch and is able to piece together what has happened. He confronts Bert on his return, and Bert has to admit to what he has been up to. He also has to inform Tooth that the balance of his account with Downtown Bank is just about down to zero and that he has no other funds to repay Tooth what he has stolen. Bert, needless to say, is fired on the spot. Tooth quickly writes a check, which he personally delivers to Oscar, covering all the money owed to Oscar that Oscar has never received. Tooth now concerns himself with how, if at all, he can recover from some other party the money stolen by Bert. Will Tooth have to bear the loss, or can he shift it to some other party?

6.   Return to the basic situation of Example 2: Hamilton, as treasurer of the DotCom Corporation, is authorized to sign, without the co-signature of

any other officer, checks for up to $50,000 drawn on the company's account with the Payson State Bank. Hamilton draws a check payable to HAL Systems for $36,724. The check in this instance is written in response to an invoice sent by HAL for some computer equipment actually received by DotCom. At the time he prepares the check, Hamilton fully intends to send it on to HAL. After staring at the check for some time, however, all the while dwelling on the mounting bills that he has been personally running up trying to live the life of a successful Internet executive, he decides to make it his own. He takes the check, forges a signature purporting to be that of an authorized representative of HAL on its back, and deposits the check in his own account with Delwood Bank.

(a) Is this situation covered by §3-404?

(b) What about §3-405?

(c) What party ends up bearing the loss of the money should Hamilton, when his misdeed is discovered, be in no position to repay anything like $36,724? He's still up to his ears in debt from other sources.

7.   Franklin, the new treasurer of the DotCom Corporation, writes out a check for $28,456 payable to HiTech Supplies Incorporated to cover a bill for supplies that HiTech has furnished to DotCom. Franklin puts the check in an envelope correctly addressed to HiTech and delivers this envelope, along with other outgoing mail that has piled up during the day, to DotCom's mailroom. Pierce, an employee in the mailroom, takes the envelope for himself. He signs the reverse of the check inside first with the words "HiTech Supplies Incorporated" and under that with his own name. He deposits this check into his own personal account at Delroy Savings and Loan. When the amount of the check has been made available to him by Delroy, he cleans out all that he has in this account and vanishes, never to return to his lowly job at DotCom. DotCom eventually discovers what has happened when HiTech sends a second bill for the amount it is owed.

(a) Does §3-404 cover this situation?

(b) What about §3-405?

(c) What about §3-406?

(d) What party or parties do you believe will end up bearing the loss of the $28,456 Pierce has made off with?

8.   Franklin writes another check, this one for $2,567, to another of DotCom's suppliers, the Ebiz Corporation. He leaves this check on top of his "to-do" pile at the end of work on Thursday, fully intending to mail it to Ebiz on the following day. Polk, one of the members of the staff that cleans the DotCom offices overnight, spots the check on top of Franklin's desk and pockets it. Polk forges the signature of Ebiz on the back of the check. He then takes it to the offices of Main Street Check Cashing, where he signs his own name to the back of the check and receives in exchange $2,361 in cash (having been charged an 8% fee by the check cashing firm). Main Street

forwards the check for collection and Payson State Bank pays it out of DotCom's account in the ordinary course of affairs. How do you analyze this situation? What party or parties should bear the loss of Polk's theft of this check?

9.   Andrew has a personal checking account with Payson State Bank. He keeps his checkbook on top of the desk in his home office. Thad, a decorator whom Andrew has hired to do some work in the apartment, is able to steal a blank check out of this checkbook when he is alone in the room. He fills this check out for $700, naming himself as payee and forging Andrew's name on the drawer line. He deposits this check in his own account with Depot National Bank and the check is paid by Payson. When Andrew discovers what has happened, he quickly contacts Payson and demands that it recredit his account with the $700, because this check bore a forged drawer's signature and hence was not a properly payable item. Can the bank make an argument based on §3-406(a) that would preclude Andrew from getting the $700 recredited to his account?

10.   Bernie writes a check out of his account with Payson State Bank, payable to one Cara for $1,200, and sends it to Cara at her home. Cara puts the check in the top drawer of her desk intending to deposit it the next time she goes to her bank. Before she can do so, Thelma, a niece of Cara's who is paying her a brief visit, comes across the check while rummaging through the drawers of her aunt's desk. Thelma takes the check and leaves for home, cutting her visit with her aunt even shorter. Once home, Thelma forges Cara's name on the back of the check and deposits it into her own account with Distant Bank and Trust. Distant Bank forwards the check for collection to Payson, which pays it in the ordinary course of its operations. When Cara discovers the loss and finds out what has become of the check, she brings an action of conversion against Distant Bank for its role in obtaining payment on an item that bore a forged signature. Do you think Distant Bank has any response to this claim, by which it could avoid at least part of the loss, based on §3-406(a)?

EXPLANATIONS

1a.   As always, it pays first to get a good look at the situation:

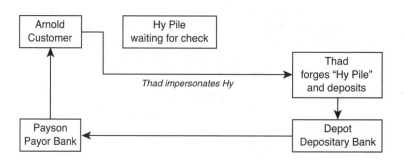

No, Payson does not have to recredit Arnold's account. In the normal course of events, the payor bank would have to recredit the account, because the check it paid bore a forged indorsement. In this case, however, Payson can point to §3-404(a) and what is known as the *impostor rule* or *impostor defense*. Thad was clearly an imposter, impersonating Hy Pile, the payee of the check. That being so, "an indorsement *by any person* in the name of the payee *is effective* as the indorsement of the payee in favor of a person who, in good faith, pays the instrument or takes it for value or for collection." So Payson can legitimately argue that the drawer's signature on the check was valid — as Arnold had himself signed it — and that the indorsement of "Hy Pile" was effective as if Pile himself had signed or authorized another to sign for him. This check was properly payable, and hence Payson did no wrong in paying it and charging the amount against Arnold's account.

Arnold, as the party who was duped into personally handing over the check to a thief, will have to bear the loss stemming from the theft. Notice that this all follows from §3-405(a) and does not depend on any showing that Arnold acted negligently in turning the check over to Thad believing him to be Pile. Arnold may have simply taken Thad at his word that he was Pile, or Arnold might have asked for and been shown a super set of phony ID. The result is once again a matter of strict liability; it follows from the basic pattern of the theft.

Arnold may try to shift at least some portion of his $38,000 loss onto another party by bringing into play the concept of comparative actual negligence, in this case by invoking subsection (d) of §3-404:

> With respect to an instrument to which subsection (a) [as here] or (b) applies, if a person paying the instrument or taking it for value or collection fails to exercise ordinary care in paying or taking the instrument and that failure substantially contributes to loss resulting from payment of the instrument, the person bearing the loss [here Arnold] may recover from the person failing to exercise ordinary care to the extent the failure to exercise ordinary care contributed to the loss.

The problem for Arnold here is that there does not seem to be another party that failed to exercise ordinary care in handling the check. Recall the definition of §3-103(a)(7). The fact that Payson may have paid the check without individually examining it would not constitute a lack of ordinary care unless that failure to examine violated the bank's prescribed procedures "and the bank's procedures do not vary unreasonably from general banking usage not disapproved of by" either Article 3 or 4. See Comment 5 to §3-103. Apparently many banks today do not set their automated check processing equipment to cull out for individual inspection checks unless they are in the $50,000 or more range. So unless Payson's own procedure called for individual inspection of items with amounts as large as this one, and the bank then failed to follow its own procedure, Payson would not have failed to exercise ordinary care on that score. Even if someone at Payson Bank had individually examined the check, what would he or she have seen? The one thing he or she would be expected to check is the authenticity of its customer's signature, and here Arnold's signature is valid. There is no way reasonably to expect Payson to be able to catch the forgery of Hy Pile's signature, as it does not have a specimen signature on file for everyone in the community.

Perhaps Arnold could argue that Depot National Bank did not act with ordinary care in allowing Thad to deposit into his account a check initially issued to Hy Pile and bearing a forged indorsement of Mr. Pile, but this seems unlikely to succeed. General banking practice in the area in which Depot operates probably does not call for the bank to turn away such third-party checks, or to insist on any verification that the payee's indorsement is genuine, when they are presented for deposit to a customer's account. Unless Depot had some special reason to believe that Thad might be depositing stolen checks into his account (in which case, why are they still doing business with him?), it does not seem a lack of ordinary care for the depositary bank to take for deposit a check under the circumstances we have here. Arnold is going to have to bear the full loss.

1b. The result here should be the same as in 1a. Subsection 3-404(a) comes into play whenever "an imposter, *by use of the mails or otherwise*, induces the issuer of an instrument to issue the instrument . . . by impersonating the payee of the instrument." Here Thad, posing as Pile, made use of the telephone and the mail to carry out his scheme, but it is still a classic case in which the impostor rule governs. If anything, a situation such as this may be more common than what we saw in 1a. It is, after all, probably easier in most situations for an impostor to get away with an impersonation of someone else when the transaction is carried out at a distance, as here, rather than face-to-face as in 1a.

1c. Again the result remains the same. Arnold bears the loss unless he is able to shift all or some of it onto another party by proving that party to have acted without ordinary care in its handling of the check. Subsection 3-404(a) specifically covers the situation in which an impostor is able to get his or her hands on a check "by impersonating the payee of the check *or a person authorized to act for the payee*." The real Ms. Knapp was authorized to act for Hy in picking up the check. Thelma's impersonation of Ms. Knapp is covered by §3-404(a) and has the same result as Thad's impersonation of the real Hy Pile in the two previous parts of this example.

1d. The risk of loss here will fall on the Deep River bank, as the party who took an instrument bearing a forged indorsement directly from the forger. Deep River may try to invoke the impostor rule of §3-404(a), to argue that the indorsement was "effective" under the circumstances and that hence the loss should fall on Arnold, but this attempt, at least if the court follows prior decisions on the question, will fail. Neither that section nor any other part of

Article 3 defines exactly what is meant by the word *impostor*, but the courts have generally ruled that the word connotes the impersonation of one person by someone else. Here Ms. Knapp is really Ms. Knapp. True, she has made a serious misrepresentation to Arnold; she has told him that she has the authority to act on behalf of Pile in picking up the check when in fact she has not been given that authority. She has not, however, impersonated anyone else, nor has anyone else impersonated her. A good review of this issue was given by the Kansas Supreme Court in *King v. White*, 265 Kan. 627, 962 P.2d 475, 38 U.C.C.2d 469 (1998). The court concluded:

> It does seem clear from cases both before and after the [1990] revision that someone must still impersonate someone else in order for the imposter defense to apply. There must be impersonation of an actual agent; a misrepresentation of agency authority is generally not sufficient to invoke the defense.

2a. The loss of the $36,724 will probably be borne in its entirety by the DotCom Corporation. Under §3-404(b)(i), if the person whose intent determines to whom an instrument is payable — which would be Hamilton here — "does not intend the person identified as payee to have any interest in the instrument," then "an indorsement by any person in the name of the payee stated in the instrument is effective as the indorsement of the payee in favor of any person who, in good faith, pays the instrument or takes it for value or collection." The drawer's signature on this check is valid, as Hamilton had the authority to sign and issue checks on behalf of DotCom. The indorsement purporting to be that of HAL Systems is effective under the language of §3-404(b). This check was properly payable out of DotCom's account, and thus that corporation will have to bear the loss. One of DotCom's trusted principal officers has turned out to be a thief, and it certainly makes sense that the company should bear the loss stemming from his deviation from the straight and narrow.

DotCom's one chance for recouping at least part of this loss is to argue that Decoy National Bank acted without ordinary care in handling the check, and that under subsection (d) of §3-404 DotCom should be able to recover from Decoy "to the extent that the failure [by Decoy] to exercise ordinary care contributed to the loss." How might Decoy have been lacking in ordinary care? DotCom would have to show that Decoy did not observe "reasonable commercial standards, prevailing in the area in which [Decoy] is located, with respect to the business in which [Decoy] is engaged" (§3-103(a)(7)) by allowing Hamilton to open an account in the name of "HAL Systems, Incorporated" with himself as the authorized signatory for that account. Banks usually demand certain back-up documentation when opening up a corporate account: proof that the corporation actually exists, proof that the corporation's board has authorized the opening of the account, and the identity of the persons it has authorized to act with respect to the account. If Decoy failed to follow this routine and allowed Hamilton to open the HAL account too easily, perhaps it could be shown to have acted with less than the ordinary care required of it. See Comment 4 to §3-405, which deals with just such a possibility, and *K.I.M. Refrigeration Corp. v. C.F.S. Bank*, 2001 N.Y. Misc. LEXIS 371, 45 U.C.C.2d 1138. If, however, Hamilton had done his homework, he no doubt could have produced, without too much effort, the kind of documentation that even the most finicky bank would have found satisfactory. (If nothing else, he could have, at no great expense, considering what he may have planned to gain by the ruse, created a corporation named "HAL Systems Incorporated" under the laws of some state other than the one in which the "true" HAL was incorporated. Then it would just be a matter of creating the standard paperwork to hand over to Decoy.) As will always be the case once the rules of Article 3 steer us into any inquiry about whether a party was "lacking in ordinary care" in its handling of a particular instrument, it will all depend on the facts of the situation and a comparison with what "reasonable commercial standards" would be in such an instance, in the place in question, and given the nature of the business in which that party is engaged.

2b. The result is the same as in 2a, even if the reasoning is slightly different. Here §3-404 governs not because of the rule we looked at in 2a, but because of the so-called *fictitious payee* rule of (b)(ii). Any time a person identified as a payee of an instrument is a "fictitious person," an indorsement by any person in the name of that payee is deemed effective as the indorsement of the payee "in favor of a person who, in good faith, pays the instrument or takes it for value or collection." You will notice that this example is basically the same as that given in Case #1 of Comment 2 to §3-404. For that matter, Example 2a paralleled Case #2 in the same comment.

3. NewEco bears the loss. This is an example of the classic *padded payroll* scam. Jackson has been conned by Lincoln into issuing a check payable to a fictitious payee. By virtue of §3-404(b)(ii), anyone, including Lincoln, can effectively indorse on "Mary Todd's" behalf. The check is therefore properly payable out of NewEco's account with Payson. Any attempt by NewEco to place some of the responsibility (and some of the loss) on either Payson or Depot Bank via §3-404(d), claiming a lack of ordinary care by either or both banks, seems very unlikely to succeed. Payson just paid the check written on the payroll account automatically; it certainly is under no obligation to check out exactly who is and who is not an employee of NewEco and how much he or she may be owed. Depot accepted for deposit at various times into one of its customer's account a single third-party check seemingly indorsed over to that customer. It would be exceptionally difficult to prove that in doing so Depot was acting outside the bounds of reasonable, customary practice. The lesson for NewEco is that it ought to set up more rigorous internal controls over its payroll procedures — some system that does not put all the responsibility (and opportunity for mischief) into the hands of a single employee — rather than try to blame others for its misfortunes.

4. We now turn to the workings of §3-405. The picture with respect to any one of the checks made out to Tooth that Ernie took for himself looks like this:

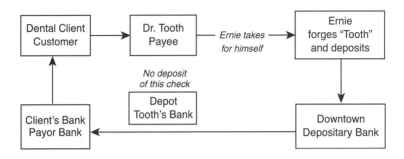

Tooth will most likely have to bear the full loss occasioned by Ernie's theft of this check and all the others. The check would be properly payable out of the client's account with his or her own bank. There is no question that the drawer's signature is valid. Ernie has made a "fraudulent indorsement" under §3-405(a)(2)(i), but the forged signature of Tooth is considered "effective as the indorsement of the person to whom the instrument is payable if it is made in the name of that person" under §3-405(b) if the forger is an employee of the named payee "entrusted with responsibility with respect to the instrument." You should read over subsection (a) carefully to see how this section defines who is an *employee* entrusted with such "responsibility," but in our scenario there seems to be no question that Ernie fits right within the mold. As Comment 1 to this section makes clear, §3-405 is based on the belief that the employer is in a far better position to avoid the loss, by taking care in choosing employees, supervising them, and adopting other measures to prevent forged indorsements on instruments payable to the employer or fraud in the issuance of instruments in the name of the employer.

The second sentence of §3-405(b) does give Tooth the right to seek contribution from any party that handled the various checks whose lack of ordinary care substantially contributed to the loss, but it is going to be hard for him to make the case against anyone else. Certainly his client's bank did not fail to use ordinary care. All it did was pay a check written by one of its customers to a "Dr. Tooth," which bore what was apparently the indorsement of that doctor. What about Downtown Bank and Trust, where Ernie deposited each of these checks? Perhaps if Ernie had tried to deposit, all at one time, a whole bundle of checks totaling some thousands of dollars, made out to another and supposedly indorsed over to him, a red flag should have gone up at the teller's window. Tooth could at least argue that whoever processed the deposit on behalf of Downtown should at least have inquired how Ernie had gotten all of these checks payable to a third party. What explanation could Ernie then have given that wouldn't in itself have sounded dubious? If, however, Ernie did not overplay his hand, and deposited checks into his own account in this fashion only one at a time and only now and then, it is unlikely that any finder of fact would conclude that the depositary bank had failed to use ordinary care.

A case that fits this pattern of skullduggery that you would do well to read is *Menichini v. Grant*, 995 F.2d 1224, 20 U.C.C.2d 959 (3d Cir. 1993). The employer, Gerald C. Menichini, had established as a sole proprietorship a firm by the name of Best Legal Services to provide various nonprofessional support services to attorneys and law firms. In 1986 Menichini hired as his first full-time employee one Lissa Grant, a law student, to serve as a receptionist. Over time, Grant's role in the firm grew to the point where Menichini left her exclusively responsible for recording all invoices and dealing with payments received. Over a period of about a year and a half, starting in April 1988, Grant intercepted some 150 checks made out to Best Legal Services and totaling $61,431.98, forged Menichini's signature to each, and deposited them in her own account. Menichini was, not surprisingly, held to be the one who should bear the loss due to his employee's embezzlement. See also *Halla v. Norwest Bank Minnesota, N.A.*, 601 N.W.2d 449, 39 U.C.C.2d 1104 (Minn. Ct. App. 1999), in which an agent charged with management of five apartment buildings was, over the course of three years, able to make her own more that $100,000 in rent checks made payable to the property owner. In this case the owner did make the argument that the bank into which the embezzling employee had deposited the rental checks acted with a lack of ordinary care by taking for deposit, into a personal account, checks originally made payable to a business and by failing to verify the business's indorsements on the checks. The Minnesota Court of Appeals upheld the trial court's grant of summary judgment to the depositary bank. It agreed with the trial court that the owner's assertion (that the depositary bank acted with less than ordinary care) was not supported by any evidence in the record. "Because a party resisting summary judgment must rest on more than mere averments, Hall [the property owner] has not established a fact issue on whether Norwest [the depositary bank] failed to exercise ordinary care."

5.   Dr. Tooth's unfortunate experience with Bert illustrates the second type of theft by a "responsible" employee for which the employer must bear the loss.

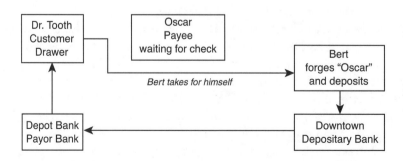

Tooth has given Bert responsibility with respect to the checks he draws to his suppliers and others to whom he owes money. Bert has made a "fraudulent indorsement" on the check, now under subpart (ii) of §3-405(a)(2). By virtue of §3-405(b), this fraudulent indorsement is effective as if Oscar himself had signed the check. The check is properly payable out of Tooth's account with Depot National Bank. Tooth may try to show that Downtown Bank and Trust, as the depositary bank that took an instrument bearing a forged indorsement from the forger, should bear at least a portion of the loss under the second sentence of §3-405(b), but to do so Tooth would have to show that Downtown failed to exercise ordinary care in accepting for deposit and sending on for collection this check bearing the forged indorsement of a third party, Oscar. If Bert has only been depositing one such check each month, and if Downtown Bank has not been given any reason to know that there is anything fishy about the situation on any occasion, I think it highly unlikely that Tooth would be able to demonstrate lack of ordinary care on that bank's part. But, again, it would all depend on the particular facts of the situation.

For a good review of the workings of §3-405, seen here in the operations of a couple of faithless employees of a doctor who were not choosey — working in tandem they engaged in the type of misbehavior we have seen in both Ernie in the previous example *and* Bert in this one — see *Lee Newman, M.D. v. Wells Fargo Bank*, 87 Cal.App. 4th 73, 104 Cal.Rptr. 2d 310, 43 U.C.C.2d 912 (2001).

6a. No. There are no impostors or fictitious payees. Subsection 3-404(b)(i) does not apply because at the time he wrote up and signed the check payable to HAL Systems, Hamilton fully intended that company to receive and therefore "have an interest" in the instrument.

6b. Yes. Hamilton as treasurer of DotCom was clearly a person with "responsibility" with respect to the item. He made a "fraudulent indorsement" of the payee's name and took the money for himself. See Case #6 in Comment 3 to §3-405.

6c. DotCom will end up bearing the loss of the $36,724 unless it can shift some of the loss, on a comparative negligence basis, onto the Delwood Bank, which took the check for deposit into Hamilton's personal account bearing a forged indorsement of HAL Systems. Look once again at Comment 4 to §3-405, which tries to illustrate the ways in which a depositary bank may be shown to have acted with less than ordinary care in taking a check under circumstances such as this. The example we have before us is not as dramatic as that set forth at the end of the comment: HAL Systems may not be "well-known national corporation"; Hamilton has not attempted to open an account in HAL's name at Delwood; and as far as we know this check is not the only one being deposited into the account, but is only one of many (some of which may be for amounts in the tens of thousands if Hamilton is really trying to live like an Internet millionaire) that have been moving in and out of Hamilton's personal account. I tend to doubt that DotCom would be able to establish any lack of due care on Delwood's part. We should remember, however, as the comment makes clear, "Failure to exercise ordinary care is to be determined in the context of all the facts relating to the bank's conduct with respect to the bank's collection of the check."

7a.   No. There are no impostors or fictitious payees, nor does §3-404(b)(i) apply. Franklin fully intended that HiTech Supplies would receive and therefore "have an interest" in the instrument.

7b.   No. Pierce would not be considered an employee with "responsibility" with respect to the instrument just because it passed through the mailroom of the company where he worked. Look at the last sentence of §3-405(a)(3): "'Responsibility' does not include authority that merely allows an employee to have access to instruments or blank or incomplete instrument forms that are being stored or transported or are part of incoming or outgoing mail, or similar access."

7c.   Section 3-406 may come into play here, though with what success is questionable. So far we have found no reason that Pierce's theft and forgery of the payee's name would not result in the loss falling, simply under the standard rules, on the party that took the check from the forger, which here is Delroy Savings and Loan. Delroy may, however, argue under §3-406(a) that DotCom somehow failed to exercise ordinary care in its hiring or supervision of its mailroom employees and that this failure "substantially contributed" to the making of the forged signature on the instrument. If it could show as much, then DotCom would be "precluded" from asserting the forgery when it tried to recover the money it has lost in a conversion action against Delroy, as in its bid to get its account with Payson recredited for the amount of the improperly paid check (which, if it had to recredit, would naturally go against Delroy on a breached warranty of presentment). Under subsection (c), the bank asserting this preclusion would have the burden of proving DotCom's failure to exercise ordinary care. It would have to prove that DotCom's mailroom procedures and safeguards failed to meet "reasonable commercial standards, prevailing in the area in which [DotCom] is located, with respect to the business in which [DotCom] is engaged" (Section 3-103(a)(7) once again). It is possible that the bank could do so, but I think it highly unlikely unless DotCom is running a particularly careless and sloppy mailroom operation.

Suppose that the bank against which DotCom is proceeding to recapture the stolen money was able to demonstrate a lack of ordinary care on DotCom's part in handling the item, which lack of care substantially contributed to Pierce's ability to get his hands on and forge the payee's signature on this check. This would preclude DotCom from relying on the forgery to avoid payment of the check. DotCom might then, in turn, assert under §3-406(b) that the bank in question had *itself* failed to exercise ordinary care in its handling of the item. If DotCom could prove this, then the two parties, DotCom and the bank, would have to share the loss on a comparative negligence basis. All this, at least in the example we have before us, appears to me to be getting more and more unlikely, but of course it all depends on the facts in context.

7d. If DotCom cannot be proven to have been running its mailroom with a lack of ordinary care, and that this failure substantially contributed to Pierce's opportunity to act as he did, the loss falls on Deloy as the party that took the check directly from the forger.

8.   Under the basic rules of loss allocation, the check cashing firm, as the party that took a check bearing a forged indorsement from the forger, would normally have to bear the risk of this loss. (This is one of the principal reasons why cashing a check at such an establishment is so relatively expensive.) That firm would have no success in calling upon either §3-404 or §3-405 for relief. This may, however, be one of the cases in which §3-406(a) should apply, allowing the check cashing service to establish that DotCom was, because of its failure to use ordinary care in its handling of the check, precluded from relying upon the forgery of Ebiz's name to avoid having the check charged to its account. Franklin does seem to have acted outside of what we would guess to be "reasonable commercial standards" for the treasurer of a major corporation, in that he left the check so casually on the top of his desk overnight and in addition apparently did not notice and immediately act upon its disappearance when he came in the next day. Had Franklin been aware that the check had been stolen, or at least that it was missing, he could have placed a stop-payment order on the check, which would have avoided the loss to DotCom. Franklin's actions appear to amount to a lack of ordinary care with respect to the item. DotCom should be made to bear the loss. Comment 3 gives as illustration three cases in which a business entity might be found lacking in ordinary care with respect to a check that is later stolen, upon which a forger has worked his or her particular type of transgression, or that has all too easily been altered. The particular hypothetical we are dealing with here does not follow any of these three cases, but taken together they suggest that DotCom's behavior here was indeed "lacking in ordinary care."

DotCom may, of course, argue under §3-406(b) that Main Street Check Cashing was itself negligent in the way it handled the check, and that this negligence substantially contributed to the theft by Polk. If that could be proven by DotCom (which I tend to think would be difficult, but then you never know), the two negligent parties, DotCom and Main Street, would be made to bear the loss allocated "between the party precluded [DotCom] and the person asserting the preclusion [Main Street] to the extent to which the failure of each to exercise ordinary care contributed to the loss."

9.   The bank can make an argument against Andrew based on §3-406(a) — anybody can argue just about anything — but it is extremely unlikely that the bank would find any takers for a result that would put any of the loss on Andrew. The bank would have to show that Andrew was acting with less than ordinary care as a consumer by keeping his checkbook on top of his desk at home and allowing someone unaccompanied access to his home office so that the theft of one of his blank checks was thereby made possible. But where else is Andrew going to keep his checkbook? Even if he placed it in a drawer, a wily character like Thad would not have been stopped from finding it and taking one of the blank check forms to use later in this way. Does it seem to you reasonable to insist that a regular guy like Andrew keep his personal checkbook under lock and key? Or that he should never leave anyone in his apartment alone in any of his rooms? What is Andrew supposed to do, follow his decorator around from room to room during the entire course of the job?

When you first read this example, you might have been tempted to conclude that Andrew must have been negligent in some way in failing to prevent Thad from making off with the blank check as he did, but I think this is being much too hard on Andrew and asking too much of him. Ask yourself this simple question: As you are reading this, are you *absolutely sure* that every single one of your own personal blank checks is exactly where you assume it to be? The intent of my asking this is not to make you paranoid. It does demonstrate, I think, that it would be unduly harsh and unrealistic to treat Andrew as having been lacking in ordinary care under the circumstances here. Perhaps if for a number of days Andrew had been noticing that some of his valuable smaller items had gone missing from just the room or rooms in which Thad had been working, it would reach a point at which it would be fair to say that Andrew was acting negligently in still allowing Thad to hang around the place unattended. Short of that, however, all we have is that Andrew has put some trust in Thad, and that trust has turned out to be misplaced. This only makes Andrew human, and now perhaps a bit more cynical. It doesn't make him negligent.

10.   Unless Distant Bank can come up with some facts that we don't have here (for example if Cara had actually seen Thelma taking things from her desk and had done nothing to stop it, or if Thelma had stolen things from her aunt in the past and Cara had just chosen to turn a blind eye), it is doubtful that it would be able to shift any of the loss onto Cara by arguing that she had somehow failed to use ordinary care in the situation. It certainly is a good rule of thumb that to deposit any check you receive as soon as possible, but we can't expect a consumer like Cara to drop everything and run to her bank every time she gets a check in the mail. And storing a check in a drawer of her desk, even if isn't protected by lock and key, doesn't ring of negligence. Neither does Cara's willingness to let her niece stay in her apartment for a while. When you look at cases of this type, you will find that a disconcerting number of them involve theft by a family member. The courts

are not inclined to hold that simply being trusting of and hospitable to one's own kin allows a finding that a party has been lacking in ordinary care.

I feel reassured in my assessment that Andrew should be able to get his account recredited for the $700 stolen by Thad — but only slightly reassured — by the recent decision of the Court of Appeals of Arizona in *Mercantile Bank of Arkansas v. Vowell*, 2003 Ark.App.Lexis 498, 50 U.C.C.2d 631. The case makes interesting, if awfully disturbing, reading. In June of 1997, Dr. John G. Vowell and his wife allowed their daughter Susan and her boyfriend to move in with them, even though they knew that the two had a history of involvement with "drugs, alcohol, writing bad checks, and stealing." They also were aware that Susan had in the past stolen checks from them and forged both of their signatures to get her hands on some money. The trial court found that the only precaution they took was to hide Mrs. Vowell's purse, which contained their checkbook, under the sink. Mrs. Vowell was seriously ill at the time and mostly bedridden. Yet her husband continued to rely on her to review their bank statements and to balance the checkbook. In addition, it has to be noted, the PIN they used in connection with their ATM card was identical to that which they used for their home security system. Not surprisingly, Susan proceeded to draw two unauthorized checks and make nine unauthorized ATM withdrawls in the aggregate of $12,028.75 over a period of approximately three months. By a vote of 3 to 3 the Appeals Court upheld a ruling of the trial court that the bank could not successfully invoke §3-406(a) against Dr. Vowell as his conduct did not "substantially contribute" to the forgery of the checks and the unauthorized ATM withdrawals. The doctor, who was the sole plaintiff (as by this time his wife had died), did not recover from the bank all that Susan had stolen, however. The reason that he had to bear a good portion of the loss had to do not with anything we have studied in this chapter, but with the so-called Bank Statement Rule of §4-406, the subject of the next chapter. A fourth judge, while concurring with the ultimate disposition of the matter based on the Bank Statement Rule, found himself in serious disagreement with the three judges who saw §3-406(a) as inapplicable.

> It is quite understandable that loving parents will try to provide shelter to their prodigal children, even though the children remain unrehabilitated from propensities that are unsavory. Nevertheless, the decision to house a thieving relative does not absolve one of the duty to exercise ordinary sense involving family valuables. . . . I fear that our refusal to reverse and remand under [§3-406] sends a powerful, and unsound, message. If the facts of this case do not demonstrate failure to exercise ordinary case under [§3-406] [and remember three judges had found they did not], what set of facts would ever do?

A good point. In any event, I think the facts surrounding Andrew's loss to the seeming trustworthy Thad are nothing like what the court was faced with in this case, and that Andrew should be able to recover fully from his bank.

18

The Bank Statement Rule

The Bank Sends the Statement

Article 4 itself imposes no duty on a bank to provide its checking account customer with periodic statements of the activity recorded relating to the account and the current status of the account. This is strictly a matter of what is called for in the contract between the customer and the bank. Most account agreements do, however, call for the bank to prepare and mail statements on a regular basis. Furnishing a statement of the account is considered a service that the bank makes available to its customers, and it would be the rare customer who would agree to opening an account that did not include this feature. The provision of regular statements is, as we will see in this chapter, also in the interest of the bank. *If* the bank does make such statements available, and the customer thereafter does not bring to the bank's attention checks that bear an unauthorized drawer's signature or alteration and therefore are not properly payable, the customer may be foreclosed by his, her, or its failure to give proper and timely notice of the irregularity from insisting that the bank recredit the account. Banks make available periodic statements for the convenience and security of their customers but also for their own protection.

Section 4-406(a) does provide that:

> A bank that sends or makes available to a customer a statement of account showing payment of items for the account shall either return or make available to the customer the items paid or provide information in the statement of account sufficient to allow the customer reasonably to identify the items paid. The statement of account provides sufficient information if the item is described by item number, amount, and date of payment.

Notice that the bank is not obligated by this provision physically to return the canceled checks with the statement. This again is a matter dealt with in the customer's contract with the bank. Some banks agree to and do furnish canceled checks with the statement. Some do not. Some banks now include with the statement an image of any check (front and back) charged to the account, but not the canceled check itself. If the bank does not return the paid items with the statement, subsection (b) of §4-406 sets out what the bank must do by way of retaining the item or a "legible copy" thereof and also how the bank must furnish the customer, upon request, with either the item or the copy.

What §4-406(a) does require is that, one way or another, the bank furnish, along with or as part of the statement of account, information "sufficient to allow the customer reasonably to identify the items paid." Actual return of the canceled checks or inclusion of a legible copy of each will in and of itself meet this criterion. If the bank does not include the checks or copies of them, then the last sentence of the section provides what is referred to as a *safe harbor rule* for the bank: "The statement of account provides sufficient information if the item is described by item number, amount and date of payment." You will have noticed that, by virtue of this safe harbor rule, a bank will have provided "sufficient information" about the item even though it does not include either the name of the payee or the date written on the check. These two bits of information, especially the former, would probably be the most helpful to a customer in spotting a check he or she has not authorized but which has been written as part of an embezzlement scheme or theft. The justification for the safe harbor rule as written is given in the concluding paragraph of Comment 1, which I suggest you read at this time. Note particularly the policy decision "that accommodating customers who do not keep adequate records is not as desirable as accommodating customers who keep more careful records." This should be heartening to customers like me — and I have to assume you — who take the time and effort to keep adequate records of the checks we write out of our accounts.

The Customer Examines the Statement

Once a bank sends or makes available to its customer a statement of account that satisfies subsection (a) of §4-406, then under subsection (c) the customer

> must exercise reasonable promptness in examining the statement or the items to determine whether any payment was not authorized because of an alteration of an item or because a purported signature by or on behalf of the customer was not authorized.

If, based on this examination, the customer should have discovered the unauthorized payment out of his, her, or its account, then the customer "must promptly notify the bank of the relevant facts."

You will sometimes hear this spoken of as the customer's "duty" to examine the statement and recognize unauthorized items, but the important thing to remember is that this "duty" is a duty the customer *owes only to himself, herself, or itself.* The reason we make sure to open our bank statements soon after they arrive and give them a careful and complete examination is not because the bank has any right to insist that we do so. No one is going to come and get you, haul you to jail, or bring suit based on your failure to review your bank statement and any accompanying canceled checks. The duty you owe to yourself to take such care on your own behalf follows from the consequences of your (totally hypothetical) failure to do so. Pursuant to subsections (d)(1) and (2), under certain specified circumstances, as we will explore more fully in the examples, a customer's failure to "comply with the duties imposed . . . by subsection (c)" will preclude the customer from asserting the bank's wrongful payment of a not-properly-payable item. The customer may forfeit the right to have the account recredited for the amount of an item or items if it fails to promptly notify the bank "of the relevant facts" regarding an irregularity that could have been discovered by reasonably prompt and careful examination of the statement.

Subsection (e) continues the comparative negligence approach that we encountered often in Chapter 17. If the customer is precluded under subsection (d) from asserting the unauthorized signature or any alteration of an item, because of a lack of diligence in dealing with the statement provided, the customer may try to show that the bank also failed to exercise ordinary care in paying the item and that this failure by the bank "substantially contributed" to the loss. If the customer is able to make out a case for the bank's negligent treatment of the item — and it is probably only the very exceptional case in which this is a realistic possibility — then the customer and the bank share in the loss on a comparative negligence basis. Subsection (e) also states that if the customer can prove that the bank did not act in good faith in paying the item — and such cases have to be rarer still — then "the preclusion of subsection (d) does not apply." Subsection (e) may offer some limited consolation to the customer who has failed to exercise the care called for in (c), but it is surely no substitute for carefully reviewing the bank statement soon after it arrives and giving prompt notice to the bank of any problems.

The One-Year Preclusion

The separate rule set out in subsection (f) of §4-406 carries even greater consequences for the careless or lackadaisical customer.

Without regard to care or lack of care of either the customer or the bank, a customer who does not within one year after the statement or items are made available to the customer (subsection (a)) discover and report the customer's unauthorized signature on or any alteration on the item is precluded from asserting against the bank the unauthorized signature or the alteration.

This subsection means what it says, and there are any number of decided cases in which the payor bank has been able to gain summary judgment, dismissing an action brought against it for wrongful payment of an item, simply by showing that no problem of the type covered by §4-406(f) was brought to the bank's attention until more than one year after the bank sent a statement from which the customer should have been able to detect the problem. You should be aware that several states, in adopting Article 4, have shortened this absolute preclusion period to less than one year.* A separate question, which we will deal with in the last example of this chapter, is whether the periods set forth in this section — either the vague "reasonable promptness" of (c) or the strict one year of (f) — may be varied or shortened by the account agreement entered into between the bank and its customer.

EXAMPLES

1.   Andrew has a personal checking account with Payson State Bank. He keeps his checkbook on top of the desk in his home office. Thad, a decorator Andrew has hired to do some work in the apartment, is able to steal a blank check (#1084) out of this checkbook when he is alone in the room. He fills this check out for $1,500, naming himself as payee and forging Andrew's name on the drawer line. He deposits this check in his own account with Depot National Bank and the check is paid by Payson on January 13, 2004. By the end of the first week of February, Thad has cleaned out his account with Depot and vanished from the scene. Payson sends Andrew a monthly statement of his account activity for the month and his balance as of the end of January. This statement is mailed off by the bank on February 3 and received by Andrew on February 6. It clearly shows that check #1084, in the amount of $1,500, was paid by the bank on January 13. Andrew reviews this statement on February 9 and immediately notices this entry. He has no recollection or record of drawing any check in this amount. Furthermore, he looks at his checkbook and finds that the blank check numbered 1084 is indeed missing. The next day he goes into his bank and speaks to a bank officer. Together they look at the check itself, which was retained by the bank as are all checks paid out of Andrew's account, as provided for in the account agreement. Andrew is willing to sign an "Affidavit of Forgery" to the effect that the signature on the drawer's line

---

* Alabama and Oregon have shortened the period to 180 days and Georgia to 60 days. Washington has reduced the period to "sixty days" for any customer other than "a natural person whose account is primarily for personal, family, or household use."

of check #1084 is not his. Indeed, as the bank officer herself can see, the signature is nothing like Andrew's normal signature. Andrew demands that Payson recredit his account with the $1,500, because this check bore a forged drawer's signature and hence was not a properly payable item.

(a) Would anything in §4-406 give Payson justification for refusing to comply with this demand?

(b) What if instead Andrew had left his January bank statement unopened on his desk for a month or so? He does not notice the questionable item until early March, when he immediately brings it to the attention of the bank. May Payson refuse to recredit Andrew's account under these facts?

(c) Finally, suppose that Andrew either does not spot the problem or chooses not to do anything about it until he reviews his various financial records in preparation for doing his taxes for the year 2004. He does not go to the bank complaining of the payment of this forged check until March *of 2005*. What result here?

2.   In mid-August of 2004, Andrew (of the previous example) mails a check (#1064) for $12,000 to one Beatrice in payment for some free-lance work she did for him. The statement that Payson sends to Andrew covering the month of August indicates that check #1064 for $12,000 was paid by Payson on August 24, 2004. In October Beatrice phones Andrew and asks when she is going to be paid by him for the work she did. Andrew assures her that he long ago sent her a check for her services and that indeed the check has been paid. Beatrice adamantly insists that she never received any such check. Andrew asks for and receives from Payson a copy of his check #1064. When he and Beatrice examine it together, they determine that the check must somehow have been pirated from Beatrice's mail before she even got a chance to see it. The back of the check bears an obviously forged indorsement in the name of "Beatrice" and indicates that the check was then deposited into an account with Decoy Bank and Trust by one Thelma. The two contact the Decoy bank, which tells them that Thelma closed her account with that bank sometime in September and did not leave a forwarding address. Andrew contacts Payson and demands that the bank recredit his account for the $12,000, because the check was not a properly payable item, bearing as it did a forged indorsement of the payee's name. Does §4-406 offer Payson any basis for resisting Andrew's demand? Consult the second point made in Comment 5 to that section.

3.   Cara, who also has a checking account with Payson, invites her nephew Theo to live with her while he attends a local college. In March of 2004 Theo steals a blank check (#2345) from his aunt's checkbook, makes it out to himself for $500, and forges Cara's name as the drawer of the check. The account statement for the month of March, mailed by Payson on April 2 and received by Cara a few days later, indicates that check #2345 for $500 was paid out of her account on March 26. In early May Theo steals another check form (#2372)

from his aunt's checkbook, makes it out to himself for $600, and forges Cara's name on the check. In late May he repeats the trick, this time with check form #2385 made out for $2,000. Payment of both of these checks is reported to Cara on her May statement of account from Payson. Only then does Cara go into Payson and look at what she now realizes are three questionable checks paid out of her account. She discovers the forgery of her signature on all three (#2345 paid in March and #2372 and #2385 both paid in May). She confronts her nephew with what she has learned, and he is deeply apologetic. He is also totally broke and in no position to repay her what he has admittedly stolen. Cara makes a formal demand that Payson recredit her account for the amount of each of these three checks, as each bore a forged drawer's signature. Under §4-406, is Payson required to recredit her account with any or all of the total of $3,100 that Theo stole from his aunt's account?

4.   Hamilton is the treasurer of the DotCom Corporation. As such he is authorized to draw checks for up to $2,000 out of that company's checking account at Payson State Bank. DotCom's agreement with Payson calls for the signatures of both Hamilton as treasurer and Washington, the president of DotCom, on any checks for amounts greater than $2,000. Beginning in January of 2004, Hamilton writes a number of checks on the DotCom account for amounts in excess of $2,000 and running up to $15,000 payable to a friend of his, one Burr. He signs the checks in his own name and also forges Washington's signature on them. Each month, when the statement of account prepared by Payson bank is received at DotCom, it is directed to the desk of Hamilton, who himself reviews it. Needless to say, he makes no mention to anyone else of the checks he has written to Burr, his confederate, who has been cashing the checks and turning the proceeds over to Hamilton. In March of 2004, after he has embezzled a total of more than $100,000 by this means, Hamilton resigns from his position with DotCom and leaves its employ, stating that for personal reasons he must relocate to another part of the country. In February of 2005, the accounting firm that does DotCom's annual audit begins to look at the company's transactions for the year 2004. They bring to the attention of Washington, still president of DotCom, "questions" about "several checks written during the earlier part of the year," but at this point they are not able to pinpoint which checks, if any, may have been improperly drawn. On February 12, Washington contacts the officer at Payson who handles the DotCom accounts and tells her that he has been given reason to believe that "some improper items may have been paid out of our account during the first months of last year." The auditors eventually give Washington a detailed listing of the checks that Hamilton wrongfully issued — listing them by number, amount, and date paid by Payson — in May of 2005. Washington immediately forwards this list to Payson and demands that the bank recredit the company's account for the full amount of each check. Payson refuses to do so, citing the one-year rule of §4-406.

(a) Can DotCom successfully argue that it never received the statements covering the months in question, as they were delivered to and examined by Hamilton, the perpetrator of the scheme?

(b) Can DotCom successfully argue that the conversation Washington had with the bank officer in February should be considered a sufficient report of the unauthorized signatures on the checks in question, so that the company had in fact given notice within one year of its receiving the statements on which these checks were listed?

5.   Arnold Moneybucks has an account with Payson State Bank. Arnold decides to purchase an expensive statue ("Hypothetical Figure #5") created by the up-and-coming modern artist John Roc directly from the artist. In late 2003, Arnold and Roc agree that Arnold will receive immediate delivery of the statue and will pay for it by sending a series of 12 monthly checks for $5,000 each following his receipt and inspection of the item. Arnold gets delivery of the statue in early January and immediately sends a check made out to "John Roc" for $5,000 to Roc at the address the artist has given him. Arnold's bank statement for the month of January indicates that this check was paid by Payson on January 20, 2004. In each of the next 11 months, February through December of 2004, Arnold sends Roc a similar check, and each time his monthly statement indicates that the check was paid a week or so after Arnold mailed it off to the artist. In March of 2005, Roc is doing his bookkeeping and comes to the conclusion that he has received only 11 checks in total from Arnold. He calls Arnold to ask where the twelfth check is. Arnold consults his own checking account record and confirms that he has indeed sent Roc 12 checks for $5,000 each and that each check was paid by his bank. Upon further examination, Arnold and Roc are able to determine that the first check — the one sent in January 2004 — was apparently stolen from Roc by one John Roebuck, whom Roc can now recall was a visitor to and "had a good look around" his studio at about that time. Roebuck altered the name on the payee line to read as his own and deposited the check in his own account with Distrust Savings and Loan. Distrust forwarded the check onto Payson, which paid it without question. In late March 2005, once the facts are all in, Arnold contacts Payson and demands that the bank recredit his account for the amount of the January 2004 check, asserting that it was not payable because of the alteration made by Roebuck. The account officer at Payson points out to Arnold that the bank is not obligated to accede to this demand, because Arnold was informed of the payment more than one year previously in his January 2004 statement. The officer agrees, however, to recredit the account with the amount stolen, in recognition of Arnold's long history and importance as a major customer of the bank. If Payson does recredit Arnold's account with $5,000, the amount stolen by Roebuck's alteration of the January 2004 check, can Payson then recover this amount from Distrust Savings and Loan based on that bank's breach of one of the warranties of presentment? See the last sentence of §4-406(f).

6.   Martin opens a checking account with the Payoff Bank of Springfield. The written deposit agreement that Martin signs at the time of opening this account provides that the bank will furnish the customer with monthly statements, which will include copies of each check processed during the month. The agreement also includes the following language:

> Because you are in the best position to discover an unauthorized copy of your signature or a material alteration made to any check, you agree that we will not be liable for paying such items if you have not reported such an unauthorized signature or alteration to us within 60 days of the mailing date of the earliest statement describing these items.

A check (#2317) is stolen from Martin's checkbook in early June 2004. The thief, who writes out the check payable to herself and forges Martin's name on the drawer line, deposits this check into an account at Distrust Savings and Loan. The check is paid by Payoff Bank on June 20. Martin's June statement records payment of this check, a copy of which is made part of the statement. This statement is mailed to Martin on July 3. It is delivered to his home on July 7. Martin is away for an extended vacation during the month of July. When he returns home in mid-August, he sorts through his mail and finds both this statement and his July statement from Payoff, but does not open either. When his August statement arrives, on September 6, Martin decides that it is finally time to look at all these statements. He immediately discovers the problem with check #2317. He reports this to the bank, giving all the proper details, on September 7. Payoff Bank refuses to recredit his account for the amount of this check, citing as its reason for doing so the language in the deposit agreement and pointing out that the statement detailing this item was mailed to Martin on July 3 and that his report of the unauthorized signature on the item was not made to the bank until September 7, more than 60 days later. Is the bank's reliance on the 60-day reporting period provided for in the deposit agreement effective?

EXPLANATIONS

1a.   No. Upon receipt of his January statement, Andrew did all that could be expected of him under §4-406(c). He exercised "reasonable promptness in examining the statement" and "promptly" notified the bank of the relevant facts regarding the improper payment. Payson would have no grounds for claiming that he is precluded, under subsection (d), from asserting against the bank its payment of an item bearing a forged drawer's signature. Because Andrew's report to the bank came well within one year of the bank's mailing of the statement, subsection (f) is also inapplicable.

1b.   Payson will probably have to recredit Andrew's account with the $1,500 even though it also is probably fair to say that Andrew did not meet his responsibility to exercise "reasonable promptness" in examining the January statement. Payson would try to assert the right to place the loss on Andrew by virtue of §4-406(d)(1):

> If the bank proves that the customer failed, with respect to an item, to comply with the duties imposed on the customer by subsection (c), the customer is precluded from asserting against the bank . . . the customer's unauthorized signature . . . , if the bank also proves that it suffered a loss by reason of the failure.

The problem for Payson will not be proving that Andrew failed to meet his subsection (c) responsibilities, but in proving in addition that Payson *suffered a loss* by reason of Andrew's failure. Imagine that Andrew *had* immediately looked at his January statement as soon as he received it and then promptly reported the unauthorized signature to Payson. Even assuming this to be so, Payson would have been made aware that it had paid an item bearing a forged drawer's signature no earlier than February 6 or so. Under the rule of *Price v. Neal*, Payson would normally have to bear this loss. The only party against whom it could proceed, asserting a breach of a warranty of presentment, to recover its loss would be Thad, the thief himself. But by this time, Thad has taken the money and run. (Thieves are wont to do just this.) So even if Andrew had promptly discovered and notified the bank of the improper payment, the bank would have had to bear the loss with nowhere else to turn. Thus, as Andrew will argue, Payson did not "suffer a loss by reason of [his] failure" to give prompt notice. It would have suffered that loss even if Andrew had not failed to comply with subsection (c). Only if Payson could prove that, had it been given prompt notice of the unauthorized signature, it would have been able to catch up with Thad before he left town and made him reimburse the bank for what he had stolen (unlikely indeed) would Andrew be precluded by subsection (d)(1) from asserting the unauthorized signature against the bank.

1c. Under subsection (f) of §4-406, Andrew would have to bear the loss and could not make Payson recredit his account for the $1,500, even though it paid a check bearing a forged drawer's signature. Because Andrew did not discover and report to the bank the unauthorized signature until more than one year after the statement on which it appeared was made available to him, he is absolutely precluded from asserting against the bank the unauthorized signature. This is true, as the subsection states, "[w]ithout regard to care or lack of care of either the customer or the bank."

The Supreme Court of Virginia has even recently held that the preclusion of §406(f) applied irrespective of whether or not the bank has paid the contested items in good faith. *Halifax Corp. v. First Union Nat. Bank*, 261 Va. 91, 546 S.E.2d 696, 44 U.C.C.2d 661 (2001). The plaintiff, a corporation, was made to bear the loss of all of the $15,445,230.49 embezzled by its comptroller — via 88 bogus checks she was able to create on her home computer — between August 1995 and January 1997, without even the possibility of getting some contribution from the bank. The corporation did not discover "accounting irregularities" until January 1999. When it sued its bank, which had paid all of the bogus checks out of its account without question, the bank sought and was granted a summary judgment in its favor on the basis of §4-406(f). The corporation argued that it had raised a triable issue of whether the bank had acted in good faith in paying some of the checks, at least some of the very largest ones, but the court held that good faith is simply not relevant as far as the §4-406(f) preclusion is concerned. I'm not sure everyone would agree with this conclusion; after all the obligation of good faith applies to every "performance or enforcement" under the Code, O§1-203 or R§1-304. But the Virginia Supreme Court, noting the absence of any reference to good faith in subsection (f) of §4-406, and comparing this to subsections (d) and (e), concluded its state legislature had left it out intentionally. The court stated, "If the General Assembly had intended to limit the preclusion contained in [§4-406(f)] to items paid in good faith, the General Assembly would have done so explicitly." That being so, the court did not believe itself authorized to, in effect, add the phrase to §4-406(f) of its own volition.

2.   Section 4-406 does not come into play here at all. Subsection (c) requires that the customer act reasonably promptly to discover or report only when "any payment not authorized because of an alteration of an item or because a purported signature by or on behalf of the customer was not authorized." Similar language appears in subsection (f). As Comment 5 states:

> Section 4-406 imposes no duty on the drawer to look for unauthorized indorsements. Section 4-111 sets out a statute of limitations allowing a customer a three-year period to seek a credit to an account improperly charged by payment of an item bearing an unauthorized indorsement.

It is not hard to appreciate why the drafters made the bank statement rule apply only to unauthorized drawer's signatures and alterations; these are the types of transgressions that a diligent customer should be able to catch by a careful examination of his or her bank statement and the canceled checks or copies of those checks that usually accompany the statement. The drawer is normally in no position to detect a forged indorsement of the payee. In our case, Andrew could have spent all the time in the world looking over his statement and canceled check #1064, but all he would have seen was a signature purporting to be that of Beatrice and the fact that it was deposited into Decoy Bank for collection. There is no reason to think that he would be able to spot a forged signature purporting to be that of Beatrice (he may never have seen her signature before under any circumstances) or that Decoy Bank and Trust was not her bank.

3.   Payson may have to recredit Cara's account for the $500 lost to Theo via check #2345 paid in March, but this ultimately will depend on facts we don't have here. The bank can rightfully claim that Cara failed to carry out her duties of reasonably prompt inspection and notification after receipt of the March statement. To preclude Cara from asserting against it the forged signature on that check under subsection (d)(1), however, the bank will also

have to prove that Cara's failure to notify it within a reasonable time caused it to suffer a loss of $500 that it would otherwise not have had to bear. This requires a showing by the bank that had Cara reported the forgery to it by sometime early in April, it would have been able to locate the thief (which might not be hard here, as Theo continued to live at Cara's place) and that Theo would have had sufficient financial resources at that time to pay back the $500 he had stolen. This involves questions of fact, evidence of which both Cara and Payson will have to explore.

Payson will definitely not be required to recredit Cara's account for the two later checks, #2372 and #2385, both forged by Theo and paid by Payson in May. This is so even though Cara promptly caught the problem and reported the relevant facts to the bank. Subsection (d)(2) of §4-406 provides:

> If the bank proves that the customer failed, with respect to an item, to comply with the duties imposed on the customer by subsection (c) [as Cara clearly did with respect to check #2345], the customer is precluded from asserting against the bank . . . the customer's unauthorized signature or alteration *by the same wrongdoer* on any other item paid in good faith by the bank [here payment on both #2372 and #2385] if the payment was made before the bank received notice from the customer of the unauthorized signature or alteration, and after the customer had been afforded a reasonable period of time, not exceeding 30 days, in which to examine the item [#2345 again] or statement of account [here the March statement] and notify the bank.

The justification for this rule seems clear enough. Had Cara diligently examined her March statement and promptly given notice of the first forged check to the bank sometime in early April, it may not have given the bank the chance to retrieve the $500 amount of that check from Theo, but it certainly would have put Cara (as well as the bank) on notice that she had a thief in her house who was not averse to stealing from her and knew where she kept her checkbook. As Comment 2 observes at one point:

> The rule of subsection (d)(2) follows pre-Code case law that payment of an additional item or items bearing an unauthorized signature or alteration by the same wrongdoer is a loss suffered by the bank traceable to the customer's failure to exercise reasonable care . . . in examining the statement and notifying the bank of objections to it. One of the most serious consequences of failure of the customer to comply with the requirements of subsection (c) is the opportunity presented to the wrongdoer to repeat the misdeeds. Conversely, one of the best ways to keep down losses of this type of situation is for the customer to promptly examine the statement and notify the bank of an unauthorized signature or alteration so that the bank will be alerted to stop paying further items.

Cases in which this "repeater rule" applies — and where the customer's chances of getting most of what has been looted out of his, her, or its account become very slim — tend to come in two basic configurations, neither of which does much to bolster the confidence we would like to feel justified in placing on our fellow men and women. The first pattern that arises with distressing frequency is the relative or trusted companion who takes advantage of the hospitality of another, as was the hypothetical given here. For a good recent example, see *Mercantile Bank of Arkansas v. Vowell*, 2003 Ark. App. LEXIS 498, 50 U.C.C.2d 631. The second pattern that you'd end up seeing a lot of if you spent more time with the cases is, of course, the embezzling employee. See, for example, *Reliance Ins. Co. v. Bank of American Nat. Trust & Savings Ass'n*, 56 Fed.R.Serv. 3d 414, 43 U.C.C.2d 946 (N.D.Ill. 2001), or *Espresso Roma Corp. v. Bank of America, N.A.*, 100 Cal.App.4th 525, 124 Cal.Rptr.2d 549, 48 U.C.C.2d 265 (2002).

4a.   No. The customer's responsibilities under subsection (c) are triggered when a bank "sends or makes available" a statement of accounts. Subsection (f), the one-year preclusion provision, is written so that the critical period commences upon the statement or items are "made available" to the customer, but the courts have sensibly read this as being equivalent to the "sends or makes available" of subsection (c). What else could it mean? Now look at the definition in O§1-201(38) (or its equivalent in R§1-201(b)(36)(A)), which, coming as it does in Article 1, is applicable to Article 4 as well as any other article of the Code:

> "Send" in connection with any writing or notice means to deposit in the mail or deliver for transmission by any other usual means of communication with postage or cost of transmission provided for and properly addressed. . . .

In this case, Payson apparently sent each monthly statement to the address given to it by the customer, the DotCom Corporation, in connection with the account. The corporation did in fact receive the statements. There is no argument about that. The problem — for the corporation — is that the wrong person within the corporation, the embezzler himself, was the only one to review the statements as they came in. But this just shows that the corporation did not set up the proper internal safeguards to protect itself against the relatively rudimentary mode of embezzlement perpetrated by its treasurer. A more carefully thought-out procedure would have provided for a person other than one who had authority to issue checks on the account to receive and review the statements as they came in.

The bank, by sending the statements to the proper address with the proper postage, did all that it needed to do to place upon the customer (in this case the DotCom Corporation) the responsibility to review the statements and to report irregularities to avoid the preclusions provided for in (c) and (f) of §4-406. See *Dow City Cemetery Ass'n v. Defiance State Bank*, 596 N.W.2d 77, 38 U.C.C.2d 1267 (Iowa 1999), in which the Supreme Court of Iowa observed, "The fact that the cemetery [the customer] relied on Starla [the crooked employee] to examine the bank statements did not relieve it of its own duty to examine the statement and notify the bank of any unauthorized signatures or alterations," citing a goodly number of cases to back up its statement.

In *Lowenstein v. Barnett Bank of South Florida, N.A.*, 720 So. 2d 596, 36 U.C.C.2d 1139 (Fla. Dist. Ct. App. 1998), the customer sought to recover in 1995 against his bank for more than 81 forged checks created and cashed by a family member between 1991 and 1994, totaling some $100,553.20. The court held that he was barred from recovering as to all but the last six of these checks by the one-year rule, despite the fact that statements including information about all the checks had been delivered to his home during a period when the customer "was in federal custody at two different correctional institutions." The evidence indicated that each of the statements had been sent by the bank to the proper address last given it by the customer.

4b. No. Subsection (f) is avoided only if the customer "discover[s] and report[s]" the irregularity within the one-year period. This is usually read as being equivalent to the customer's responsibility to promptly "notify the bank of the relevant facts" under subsection (c). The customer does not meet this obligation by vague statements that something seems to be wrong with some items. The customer meets the responsibilities of (c) and avoids the preclusion of (f) only by giving specifics as to exactly which items it claims were wrongfully paid. See, for example, *First Place Computers, Inc. v. Security National Bank*, 251 Neb. 485, 558 N.W.2d 57, 31 U.C.C.2d 843 (1997) ("general concerns about possible irregularities in the account" did not meet the requirement of the one-year rule), and *Villa Contracting Co. v. Summit Bancorporation*, 302 N.J. Super. 588, 695 A.2d 762, 33 U.C.C.2d 1177 (1996) (the customer "must deal in specifics rather than generalities" and "must notify the bank of exactly which items bear the forged signatures").

5. No. The last sentence of subsection (f) makes clear that Payson cannot recover from Distrust for breach of the presentment warranties of §4-208. The first part of Comment 5 speaks to this situation:

> [I]f a drawer has not notified the payor bank of an unauthorized check or material alteration with the one-year period, the payor bank may not choose to recredit the drawer's account and pass the loss to the collecting bank on the theory of breach of warranty.

See also subsection (c) of §4-208.

6. The language in the deposit agreement that Martin has signed is based on the provision before the court in the case of *W.J. Miranda Construction Corp., Inc. v. First National Union Bank*, 40 U.C.C.2d 8 (Fla. Cir. Ct. 1999). The court there held that the so-called "cut-down" clause made part of the deposit agreement between the customer and the bank, reducing the time the customer had to report irregularity in any items paid from the one year after the mailing date of a statement provided for in §4-406(f) to 60 days, was enforceable against the customer and hence blocked any recovery when the customer gave notice more than 60 days after receipt of the statement describing the items under dispute. The court first concluded that the one-year notice requirement of §4-406(f) was not in the nature of a statute of limitations; had it been so, the parties would not have been free to shorten it by their personal agreement.

Rather, subsection 4-406(f) sets out "a notice requirement, which acts as a condition precedent to [the customer's] right to sue" on the contract with the bank. As a term of the contract entered into between the bank and its customer, this provision is to be judged in light of §4-103(a):

> The effect of provisions of this Article may be varied by agreement, but the parties to the agreement cannot disclaim a bank's responsibility for its lack of good faith or failure to exercise ordinary care or limit the measure of damages for the lack or failure. However, the parties may determine by agreement the standards by which the bank's responsibility is to be measured if those standards are not manifestly unreasonable.

The court then held that the particular cut-down language in the agreement was not a "manifestly unreasonable" alteration of the one-year preclusion provided for, in the absence of other agreement, in §4-406(f), at least when the agreed-upon time limitation was not being asserted in an attempt to absolve the bank of its duty to act in good faith and use due care. No argument was being made by the customer under the circumstances that the bank had failed to do either.

This decision is in keeping with the majority of those that have had to rule on the validity of such cut-down provisions, which are found in many bank-customer deposit agreements and in some instances call for notice by the customer of any irregularities that the statement should have brought to light in as few as 14 days. *See,* for example, *National Title Ins. Corp. Agency v. First Union Nat. Bank,* 263 Va. 355, 559 S.E.2d 668, 47 U.C.C.2d 318 (2002), and *Borowski v. Firstar Bank Milwaukee,* 217 Wis.2d 565, 579 N.W.2d 247, 35 U.C.C.2d 221 (Wis. App. 1998). A particularly well-known, and generally well-regarded, opinion on point was rendered by the Minnesota Supreme Court in *Stowell v. Cloquet Co-op Credit Union,* 557 N.W.2d 567, 31 U.C.C.2d 623 (Minn. 1997). The court there read the cut-down provision (to 20 days) before it not as an attempt to vary the terms of subsection (f) of §4-406, but rather as a specification by the parties of what would constitute "reasonable promptness" by the customer in the examination of his or her account statements and notification of the bank of any forged checks as required by subsection (c). Applying §4-103(a), as quoted earlier, the court held that an agreed-to 20-day term for "reasonable promptness" was not "manifestly unreasonable" under the circumstances.

Notice that neither the *W.J. Miranda* case nor *Stowell,* and the slightly different ways they approached such provisions, would allow a bank to shorten to less than the one year statutorily provided for in §4-406(f) the period in which it could assert a preclusion against its customer *without regard* to the bank's possible lack of care. Nor does either decision dictate the result should a bank try getting its customers to agree to an even shorter period for reporting irregularities (say, one week or ten days). I can well imagine a court determining that such an extreme cut-down was in fact "manifestly unreasonable," at least in a consumer context.

PART SIX

Electronic Means of Payment: The Consumer Context

19

Credit Cards

How Credit Cards Work

Believe it or not, there are those of us who can remember (if only dimly) a time before the availability and widespread use of the universal credit card, such as Visa or MasterCard, of the type we will be considering in this chapter. In the earlier part of the twentieth century, individual retailers might issue to regular customers charge cards, or as they were often called, charge plates (being made of metal!) that the customer could use in making purchases at the store in question. On a periodic basis, the customer would receive a bill for all that had been charged on that customer's account, and the customer was expected to pay the bill in full. If the agreement between the customer and the individual retailer allowed the customer to pay only a portion of what had been charged in any given period, spreading payment of the remainder into the future on established credit terms, the card would then be more properly called a *credit card*, rather than simply a *charge card*. Such restricted-use cards — ones that are accepted by only a particular retailer (for instance Macy's or Wal-Mart), or at gasoline stations selling a particular brand of gas — still exist, of course. You may have one, two, or a whole slew of them in your wallet.

The real boom in the use of credit cards began in the 1960s with the introduction of the so-called *universal use credit card*, a card that was "universal" in that it could be used to charge purchases from a wide variety of retailers and service providers and that incorporated a "credit" agreement allowing the cardholder, in effect, to borrow from the issuer of the card so that not all purchases made within a given billing cycle had to be paid for upon receipt of the bill. This type of card provides the customer with greater flexibility; he or she does not have to open a charge account in advance with each retailer where he or she may end up shopping. It also cuts down on the bulk of the customer's wallet.*

---

* At least that is the idea. It is, of course, fairly easy nowadays for a person to end up acquiring and carrying around any number of credit cards — and all too easy for that

Our first goal is to get a good overview of exactly how the universal credit card works from the point of view of all the parties involved. How do funds eventually get from A, the credit card user, to B, the merchant taking the card in exchange for goods or services? The basic plan looks like this:

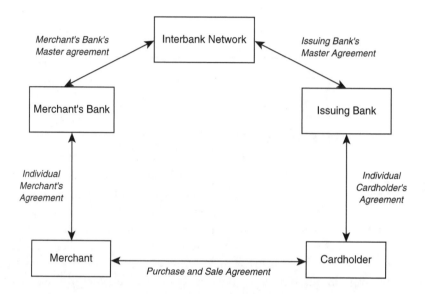

The interbank network placed at the top of this diagram — for example, Visa USA or MasterCard International, the two largest players in this field, which together account for a large majority of all credit cards now in the hands of users in the United States — is not itself directly involved in any individual transaction where the card is used to pay for goods or services. Its function is to provide the technological infrastructure that binds together the various banks and merchants in the system. The network enters into agreements with banks, such as the issuing bank in our diagram, authorizing the bank to enter into the system and to issue cards to end users. An issuing bank is then free to enter into contracts with individuals and businesses under which it issues the type of card in question to these users, agreeing to bill them on a periodic basis, extend them a line of credit up to a specified amount, charge them interest for any outstanding balances, and so on.

The master agreement under which banks become members of an interbank network permits the banks to serve a separate function, as with the merchant's bank of our diagram. Acting in this capacity, a member bank will

---

person to run the charges on each of those cards up to the maximum credit limit provided. Such scenarios are more properly dealt with in another course, namely bankruptcy. For our purposes, we will assume that the credit card holder has been judicious, at least with respect to how many cards he or she has been using and how much debt has been piling up.

solicit the participation of and then contract directly with the individual merchants in the system, each of which agrees "to accept" the card, taking it for payment for the goods or services it offers to the public. At the end of each business day, the participating merchant will collect all the charges it has taken in during the day on the card into a bundle — either literally, if the merchant is still asking purchasers to sign paper "charge slips" at the time of the transaction, or metaphorically if, as is increasingly true, the record of each charge has been created electronically by the user's card being "swiped" through a card reader, with the rest of the information regarding the charge input directly to fill out the electronic record. One way or another, this bundle of all the day's charges is by agreement forwarded to the merchant's bank for processing. Information about each separate charge is sent on by the merchant's bank, via the technological roadways maintained (for a small fee) by the interbank network, to the bank that issued the card used in that particular transaction. That issuing bank periodically compiles a listing of all the charges made on the card, totals the amount due, and sends all this information, in the form of a bill, to the cardholder for payment. This is the one part of the process with which you are most probably familiar.*

Fortunately for the merchant, it does not have to wait until each bill is paid and the amount due it on each transaction is fed back into the system to get its hands on the money representing the charges it has collected. Under its agreement with its bank, the amount of the charges it has collected on any given day (minus a small fee, of course) is within a few days made available to the merchant by deposit into an account it holds at the bank. The exact availability schedule, determining how much and when the accumulated charges delivered to the bank will result in money credited to the merchant's account, is set forth in detail in the contract between the merchant and its bank. Under the contract, the merchant must also agree that any charges reported in error, or that are eventually not collected because of a legitimate defense on the part of the cardholder, can be "charged back" or debited from its account.

The Law Regulating Credit Card Transactions

The law governing this entire multiparty arrangement is principally the traditional common law of contract. Notice the variety of contractual relationships

---

* The issuing bank does not make its money by taking a cut of the action or percentage of the amounts charged. It finds its reward in any annual fee it charges for use of the card and, much more significantly, in the interest fees it collects from those cardholders who in effect borrow on the card by carrying a credit balance from month to month.

that serve as background to and make possible any single credit card transaction. The issuing bank has entered into a contract with the interbank network, as has the merchant's bank. The issuing bank has also entered into a contract with the cardholder upon issuance of the card. The merchant's bank has a contract with the merchant. Each of these contracts is in place before the cardholder ever enters the merchant's shop or (as is increasingly true) makes contact with the merchant over the phone or via the Internet. When the cardholder and the merchant do make contact and come to some agreement about the sale or lease of goods or services, this is itself a distinct contract. Only this last contract, the one between the cardholder and the merchant, is even potentially governed by the Uniform Commercial Code; if the contract is for the sale of goods, it is subject to Article 2 of the Code; if for a lease of goods, by Article 2A. (If the cardholder-merchant contract is for the provision of services by the merchant, then of course it falls outside of the U.C.C. and is governed by the common law as it is applicable to service contracts.) Other than this, the various contracts that figure in our diagram are not dealt with at all by the Uniform Commercial Code. Nor, for the most part, does any federal law pertain to them. They are contracts entered into between supposedly savvy business parties (banks and the like), and the rules of the game will be the terms of the agreements entered into. The one exception to this statement is that federal statutory and regulatory law does affect the possible terms and enforcement of the issuing bank's contract with the individual cardholder, at least when the cardholder is a consumer. As we will see, the underlying purpose of this limited regulatory regime is consumer protection.*

In the early 1970s, Congress passed the federal *Truth-in-Lending Act* (TILA), which has been codified as Title I of the comprehensive Consumer Credit Protection Act (15 U.S.C. §1601 *et seq.*).† Acting pursuant to its authority under the TILA, the Federal Reserve promulgated *Regulation Z* (12 C.F.R. Part 226) to enforce the Act's provisions.‡ The first thing to

---

* Many states also have passed legislation that supplements but does not replace the federal law and rules discussed in this chapter. Again, these state statutes focus on the issuing bank-cardholder relationship in attempting to protect the consumer from what might be considered unfair or predatory aspects of the relationship.

† Some of the casebooks and other books in this area rely on the section numbers of the TILA directly (as in TILA §103). Others cite to the same section as codified in the United States Code (so TILA §103 is also 15 U.S.C. §1602). For your convenience, I have decided to include both cites, giving the TILA section first followed by the U.S.C. cite in brackets. So, for example, "TILA §103 [15 U.S.C. §1602]."

‡ Just to make life interesting, it has been my experience that not all of the selected commercial statute books, of the type you have available to you reproducing the Uniform Commercial Code and other related materials, include copies of both the TILA and Regulation Z. Some contain both, some one, and some the other. In truth, the text of the TILA and Regulation Z are almost identical, and I can appreciate why the editors of these volumes may have decided not to reproduce both just to make these statutory supplements even bulkier than they already are. For our purposes,

notice about the provisions of the TILA is that, with only rare exception, they apply only to consumer users of credit cards.* TILA §104(1) [15 U.S.C. §1603(1)] and Reg. Z §226.3(a) specifically provide that the Act does not apply to

> Credit transactions involving extensions of credit primarily for business, commercial, or agricultural purposes, or to government or governmental agencies or instrumentalities, or to organizations.

Note also that under subsection (3) of the same section, the TILA does not apply to even a consumer transaction (except of one unique type) "in which the total amount financed exceeds $25,000." It will be handy to remember that for definitions of just about all of the terms used here or elsewhere in the TILA, you can look to TILA §103 [15 U.S.C. §1602] and Reg. Z §226.2.

A large part of the TILA and Regulation Z are taken up with making sure that the card issuer makes certain prescribed *disclosures* to the cardholder every step along the way. Disclosure of certain key aspects of the relationship is required in any advertisement or direct solicitation of potential cardholders by the issuer or accompanying any application that the prospective cardholder is asked to fill out. It is also required upon initial issuance of the card, when a renewal card is sent, and on each bill. The type of information that is the subject of mandatory disclosure includes what rights the cardholder has to dispute any charge reported to him or her on a bill, the method for handling such a dispute, whether there is any annual fee for use of the card, and the extent of the cardholder's potential liability for unauthorized use of the card. Because the cardholder may also be carrying a balance over from one month to the next, and thereby taking advantage of the issuer's offer of credit, disclosure has to be made of the terms of the loan, using the TILA's detailed definitions and Regulation Z's further explication of the "finance charge" and the "Annual Percentage Rate" that the issuing bank intends to extract.

In the following examples we consider three other aspects of the TILA's regulation of credit card use. First we deal with issues involving the *unauthorized use* of a credit card by one other than the cardholder. What constitutes an unauthorized use?[†] To what extent may the cardholder be held liable for any

---

I will cite both the statutory section *and* the parallel provision in Regulation Z. So, for instance, I might refer you to "TILA §132 [15 U.S.C. §1642] or Reg. Z §226.12." If you can track down and carefully read just *one* of these references in the materials you have available to you — and that you certainly should be able to do — it should be sufficient to analyze the examples I will place before you.

* The exceptions, in which other than consumer users may rely upon TILA, are set out in TILA §135 [15 U.S.C. §1645]. A nonconsumer cardholder is protected from the issuance to it of a credit card for which it has not applied and from liability for unauthorized use of its card, a significant part of TILA that we will take up in the examples. The nonconsumer is also subject to TILA's provision dealing with the fraudulent use of credit cards.

[†] As you will discover when you look at the definition of unauthorized use in either the TILA or Regulation Z, the key question will be whether a user of the card other

or all of the charges made by the unauthorized party? Secondly, we take up the method of *error resolution* provided for by the statute. If the cardholder discovers a charge on his or her statement that he or she believes to be in error, what must be done to contest the charge? What must the issuing bank do once a charge is put in dispute? How, if at all, does the dispute get peacefully resolved by this mechanism? Finally, we consider under what conditions the cardholder may assert *against the credit card issuer* any claims or defenses that it would have against the merchant, when the issuer continues to insist that the charge be paid after an attempt at error resolution has failed to wipe the charge off the cardholder's account.

EXAMPLES

1.   Angela, who is a very handy type, is personally remodeling and repainting her bedroom, with the help of her friend Bella. At one point Angela asks Bella to go to the local hardware store to purchase some paint for the next phase of the job. Saying, "You'll need this," she hands over to Bella a MajorCard card that was issued to her by Shelbyville Bank. Bella goes to Cogland's Hardware, where she purchases a quantity of paint. She hands Angela's card over to Cogland, who rings up the purchase by charging the card. Bella signs her own name on the charge slip. Bella returns with the paint to Angela's. After it is applied to the walls, Angela decides that the color is not at all to her liking. She is going to have to repaint the whole room. When Angela's next MajorCard bill arrives from Shelbyville Bank, it contains the charge from Cogland's Hardware for the paint Bella purchased. Does Angela have any argument that she is not responsible for this purchase because it was an "unauthorized use" of her card? See TILA §103(o) [15 U.S.C. §1602(o)] or Reg. Z §226.12(b)(1), n.22.

2.   Angela, of the previous example, has to go away for a weekend. Bella offers to come over to her house on Sunday and continue work on the remodeling of the bedroom. Angela gives Bella the key to her house. When Bella arrives on Sunday, she finds a note from Angela thanking her for all her help. Next to the note is Angela's MajorCard card. During the course of her work, Bella determines that she needs a taller stepladder to do work on the ceiling. She takes Angela's MajorCard card to Cogland's, where she purchases a ladder, again using the card for payment but this time signing Angela's name to the charge slip, creating a fairly good likeness of Angela's signature as it appears on the back of the card.

---

than the cardholder himself or herself had the "actual, implied, or apparent authority" to use the card. If you are not familiar with these terms — and how the concepts they represent play out under the common law of agency to which the statute and the regulation refer — you should look at the brief discussion of the basic rules of agency law given in the introduction to Chapter 4, where actual, implied, and apparent authority came up in a different context.

    (a) Would this constitute an unauthorized use of the card?

    (b) Suppose that in addition to buying the stepladder for Angela's home remodeling project, Bella also charged to the card a bread-making machine that she happened to see on sale at the hardware store and that she determined she simply must have for her own use. Would *this* charge, for the appliance, be an unauthorized use of the card?

    (c) Would your answer to part (b) remain the same if instead Bella had signed her own name to the charge slip handed to her by Cogland?

3.   Darrel applies for a MajorCard card from Shelbyville Bank. The bank puts a card issued in Darrel's name into the mail, sending it to the address given the bank by Darrel on his application. This card is apparently stolen from Darrel's mailbox by some unscrupulous character. The first mail Darrel actually receives from the bank relating to the card is a first month's statement indicating that more than $3,500 in purchases have been charged to the card. Is Darrel responsible for paying any of this? For this and the example to follow, see TILA §133(a)(1) [15 U.S.C. §1643(a)(1)] or Reg. Z §226.12(b).

4.   Emily applied for, received, and accepted a MajorCard card issued by the Shelbyville Bank. At one point some crooked character comes into Emily's office while she is not there, rifles through her wallet, and extracts the MajorCard card. When Emily finally becomes aware that the card is missing, she checks with her bank and finds that more than $10,000 in charges have been made on the card by whoever took it.

    (a) Is Emily responsible for any of these charges?

    (b) What if Emily had immediately noticed that her wallet had been tampered with and, upon carefully checking, found that the MajorCard card was missing? She quickly calls the telephone number provided by the bank to report the stolen card. All of these hefty charges on the card are made by the thief after Emily has notified the bank of the theft of the card. Does Emily bear any of the loss under these circumstances?

5.   Frederick has a MajorCard card issued to him by the Shelbyville Bank on which he is billed monthly. On his statement for September 2004, which the bank mails on October 3 and Frederick receives on October 5, 2004, there is a charge of $123.57 from a "Metro Diner" of Shelbyville, the date of the transaction being September 15, 2004. Frederick is sure this is some sort of mistake. He has never been to the Metro Diner, and certainly not on the date in question.

    (a) Would this charge constitute a "billing error"? See TILA §161(b) [15 U.S.C. §1666(b)] or Reg. Z §226.13(a).

    (b) What should Frederick do to officially register his dispute of this item? See TILA §161(a) [15 U.S.C. §1666(a)] or Reg. Z §226.13(b).

    (c) What must Shelbyville Bank do upon being made aware that Frederick considers this item to be in error? See TILA §161(a) and (c) [15 U.S.C. §1666(a) and (c)] or Reg. Z §226.13(c), (d), and (f).

(d) Suppose that upon inquiry to the Metro Diner, the bank is informed by the manager of the diner that its report of a charge in this amount on Frederick's card was indeed an error. The meal was eaten and the charge incurred by someone else whose card number was mistakenly read as that of Frederick's. What is the bank obligated to do now? See TILA §161(a) [15 U.S.C. §1666(a)] or Reg. Z §226.13(e).

(e) Suppose instead that the manager of the diner, upon checking her records, insists that the charge was not made in error. She forwards to the bank a copy of a charge slip, bearing the date and amount in question, which does indeed carry the imprint of Frederick's card and a signature that appears to be that of Frederick. The bank concludes that its inclusion of the charge on Frederick's September bill was not in error. What may and must it do then? See TILA §161(a) [15 U.S.C. §1666(a)] or Reg. Z §226.13(f) and (g).

6.   Gabriella, a resident of Baltimore, has a MajorCard issued to her by Maryland Bank and Trust. She uses the card to purchase, for $1,200, from Hopkins Fine Jewelry of Baltimore what she is assured by Hopkins is a unique antique watch made sometime in the late 1800s. She begins to wear the watch immediately and receives many compliments on it. One friend, however, tells Gabriella that she almost bought "the exact same thing" at a jewelry store other than Hopkins. Gabriella goes to this other store and does see a watch there that appears to be identical to hers. The owner of the shop looks at her watch and tells her that although it is a fine watch (as is the identical watch he has on display), it is not an antique but a recent reproduction. He is asking $800 for that particular model. When Gabriella gets home that day, she finds her most recent MajorCard bill, which includes the $1,200 charge she made at the Hopkins jewelry store. She goes to Hopkins's store the next day and demands that he take back the watch and credit her MajorCard with $1,200. Hopkins insists that whatever anyone else may have told her, this particular watch is indeed an antique and worth every penny she paid for it. Gabriella notifies Maryland Bank and Trust that she is disputing the $1,200 on her bill, and the bank investigates, but ultimately it decides (in light of her admission that she made the charge for $1,200 on the date in question and Hopkins's insistence that there was nothing faulty or questionable about what she purchased that day) that there was no billing error and that Gabriella should pay the $1,200 as part of what she owes on her MajorCard account.

(a) If Gabriella refuses to pay this part of her MajorCard bill and is eventually sued for the amount by Maryland Bank and Trust, can she use as a defense against that bank the breach of warranty she claims she was given by Hopkins? That is, could she defeat or lower the bank's claim by proving, by whatever means, that the watch is not a genuine antique made in the late 1800s but rather a cheaper reproduction? Remember, no one at the bank ever gave her any assurances about the nature of the watch. See TILA §170(a) [15 U.S.C. §1666i(a)] or Reg. Z §226.12(c).

(b) Would your answer be the same if Gabriella had purchased the watch not at a jewelry store located in her hometown of Baltimore but rather at a store in Los Angeles when she happened to be visiting that fair city?

(c) What if Gabriella had not immediately become aware of the questionable nature of her purchase from Hopkins? She pays the MajorCard bill, including the $1,200. Only later does she have reason to believe that Hopkins breached a warranty in the sale of the watch to her. She tries to get relief from Hopkins, but to no avail. Can she sue the bank for return of the $1,200 or for $400 in damages, asserting against the bank the breach of warranty by the merchant? See TILA §170(b) [15 U.S.C. §1666i(b)] or Reg. Z §226.12(c).

EXPLANATIONS

1.   No. Angela must pay for this purchase with her card, as this was clearly an *authorized* use. As you see in either the TILA or the Reg. Z cite, the term *unauthorized use* means

> a use of a credit card by a person other than the cardholder who does not have actual, implied, or apparent authority for such use and from which the cardholder receives no benefit.

This was a use by a person other than the cardholder, so the question comes down to whether, under the common law of agency, Bella had the authority to make the charge. In this instance it seems undeniable that Bella was given actual authority by Angela to use Angela's card to purchase the paint.

2a.   No. This should also be considered an authorized use of the card. Cogland and the issuing bank could argue that Angela, by leaving her card next to the note as she did, and in light of Angela's past practice of giving Bella actual authority to use the card to buy supplies for the remodeling projects, had given Bella the implied authority to use the card to buy the stepladder. The fact that Bella signed Angela's name rather than her own does not change things. Angela, it could be argued, has impliedly authorized Bella not only to use the card in connection with the work being done, but also to sign Angela's name in connection with the use of the card. This is not a forgery or an unauthorized signature. It is an example of an agent, here Bella, having the authority to sign the name of her principal, Angela, under the circumstances.

2b.   Bella was authorized to use the card at Cogland's, but she went overboard and charged an item that she had no reason to think Angela would have authorized her to buy and that she plans on keeping for her own use. The courts have generally held that in a situation such as this, the *misuse* of a card voluntarily made available to another does not constitute an unauthorized use.

A well-known case addressing the problem is *Stieger v. Chevy Chase Savings Bank*, 666 A.2d 479 (D.C. 1995). Stieger, the cardholder, voluntarily gave his card to one Ms. Garrett for the limited purpose of renting a car and for a stay in a hotel during a business trip being made on Stieger's behalf. Garrett made a number of other charges not specifically authorized by Stieger, in most cases signing "P. Stieger." Stieger contended that these additional charges were unauthorized, but the court ruled that, at least with respect to the charges for which Garrett signed Stieger's name, the doctrine of apparent authority applied and the charges were authorized.

> Our cases reveal that apparent authority arises when a principal places an agent in a position which causes a third person to reasonably believe the principal had consented to the exercise of authority the agent purports to hold. . . . [A]pparent authority of an agent arises when the principal places the agent in such a position as to *mislead* third persons into believing that the agent is clothed with authority which in fact he does not possess.

The court noted that this was not a case in which the acquisition of the card by the user was without the cardholder's consent, such as when the card has been stolen, lost, or obtained from the cardholder by fraud. In such situations, the mere possession of the card by the user does not support a finding of apparent authority in the user; the cardholder has himself or herself done nothing to give the third party the impression that the use is authorized. As the *Stieger* court concluded, however, the situation is different if the cardholder has voluntarily made the card available to the user, even if for a limited purpose.

> Nearly every jurisdiction that has addressed a factual situation where a cardholder voluntarily and knowingly allows another to use his card and that person subsequently misuses the card has determined that the agent has apparent authority, and therefore was not an "unauthorized" user under [the TILA].

So Bella's purchase of the bread-making machine would likely be considered an authorized use of the card, because Angela voluntarily and knowingly allowed Bella to use the card. The fact that Bella misused it, going beyond what she could have reasonably believed Angela intended her to use the card for, does not render this an unauthorized use.

2c.   At least according to the *Stieger* case, this would make a difference and Bella's misuse of the card to obtain the bread-making machine for herself would constitute an unauthorized use.

> To a merchant, voluntary relinquishment combined with the match of a signature is generally reasonable identification of apparent authority to utilize the credit card. . . . [T]he same cannot be said of the two charges where Ms. Garrett signed her own name rather than "P. Stieger." It is an unreasonable extension of the apparent authority provided to Ms. Garrett for a merchant to accept charges, where the signatures do not match, without any additional factors to mislead the

merchant into believing that the person presenting the card is the agent of the cardholder. . . .

3.   Darrel is not responsible for any of the unauthorized charges made with this card, not a penny. Liability of a cardholder for unauthorized use of the card is predicated (under TILA §133(a)(1)(A) [15 U.S.C. §1643(a)(1)(A)] and Reg. Z §226.12(b)(2)(i)) on the card having been "accepted." The term *accepted credit card* (which you should be able to find for yourself in either the statute or the regulation),

> means any credit card which the cardholder has requested and received or has signed and used, or authorized another to use, for the purpose of obtaining money, property, labor, or services on credit.

Darrel requested but never received the card, so he is not at all liable for any charges made on it. Up until fairly recently, a large percentage of the losses merchants or issuers suffered from the unauthorized use of cards could be traced to situations like this one, when an initial or replacement card is sent to the cardholder but is stolen before it ever reaches the intended recipient. That is why, as you may have yourself experienced, most issuers now require that the card, once received, be "activated" by the cardholder through a call from his or her home phone and the giving of personal information (such as a Social Security number or mother's maiden name) that a thief would presumably not readily have available. This practice has apparently cut down on at least this one type of credit card fraud considerably.

4a.   The crook's charges against the card were clearly unauthorized and hence Emily is responsible for only $50 of these unauthorized charges, but no more. See TILA §133(a)(1)(B) [15 U.S.C. §1643(a)(1)(B)] and Reg. Z §226.12(b)(1). The policy decision behind this important aspect of TILA is to have the principal brunt of loss due to unauthorized use (amounting to something like $1.5 billion in 1995) borne by the credit card industry rather than individual users. This is, of course, all the more reason why the question of whether a particular charge will be deemed authorized or unauthorized is so important to the cardholder. The cardholder is fully liable for any authorized charges, but can be held responsible for no more than $50 of unauthorized charges, even if he or she fails to report the loss of the card in a timely fashion.

4b.   No. Now Emily does not even have to bear $50 worth of the loss. A cardholder can be liable for unauthorized use only if the use occurs "before the card issuer has been notified that an unauthorized use of the credit card has occurred or may occur as the result of loss, theft, or otherwise" (TILA §133(a)(1)(E) [15 U.S.C. §1643(a)(1)(E)] and Reg. Z §226.12(b)(1)). Emily's timely reporting of the loss has saved her $50. The $50 amount may not seem like more than a token, but it is something. More important from Emily's point of view is that the sooner she discovers and reports the loss, the sooner she can put a stop to unauthorized charges on the card. Although she will not be responsible for more than $50 of these charges, anything she can do to minimize the hassle she will have to go through because of unauthorized charges is more than worth the time and effort expended in reporting the loss as soon as she can.

5a. Yes. As of this point, Frederick believes this item on his bill reflects "an extension of credit [by his bank to pay a bill at the Metro Diner] that was never made" to him or to someone authorized to use the card. As you can see, not all "billing errors" that require both the cardholder and the issuing bank to comply with the billing resolution procedures of the TILA are of this type. The cardholder may be disputing only the amount of a particular item, rather than claiming that he or she never used the card at the merchant's place of business on the date in question. The cardholder himself or herself may not in fact be sure what the listed item stands for and may not know whether it is legitimate, in which case he or she may request "additional clarification, including documentary evidence," about the particular item.

Notice, however, that the term "billing error" does not include a dispute relating to the quality of property or services that the cardholder has accepted or to which they have been delivered. See *Beaumont v. Citibank (South Dakota) N.A.*, 2002 U.S.Dist.LEXIS 5276 (S.D.N.Y. 2002). That is, if the cardholder acknowledges making the charge and getting the goods or services but is dissatisfied with them, even if rightfully so, he or she cannot claim that a billing error has been made. So, for example, if Frederick does remember eating at the Metro Diner on that day, and using his MajorCard to pay for the meal, he can't initiate the billing error procedure, even if his memory of the meal is particularly vivid because he later had reason to believe he was served tainted food. If he believes that for this reason he should not have to pay any or all of the $123.57, his remedy lies in a different part of the TILA and Regulation Z. See Example 6.

5b. Frederick must send the Shelbyville Bank a written notice that is received by the bank within 60 days of October 3. This notice should contain information sufficient to allow the bank to identify Frederick and his account number, and to make the bank aware of which item on his September bill he believes to be in error, as well as the reasons for his belief that the item is in error.

As a practical matter, many issuers now provide on the monthly statement a telephone number for cardholders to call if they believe a billing error has occurred. The issuer usually immediately puts the amount "in dispute," meaning, as we will see, that the cardholder does not have to pay it as part of that month's bill. The issuer then itself sends the cardholder a form to fill out, sign, and return which acts as the written notice required by the TILA asserting the existence of a billing error.

5c. The bank has to send a written acknowledgment of receipt of the billing error notice sent by Frederick within 30 days after receipt of that notice. The bank may not, during the time the dispute is still pending, require payment of the amount in dispute, make any efforts to collect the disputed amount, or directly or indirectly make or threaten to make an adverse credit report about Frederick's credit status because he has failed to pay the disputed charge. Within two complete billing cycles (two months in this case), the bank must do one of two things. It may resolve the dispute in Frederick's favor and make the appropriate correction to his account, notifying Frederick of the fact. Or it may "send a written explanation or clarification" to Frederick "after having conducted an investigation, setting forth to the extent applicable the reasons why [it] believes [Frederick's] account was correctly shown in the statement," and upon request provide copies of documentary evidence of his indebtedness. I am quoting here from the TILA itself. Regulation Z adds the not unreasonable requirement that the bank's investigation be a "reasonable investigation" (Reg. Z §226.13(f), n.31).

It is important to recognize that the role of the issuing bank in this dispute resolution process is that of impartial arbiter. For a cardholder, disputing an item is not the same as having it wiped off the books. How could it be? The issuer's investigation may indeed cause the merchant to realize that a mistake has been made and that the charge was submitted in error. But that will not invariably be the case. Should the merchant insist that the charge was valid, and give the bank evidence appropriate to the situation to back up its claim, then the bank is well within its rights, and may be under an obligation, to conclude that the cardholder's claim of a billing error cannot be sustained. The charge goes back on the bill. Were any individual issuer to consistently rule in favor of its own cardholders when disputes arise, we have to assume that merchants would soon learn not to accept cards issued by that bank.

5d. Shelbyville Bank should correct the billing error and credit Frederick's account with the disputed amount and any related finance charges. It must further mail a correction notice to him.

5e. The bank should then mail to Frederick an explanation of why it has determined that no billing error occurred, and must also furnish copies of documentary evidence (in this case the signed credit card slip) of Frederick's indebtedness to him if he so requests. The bank can then add back to the amount due on Frederick's account the disputed $123.57, notifying him of the time when this payment is due and of the amount, including any relevant finance charges, that he now owes. As TILA §161(a) concludes:

> After complying with the provisions of this subsection with respect to any alleged billing error, a creditor [the issuing back] has no further responsibility under this section if the obligor [the cardholder] continues to make substantially the same allegation with respect to such error.

I think it is important to recognize that a finding against Frederick in such a situation is *not* necessarily equivalent to a clear-cut determination that he must have been lying all along about not having gone to the Metro Diner, and that he is just trying to get out of paying for a meal that he did in fact agree to pay for. Even if the dispute resolution process ends up finding that no billing error occurred, the further information Frederick may have obtained may by now have cleared up the mystery. Sometimes the process just jogs the (perfectly honest) cardholder's memory about a charge that he or she had really forgotten. Perhaps the restaurant that was still officially listed as "Metro Diner" on the MajorCard merchant's directory, and hence showed up on the bill by that name, had by the time in question been operating under another name, say, "International Villa." Or perhaps Frederick, when he gets a chance to see a copy of the charge slip itself and the signature on it, comes to the unhappy realization that the charge occurred during a period when he lent his son the card in order to gas up the car — and his son misused the card to get a meal for himself and some friends at a local diner while he was at it. This would make the charge, as we have already determined, an authorized charge on the card and one for which Frederick really is responsible. How Frederick sorts out the affair with his son is his business. It does not come within the scope of any federal statute or regulation, as far as I am aware.

6a. Yes. Subject to certain limitations, none of which apply here, the TILA provides that the issuer "shall be subject to all claims (other than tort claims) and defenses arising out of any transaction in which the credit card is used as a method of payment." The TILA provides that one of the preconditions to Gabriella's being able to assert the defense against the bank is that she have made "a good faith attempt to obtain satisfactory resolution of a disagreement or problem relative to the transaction from the person honoring the credit card." Similar language is found in Reg. Z §226.12(c).

6b. If, as here, Gabriella's use of the card was in another state or more than 100 miles from the billing address that she has given the bank in connection with her card, then Gabriella would *not* be able to assert against the bank any breach of warranty arising out of her transaction with the Los Angeles jeweler. What justification there is for the "100 mile rule," as this limitation is sometimes called, is not altogether clear. It is usually asserted that the effect of the limitation is to make credit cards more easily used (that is, more acceptable to merchants) when the cardholder is far away from home. Whether this is indeed the case, and if so exactly why, is subject to dispute. The need, if any, for the 100-mile rule has become even more questionable in recent years, as more and more credit card transactions take place over the telephone or via the Internet. Where exactly is the location of the transaction when the card is used in this way? The few cases that have had to deal even tangentially with such metaphysical questions give no clear or consistent answer. As for Gabriella in our example, the answer is not in dispute. She has no defense based on any alleged breach of warranty if she is sued by Maryland Bank. She is going to have to pay the bank the charge resulting from the purchase of the watch. Any relief she may hope to gain will have to be had by her going against the California seller on a breach of warranty action under Article 2.

6c. No. The cited provisions grant the cardholder no right to institute a suit against the issuer under any circumstances. They provide only for the cardholder's assertion of certain claims and defenses should he or she be sued by the issuer.

20

Debit Cards and ATM Transactions

Introduction to Debit and ATM Cards

A *debit card* differs from a credit card in one fundamental respect from which a whole series of consequences flows. Debit cards (or, as some banks have taken to calling them, "check cards") are necessarily linked to an account that the cardholder has with the issuing bank. As we have spent no small amount of time investigating in prior parts of this book, one way in which a bank's customer can pay for something using money in his or her account is by the issuance of a paper check. Another way is for the customer to make use of a debit card issued in connection with the account. When the customer makes a purchase at a merchant that is equipped to accept payment by this method, having available what is referred to as a *point-of-sale* (POS) terminal, the customer first swipes the debit card through the terminal. The customer then enters on a numeric pad adjacent to the terminal his or her own *personal identification number* (PIN), which he or she was initially given by the bank or later chose to be associated with the card.* The terminal is connected to a network that allows it to transmit information regarding the attempted use of the card to the bank at which the account is held. The terminal should receive, within seconds, a confirmation that the account with which the card is linked is still active, that it has sufficient funds to cover the charge, and that the card has not been reported lost or stolen. Once the use of the debit card is "authorized" in this way, the merchant is free to let the user take the goods he or she

---

* In recent years the Visa and Mastercard networks have begun to market through their member banks debit cards that don't depend on the use of a PIN to complete a transaction. Use of such "PIN-less" debit cards relies only on the signature, or sometimes a picture, of the cardholder as a means of identification and theft-protection device.

has purchased out of the store, just as if he or she had paid cash. The amount of the purchase is instantaneously deducted from the customer's bank account. The merchant's own account with its bank is credited, either immediately or (in some systems) at the end of the business day, with the amount of the purchase. Using a credit card, a consumer buys now but pays later, when the bill comes in. Even then, he or she may use the credit feature of the card to spread out payments over a longer period of time. When a customer uses a debit card to pay for goods or services, he or she pays on the spot. The cost is immediately deducted from his or her checking account.*

An *ATM card* is like the debit card (and in fact many banks issue a single card that can function as both a debit card and an ATM card) in that it is issued and functions only in connection with an account or accounts the customer has with the issuing bank. The ATM card, inserted into the slot of an *automated teller machine* (an ATM) which is then "given" the customer's PIN number previously associated with the card, allows the customer to check his or her balance and make transfers between accounts. And, oh yes, to withdraw cash from the account, which cash is presented to the customer right then and there.

The debit card and the ATM card, along with other even more recently invented ways for the customer to make use of funds in his or her account (such as automated telephone bill payment service, direct deposit of the customer's paycheck or preauthorized payment of his or her recurrent bills, and payment of bills and transfers between accounts that the customer initiates through a bank-by-computer system) all are part of a growing phenomenon. The customer carries out his or her banking without ever having come into contact with any human representative of the bank, either face-to-face or by a conventional phone call. This can be very convenient and efficient. It also opens up whole new avenues for possible fraud and error in the transaction.

The Law Governing Consumer Electronic Fund Transfers

In 1978 Congress passed the *Electronic Fund Transfer Act* (EFTA), which was codified as Title IX to the comprehensive Consumer Credit Protection Act (15 U.S.C. §1601 *et seq.*). As authorized and directed by the EFTA, the

---

* Just to make things more interesting, some banks have taken to issuing cards that can serve as either a credit or a debit card. If that is the case, the customer will have to determine at the time of purchase in what way the card is being used. Whenever the card is functioning as a credit card, its use is governed by the Truth-in-Lending Act and Regulation Z, which we discussed in Chapter 19. When the card is put to use as a debit card, the governing law is the Electronic Fund Transfer Act and Regulation E, which we are about to look into.

Federal Reserve issued *Regulation E* (12 C.F.R. Part 205) to further expli-
cate the workings of the Act.* Key to understanding the workings of the Act
and its scope is its definition of *electronic fund transfer* in §903(6) [15 C.F.R.
§1693a(6)], as elaborated upon in Reg. E §205.3. The core of the definition
reads as follows:

> [T]he term "electronic fund transfer" means any transfer of funds,
> other than a transfer originated by a check, draft, or similar paper
> instrument, which is initiated through an electronic terminal, tele-
> phonic instrument, or computer or magnetic tape so as to order,
> instruct, or authorize a financial institution to debit or credit an
> account. Such term includes, but is not limited to, point-of-sale
> transfers, automated teller machine transactions, direct deposits or
> withdrawals of funds, and transfers initiated by telephone.†

Although this definition does not appear to limit the scope of the act to individual consumers and their transactions, look at the definition given in EFTA
§903(2) [15 U.S.C. §1693a(2)] and Reg. E §205.2(b)(1) for the word
account. Reading from the Act, "[T]he term 'account' means a demand deposit,
savings deposit, or other asset account . . . , established primarily for personal,
family, or household purposes." Just so that there is no doubt, the Act also
defines *consumer* as meaning "a natural person" (EFTA §903(5) [15 U.S.C.
§1693a(5)] and Reg. E §205.2(e)).

A large part of the EFTA is taken up with the *disclosure requirements*
imposed upon any bank that agrees to process electronic fund transfers on
behalf of its customers. Specified disclosure is initially required at the time
the consumer contracts for an electronic fund transfer service or before the
first electronic transfer is made through the service. The bank is also obligated to make disclosure of any change in the terms of the service, as well as,
at least once a year, to furnish the customer details of the error resolution

---

* Some of the statutory supplements and other books covering this topic reproduce
or cite only to the language of Regulation E. Some contain or cite to the EFTA itself,
sometimes to the section number of the EFTA and sometimes to the parallel section
number of the United States Code. The exact language of the Regulation is, of
course, not precisely the same as that of the Act. Its purpose is, after all, to clarify and
make the EFTA more coherent. Still, for our purposes, looking at either the
Regulation or the Act should serve equally well. I will try to cover all bases by directing you when I can to the rule we seek in all three ways. So, for example, we are just
about to look at the definition of *electronic fund transfer*, which can be found in
EFTA §903(6) [15 U.S.C. §1693a(6)] and Reg. E §205.3.
† Notice that, under the exclusion listed as (E) following this language, an instruction
given for a one-time transaction in the course of a telephone conversation between the
consumer and an officer or employee of the bank is not covered by the Act. Once a
real live person at the bank is involved in taking the instruction from the customer, the
transaction is not truly "electronic" and is not within the scope of the Act.

process available to the customer in connection with the service. The EFTA also requires that for any transfer initiated at an electronic terminal (such as a POS terminal or an ATM machine), the system shall provide at the time of the transaction written documentation of the transfer (being the debit card receipt or the ATM record, which, in theory at least, should come out of the ATM at the end of your session with the machine). The Act also requires that the bank provide the consumer with a periodic statement, usually on a monthly basis, for each account that can be accessed by means of an electronic fund transfer mechanism. In most instances this requirement is met by the bank's including information about any electronic fund transfers on the monthly statement of account that it produces and mails in connection with the typical checking account.

One other concept that is crucial to an understanding of the workings of the EFTA is that of the *access device*. The Act itself does not define this term. Regulation E §205.2(a)(1) does contain a definition: "'Access device' means a card, code, or other means of access to a consumer's account, or any combination thereof, that may be used by the consumer to initiate electronic fund transfers." Not all electronic fund transfers make use of an access device. Direct deposit of a paycheck or preauthorized payment out of the account of recurring bills, for example, do not. The debit card and the ATM card are, of course, the prime examples of the access device. As you can see, the actual definition of *access device* does not require any special means of verification, such as the PIN we are most familiar with, to be issued along with the card itself. The Act does, however, condition the customer's potential liability for any unauthorized transfers out of the account on the card issuer's having provided along with the access device, "a means whereby the user of such card, code, or other means of access can be identified as the person authorized to use it, such as by signature, photograph, or fingerprint or by electronic or mechanical confirmation" (EFTA§909(a) [15 U.S.C. §1693g(a)]). Or see Reg. E §206.(a).*

In the following examples, we consider a series of issues. First of all, what constitutes an *unauthorized use* of the access device? Second, if there is an unauthorized use of the card, to what extent, if any, may the customer be liable for the amount transferred out of his or her account without his or her permission? Third, what mechanism is required by the EFTA for *dispute resolution* when the customer believes that an amount reported as electronically

---

* Notice that nothing in the Act or the Regulation requires that a debit or ATM card be usable only with a PIN. In recent years both MasterCard and Visa have introduced their own form of debit card, which normally requires verification by the merchant only through comparison of the signature of the user with the signature on the reverse of the card. Such PIN-less systems impose, of course, a higher risk of loss on the issuer, but these networks obviously believe that the additional risk is justified by the greater convenience offered to the user, making it just that much easier to spend, spend, spend.

transferred out of his or her account is in error? Finally, we consider the question of when, if ever, the customer can *stop payment* of or *reverse* an authorized transfer.

EXAMPLES

1.   Cesar is in need of some cash, but finds he does not have time during the day to make it to his bank. He gives his niece Nina his ATM card and tells her his PIN number. He asks her to go to the bank and withdraw $300 from his account. Nina does as she is asked, and returns the card to Cesar along with the $300 she has withdrawn from the bank's ATM machine.
   (a) Is this an unauthorized electronic fund transfer? For this and the next three examples, see EFTA §903(11) [15 U.S.C. §1693a(11)] or Reg. E §205.2(m).
   (b) What would be your answer if Nina had in fact withdrawn $500 from Cesar's account at the ATM, keeping $200 for herself?

2.   Ralph has received an ATM card from his bank. Fearing that he will forget the PIN number he has been given, he writes the number on a piece of paper, which he keeps "safely" in his wallet along with the card. Ralph has his pocket picked by one Thelma. Thelma immediately goes to a branch of the bank by which the card was issued and tries using the card at an ATM in conjunction with the number written on the scrap of paper that she finds in the wallet. It works! Thelma withdraws $1,000 in cash from the ATM.
   (a) Is Thelma's transaction an unauthorized transaction?
   (b) Suppose that Thelma then goes to a local electronics store, which has a sticker on the door indicating that it takes this brand of debit card. She uses the card and the PIN to purchase more than $1,400 worth of high-quality stereo equipment. Is this an unauthorized transaction?
   (c) What if Ralph had written his PIN number on the card itself? Would this change your view of either of the prior questions?

3.   Late one night, as she enters the ATM lobby at her bank, Sarah is confronted by a masked figure who claims to be carrying a gun in his pocket. He tells Sarah that she will not be hurt if she just hands over to him her ATM card and tells him her true PIN. Sarah does so. The masked figure uses the card to withdraw $1,000 from Sarah's account before vanishing into the darkness.
   (a) Is this an unauthorized use of the card?
   (b) What if instead the masked man had held the gun to Sarah's back as she, at his insistence, inserted her card into the ATM machine and punched in her PIN, then calling on the machine to release $1,000 in cash? The thief takes the money and runs.

4.   Joel takes his 16-year-old son, Junior, shopping with him. Before they hit the stores, Joel goes to his bank and uses the ATM machine to withdraw some cash. Junior looks over his shoulder and is able to make out the PIN as Joel enters it into the machine. Several days later, while Joel is in bed with a high fever, under doctor's orders to rest as much as possible, Junior takes his father's ATM card from Joel's wallet. He goes to the bank and withdraws $300 in cash, which he quickly spends on computer games, heavy metal CDs, and so on.

(a) Is Junior's use of the card an unauthorized use?

(b) Suppose instead that the reason Junior makes the withdrawal is otherwise: A plumbing emergency has come up at the house and the only plumber who is willing even to come and look at the problem demands that she be paid $300 in cash upon arrival. Rather than bother his sick father with the problem, Junior goes to the bank, gets the $300 in cash, and uses it to pay the plumber. Would Junior's use of the card be deemed unauthorized under this very different set of facts?

5.   Lenore has been issued and accepted a combination ATM and debit card for use in conjunction with her checking account at Shelbyville Bank and Trust. On Monday, May 2, while he is visiting in her home, her son-in-law Thad surreptitiously sneaks Lenore's card from her wallet. Later that day, Thad goes to a Shelbyville Trust ATM and, guessing correctly that Lenore has picked the last four digits of her telephone number as her PIN, withdraws $450 from the account. He once again uses the card to withdraw $200 from Lenore's account on the following Monday, May 9, and $400 on Wednesday, May 11. Lenore does not discover the loss of her card until May 12. She immediately calls the telephone number she has been given by the bank to report the loss of her card.

(a) When Lenore becomes aware of the total of $1,050 that Thad has transferred out of her account, she demands that the bank recredit the account with this amount. Is the bank obligated to do so? For this and Example 6, consult EFTA §909(a) [15 U.S.C. §1693g(a)] or Reg. E §205.6.

(b) What if Lenore had discovered the loss of her card soon after Thad's visit, on May 3, but failed to notify the bank until May 12?

6.   Homer has been issued and accepted a combination ATM and debit card for use in conjunction with a checking account he maintains at Shelbyville Bank and Trust. On his September 2004 statement of account, mailed to him by the bank on October 3 and received by Homer on October 6, there is recorded an $80 ATM withdrawal on September 23. Homer cannot remember making this withdrawal. In fact, he finds it curious as he very rarely uses the ATM card associated with this account. (Homer lives in Springfield and also has an account with Springfield State Bank, from which he normally makes his ATM withdrawals.) Homer gives no notice of this questionable $80 withdrawal to the Shelbyville Bank, nor does he check to

see that he still has the card. It turns out that the withdrawal was made by Homer's friend, one Barney, who stole the card from Homer's wallet while the two were together at a local bar, just after Homer bragged about his cleverness in picking "1234" as his PIN. Several months later, Barney begins to use the card again, first withdrawing $600 from the account at an ATM on December 22 and then running up bills totaling more than $500 at the local mall on December 23, using the card as a debit card. Then these transactions are reported to Homer on his December 2004 statement, which he receives in early January 2005, Homer is sure that they are in error and finally discovers that his card is missing. He quickly reports the loss of the card and the unauthorized transactions to the bank. Is Shelbyville Bank and Trust required to recredit Homer's account with any of the amounts transferred out of it by Barney?

7.   Flanders has a checking account with Springfield State Bank. He has been issued and has accepted a combination ATM and debit card in connection with this account. When he receives his September 2004 statement of account, he carefully examines each entry. He quickly focuses on a debit in the amount of $246.79 reported to be for use of the debit card on September 4 at a store identified as "Wiggum's Gun Shop." Flanders knows he never made any such purchase.

   (a) What should Flanders do to get this debit wiped off his account? See EFTA §908 [15 U.S.C. §1693f] or Reg. E §205.11.
   (b) Is the bank under an obligation to immediately recredit Flanders's account with the disputed amount pending the results of its investigation?
   (c) Suppose that the bank does determine, within a couple of days of its receipt of Flanders's notice of the claimed billing error, that this debit was indeed an error. What must it do then?
   (d) Suppose instead that the bank determines it will need more than 10 business days to investigate the situation. What must it do?
   (e) Two weeks later, after completing its investigation, the bank determines that no error occurred. As far as it can determine, Flanders's card was used to make a purchase at Wiggum's on the date and in the amount as indicated, and there is no reason to believe this was other than an authorized use of the card. What may and must the bank do now?

8.   Moe also has a checking account with Springfield State Bank, in connection with which he been issued and has accepted a combination ATM and debit card. Moe goes to Selma's Appliance City and purchases a wide-screen TV, paying the $1,699.99 price with his debit card. As soon as he gets home, he sets up the TV and turns it on. Nothing happens. As he fiddles with the set, trying to get it to work, it begins to heat up noticeably and the faint smell of burning metal begins to fill the air. Moe unplugs the TV and rushes

to his phone. He calls Springfield State Bank to find out how he can "stop payment" of the price to Selma on the purchase he made just hours ago. What will the bank tell him?

EXPLANATIONS

1a. Obviously not. This is an authorized transaction. An *unauthorized transaction* is defined (basically the same way in both the EFTA and Regulation E) as

> an electronic fund transfer from a consumer's account initiated by a person other than the consumer without actual authority to initiate the transfer and from which the consumer receives no benefit, but the term does not include any electronic transfer . . . initiated by a person other than the consumer who has been furnished with the card, code or other means of access to such consumer's account by such consumer, unless the consumer has notified the financial institution involved that transfers by such other person are no longer authorized. . . .

Here Nina was given the *actual authority* by her uncle to use the card as she did. Hence this does not come within the definition of an unauthorized transfer, even though it is made by a person other than the customer whose account is affected.

1b. This also would not be an unauthorized transfer, even though Nina went beyond the bounds of her actual authority in withdrawing the additional $200. Nina has still been "furnished" the access device, the card, directly by her uncle. The latter part of the definition of *unauthorized transfer* quoted in Example 1a covers the situation.

2a. Yes, this is an unauthorized transfer. Thelma has certainly not been invested with any actual authority by Ralph to use the card. Nor would we say that he has "furnished" her the card. She stole it from him. The fact that he may have made actual *use* of the card that much easier by writing the PIN down as he has does not turn this into an authorized transaction — a point we'll return to in Example 2c.

2b. Yes, this use of the card as a debit card is also an unauthorized transfer, and for just the reasons given in the explanation of Example 2a. This question is intended to remind you that for the purposes of the EFTA and Regulation E, use of a card as an ATM card or as a debit card, is treated identically. The customer or someone whom he or she has authorized can use the card to get cash or merchandise. It is all one and the same as far as the Act goes. Similarly, an unauthorized transfer can take place at an ATM machine or at the debit card terminal of a merchant.

2c. Ralph's actually writing his PIN directly on the card might change your opinion of exactly how bright he is, but it does not render either use of the card an authorized use. Ralph has still neither given Thelma the actual authority to use the card nor furnished her with the card itself. The Federal Reserve issued a series of interpretations concerning the liability of consumers for unauthorized use in the form of a supplement to §205 of Regulation E. Included in these interpretations is the following:

> *Question:* Consumer negligence. A consumer writes the PIN on the ATM card or on a piece of paper kept with the card — actions that may constitute negligence under state law. Do such actions affect the liability for unauthorized transfers that may be imposed on the consumer? *Answer:* No. The extent of the consumer's liability is determined by the promptness in reporting loss or theft of an access device or unauthorized transfers appearing on a periodic statement [as we will see in Examples 5 and 6]. Negligence on the consumer's part cannot be taken into account to impose greater liability than is permissible under the act and Regulation E. (§205.6(b)).

Even if the ill-advised way in which Ralph has chosen to keep track of his PIN does not render Thelma's use of the card an authorized transaction, that is of course no reason for any of us to follow his lead. The prudent cardholder will do whatever he or she reasonably can to keep his or her PIN as secret and as hard to guess as possible. For one thing, as we will deal with in later examples, the cardholder will bear up to at least a token $50 of any loss due to unauthorized use, and can bear liability beyond this amount if he or she doesn't deal with the loss of the card or any reported unauthorized use in the correct way. Beyond this, of course, having to deal with any unauthorized use (reporting the theft of the card, convincing the issuer of the card as to which uses were unauthorized, simply waiting for the whole unhappy matter to be cleared up and the money recredited to the account) is enough of a hassle that the advisability of closely guarding one's card and keeping one's PIN separate and secret cannot be stressed too strongly.

3a. Yes, of course this is an unauthorized use. Sarah has certainly not given the masked figure the actual authority to use her card, nor does it make any sense to say she has "furnished" him with the card. That word, as used in the definition of an unauthorized transfer, is taken to mean that the cardholder turned the card over to another voluntarily. Had the robber accosted Sarah on the street outside the ATM and demanded that she turn over her purse, we would not say that she had "furnished" him with her card simply because it was in the purse at the time of the robbery.

3b. I would say that this is an unauthorized transfer even though the cardholder herself did plug the card into the machine and enter her PIN. True, the definition of *unauthorized transfer* contemplates that the transfer be "initiated by a person other than" the cardholder, but I would argue that this transfer was really "initiated" by the masked man and not Sarah. I know of no case in which an issuer has even tried to argue that the transfer was authorized in a situation such as this.

4a. Yes, this is an unauthorized use. Junior did not have any actual authority from his father to use the card as he did, nor did Joel furnish him with it.

Joel may have been careless in letting someone else, even his own flesh and blood, discover his PIN as Junior has, but as we have already discovered such carelessness does not turn this into an authorized transaction.

4b. Under these facts, Junior's use of the card would not be deemed an unauthorized transfer. The definition of the term requires both that the transfer be initiated by someone without the actual authority to use the card and that "the consumer receive[] no benefit" from the use. Here Joel has gotten the benefit from the card's use, even if Junior was never given actual authority to use the card as he did.

5a. We deal in this and Example 6 with the question of what liability the cardholder has for unauthorized use of the card. (The cardholder is naturally fully liable for any *authorized* use.) The EFTA establishes a three-tiered system of liability in §909(a) [15 U.S.C. §1693(a)], even if it is not immediately apparent from the awkward way in which the subsection is written. Regulation E, in §205.6(b)(1) through (3), sets out the same matter and is a much easier read. The first level of liability is that of the cardholder for any unauthorized use when the loss of the card is reported to the issuer within two business days after the cardholder learns of the theft or loss of the card. In such a case the cardholder is liable for *the lesser of* the amount of the unauthorized transfers made that occurred before notice to the issuer or $50. In this part of the example, Lenore gave notice to the bank promptly after she became aware of the loss of her card. (Note that the two-business-day period begins to run not when the card is lost or stolen but when the cardholder "learns of the loss or theft.") Lenore is liable for $50 of the unauthorized transfers made by Thad, but no more. Having given timely notice, she is protected by the $50 cap on the cardholder's potential liability for unauthorized use. The bank will have to recredit her account with all but $50 of the transfers made out of her account by Thad. As a practical matter, many issuers will waive the $50 they are entitled to in situations such as this, as a matter of good customer relations.

5b. By failing to give notice to the bank within two business days after having learned of the disappearance of her card, Lenore has lost the protection of the $50 cap on her potential liability. She can be held liable by the bank for the lesser of (1) $500 or (2) up to $50 in unauthorized use in the first two days after the cardholder becomes aware of the loss plus "[t]he amount of unauthorized transfers that occur after the close of two business days and before notice to the [issuing] institution, provided the institution establishes that these transfers would not have occurred had the consumer notified the institution within that two-day period." Here the bank would argue that, had Lenore given notice to it by the close of business on May 5, it would have deactivated the card and Thad would not have been able to use it as he did on May 9 or May 11 (for a total of $600). So Lenore is potentially liable for the lesser of $500 or the sum of $50 (for the use on May 2) and $600 (for the uses after May 5). The lesser of $500 and $650 is of course $500. Lenore will be able to insist on her account being recredited for all but $500 of the various transfers Thad made with her card. This is an example of the second tier of cardholder liability established by the EFTA; the cap on the loss that the cardholder may be made to bear is raised to $500 if the cardholder is not prompt in reporting the loss or theft of the card. As to what constitutes notice for the purposes of this rule, and for the possibility that the period in which notice must be given may be extended "due to extenuating circumstances," you can check out paragraphs (4) and (5) of Regulation E §205.6(b).

6. The bank is obligated to recredit Homer's account with only $30. Homer is protected by the $50 cap with regard to the first unauthorized transfer made by Barney (the $80 taken on September 23). With respect to Barney's later uses of the card in December, Homer will be fully liable. This unlimited liability — based on Homer's failure to report the unauthorized transfer appearing on his bank statement within 60 days of the bank's transmittal of the statement on October 3 — is the third tier of responsibility, which the cardholder has to be aware of and particularly careful to avoid. Quoting from Regulation E §205.6(b)(3):

> A consumer must report an unauthorized electronic fund transfer that appears on a periodic statement within 60 days of the financial institution's transmittal of the statement to avoid liability for subsequent transfers. If the consumer fails to do so, the consumer's liability shall not exceed the amount of the unauthorized transfers that occur after the close of the 60 days and before notice to the institution, and that the institution establishes would not have occurred had the consumer notified the institution within the 60-day period. When an access device is involved in the unauthorized transfer, the consumer may be liable for other amounts set forth in paragraphs (b)(1) [the $50 token liability for any unauthorized use] or (b)(2) [the liability of up to $500 for the cardholder's failure to promptly report loss or theft of the card] of this section, as applicable.

Here the bank should be able to establish that had Homer given it notice within 60 days of the unauthorized transfer reported to him on his September statement, it would have deactivated the card in time to prevent Barney's use of it in late December. So Homer is liable under (b)(1) for $50 based on the unauthorized use of the card in September and under (b)(3) for the total of $1,100 in use of the card in late December.

7a. Flanders should, within 60 days of the date on which the September statement was mailed to him, give notice to the bank that he believes this particular entry to be in error. His initial notice may be oral or written, as long as it enables the bank to identify him and his account; gives the date, type, and amount of the supposed transaction; and indicates why he believes the entry is in error. The bank may, however, require Flanders to give a written confirmation of all this information within 10 days of his giving any oral notice.

7b. No. The bank is under no obligation to immediately recredit the account with the amount of the claimed error. Rather, it is under an obligation to promptly investigate the alleged error and is required to determine whether an error has indeed occurred. The bank must make this determination within 10 business days after it receives notice from Flanders.

7c. If the bank determines the claim of error to be valid within the 10-day period, it must correct the error, in this case by recrediting Flanders's account with the $246.79, within one day after it determines that an error has occurred. It must also report the result of its investigation to Flanders within three business days after completing its investigation.

7d. The bank is normally given only 10 business days to investigate without recrediting the account with the disputed amount. (This period is extended to 20 days if the transfer was into or out of an account within 30 days of the first deposit being made to the account. Reg. E §205.11(c)(3)(i).) If the bank is not ready to conclude its investigation within the 10 business days, it is required to provisionally recredit the account with the amount in dispute, withholding a maximum of $50 from the account if it has a "reasonable basis" for believing that an unauthorized transfer may have occurred. The bank must inform Flanders, within two business days of the provisional crediting, of the amount and date of the credit, and must give him full use of the provisionally credited funds during the continuation of the investigation. The bank will normally then have up to 45 days from the date of receipt of the notice it got from Flanders to complete its investigation. This 45 days is extended to 90 days in §205.11(c)(3)(ii) of the Regulation in some situations, including one such as this when the electronic fund transfer "resulted from a point-of-sale debit card transaction." Within this period, be it 45 or 90 days depending on the circumstances, the bank must conclude its investigation. Should it at any time within this period determine that the debit card charge posted at Wiggum's was indeed in error, it must correct the error within one day after making that determination and so inform Flanders within three days. Flanders will be informed that the provisional credit of funds made pending the extended investigation has been made final.

7e. The bank, having determined that no error has occurred, must give Flanders a written explanation of its findings and note his right to request any documents on which the bank relied in making its determination. Should Flanders so request, the bank must promptly provide him with copies of any such documents. The bank may also not debit his account the amount of the provisional credit that it added during the course of the extended investigation. The bank must give Flanders notice of the date and the amount of this debit and must also give him what amounts to overdraft privileges equal in amount to the debit for a period of five business days following the notice. See Reg. E §205.11(d).

What can Flanders do now if he is still sure that the bank made an error that is costing him money? He is going to have to take the bank to court. The EFTA and Regulation E set out a dispute resolution process that both the customer and the bank have to follow in an attempt to resolve any asserted billing error; neither mandates that the bank must always find in favor of the customer. As set forth in §205.11(e) of the Regulation:

> A financial institution that has fully complied with the error resolution requirements has no further responsibilities under this section should the consumer later reassert the same error.

If Flanders does take the bank to court, and *if* he is able to establish that the bank "knowingly and willingly concluded that [his] account was not in error when such conclusion could not reasonably have been drawn from the evidence available to [the bank] at the time of the investigation" — a tall order indeed — Flanders would be entitled to treble damages. EFTA §908(e)(2) [15 U.S.C. §1693f(e)(2)].

8.   The bank will have to tell him that there is no way for him to "stop" payment made by use of a debit card once the payment has been made. The transaction, including the payment for the goods, is conceived of as completed at the moment the debit card's use was authorized at the point of sale, Selma's Appliance City. It is the same as if he had paid in cash. He's going to have to take his problem with the TV up with Selma.

PART SEVEN

Electronic Means of Payment: The Commercial Context

21

Introduction to Commercial Electronic Funds Transfers and Article 4A

The Commercial Electronic Funds Transfer

Although the use of cash, check, or consumer credit or debit card still accounts for the large majority of payment transactions that take place every day in the United States, when measured by the total *dollar volume* of transactions, all these means pale in comparison to the so-called *wholesale wire transfer* used by businesses and financial institutions to move money around from one party to another. Something like 85 percent of all payment transactions, measured by the total amount of money involved, are carried out through the wire transfer system. Latest estimates have it that payments totaling more than $2 trillion are carried by this system every day in the United States alone. Taking into account international wire transfers would raise this number considerably. A typical commercial wire transfer can easily be for an amount in the millions of dollars, which is certainly something we couldn't say for payment by cash, check, credit card, or debit card.

Commercial wire transfers are characterized not only by their size but also by the high speed and efficiency with which they are carried out. A wire transfer of funds is usually completed within one day, and often in only an hour or two at the outside. Equally important from the point of view of the recipient, funds received by wire become final and available for use with practically the same speed. Compare this to the check, which (as we have seen) has to be deposited and then forwarded for collection, and may in some instances *never* turn into available funds if it is not accepted for payment by the payor bank. Furthermore, the cost of carrying out a wire transfer, especially considering the amounts involved, is amazingly low. Wire transfer of funds as a means of payment is said to be particularly appropriate to the modern, large-scale business operation because it is, as the saying goes, cheap, fast, and final.

Given the amounts involved and the obvious importance of this means of making payment to the economy as a whole, it is disconcerting to find that prior to the past decade there was no comprehensive body of law — common law, statute, or regulation — governing the electronic wire transfer. The technological developments that made large-scale electronic transfer of funds possible had leapt ahead of what the law was prepared to deal with. This situation was rectified in 1989 by the addition to the Uniform Commercial Code of an Article 4A, Funds Transfers, which has by now been adopted by all the states. You should at this time read the Official Comment to §4A-102. It gives a good summary of the reasons for and the underlying philosophy behind the creation of Article 4A. As that Comment says,

> In the drafting of Article 4A, a deliberate decision was made to write on a clean slate and to treat a funds transfer as a unique method of payment to be governed by unique rules that address the particular issues raised by this method of payment.

It is our task in this and the next two chapters to see what has been written on this clean slate and the "unique rules" that apply to this rather remarkable means of moving money from one party to another.*

---

* A continuing controversy surrounding Article 4A in the courts is whether its provisions are the sole law applicable to issues arising out of the use of wire transfers. You can see, in the concluding sentence to the Official Comment to §4A-102, that the drafters thought that their work should essentially cover the field and in effect preempt any claims based on law extrinsic to 4A. "[R]esort to principles of law and equity outside of Article 4A is not appropriate to create rights, duties and liabilities inconsistent with those stated in this Article." Most courts have followed the intention of the drafters and have ruled that any arguments based on principles not found in Article 4A itself were "displaced" (see the general principle set forth in §1-103) by the enactment of 4A and hence are no longer relevant to a controversy governed by that article. A few courts, however, have found room for claims based on common law principles that the courts determined were not "inconsistent with" but rather still valid and supplemental to the rules of 4A. *See, e.g., Sheerbonnet, Ltd. v. American Express Bank, Ltd.*, 951 F. Supp. 403, 28 U.C.C.2d 330 (S.D.N.Y. 1995). Such decisions are, it seems fair to say, in the minority and can perhaps best be thought of as limited to their very distinctive facts. Most Code commentators would argue that

The Scope of Article 4A

First look to §4A-102: "Except as otherwise provided in Section 4A-108, this Article applies to *funds transfers* defined in Section 4A-104." So it is to that section we next turn. In subsection (a) we find that

> "Funds transfer" means the series of transactions, beginning with the originator's payment order, made for the purpose of making payment to the beneficiary of the order.

We are obviously dealing here with a whole different set of terms than those we encountered in the checking context. (That's the "clean slate" the drafters of Article 4A referred to.) We start with the simple observation that the *originator* (§4A-104(c)) of any particular funds transfer is the party who is initiating the transfer for the purpose of making payment to another, the *beneficiary* (§4A-103(a)(2)) of the transfer. The originator starts the whole process rolling by issuing a payment order to its bank, the *originator's bank* (§4A-104(d)), instructing it to wire a certain amount of money to a specified account held by the beneficiary in the *beneficiary's bank* (§4A-103(a)(3)). How all this actually gets accomplished, the steps along the way, is something we will explore in detail in this chapter. For now, just look at the big picture and note the concluding sentence of §4A-104(a): "A funds transfer is completed by acceptance by the beneficiary's bank of a payment order for the benefit of the beneficiary of the originator's payment order." We will have to consider in more detail exactly what constitutes "acceptance" of a payment order, but the basic idea should not be that hard to grasp. An individual funds transfer commences with the originator instructing its bank to send some money into the beneficiary's account held at the beneficiary's bank. The funds transfer is successfully completed when the money has made its way into that account and is available for the beneficiary's use.

A single funds transfer is, as you could see in the quoted definition, a *series* of transactions. Each one of these will be what the article defines as a *payment order* in §4A-103(a)(1):

> "Payment order" means an instruction of a sender to a receiving bank, transmitted orally, electronically, or in writing to pay, or to cause another to pay, a fixed amount of money to a beneficiary, if . . .

Article 4A is exactly what its drafters intended it to be: the sole comprehensive source of law relating to conflicts arising out of wire transfers. Thus, any common law claims are necessarily "inconsistent" with Article 4A as statutory law. Most courts do indeed seem to view the question in the same way and find cases such as *Sheerbonnet* distinguishable if not downright questionable. *See, e.g., Grain Traders, Inc. v. Citibank, N.A.*, 160 F.3d 97, 36 U.C.C.2d 1141 (2d Cir. 1998); *National Council of Churches of Christ v. First Union National Bank*, 1998 U.S. App. LEXIS 26392 (4th Cir. 1998); *Moody Nat. Bank v. Texas City Development Ltd., Co.* 46 S.W.3d 373, 44 U.C.C.2d 261 (Tex. App. 2001).

three conditions (which you should read) are met. Any given funds transfer may consist of one, two, three, or more payment orders, each one following from the one before, starting with the payment order given by the originator to its bank and culminating with a final payment order sent to the beneficiary's bank.*

We will leave the detailed mechanics of Article 4A for the moment, but it is important to point out two types of transaction that do not fall within its scope. Under §4A-108, the article does not apply to "a funds transfer any part of which is governed by the Electronic Fund Transfer Act of 1978." We looked at the EFTA in Chapter 20. It covers electronic transfers made into or out of bank accounts held by consumers. Such transactions are governed by the EFTA and not Article 4A. Article 4A is intended to cover only the wholesale wire transfer initiated by a business or financial institution for large-scale commercial purposes. The originator or the beneficiary of an Article 4A funds transfer may, of course, be an individual, but if so he or she will be involved not in a consumer transaction but in a commercial one. Secondly, Article 4A does not cover even large commercial wire transfers that are "debit" rather than "credit" transfers. Suppose, for example, that a large corporation has authorized its insurance company to withdraw, by electronic means, its monthly insurance premiums from a specified account the corporation has with a particular bank. Once a month the insurance company sends a directive to the bank to pay it the appropriate amount. The bank complies because it has been preauthorized to do so by its customer, the insured corporation. Such a transaction does not fall within the §4A-104(a) definition of *funds transfer*, which delineates the scope of Article 4A, because it is not set in motion by an initial payment order made by a *debtor* for the purpose of making payment owed by it to its *creditor*. A transfer such as we have here, initiated by an instruction given by a creditor, is referred to as a "debit transfer" and is not covered by Article 4A. See the first paragraph of Comment 4 to that section.

The Major Funds Transfer Systems

As you can see in the definition of *payment order*, such an order may be transmitted by its sender "directly to the receiving bank or to an agent, a

---

* It is interesting to note that Article 4A speaks only in terms of a "funds transfer" and not of an electronic or wire transfer. That is deliberate on the drafters' part. As you can see, nothing in the definition of payment order requires that the order be made electronically, whatever we take that word to mean. It is entirely possible, in a given funds transfer, for all the payment orders to be transmitted orally or in writing. Practically, of course, it is the fact that most funds transfers are carried out at least partially through electronic means that makes them suit their intended purpose — and makes them as interesting as they are.

funds-transfer system, or communication system for the transmittal to the receiving bank." A definition of *funds-transfer system* is found in §4A-105(a)(5). Although banks communicate with other banks in a variety of ways, two major funds-transfer systems now operate in the United States and take up the lion's share of the wire transfer business. The first of these systems is called *CHIPS* (for Clearing House Interbank Payment Systems). It is a privately owned and operated system maintained by the New York Clearing House Association, conducted through a single "node" or computer located in New York City. CHIPS is set up to accept messages from and can send messages to about 60 affiliated entities, primarily major banks. At last count (at least that I could find) CHIPS was said to handle more than 235,000 transactions a day, the average transaction being in the neighborhood of $7 million. CHIPS is also the principal facility through which international transfers heading in or out of the United States make their way.*

Fedwire is a telecommunications network owned and operated by the 12 Federal Reserve Banks around the country. Each bank is a "node" in the system. It allows each of the Federal Reserve Banks to communicate with and transfer funds to all the others. In addition, an individual private bank can arrange to make use of Fedwire by becoming affiliated with the Federal Reserve Bank covering the territory in which it is located and by establishing its own account with that Federal Reserve Bank, in which it must keep a given level of money on deposit. Overall, something like 10,000 financial institutions are served by the Fedwire system, which carries more than $1.5 trillion a day of funds-transfer orders, the average being something like $3 million or more.

It will be important to remember for the purposes of all that follows that Fedwire as a telecommunications systems is never a party to an Article 4A funds transfer. It is merely a means of communications that one bank may use to send a payment order to another. Individual Federal Reserve Banks, in contrast, can be and regularly are banks acting as parties as the orders and the money move from the originator's bank to the beneficiary's bank.

---

* CHIPS transfers are always denominated in U.S. dollars, no matter where they are heading or from whence they have come. Another communications system, SWIFT (for Society for Worldwide Interbank Financial Telecommunications), is an automated system set up to send international funds-transfer messages not denominated in dollars. SWIFT, unlike CHIPS and Fedwire (which we will soon encounter), serves as a message transmittal service only. It does not itself provide a means of settlement between the sender and the recipient of the message, as CHIPS and Fedwire are able to do.

Means of Settlement

So far all that we have been speaking about is how messages — orders of one sort or another to transfer money — are carried out in series to accomplish a funds transfer. Words are cheap. How does the actual money flow from the originator to the beneficiary? Any individual bank in the chain of messages is not likely to follow an order to send money to another bank or, in the case of the beneficiary's bank, to make money available to its customer — especially when you think of the sums involved — unless that bank has itself already received that amount of money from the one doing the ordering (or is virtually certain that it will do so in a short time). This is where the notion of settlement comes in. A bank receiving a payment order is only likely, simply as a matter of common sense, to carry out that order (or, as we will use the Article 4A term, "accept" the order) if has already received funds equivalent to the amount it is being ordered to pay out.

There are various ways in which the sender of a payment order can settle with the receiving bank to ensure that the sender's order will be accepted. At the very start, we know, the originator sends a payment order to its bank. The originator and the originator's bank will have signed an agreement (typically termed a Funds Transfer Agreement) under which the bank will agree to carry out such instructions provided the originator has enough in its account to cover the order. Assume first that the beneficiary happens to have an account with the originator's bank, and that it is this account into which the bank is being ordered to transfer the money. The originator's bank will simply debit the originator's account for the amount indicated and credit the beneficiary's account for that same amount (taking for itself perhaps only a very small fee). That's easy enough. Suppose next that the beneficiary's account is held with another bank, but that this is a bank with which the originator's bank normally carries on a large volume of transactions. The originator's bank may then itself actually maintain an account with the beneficiary's bank. The originator's bank will then debit the amount of the order from the originator's account at the same time as it sends a payment order directly to the beneficiary's bank. This order will authorize the beneficiary's bank to debit the originator's bank's account held at the beneficiary's bank for the amount of the transfer. The beneficiary's bank will do so, at the same time crediting this amount to the beneficiary's account. Once again, the money has moved out of the originator's account and into the beneficiary's account without either bank having to worry that it will not get paid. The money is already there and at hand.

Things get decidedly more complicated if the account into which the originator wants money to be transferred is not in the same bank or is not in a bank with which the originator's bank itself has an account. This is where CHIPS and Fedwire come into play, not merely as ways of sending messages, but as means of settling accounts by the actual transfer of funds. A payment order sent by one CHIPS-participating bank to another is not necessarily settled by the simultaneous transfer of funds equivalent to the individual order from the sending bank to the receiving one. Up until just a few years ago, in fact, settlement of *all* payment orders executed through CHIPS on any given day was done by an end-of-the-day settlement procedure referred to as "multilateral netting," which took into account all payment orders processed during the course of that day by all of the participating banks. At day's end, all activity for each participating bank — both the payment orders it has sent and those it has received — was summed up to arrive at a net figure. If a particular bank had sent in total, say, payment orders totaling $70 million and received payment orders totaling $65 million, it would have to transfer $5 million into the CHIPS pool. If another bank had received more in payment orders (say $102 million) than it had initiated (say $98 million), then CHIPS would make sure that the net of $4 million was credited to that bank's account. By the end of the day, and barring some catastrophic failure of one of the participating banks, the total of all of these net debits and credits would balance out. Settlement for each of the thousands of payment orders carried over the CHIPS system (currently around 235,000 a day) during the course of the day would have been completed.*

Starting in 2001, CHIPS introduced a new method for faster settlement of most of the orders its executes, what it refers to as "CHIPS Finality." As stated in its promotional literature

> Our patented algorithm for multi-lateral netting continually offsets and settles payments throughout the day. Payments are matched, netted, and settled usually in a matter of seconds — 85% are cleared before 12:30 p.m. This allows payments to flow faster and maximizes liquidity.

As you might guess, the smaller payments are settled the most quickly. The larger payments may still take some time to settle, but in no event later than the end of the day. One important reason for the implementation by CHIPS of this new and more complex system was to make its services more competitive with those offered by Fedwire, where settlement is instantaneous in all cases.

Settlement of payment orders sent via Fedwire is always simultaneous with receipt of the order. Any bank that has arranged for direct access to the

---

*The actual mechanism for transfer of funds into and out of what I have referred to as the CHIPS pool is in fact Fedwire. In the end-of-day settlement procedure, for example, late in the afternoon CHIPS informs banks that have a net debit for the day of the amount they owe, and the banks are expected to send this amount to CHIPS through a Fedwire transfer of funds. Early in the evening, CHIPS then sends via Fedwire the amount owed to all those banks with a net credit for the day.

Fedwire system is required to have an account with the Federal Reserve Bank through which it will be sending payment orders. When the Federal Reserve Bank receives a payment order from the participating bank, it then sends a payment order of its own to the next bank in the chain, and immediately transfers the amount of the order out of the sending bank's account. Simultaneously with its sending of a payment order to the next bank in the chain (either a bank in its own territory which will necessarily have an account at the same Federal Reserve or another Federal Reserve Bank in another part of the country), the bank will credit the same amount to the account of the bank to which it is sending the payment order. As the saying goes, with Fedwire, "the message is the money."

The Article 4A Funds Transfer

It is time now to look at the basic mechanism by which a funds transfer is carried out. By the very definition of a funds transfer, the process starts out with a payment order made by the originator to its bank, referred to naturally enough as the *originator's bank*. This payment order may be transmitted "orally, electronically or in writing" (§4A-103(a)(1)), as may indeed any payment order. Large-scale users of the system are by now usually linked up to their banks via computerized systems, but others still initiate payment orders by personally appearing at the bank or through a phone message.* The payment order must identify the intended beneficiary and specify into what account at what bank the money is eventually to be transferred.

The originator's bank will then check to make sure the originator has enough in its account or in borrowing privileges to cover the amount of the order. The originator's bank makes the decision on whether to accept the order. *Acceptance* of a payment order is a key concept in Article 4A. Look at §4A-209. The two crucial subsections are (a) and (b). Subsection (a) covers the case when the receiving bank is other than the beneficiary's bank. Subsection (b) deals with the question of when acceptance has occurred when the bank receiving a payment order is the beneficiary's bank. If the originator's bank does not happen also to be the beneficiary's bank, then it will accept the order issued to it by the originator by "executing the order." As to what it takes for a bank to *execute* a payment order it has received, see §4A-301(a): "A payment order is 'executed' by the receiving bank when it issues a payment order intended to carry out the payment order received by the bank."

---

* The communication between the originator and its bank must be carried out using previously designated security procedures; we will deal with what those procedures may be, and how they affect potential liability for fraudulent transactions, in Chapter 22.

If the originator's bank is in a position to send a payment order directly to the beneficiary's bank, either directly or through a systems such as CHIPS or Fedwire, it will accept by doing so. If not, it will issue a payment order to an *intermediary bank* (§4A-104(b)), which will itself then accept (if it determines it is right to do so) by executing the order. It will execute the order either by sending its own payment order to the beneficiary's bank, if it is in a position to do so, or to another intermediary bank that it has reason to believe is in a better position to get the message (and the money) to the beneficiary's bank.

A given funds transfer may occur using no intermediary banks or several. Eventually, one receiving bank will be in a position to communicate and settle directly with the beneficiary's bank. It will send a final payment order to the beneficiary's bank directing that the given amount be credited to the beneficiary's account with that bank. The beneficiary's bank will then either accept or reject this order (acceptance to be judged by §4A-209(b)), its main concern being whether it has any reason to doubt that it will receive settlement for this amount prior to having to make the funds available to the beneficiary. If all goes according to plan, as is true with the overwhelming majority of funds transfers, the beneficiary's account with its bank will be credited with the amount of the transfer. Even if several intermediary banks are involved, this entire process will typically have taken no more than an hour or two.

The important thing to remember is that a single funds transfer will consist of a *series* of payment orders, each of which has to be separately identified. If all goes well, as it normally does, dissection of the exact route the funds transfer took soon becomes no more interesting than the exact route a valid check takes in being forwarded from the depositary bank to the payor bank, which pays as a matter of course when sufficient funds are available in the customer's account. Should issues arise, however, each and every step along the way could become relevant and enter into the dispute.

Let us look at the diagram on the following page of a funds transfer involving two intermediary banks and hence four payment orders. Here the Originator owes the Beneficiary some amount of money. It has been agreed between the two that the Originator will pay by wiring the money into the Beneficiary's account with the Beneficiary's bank. The Originator initiates the payment by making Payment Order #1, its order to the Originator's Bank, which has presumably agreed to handle this type of transaction for the Originator. The Originator's Bank is the receiving bank of Payment Order #1. It accepts this order by execution, sending Payment Order #2 to Intermediary Bank One. That bank is the receiving bank of Payment Order #2, which it accepts by sending Payment Order #3 to Intermediary Bank Two. That bank in turns accepts by sending Payment Order #4 to the Beneficiary's Bank. Once the Beneficiary's Bank accepts Payment Order #4, the amount of the payment is credited to the Beneficiary's account with that bank.

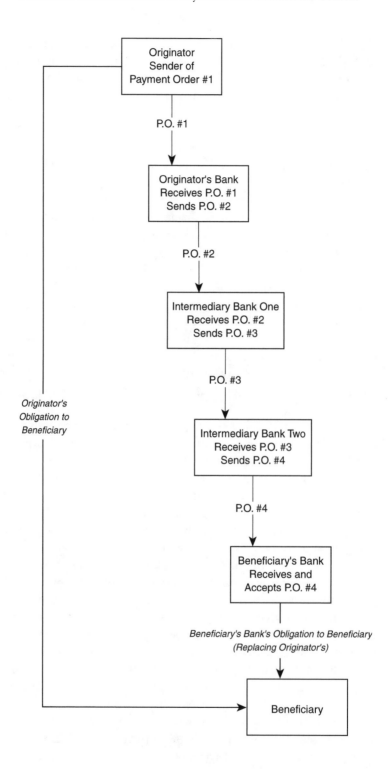

And that's the story. As the last sentence of §4A-104(a) states: "A funds transfer is completed by acceptance by the beneficiary's bank of a payment order for the benefit of the beneficiary of the originator's payment order." And the result? Look first to §4A-404(a). Setting aside certain rare exceptions that need not concern us here, "if a beneficiary's bank accepts a payment order, the bank is obligated to pay the amount of the order to the beneficiary of the order." The beneficiary may not immediately withdraw all the money, but these funds are as secure as any other money that the beneficiary has parked in this account at that particular bank (and remember, the beneficiary was the one to pick where it wanted to do its banking and have this payment sent). Furthermore, under §4A-406(a),

> [T]he originator of a funds transfer payment pays the beneficiary of the originator's payment order (i) at the time a payment order for the benefit of the beneficiary is accepted by the beneficiary's bank in the funds transfer, and (ii) in an amount equal to the amount of the order accepted by the beneficiary's bank, but not more than the amount of the originator's order.

The originator's initial obligation to pay the beneficiary under some underlying contract, perhaps for goods or services rendered or something of the sort, is extinguished. Payment has been made. In place of the right of the beneficiary under this underlying contract, the beneficiary now has its right against the beneficiary's bank for the amount of the payment order accepted by that bank and credited to its account.

EXAMPLES

1.   Under an agreement between the Big Apple Manufacturing Company, located in the suburbs of New York, and Gotham Bank, a major New York bank in which Big Apple has an account, the treasurer of Big Apple is authorized to initiate funds transfers out of the company's Gotham account. In late April, Big Apple enters into a purchase and sale agreement with San Francisco Sheet Metal, one of its principal suppliers, under which the sheet metal firm will ship a large quantity of product to Big Apple, delivery to be completed by Tuesday, May 31. Big Apple agrees to pay by a transfer of $765,000 into a specified account the supplier has at Golden Gate Bank of San Francisco. On May 10, Big Apple's treasurer sends a written instruction to Gotham Bank calling for it to transfer $765,000 to the designated Golden Gate account "upon the delivery to Big Apple of merchandise to be provided by San Francisco Sheet Metal under contract with our firm."

(a) Is this instruction a valid payment order under Article 4A? Review §4A-103(a)(1).

(b) What if instead the instruction had said that the transfer of funds was to be made on May 31, with no other condition attached?

(c) What if the instruction in part (b) had been made orally, over the telephone, and not in writing?

2.   Big Apple, of the preceding example, also arranges to buy a large quantity of component parts to be specially manufactured to its specifications by Brooklyn Cogs and Widgets (BC&W). The purchase and sale agreement calls for Big Apple to pay $1 million into a specified account that BC&W has with Dodger National Bank of Brooklyn. On October 1, Big Apple's treasurer sends an instruction via computer to Gotham Bank telling it to immediately transfer $1 million into BC&W's account with Dodger National Bank.

(a) Is Gotham legally obligated to comply with this instruction, simply by virtue of having received it from Big Apple? Why might it not want to do so? Should it decide not to comply with this order, what must it do? See Comment 3 to §4A-209 and §4A-210.

(b) Suppose the person at Gotham in charge of receiving and processing computer instructions such as that sent by Big Apple replies to the message with one of his or her own. The message sent to Big Apple reads, in effect, "Will do as you have instructed." Has Gotham "accepted" the payment order as that term is used in Article 4A? Look to §§4A-209(a) and 4A-301(a).

(c) Suppose that Big Apple's computer instruction is received by Gotham at 10:30 a.m. At 10:45 a.m., Gotham, having determined that Dodger National Bank participates in the CHIPS system, sends a computerized message via CHIPS to the Dodger National Bank instructing it to credit BC&W's specified account with that bank with $1 million. Has Gotham now accepted the payment order sent to it by Big Apple? If so, as of what time?

(d) Dodger National Bank receives the computer message sent to it by Gotham at 10:46 a.m. By its receipt of this message, has Dodger accepted the payment order? See §4A-209(b).

(e) Is Dodger National Bank obligated to immediately credit BC&W's account with the $1 million? Is it obligated to get into contact immediately with BC&W and inform BC&W that it has received payment of $1 million from Big Apple? See Comment 5 to §4A-209.

(f) Assume that Dodger neither credits the money to BC&W's account nor gets in touch with that firm on October 1. As of when will it be deemed to have accepted the payment order sent to it by Gotham? What obligations does Dodger National Bank then have to its customer, Brooklyn Cogs and Widgets? See §§4A-404(a) and 4A-405(a) and (b).

(g) Upon acceptance by Dodger National Bank, what is the effect on Big Apple's obligation to pay $1 million to BC&W under the terms of their purchase and sale agreement? See §4A-406(a) and (b).

3.   To complete a major expansion of its plant in 2004, Big Apple Manufacturing Company negotiated a loan of $100 million (secured of

course by a mortgage on its property) from a major mortgage lender, The Moneymen Group, with headquarters in New England. Big Apple is to make payments of $2 million into a specified account held by Moneymen with Patriot National Bank of Boston by the end of each month over a period of years. On March 25, 2005, the treasurer of Big Apple sends a computer message to Gotham Bank instructing it to transfer $2 million into the specified account at Patriot National Bank on March 30, which is the last business day of the month. At 10:30 a.m. local time on March 30, Gotham sends a Fedwire to the Federal Reserve Bank of New York, instructing it to pay or cause to be paid $2 million into this account at Patriot National Bank of Boston. This message is received by the New York Fed at 10:31 a.m. At 10:45, the New York Fed sends a message by Fedwire to the Federal Reserve Bank of Boston, carrying along the instruction, which message is received by the Boston Fed at 10:46. At 11:00 a.m. the Boston Fed sends a Fedwire to Patriot National Bank instructing it to credit $2 million to the designated account. At noon, the account representative at Moneymen who is responsible for the loan to Big Apple calls Patriot National Bank. She inquires whether a payment of $2 million has been received from Big Apple by that bank and credited to her company's account. She is told that, yes, this has occurred. Carefully outline the course of this particular funds transfer. Who is the originator and who is the beneficiary? Describe each payment order: Who was the sender, which was the receiving bank, and how and when was the order accepted by the receiving bank? What is the end result of the entire process?

4.   Big Apple carries a worker's compensation insurance policy with Big Orange Insurance Company of California. During the first week of each month, Big Apple receives a statement from Big Orange giving it the amount of premium it owes for the month. Payment is owed by the 20th of the month, or on the first business day following the 20th if the 20th falls on a weekend or a holiday. On September 8, having received and reviewed the premium statement for that month, the treasurer of Big Apple sends an instruction to Gotham Bank to transfer the billed amount into an account held by Big Orange Insurance with the Sunshine Bank of Los Angeles, "payment to be credited to that account Tuesday, September 20."

   (a) What is the "payment date" of Big Apple's payment order to Gotham Bank? See §4A-401.

   (b) What is the "execution date" of that payment order? See §4A-301(b).

   (c) Suppose that on September 8, immediately upon receiving the payment order from Big Apple, an authorized representative of Gotham Bank had sent a payment order intended to carry out Big Apple's instructions to the New York Federal Reserve. Would it be correct to say that Gotham had executed Big Apple's order on September 8? What are the consequences for Gotham of its representative's having jumped the gun in this way? See §4A-209(d) and §4A-402(c).

5. Jules Moneybucks owns and operates a fashionable jewelry store, dealing in both new and antique jewelry, in the heart of New York City. He is contacted by one Ellie Diamond, a broker in jewelry and gems known to Jules, who tells him that she has just made arrangements to purchase a particularly fine piece, a diamond tiara once owned by the Queen of Romania, which she would be willing to sell to Jules for $250,000. Jules is aware of the piece (news of its availability has been circulating in the jewelry business over the past few weeks) and agrees to buy it for that price. It is agreed that Ellie will have the piece delivered by special courier to Jules's shop and that he will then wire the price into a specified account at Ellie's bank, Golden State Bank of Los Angeles. The tiara is delivered to Jules's place of business by (heavily armed) couriers around noon the next day. Jules opens the package and gives the piece a quick look over to determine that it is indeed what he has been promised. He then makes a call to his bank, Gotham National Bank, instructing it to arrange for the immediate transfer of $250,000 into Ellie's account at Golden State Bank. This call is made by Jules at 12:15 p.m. Jules then goes back to bask in the glory of his new acquisition and to arrange for its display. It is only then, upon giving the piece more attention, that he becomes concerned that one of the largest diamonds in it appears to be a replacement and not part of the original piece as it has always been described in the literature. At 12:45 p.m., he places a second urgent call to Gotham Bank and orders it not to go through with the wire transfer that he ordered only half an hour earlier. As it turns out, Gotham Bank had itself already sent a payment order to the Federal Reserve Bank of New York, following up on its instruction from Jules at 12:30 p.m.

(a) Does Jules's countermand of his original order come too late to stop payment to Ellie? See §4A-211.

(b) Can Jules, upon being told that this order has already been accepted by Gotham's sending of a payment order to the New York Fed, try to call that bank and cancel the order sent in furtherance of his originating instruction?

(c) Suppose that when Jules makes his second call at 12:45 p.m., Gotham Bank has yet to issue a payment order of its own carrying out the instruction it received from Jules at 12:15 p.m. What is the result?

6. Arnold Moneybucks owns and operates a venture capital firm, the Moneybucks Money Fund, which specializes in buying interests in start-up Internet companies. For several months, Andrea Hotshot has been trying to convince Arnold to put some money into her new firm, Horseshoes.com. Eventually Arnold decides to make an investment in Andrea's firm if the right terms can be negotiated. Lawyers for Arnold and Andrea enter into

negotiations and eventually arrive at an agreement they think will be suitable to the two parties. A closing is arranged to take place in Chicago, at the principal offices of the Moneybucks firm. Arnold and Andrea are in attendance, along with their various advisors and lawyers. As the closing progresses, the parties make minor changes to the terms of the agreement under which Arnold's firm will buy a stated number of shares for a given price. The exact amount that Arnold is to pay for the shares has to be adjusted to take into account these last-minute changes, as well as the most current information regarding Andrea's firm. After all the various calculations are performed and the paperwork is signed, the last thing necessary to close the deal is for Arnold to pay the sum of $5,230,000 to Horseshoes.com. Arnold goes into the office of the treasurer of his firm and instructs her to have this amount immediately wired into an account that Horseshoes.com has with Palo Alto Bank for Entrepreneurs, located in California. Arnold returns to the conference room where the closing is being held. The participants sit around chatting (and perhaps trying to accomplish other business) for about an hour. At that time a call comes in for Andrea. It is from an officer of the Palo Alto bank, who tells Andrea that a wire transfer for $5,230,000 has just come into the bank via Fedwire and has been credited to her company's account.

(a) Is the attorney in charge of the closing now free to release to Arnold the share certificates in Horseshoes.com which represent his firm's interest in that company? What happens next?

(b) Suppose that the officer of the Palo Alto bank informs Andrea that it has received and credited to her company's account only $5,229,980. It seems that the various banks that have handled the wire transfer have each taken a small fee for their services, and the end result is that $20 less has been credited to Horseshoes.com's account than had been deducted from the Moneybucks' account at the initiation of the transfer. Is Andrea free to consider Arnold in breach of their agreement and call the deal off? See §4A-406(c) and Comment 5 to that section.

EXPLANATIONS

1a. No. This written instruction to Gotham Bank does not constitute an Article 4A payment order, because it "state[s] a condition to payment to the beneficiary [the San Francisco firm] other than time of payment." As the drafters of 4A point out in Comment 3 to §4A-104,

> The function of banks in a funds transfer under Article 4A is comparable to the role of banks in the collection of checks in that it is essentially mechanical in nature. The low price and high speed that characterize funds transfers reflect this fact.

1b. This would be a payment order under Article 4A. The only "condition" attached to the instruction given by Big Apple was the time of payment.

1c. Under §4A-103(a)(1), a payment order may be "transmitted [to a receiving bank] orally, electronically, or in writing." So the fact that the instruction was made orally would not prevent it from being a valid payment order initiating a funds transfer governed by Article 4A.

2a. Gotham is not obligated to comply with Big Apple's instruction under any rule of Article 4A. As the cited comment says,

> A receiving bank has no duty to accept a payment order unless the bank makes an agreement, either before or after issuance of the payment order, to accept it, or acceptance is required by a funds transfer system rule. If the bank makes such an agreement it incurs a contractual obligation based on the agreement and may be held liable for breach of contract if a failure to execute violates the agreement.

Assuming as we are that Big Apple does have an account with Gotham, and furthermore that the bank has entered into an agreement to comply with payment orders issued to it by the appropriate party at Big Apple, the principal reason why the bank might not want to comply with the order given it would be that Big Apple might not at the moment have $1 million in its account to cover the order. Just as a bank will usually not honor a check written on an account of one of its customers for which there are insufficient funds in the account, it would usually not want to execute an Article 4A payment order that would put it at risk of itself incurring liability when its customer could not "cover" the transfer of funds. The amounts involved in funds transfers are typically much greater than with your average, or even above average, check, so the bank has to be that much more careful.

Unless Gotham has by agreement agreed to execute orders, at least up to a certain predetermined amount, for which there are not currently sufficient funds in Big Apple's account, it is not obligated to accept the order and most likely will not do so. The means Gotham may use to *reject* the payment order it has received are set out in §4A-210(a). Comment 1 to this section, which you should be sure to read in full, states that notice of rejection, when the receiving bank is other than the beneficiary's bank, is not necessary to prevent acceptance of the payment order. "Acceptance can occur only if the receiving bank executes the order." Notice of rejection, however, "will routinely be given by such a bank in cases in which the bank cannot or is not willing to execute the order for some reason." The bank, after all, wants to keep up its good relationship with its customer and not just ignore communications from it.

2b. No. This message back to the sender of the payment order, here the party intending to originate the funds transfer, does not constitute acceptance of the payment order. That can happen, under §4A-209(a), only upon the receiving bank's *execution* of the order. Under §4A-301(a), "[a] payment order is 'executed' by the receiving bank when it issues a payment order intended to carry out the payment order received by the bank."

2c. Yes. Gotham now has accepted the payment order by its execution of that order. It accepted at 10:45 a.m., the time when it initiated its own payment order.

As the funds transfer we are investigating has now gotten going in earnest, it is time for a diagram.

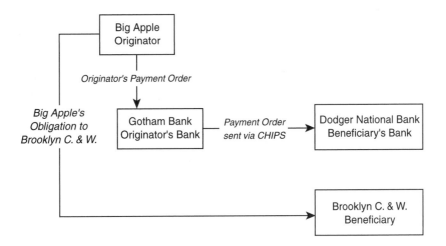

The originator's payment order was followed up by a second payment order, sent through the CHIPS system, from Gotham to Dodger National Bank, which in this case happens to be the beneficiary's bank.

2d. No. Subsection (b) of §4A-209 governs when a payment order sent to the beneficiary's bank is accepted. Acceptance does not occur simply because that bank has received the payment order directed to it. Acceptance occurs upon the earliest of three possible events. Here the Dodger bank has not yet paid Brooklyn Cogs and Widgets (which would require either that it inform that firm that the money is available in its account, or that it actually apply the $1 million to meet some obligation of BC&W, such as covering BC&W's own transfers out of its account). So an event meeting subsection (b)(1) criteria has not yet occurred. Because this transfer used the CHIPS system, the Dodger bank may not have received settlement at the same time. So (b)(2) can be used to set a moment of acceptance only if we know exactly when Dodger does receive settlement through CHIPS, which might, in fact, be after the cutoff hour the Dodger bank has established as the end of its "funds-transfer business day." See §4A-106. The workings of (b)(3) are explored in Example 2f.

2e. No. Dodger is not obligated to credit BC&W's account with the $1 million immediately. It will not have to do so until it has accepted the payment order that it received from Gotham, and as we've seen it has not necessarily done so yet. Nor is Dodger required immediately to notify BC&W that the order has been received. In fact, it will want to be careful not to do so until it is sure the money has arrived. Should it notify BC&W that the payment order has been received on October 1, it will then have accepted the order and be itself obligated to BC&W for the $1 million as of that moment, under §4A-209(b)(ii), "unless the notice indicates that the bank is rejecting the order [unlikely] or that funds with respect to the order may not be withdrawn or used until receipt of payment from the sender of the order." The concluding part of Comment 5 to this section — beginning with "If the beneficiary's bank wants to defer incurring liability to this beneficiary until the beneficiary's bank receives payment, it can do so." — deals with this crucial matter of timing.

2f.   Under §4A-209(b)(3), Dodger will have accepted the payment order sent to it on October 1 as of the opening of its next funds-transfer business day following that date, "if, at that time, the amount of the sender's order is fully covered by a withdrawable credit balance in an authorized account of the sender or the bank has otherwise received payment from the sender." If CHIPS effected settlement by the end of October 1, (even to imagine otherwise is to assume the occurrence of the "doomsday scenario" of the CHIPS system failing on a given day, an event we are assured in Comment 4 to §4A-405 "should never occur"), then the order to Dodger is automatically accepted as of the opening of business on October 2 if that is a funds-transfer business day as defined in §4A-105(a)(5).

Note in general that if a beneficiary's bank has not already accepted via subsections (b)(1) or (b)(2) of §4A-209, and if for some reason it has not been paid the amount of the transfer as of the beginning of the next funds-transfer business day, then it can still be held to have accepted the order by the passage of time, unless the order is rejected (under §4A-210) "before that time [the opening of its next funds-transfer business day] or is rejected (i) within one hour of that time, or (ii) one hour after the opening of the next business day of the sender following the payment date if that time is later." Most payment orders to a beneficiary's bank are probably accepted in this way, by that bank's doing nothing to reject the order within the time-frame allowed, just as most checks are accepted by a payor bank by that bank's failure to dishonor and return the item within the time limits laid out in Article 4. You should read over Comments 7 and 8 to §4A-209.

Under §4A-404(a), with only some minor exceptions with which we need not concern ourselves, "if a beneficiary's bank accepts a payment order, the bank is obligated to pay the amount of the order to the beneficiary of the order." As that subsection goes on to detail, the beneficiary's bank can and will be held liable for damages, including in some instances consequential damages, for its failure to pay what *it* now owes the beneficiary. You should recognize your old friend, the rule of *Hadley v. Baxendale*, as it has made its way into that subsection. What it means for the beneficiary's bank to "pay" the beneficiary is set forth in §4A-405(a). Under §4A-404(b), the beneficiary's bank is also responsible for giving notice to the beneficiary "before midnight of the next funds-transfer day following the payment date" when the order has been accepted. If the beneficiary's bank fails to give this notice, it will be liable to the beneficiary for interest on the amount of the payment for any delay in the beneficiary's learning of the payment.

2g.   Under §4A-406(a),

> the originator of a funds transfer [Big Apple] pays the beneficiary of the originator's payment order [BC&W] (i) at the time a payment order for the benefit of the beneficiary is accepted by the beneficiary's bank [Dodger], and (ii) in an amount equal to the amount of the order accepted by the beneficiary's bank, but not more than the amount of the originator's order.

Under subsection (b), this discharges the obligation Big Apple had to BC&W under the purchase and sale agreement the two entered into. See Comments 1 and 2 to this section. With Dodger National Bank's having accepted the payment order received by it, thus concluding the funds transfer, our earlier diagram is transformed to the following:

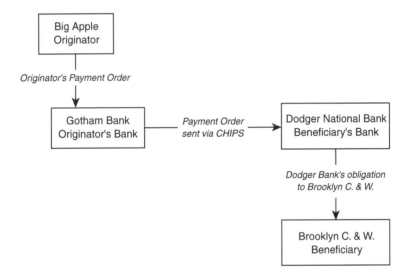

3.   Once again, a diagram will be worth, if not exactly a thousand words, a goodly number of them. See the following page.

The first payment order was sent on March 25 by Big Apple, the originator, to Gotham, the originator's bank. This payment order was accepted by Gotham at 10:30 a.m. on March 30, by Gotham's execution of the order. It did so by sending a second payment order at that time via Fedwire to the Federal Reserve Bank of New York, which is the receiving bank of this order. This order is accepted by the New York Fed at 10:45 when it sends, via Fedwire, a third payment order to the Federal Reserve Bank of Boston. This order is in turn accepted by the Federal Reserve of Boston when it sends a fourth payment order, again via Fedwire, to Patriot National Bank at 11:00 a.m. This last payment order is accepted by the bank when it receives payment of the amount indicated in the Fedwire message, which will

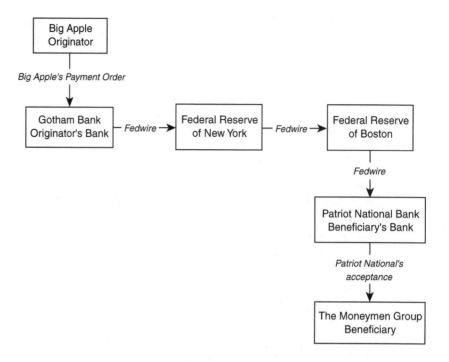

presumably come to it (that is, be credited to its account with the Boston Fed) virtually simultaneously with the message send to it by that bank at 11:00 a.m. Thus, when the representative of Moneymen calls Patriot at noon, the payment order sent to its bank has almost assuredly already been accepted by full payment to the bank, sometime within minutes of 11:00 a.m. If for some reason it has not, it is then accepted at the moment the person at Patriot tells the person at Moneymen at noon that the $2 million has arrived and has been credited to the Moneymen account. The end result? Patriot National Bank owes Moneymen $2 million and Big Apple's obligation to pay $2 million on its mortgage to Moneymen by the end of March has been discharged. All is well.

4a.   The payment date has in this instance been determined, by the instruction sent by Big Apple, to be Tuesday, September 20.

4b.   The execution date of a payment order

> means the day on which the receiving bank [here Gotham] may properly issue a payment order in execution of the sender's order. . . . If the sender's instruction indicates a payment date, the execution date is the payment date or an earlier date on which execution is reasonably necessary to allow payment to the beneficiary on the payment date.

So here the execution date would also be Tuesday, September 20, unless for some reason the Gotham bank thought and was reasonable in thinking that execution on a prior day was necessary to ensure that payment would be made into Sunshine Bank of Los Angeles for the benefit of Big Orange Insurance on time. It is hard to think of a reason why execution even one day ahead of September 20 would be reasonably necessary in this instance, especially when the funds are traveling east to west and into a part of the country where the days end three hours later.

4c. Gotham has not accepted Big Apple's payment order by sending out an order of its own on September 8. Under §4A-209(d), "[a] payment order issued to the originator's bank cannot be accepted until the . . . execution date if the bank is not the beneficiary's bank." One risk that Gotham faces here is that Big Apple, as the originator, will cancel the order prior to the execution date of September 20 and Gotham will be left holding the bag. Its order will have been carried out almost two weeks earlier and the money will be in the beneficiary's account. Gotham will have no right to payment from Big Apple, because Big Apple has effectively canceled its order. Gotham is left with the right to "recover from the beneficiary any payment received to the extent allowed by the law governing mistake and restitution." Granted, the chances that Big Apple will want to cancel payment of an insurance premium are small, but in other circumstances this could be a greater possibility, and Gotham has incurred a significant risk by acting before the execution date. In addition, under §4A-402(c), "[p]ayment by the sender [Big Apple] is not due until the execution date of the sender's order," so Gotham will have no right to debit Big Apple's account with the amount of the order until September 20. It takes the risk that on that date Big Apple's account will not have enough in it to cover the payment already made by Gotham earlier in the month. At the least, because money in the bank in the amounts typically involved in wholesale wire transfers is money earning interest, Gotham will have to bear the loss of whatever interest would have been attributable to the amount of the transfer because it paid this large amount of money on September 8, and will not be entitled to payment from its customer, Big Apple, until the 20th. See Comment 9 to §4A-209.

5a. Yes, Jules is too late. Here, because no different payment date was specified by Jules, the execution date was, under §4A-301(b), the day the order was received. Gotham executed and by doing so accepted the order at 12:30 p.m. Pursuant to §4A-211(c), "[a]fter a payment order has been accepted, cancellation or amendment of the order is not effective," unless the receiving bank agrees or a funds-transfer system rule allows for cancellation or amendment without the agreement of the bank. This last condition would not be applicable to any order sent via Fedwire. And it is awfully hard to imagine why Gotham would agree to Jules's cancellation of his already accepted payment order unless Gotham itself could be sure that *its* payment order to the New York Fed could in turn be canceled, relieving Gotham of any obligation to pay that bank $250,000. See the concluding paragraph of Comment 3 to this section.

5b. Jules can place the call, but it will have no effect, even if he can find someone at the Fed willing to talk to him and even if the New York Fed has not yet accepted Gotham's order. Looking at §4A-211, we note that a communication attempting to cancel or amend a payment order may be made only by the *sender* of that order. Jules has no authority to cancel an order sent by Gotham, which is what he would be attempting to do.

5c. Under §4A-211(b), Jules's cancellation would be effective "if notice of [his] communication is received at a time and in a manner affording the receiving bank a reasonable opportunity to act on the communication before the bank accepts the payment order."

6a. Yes. If all other aspects of the closing have been taken care of, this payment by wire is the final step in the transaction and the closing can be completed by the attorney's release to Arnold of the share certificates. What happens next? Well, everybody can go home or back to work, unless they want to go out for a meal together to celebrate the closing of the deal. As to what the future will bring for Horseshoes.com and Arnold's investment in that firm, only time will tell.

This example is meant to illustrate one of the principal ways in which the present ability to wire large sums of money from one party's account into another's greatly facilitates modern business practices. Imagine what this closing would have been like if wholesale wire transfer of funds in amounts as large as this were not feasible, or if they took days to accomplish. Andrea and her attorneys certainly could not agree to close the deal with a personal check from Arnold or his firm. Also, because the exact amount that Arnold is going to have to come up with is typically not determined until the time of the closing, it would be impossible for him to have brought a bank check for the exact amount to the table. The participants in this closing may have had to waste an hour or so just chatting while they waited for the $5,230,000 to be paid, and we acknowledge of course that they are busy people, but this really is an amazingly effective way for the exact amount that ultimately must change hands to be paid — quickly, efficiently, and cheaply.

6b. No. Subsection 4A-406(c) provides that "if the beneficiary's bank accepts a payment order in an amount equal to the amount of the originator's payment order less charges of one or more receiving banks in the funds transfer," payment to the beneficiary and hence discharge of Arnold's obligation to pay $5,230,000 to close the deal "is deemed to be in the amount of the originator's payment order unless upon demand by the beneficiary the originator does not pay the beneficiary the amount of the deducted charges." So Andrea does have the right, if she wishes to insist upon it, to demand that Arnold's firm come up with and pay to her firm the $20 in fees. Arnold can settle it then and there by giving Andrea a $20 bill (if he happens to be carrying around any such small bills).

22

Security Procedures and the Risk of Theft

Introduction to Security Procedures

With all that money whizzing around the world via wholesale wire transfers and in such large amounts, it is perfectly understandable that thieves would try to get their hands on some of it. The major wire transfer systems, such as Fedwire and CHIPS, are (as you can imagine) quite well aware of the risks involved in carrying on this business, and have in place their own procedures, both in terms of personnel management and the highest level of computer security, for protecting themselves and those that use their services. Banks that regularly carry out payment orders will do likewise. The weakest link in the chain by far is the initial payment order made by the originator to its bank that starts the funds transfer on its way. Article 4A establishes the rules of loss allocation should a thief break into this weakest link and make off with some money that is not rightfully his or hers.

Central to Article 4A's handling of this problem is the concept of the *security procedure* agreed to by the originator and its bank at the time the customer and the bank enter into an agreement under which the bank will accept and execute payment orders received from the customer. Under §4A-201,

> "Security procedure" means a procedure established by agreement of a customer and a receiving bank for the purpose of (i) verifying that a payment order or communication amending or canceling a payment order is that of the customer, or (ii) detecting error in the transmission of the content of the payment order or communication. A security procedure may require the use of algorithms or other codes, identifying words or numbers, encryption, callback procedures, or similar security devices. Comparison of a signature on a payment order or communication with an authorized specimen signature of the customer is not by itself a security procedure.

Something more than signature comparison is required to constitute an Article 4A security procedure. The procedures actually in use vary widely, usually reflecting the size of the customer and the number and typical amount of wire transfers it expects to initiate over time. The largest customers, who regularly transmit many large payment orders a day, will probably have on their premises dedicated computer terminals connecting them directly with their bank; access to such a terminal is normally heavily restricted and the connection is made using a high level of encryption technology. A medium-sized user might have been supplied by the bank with a computer program, which can run on one or more of the user's desktop computers, but which requires both an identification code and a special password to enter and activate. Again, communication with the bank will presumably be by a secure modem connection. The customer who intends to initiate payment orders infrequently may agree with its bank to rely solely on oral means to communicate with its bank with respect to wire transfers. (Remember that a payment order may be "transmitted orally" under §4A-103(a)(1).) In such a case the security mechanism agreed-upon typically requires that the person representing the originator in making the telephone call use a previously agreed-upon keyword or phrase. Either the person at the bank who receives this call or another person at the bank will then call back the originator at a previously specified telephone number. The originator's representative, or a second person working at the originator's business, will then be asked to verify (perhaps by another, different keyword) that the order actually came from the originator. Requiring that two separate people at the originator's place of business, or two separate people at the originator's bank, be involved in the process does, of course, add to the complexity and time it takes to complete the transaction. It may well be justified, however, in that it makes it just that much harder for a single individual working either for the originator or for the originator's bank to pull off a scam.

Notice in the definition of *security procedure* that such a procedure may be set in place not only to make sure that the payment order or other communication has truly been initiated by an authorized representative of the originator, but also to "detect error" in the transmission. The agreement between the customer and the bank, for example, may contain a provision that any payment order for, say, more than $500,000 must be initiated by a second keyword in addition to the one which the customer normally uses. If the customer makes a mistake, and enters the amount $4,000,000 in a payment order that is supposed to be for only $400,000, this type of security procedure should be able to catch the mistake before the originator's bank accepts the order.

Bearing the Risk of Theft

Article 4A allocates the risk of loss due to unauthorized payment orders in three sections, §§4A-202 through 4A-204. Under §4A-202(a), "[a] payment order received by the receiving bank is the authorized order of the person identified as sender if that person authorized the order or is otherwise bound by it under the law of agency." Therefore, an originator's order will be deemed to be authorized by the originator, whether or not it complies with the security procedure agreed to by the originator and the bank, if the order was actually *authorized* by the originator as that term is used in the law of agency.

The originator's bank, however, is usually not in a position to know for sure whether an order it receives by phone or computer is in fact the authorized act of the originator, nor does it want to take the time or incur the risk of trying to make that determination. For most funds transfers, the originator's bank will be entitled to treat the communication as coming from the originator, to debit the originator's account for the amount of the order and to execute the order, by itself sending an order to the next bank in the chain, because the order can legitimately be considered a *verified payment order* under the terms of §4A-202(b): "If a bank and its customer have agreed that the authenticity of payment orders issued to the bank in the name of the customer as sender will be verified pursuant to a security procedure, a payment order received by the receiving bank is effective as the order of the customer, whether or not authorized," as long as certain conditions are met. For a verified order to be effective as an order of the originator, it is necessary that the security procedure agreed to between the customer and the bank be a "commercially reasonable" security procedure, on which see subsection (c). It is also necessary that "the bank prove[] that it accepted the payment order in good faith [as to which see §4A-105(a)(6)] and in compliance with the security procedure and any written agreement or instruction of the customer restricting acceptance of a payment order issued in the name of the customer."*

Thus, the originator's bank is generally entitled to treat as coming from the originator any payment order that is actually authorized *or* that is verified according to the security procedure previously agreed to by the originator-customer. The bank may accept such orders by executing them and may deduct from the account of the originator the amount of the order. In certain limited circumstances, set out in §4A-203, the bank may be barred from enforcing even a verified payment order. We will consider these situa-

---

* As an example of the type of separate written instruction that the customer may give to its bank "restricting acceptance of payment orders issued in the name of the customer," consider the following. A customer may on a regular basis supply the bank with a list of authorized beneficiaries; that is, of parties and account numbers to which it anticipates it will be transferring funds under its agreement with the bank. The bank is entitled to accept orders only if they instruct payment to these listed beneficiaries. If a crooked employee of the customer were to get his or her hands on the means normally used to transmit payment orders to the customer's bank and try to use this to funnel money into an account of his or her own, the bank would not be entitled to accept this order for payment into an unlisted account.

tions in the following examples. We will also look at the provisions of §4A-204, which sets out the liability of a receiving bank for executing what turns out to be an unauthorized and ineffective payment order.

EXAMPLES

1. The DotCom Corporation and Payson State Bank have entered into a written agreement under which the bank will execute wire transfer payment orders on behalf of the corporation. The agreement provides that all such orders will be transmitted to the bank via a computer program provided to the corporation by the bank. The program, which calls for any payment order to be accompanied by an identification number given by the bank to DotCom as well as by a password chosen by the corporation, is installed on the desktop computer that sits in the office of Hamilton, who is the treasurer of the corporation. The identification number and password are known only to Hamilton and to Washington, who is the president of DotCom. Only Hamilton and Washington are authorized to use the system to send payment orders or other communications to Payson in this way. One day while he is away from his office, Hamilton realizes that he was supposed to have sent a payment order to Payson on the previous day to pay one of DotCom's principal suppliers money it is owed. Hamilton sends the bank a fax ordering it to send a certain amount of money to the supplier at a given account in a named bank.

(a) Is Payson obligated to execute this order?

(b) If Payson does execute the order it has received by fax, is it within its rights to withdraw the amount of the order from DotCom's account with the bank?

2. The basic set-up is the same as in Example 1. Suppose that one day Hamilton is about to send a payment order to Payson when he finds he can't recall the exact identification number and password he will have to use. He goes to the door of Washington's office and asks her to remind him. Washington shouts out the information to Hamilton. Benedict Arnold, Washington's secretary, hears the conversation loud and clear. Soon after, Arnold goes into Hamilton's office when Hamilton is not there but the computer is on. He sits down at the computer and quickly figures out how to initiate a payment order to Payson, which directs the bank to wire $250,000 into a certain account that Arnold has with Distrust National Bank. Payson does as this order instructs. By the time Hamilton, as treasurer of the company, becomes aware of this transfer out of the corporation's account, when he is reviewing the company's monthly statement, Benedict Arnold has left the employ of DotCom and vanished from the scene.

(a) Who bears the loss of this $250,000?

(b) Suppose instead that Arnold had only been able to catch the identification number used by the company when Washington reminded

Hamilton of the relevant information. Arnold, however, is a good enough computer hacker that he is able, using just that information, to find a way to get the password out of the system and to send a computer message from his own home computer that perfectly mimics an authorized message sent from the computer in Hamilton's office using the correct identification number and password. Once again he orders $250,000 to be sent to his own account, takes the money, and runs. Who would be responsible for taking the quarter-million-dollar loss under this set of circumstances?

(c) Finally, suppose that after $250,000 is mysteriously wired out of DotCom's account with Payson, diligent investigation discloses that the payment order received by the bank and bearing all the indicia of an authentic payment order from the company was actually sent by one Thad Codemaster, a sophisticated computer user. Given some time and effort, Thad has been able to hack into the computer that Payson uses for receipt of payment orders and to capture the identification numbers and passwords used by a number of Payson's customers, including DotCom. Thad has then been able to send from his own computer an instruction that is read by Payson's computer as an authorized message from DotCom, instructing it to wire $250,000 into an account that Thad has with a bank in the Cayman Islands. Who bears this loss? See §4A-203(a)(2).

3.   Brooklyn Cogs and Widgets (BC&W) is one of the largest manufacturers in the New York metropolitan area. Because of the volume of its business, it regularly has to pay a large variety of suppliers, often in amounts ranging up to the millions. BC&W enters into an agreement with one of its banks, Dodger Bank, under which that bank will execute wire transfers out of BC&W's account. The agreement calls for a security procedure under which payment orders can be made over the telephone by the treasurer of BC&W, currently Mr. P. W. Reese, identifying himself and using an agreed-upon password. The bank will then call the treasurer back at his office telephone number and ask him to verify the order by using a second password. Bummer, an employee of BC&W who works in an office near Reese's, is able to overhear Reese initiating and verifying a payment order to the Dodger bank using this system. When next he finds Reese's office empty, Bummer sneaks in and, pretending to be Reese, calls in a payment order instructing the bank to transfer $100,000 into an account Bummer has at Yankee Pinstripe Bank. Within a minute, a call comes into Reese's telephone line asking for Reese to verify the payment order. Bummer is there to pick up the phone and give the needed verifying password. Bummer slips out of Reese's office. Later in the day, when he checks his balance at Yankee Pinstripe, he finds that the account has indeed been credited with $100,000. He goes out to the Aqueduct racetrack that weekend and loses the entire amount and whatever other meager savings he had. When the unauthorized transfer by

Bummer is discovered, there is no way he can repay even a fraction of the $100,000.

(a) Does Brooklyn Cogs and Widgets have to bear this loss? What argument might the firm make that it should not?

(b) Suppose further that when BC&W entered into a written funds transfer agreement with Dodger Bank, the bank had suggested and in fact urged the firm to incorporate a security procedure involving a dedicated computer terminal at BC&W's offices, or at the very least a highly secure computer program that could be installed on Reese's desktop computer. Reese insisted that he is an old-fashioned sort, uncomfortable with anything having to do with computers and preferring to do business face-to-face or over the telephone, "where I at least know who I'm talking to." Dodger Bank then wrote into the agreement the "call-back" telephone security procedure that BC&W was to use in placing payment orders. How does this affect your answer to the previous question? Look at the last sentence of §4A-202(c).

4.   The Yankee Pinstripe Bank inserts into all funds transfer agreements that it asks its customers to sign a clause that reads:

> By its signing this Agreement Customer hereby agrees that in no event shall Yankee Pinstripe Bank be liable for more than $100,000 in loss resulting from the Bank's unauthorized execution of a payment order on behalf of Customer without regard to whether the Bank has complied with its obligations under the Security Procedure set forth elsewhere in this Agreement or whether such Security Procedure is later found to be a commercially reasonable procedure in regard to use by Customer.

Is this an enforceable provision? See §4A-202(f).

5.   Steinbrenner, an employee of Yankee Pinstripe Bank who has access to the Fedwire terminal at the bank and is knowledgeable about its use, issues a payment order to the Federal Reserve Bank of New York purporting to execute a payment order that Yankee Pinstripe received from one of its customers, Uptown Fashions. In fact, Uptown Fashions has issued no such payment order. The order sent to the New York Fed instructs that bank to wire $135,000 into an account Steinbrenner has with the New Dodgers Bank of California. This funds transfer is completed by the New York Fed's sending a payment order to the San Francisco Fed, which in turn sends a payment order to the New Dodgers Bank. That bank accepts the order it receives and credits $135,000 to Steinbrenner's account. Meanwhile, Steinbrenner has caused the same amount to be deducted from Uptown Fashion's account with Yankee Pinstripe. Uptown Fashion soon becomes aware of the amount that has been taken out of its account without its permission and immediately contacts the bank.

(a) Which party should bear the loss to Steinbrenner, the thief?

(b) How much will Yankee Pinstripe have to credit to Uptown Fashion's account? See §4A-204.

(c) Suppose instead that Uptown Fashion does not become aware of the unauthorized withdrawal soon after it happens. The $135,000 debit, which was wrongfully deducted from Uptown Fashions's account on May 6, 2004, is reported on the May statement of account, which Uptown Fashion receives from the bank on June 4. No one from Uptown Fashion contacts the bank about this un-authorized withdrawal until July 28. How does this affect your answer to Example 5b? What if Uptown Fashion does not come upon the problem until it is conducting its annual audit and contacts the bank in February of 2005?

(d) Finally, what if Uptown Fashion does not complain about the unauthorized deduction from its account until June of 2006? See §4A-505.

EXPLANATIONS

1a. No. Recall that a receiving bank "has no duty to accept a payment order unless the bank makes an agreement, either before or after issuance of the payment order, to accept it" (Comment 3 to §4A-209). Payson State Bank is certainly going to have made sure that the funds transfer agreement it entered into with DotCom explicitly provides that the bank is under no duty to accept any payment order other than one sent to it and verified through the security procedure DotCom has agreed to use. See also the language in §4A-202(b) to the effect that "[t]he bank is not required to follow an instruction that violates a written agreement with the customer. . ."

1b. If Payson does execute this order, even though it is under no duty to do so, it will be entitled to withdraw the amount of the order from DotCom's account. This would be an order actually *authorized* by the customer and hence one that the bank is entitled to treat as valid. Payson, of course, took a great risk in executing an order that did not come to it via the agreed-upon secured method. In this instance, at least it did not lose by taking that risk, but it certainly isn't something you would expect the bank to do often — not if it wanted to stay in business.

2a. DotCom will bear the loss of funds. The payment order sent by Arnold was not an authorized order. It does, however, appear to be a *verified* payment order and hence, under §4A-202(b), one that is "effective as the order of the customer." For Payson to take advantage of the rule of §4A-202(b), of course, it will have to prove a number of things should DotCom want to contest the issue. First of all, was the security procedure under which Payson verified the order a "commercially reasonable method of providing [DotCom] security against unauthorized payment order"? The first sentence of subsection (c) tells us that the commercial reasonableness of a selected security procedure is a matter of law and that it is to be determined by considering a number of variables. Here, unless evidence proves to the contrary, we appear to have a commercially reasonable procedure given the context. Second, Payson must establish if called into question that it "accepted the payment order in good faith and in compliance with the security procedure" as well as with any other written agreement or instruction given to it by DotCom that would limit Payson's right to accept a payment order. Given the facts we have here, there seems no reason to doubt that Payson will be able to meet these criteria as well. DotCom has been given a security procedure to use in initiating funds transfers through Payson, and its own officers have compromised the security of the procedure by their casual way of dealing with it. DotCom should and will bear the loss occasioned by its employee's theft.

2b. DotCom will still bear the loss. You can check for yourself that all the criteria established in §4A-202(b) for a verified payment order have been met. As we will see in the next part of this example, §4A-203 provides for some limited instances in which a verified payment order will not be enforceable against the customer, but that section does not apply to this case. The security procedure was overcome by a computer hacker, but it was an inside job, and so DotCom must still take the loss.

2c. Under §4A-203(b)(2), the Payson bank will not be allowed to consider the message initiated by Thad an effective order from DotCom, although from all appearances the order will have seemed to be so as far as the bank's personnel and computers were concerned. Payson will have to bear the loss. This is all assuming, of course, that Thad did not receive any information helping him to break into Payson's system "from a source controlled by the customer [DotCom] . . . regardless of how the information was obtained or whether the customer was at fault." See Comment 5 to this section.

Although I did not include an example calling for reference to paragraph (1) of §4A-203(a), you should look it over, along with Comment 6. At first it might seem puzzling: Why would a bank agree to take on *greater* risk for verified but unauthorized payments than Article 4A requires? Banks usually try to cut their losses, not the other way around. You have to remember, however, that the customers who are most likely to contract for wholesale wire transfers service are often the largest and hence most powerful commercial entities around — the General Motorses and Time Warners of this world. Major banks will understandably compete to get the business of customers such as these. The negotiation between such a customer and its bank that leads to the final funds transfer agreement by which both are bound will not be a simple matter. The bank is in no position to insist that a mega-customer sign the bank's standard form agreement on a take-it-or-leave-it basis. Under such circumstances, it may turn out to be a prudent business decision on the part of a bank to agree in writing to "limit the extent to which it is entitled to enforce or retain payment of [an unauthorized but verified] payment order," so as to get or keep a major customer.

3a. BC&W does not necessarily have to bear the loss. The argument it would make — and it seems a good one under the circumstances — is that the security procedure was not a commercially reasonable one given the size and nature of the customer. Recall that under §4A-202(b), the customer will be responsible for the consequences of the unauthorized but verified payment order only if "the security procedure is a commercially reasonable method of providing security against unauthorized payment orders." The commercial reasonableness of the security procedure is to be considered, under subsection (c),

> by considering the wishes of the customer expressed to the bank, the circumstances of the customer known to the bank, including the size, type and frequency of payment orders normally issued by the customer to the bank, alternative security procedures offered to the customer, and security procedures in general use by customers and receiving banks similarly situated.

If this minimal procedure of oral confirmation was the only security procedure offered to BC&W, a court might well conclude that the procedure was not commercially reasonable given the particular circumstances.

3b. If BC&W was offered a commercially reasonable security procedure, but then the firm chose a riskier procedure and agreed to it in writing, then under the cited part of §4A-203(c) the bank would be protected by the security procedure and BC&W would have to bear the loss. You should read Comment 5 to §4A-203, which gives a good overview of both the working of and the policy justifications for the "commercially reasonable" security procedure aspect of §4A- 202(b).

4.   No, such a provision would not be enforceable. Subsection (f) of §4A-202 makes this clear.

5a. Yankee Pinstripe Bank, should bear the loss. It never received an authorized or verified payment order from Uptown Fashions to transfer any funds out of that firm's account, so it had no right to withdraw any money from that account. The bank has to bear the risk that one of its employees will, as has happened in this case, carry on a fraudulent transaction. Steinbrenner has stolen $135,000 from Yankee Pinstripe Bank, not from Uptown Fashions.

5b. Yankee Pinstripe is going to have to recredit Uptown Fashions's account with the full $135,000, because this "payment" purportedly received from that customer was made on the basis of a payment order that the bank was clearly "not entitled to enforce." In addition, the bank will have to pay Uptown Fashions "interest on the refundable amount calculated from the date the bank received payment to the date of the refund."

5c. Uptown Fashions will still be entitled to refund of the $135,000, but it may have lost the right to interest on this amount by its failure to exercise ordinary care under the circumstances and to "notify the bank of the relevant facts within a reasonable time not exceeding 90 days after the date the customer received notification from the bank that the order was accepted or that the customer's account was debited with respect to the order." If Uptown Fashions does notify the bank on July 28, this is within 90 days, but a question remains as to whether this delay of almost two months was outside a "reasonable time" for the customer to report the totally unauthorized transfer out of its account of this amount of money. As Comment 2 to this section (which you should read at this time) states, "Reasonable time is not defined and it may depend on the facts of the particular case." Many banks will make sure that the written funds transfer agreements they enter into with their customers set forth a specific number of days less than 90 that will constitute "reasonable time" for the purposes of §4A-204, just so that this issue doesn't later have to be litigated. Note that under (b), "[r]easonable time under subsection (a) may be fixed by agreement."

If Uptown Fashions does not notify the bank until February 2002, well beyond 90 days after it received notice of the unauthorized and unverified payment order, then it will definitely lose the right to any interest on the $135,000. It will still, of course, have the right to refund of the base amount. Nothing in §4A-204 puts in jeopardy Uptown's right to refund of money wrongfully taken out of its account. Subsection (b) of §4A-204 explicitly states, "the obligation of the receiving bank to refund payment as stated in subsection (a) may not otherwise be varied by agreement."

5d. Under the cited section, if Uptown Fashion does wait to object until more than a year has passed after its having received notice that this order was executed, it will be "precluded from asserting that the bank is not entitled to retain the payment." It will lose not only the right to interest on the $135,000, but the base amount as well. As the comment to this section remarks, "This section is in the nature of a statute of repose for objecting to debits made out of the customer's account." In this respect, it may put you in mind of the similar (if not identical in detail) §4-406(f), which we looked at as part of the "bank statement rule" covering a bank's mistaken or wrongful payment of a check out of a customer's account.

An unresolved question about §4A-505 is whether the statutory one-year period specified in that section may be shortened to something less by agreement of the parties. We saw the analogous question with respect to §4-406(f) in Example 6 of Chapter 18. The courts have typically found nothing inherently wrong with such contractually shortened "cut-off" periods, as long as the time allowed for the customer to become aware of and report problems discernible from his or her account statement is still "commercial reasonable" in the Article 4 context. The answer might not be the same when the problem to be reported is with a funds transfer governed by Article 4A. In the recent case of *Regatos v. North Fork Bank*, 257 F.Supp.2d 632, 50 U.C.C.2d 35 (S.D.N.Y. 2003), District Judge Scheindlin gives careful consideration to the question, which she characterizes as one of first impression. She holds that the one-year notice provision or "statute of repose" found in §4A-505 could *not* effectively be shortened by agreement of the parties.

> Consideration of the structure of Article 4A, along with its underlying purposes and policies, leads to the conclusion that the drafters did not intend to permit a bank and its customer to vary the one year notice period by agreement.

Judge Scheindlin then goes on to comment that even if she is wrong to hold variation of the one-year period in §4A-505 absolutely barred, a fifteen-day notice provision as she had before her would not be enforceable as it is "demonstrably unreasonable." As such it "effectively guts the invariable rights of the customer under sections 4A-202 and 4A-204" and should not stand in the way of the customer's claim for reimbursement under those sections of amounts he claimed improperly paid by the bank. Only time will tell whether this decision will be appealed, and if so what the ultimate outcome will be.

23

Errors in Execution

Introduction

Mistakes will happen. In this chapter we consider which party must bear the risk of a mistake being made somewhere along the line in the execution of a funds transfer governed by Article 4A. We also have to consider what damages a party who fails to fulfill its obligations under the article may be liable to pay for its mistake, to whom and for what amount. Finally we take on a particularly interesting question: If an error in the processing of a funds transfer results in a sum of money (and these being wholesale wire transfers, the sums involved can often be quite great) being accidentally credited to the account of someone, usually just some random figure, who was not meant to be the beneficiary of the transfer, what recourse does the party who bears the loss of the mistake have to get the money back from the recipient?

The general principle under which Article 4A operates is, not surprisingly, that the party who made the mistake should be made to bear the risk of that mistake. This general principle is carried out in a number of individual sections that attempt to take into account all the various types of errors that can occur in the funds transfer context. When you think about it — and the drafters of Article 4A did think about it a great deal — there are plenty of ways things can go awry in the wire transfer system. We have to anticipate that an error could be made by the originator itself, by the originator's bank, by any intermediary bank, or by the beneficiary's bank. Also, the error could result in a payment order being for more than was intended or for less, it could be executed in duplicate, or it could be "addressed" to the wrong recipient entirely. For each of the various possibilities that might crop up, Article 4A should provide a definitive answer about which party takes the loss occasioned by its mistake.

Having determined which party was at fault in the course of events, the article also sets out the consequences for that party. In some instances it will be enough to say that the party initially bears the loss of the amount of the transfer involved and the difficulty of trying to recover this amount from whoever is now in possession of the funds. In other situations the party making the mistake may also be liable in damages to another to whom it has failed in its obligation to execute and respond to payment orders without mistake.

Before moving into the examples, there are two particularly important parts of the Article 4A scheme worth noting at the outset. First of all, look at §4A-402. Under subsection (c), as we have already seen, the originator who sends a payment order to its bank is obligated to pay that bank upon the execution of its order. But look at the last sentence:

> The obligation of that sender [here the originator] to pay its payment order is excused if the funds transfer is not completed by acceptance by the beneficiary's bank of a payment order instructing payment to the beneficiary of that sender's payment order.

Under subsection (d), if the originator has already paid its bank on a payment order that does not eventually result in a conforming payment order being received and accepted by the beneficiary's bank effectively discharging the originator's obligation to the beneficiary under §4A-406, the originator's bank is obliged to "refund payment to the extent the [originator] was not obliged to pay" and indeed to credit the originator with interest from the date of its payment until the time of the refund. This is the so-called *money-back guarantee* provision of Article 4A. As Comment 2 to this section quite rightly points out,

> This "money-back guarantee" is an important protection of [the] Originator. Originator is assured that it will not lose its money if something goes wrong in the transfer.

To this we would add only the obvious caveat that the originator can take comfort from this protection only if *it* is not the one responsible for something going wrong.

A second noteworthy aspect worthy of the Article 4 scheme for allocating risks due to errors is that the party making the mistake and having to bear the loss is often given the right to recover from the person into whose account the funds were mistakenly delivered, "to the extent allowed by the law governing mistake and restitution." (See, for example, §4A-303(c).) Article 4A itself does not cover the law of mistaken payment and restitution; these are common law concepts, and the article invokes the common law of the state under whose laws any dispute is being considered to determine whether and to what extent the party who has received a mistaken payment is legally obligated to restore it to the party who made the mistake. In most cases there will be no question that restitution is due. If the account into which a mistaken payment has been credited is held by just some random person who is owed nothing by the originator, it should be clear under the common law of restitution that the money must be restored to its rightful owner. There do turn out to be cases, however, in which the error is such that the party receiving the mistaken payment is not an entire stranger to the originator, and may in fact be owed some money by that entity. Under the common law of restitution, a doctrine referred to as the *discharge for value rule* may come into play. Even if there was no intention on the originator's part to pay its debt to the party mistakenly receiving payment, may that party hold onto the money as long as it credits the payment to what it is in fact owed by the originator? We will look at this common law wrinkle on the right to restitution, and how the courts have dealt with it, in the last example.

EXAMPLES

1. The DotCom Corporation and Payson State Bank have entered into a written funds transfer agreement under which the bank will execute wire transfer payment orders on behalf of the corporation. The agreement sets up a security procedure that takes advantage of a computerized means for DotCom to communicate with the bank. One day Hamilton, the treasurer of DotCom, determines to pay the $800,000 his company owes one of its principal suppliers, the Wireless Corporation located in Palo Alto, California. The purchase and sale agreement between DotCom and the Wireless firm calls for a payment to be made via wire transfer into Wireless's account (#80368046) at the Sunshine Bank of Palo Alto. Using the desktop computer in his office, and following the security procedure provided for in his company's agreement with Payson, Hamilton sends a payment order to that bank. By mistake Hamilton's order directs the transfer of $8 million into Wireless's account with the Palo Alto bank. Hamilton does give the correct name, bank, and account number of Wireless. Within a few minutes of its receiving this order, Payson has deducted $8 million from DotCom's account and sent its own payment order via Fedwire to the New York Federal Reserve Bank, intending to execute this order. A couple of hours later, a payment order is received via Fedwire at the Sunshine Bank of Palo Alto from the Federal Reserve Bank of San Francisco ordering it to credit $8 million to Wireless's account #80368046. Sunshine Bank accepts the order and informs the Wireless Corporation that its account has been credited with $8 million sent to it by the DotCom Corporation.

   (a) Can DotCom insist that its bank, Payson State, recredit its account with the excess $7,200,000 that was mistakenly sent to Sunshine and credited to Wireless's account? If not, what can it do to recover this money sent in error?

   (b) Suppose that the security procedure set forth in the funds transfer agreement entered into between DotCom and Payson provided not only a means for the bank to verify that the order was truly sent by an authorized person at DotCom, but also a means of detecting certain errors. In particular, it provided that any payment order sent by DotCom for an amount in excess of $1 million would include the prefix "XXX" prior to the amount in the order. The order as sent by Hamilton indicated the amount of the order as "8,000,000 U.S. Dollars" and did not include the "XXX" prefix. As before, the Payson bank executed the order by sending its own payment order to the New York Fed, instructing payment of $8 million into the designated Wireless account. How would this affect your analysis of the situation? See §4A-205.

2.   Hamilton, the treasurer of DotCom, also decides to pay the $500,000 that DotCom owes its advertising agency, MadAve Associates. Hamilton issues a payment order, following the agreed-to security procedures, to Payson State Bank calling for $500,000 to be paid into the account of MadAve Associates at Gotham Bank. Unfortunately, Hamilton enters the number of MadAve's account as #123465 when the correct number is #123456. Payson Bank deducts $500,000 from the DotCom account and executes the order as received. When Gotham Bank receives a payment order instructing it to credit $500,000 into account #123465, its computers report that there is no account at the bank bearing that number.

  (a) What should Gotham do in this situation? See §4A-207(a). What will be the end result?
  (b) Suppose instead that there is a customer, one Larry Luckowski, who does happen to have an account #123465 at Gotham Bank. Gotham Bank credits Larry's account with the $500,000. Was Gotham wrong to do so? Would it make any difference to your answer if the payment order received by Gotham had included the name of the intended beneficiary ("MadAve Associates") as well as the (mistaken) account number? See §4A-207(b)(1).
  (c) Has DotCom paid what it owes to its advertising agency, MadAve Associates? Recall §4A-406.
  (d) Against whom is DotCom going to have to proceed to get return of the $500,000 that has gone astray? See the remainder of §4A-207.

3.   The DotCom Corporation also owes $4 million to one of its principal suppliers, Brooklyn Cogs and Widgets (BC&W). Hamilton uses the desktop computer in his office and the security procedure provided for in his firm's agreement with Payson State Bank to place a payment order to Payson, instructing it to wire $4 million into a designated account that BC&W has at Dodger National Bank. Through a foul-up at Payson, the payment order it sends intending to execute DotCom's order is for $6 million. That amount is deducted from DotCom's account at Payson, and that amount is eventually credited to BC&W's account with Dodger National Bank.

(a) Is DotCom entitled to return of the extra $2 million? From whom? See §4A-303(a).

(b) Suppose instead that Payson did at first send a payment order intending to execute the order it received from DotCom in the correct amount, $4 million. Then, later in the day, Payson sent a duplicate order for $4 million, acting on the mistaken belief that it had not yet executed its customer's order. By the end of the day, BC&W's account with the Dodger bank has been credited with each of these orders, for a total of $8 million. How do you analyze this situation?

(c) Finally, suppose that Payson's error was to send an order instructing that only $400,000 be credited to BC&W's account. That firm's account at Dodger is indeed credited with that amount but no more. What then? See §4A-303(b).

4. After a period of tough negotiations, the president of DotCom has entered into an agreement for her firm to buy all of the outstanding stock of another Internet company, the NetNet Corporation, from its current owner, one Arnold Moneybucks. She has received the approval of DotCom's board of directors to go ahead with the deal. Her agreement with Arnold calls for her to seal the deal by having $5 million wired into a designated account (#789864) held by Arnold in the Palo Alto Bank for Entrepreneurs by the end of business on Friday, November 13. Hamilton, the treasurer of DotCom, is directed to arrange for the transfer of the funds. Late in the afternoon of Thursday, November 12, Hamilton sends a payment order to Payson State Bank, ordering it to have $5 million transferred into Arnold's account as soon as possible. This order is given by Hamilton using the prescribed security procedures called for in DotCom's agreement with Payson and correctly identifies the account into which the funds are to be transferred, both by the name of the beneficiary and the bank account number. Payson deducts $5 million from the DotCom account and attempts to execute the order. Unfortunately, through a foul-up at Payson, the payment order it itself sends, intending to execute DotCom's order gives the beneficiary's account number as #864789. This happens to be the number of an account at the bank, held by Winona Windfall. The Palo Alto bank credits the $5 million it receives to Ms. Windfall's account.

(a) Is DotCom entitled to have its account at Payson recredited for this amount? See §§4A-303(c) and 4A-402(c) and (d).

(b) Assume that Arnold, having not received his payment of $5 million from DotCom by the agreed time, pulls out of the deal. By the end of the next week the aggregate value of all of the NetNet stock has shot up to more than $9 million, because that firm has come upon a method for making its product work just that much faster. Can DotCom hold Payson liable for its mistake to the tune of the

$4 million lost profit it can demonstrate it has suffered due to the bank's mistake? See §4A-305(b) and (c).

(c) Winona Windfall comes to you for advice. She wants to know if she is entitled to hold onto the $5 million that has suddenly and mysteriously appeared in her account? What do you tell her?

5.   The recently organized firm of Horseshoes Incorporated (which has just set up a Website called "Horseshoes.com") enters into a funds transfer agreement with the Palo Alto Bank for Entrepreneurs under which that bank agrees to execute wire transfers on behalf of the corporation under a prescribed security procedure. Money is tight for the start-up firm and it begins to experience cash-flow problems. The president and chief executive officer of the firm, one Smithy, has to make calculated decisions about which of its creditors to pay when, and which can be held off for a time. Smithy sees that his firm has just over $160,000 in available funds in its account with the Palo Alto bank. He decides that he can wait no longer to pay a bill for $75,000, which he owes to one of his firm's principal suppliers, the Ironbars Corporation. If he does not pay Ironbars soon, that firm has threatened to discontinue making deliveries to Horseshoes, and if this were to happen Smithy would have to discontinue critical operations. Using the required security procedure, Smithy sends a payment order to the Palo Alto bank, instructing that $75,000 be wired to Ironbars's account, which he gives as #10001 at San Francisco Federal Bank. Unfortunately, Smithy has made a mistake in referring to his list of creditors and their bank account information and in transferring the needed information onto the payment order that he sends to his company's bank. Account number #10001 at San Francisco Federal happens to be the account of the landlord who owns the building out of which Horseshoes operates — and to which Smithy's firm owes a considerable amount (more than $120,000) in back rent. Upon receiving the payment order sent by Smithy, the Palo Alto bank deducts $75,000 from the Horseshoes account. It then sends a payment order of its own instructing the recipient to transfer $75,000 into the account (given as #10001) of Ironbars at San Francisco Federal. By the end of the day, San Francisco Federal has received a payment order instructing it to accept this amount for credit to Ironbars and its account #10001. San Francisco Federal credits the $75,000 to account #10001, which is, as we know, an account held by Horseshoes's landlord, not by Ironbars.

(a) Did San Francisco Federal act in error? Recall §4A-207.

(b) Can Horseshoes demand a refund from the Palo Alto Bank for Entrepreneurs of the $75,000 previously withdrawn from its account held with that bank?

(c) Given the circumstances, does Horseshoes have a right to restitution of the $75,000 it has mistakenly put into the hands of its landlord?

EXPLANATIONS

1a. No. Payson has executed DotCom's order as it was received according to the agreed-upon security procedure. There has been no error on Payson's part. The error was obviously on the part of Hamilton, representing DotCom, and that company is initially going to have to bear the consequences and see what can be done to recover the money it overpaid by mistake from the Wireless Corporation. DotCom's present predicament is not one governed by Article 4A; the situation is no different than if it had paid by check and made the check out for the wrong higher figure (or if it had paid in cash and just happened to leave off a moneybag full of $8,000,000 instead of $800,000 at Wireless's reception desk). DotCom will first seek recovery of the extra $7,200,000, one would think, simply by contacting Wireless, explaining the mistake, and asking for return of the amount paid in error. In most cases this should probably be enough to get the mistaken payment back. What justification can Wireless have for holding onto $7,200,000 of DotCom's money to which it has no right? If Wireless balks at returning the funds, then DotCom will have to resort to the law, in this case the common law of restitution. Under the common law of restitution, a party that has been mistakenly paid an amount to which it has no right and for which it has not thereafter given value, and that has not relied upon the mistaken payment, is legally bound to return the mistaken payment to the party from whom it came. Barring some unusual circumstances, none of which appear to be present here, Wireless would be legally obligated to return the $7,200,000 to DotCom.

1b. Section 4A-205 deals with the problem of erroneous payments when the payment order was transmitted "pursuant to a security procedure for the detection of error" as was the case here. Under (a)(1), if the sender proves that it complied with the security procedure but that the receiving bank did not, and furthermore that "the error would have been detected had the receiving bank also complied, the sender [here DotCom] is not obliged to pay the order to the extent stated in paragraphs (2) and (3)." Here Payson did fail to observe the security procedure for detection of error, made part of the funds transfer agreement it entered into with DotCom. Had it correctly observed the procedure, the mistaken overpayment would have been detected and the extra $7,200,000 would not have ended up in Wireless's account. This case is covered by paragraph (3). DotCom is obligated to pay Payson $800,000 but no more. Payson will have to recredit DotCom's account for the $7,200,000 wrongfully charged through Payson's mistake. Payson is the "entitled to recover from the beneficiary the excess amount received to the extent allowed by the law governing mistake and restitution." So in this instance it will be Payson that will have to resort to the common law of restitution to recover the excess $7,200,000 from Wireless.

2a. Because the payment order received by the beneficiary bank refers to a "nonexistent or unidentifiable person or account, no person has rights as a beneficiary of the order and acceptance of the order cannot occur." Gotham Bank should reject this order, acting pursuant to §4A-210. A communication stating that the order has been rejected should soon be received by Payson, which should then notify DotCom. Under the money-back guarantee of §4A-402(c) and the rule of §4A-402(d), Payson will also have to recredit DotCom's account with the $500,000 it previously deducted from that account. Hamilton will have to try again to make the payment due MadAve, and this time we hope he'll get all the details right.

2b. Gotham was not wrong to credit the $500,000 into account #123465, even if the communication it received did also identify MadAve Associates and not Mr. Luckowski as the intended beneficiary, unless Gotham Bank *actually knew* that the name and number on the payment order it received referred to different persons. Typically, a bank will be operating on an automated system that is programmed to accept payment orders based on the given account number, which is of course more easily dealt with by computer than the name of the account holder. The bank will not even check for any possible discrepancy, and as you can see from the last sentence of §4A-207(b)(1), it is not required to do so. The justification for this rule is given in Comment 2 to this section, which is well worth your time to read.

What the receiving bank actually knew at the time of its acceptance is a question of fact, and it is not sufficient for the customer to prove that the bank "could have known" or even "should have known" of the different name and number. See *First Security Bank of New Mexico, N.A. v. Pan American Bank*, 215 F.3d 1147, 42 U.C.C.2d 206 (10th Cir. 2000), which serves as a good example of how difficult it can be for a customer to prove the bank's actual knowledge of the mix-up, even when its system is not entirely automated but involves genuine human beings retrieving and acting upon incoming information.

2c. No. DotCom has not paid what it owes to MadAve, even though it has attempted to do so. Payment to another is made by wire transfer under §4A-406(a) only when "a payment order for the benefit of the beneficiary is accepted by the beneficiary's bank in the funds transfer." Here Gotham did accept a payment order, but it was not a payment order for the benefit of MadAve. No money has come into MadAve's account. MadAve remains unpaid.

2d. Hamilton, acting on behalf of DotCom, is the one who made the mistake here, so we would expect that his firm would initially have to bear the loss of the money that was mistakenly transferred into Luckowski's account. In general that will be true. Under §4A-207(c)(2),

> If the originator is not a bank and proves that the person identified by number was not entitled to receive payment from the originator, the

originator is not obliged to pay its order *unless* the originator's bank proves that the originator, before acceptance of the originator's order, had notice that payment of a payment order issued by the originator might be made by the beneficiary's bank on the basis of an identifying or bank account number even if it identifies a person different from the named beneficiary.

At first this might seem to give DotCom a good argument that it deserves a refund from Payson of the amount deducted from DotCom's account in regard to the misdirected payment order, but that is highly unlikely. Unless the lawyers who advise Payson have done a particularly poor job, we can be sure that the funds transfer agreement entered into by it and DotCom *did* include notice to DotCom that payment of a payment order issued by DotCom might be made based solely on the account number given to Payson in any payment order, "even if [the number] identifies a person different from the named beneficiary." This provision in Article 4A is meant to make sure that anyone contracting with a bank for wire transfer services is well aware that banks generally deal with these transfer on the basis of the numbers given and not the names, and thus how exceptionally important it is for the originator to get the numbers right. Once the originator is given this notice, it will bear the risk if it specifies an incorrect account number in any payment order it communicates to its bank.

Under §4A-207(d)(2), because the beneficiary's bank rightfully paid the person identified by the number of the payment order it received, and "that person is not entitled to payment from the originator, the amount paid may be recovered from that person to the extent allowed by the law governing mistake and restitution" by DotCom, the originator. DotCom should be able to recover the full amount from Luckowski under restitutionary theory. Luckowski may understandably consider himself lucky suddenly to find $500,000 showing up in his bank account, but luck is itself no reason for him to claim a right to the mistaken payment. He has given no value for this amount. And let us hope for his sake that he has not "relied" on his all of a sudden being that much richer simply because his account balance reads as it does. It would be hard for him to argue that he had *reasonably* relied upon receipt of the $500,000 to, say, withdraw large amounts and spend it on fine dinners and extensive travel, when he had no basis for believing that the money was truly his in the first place.

3a.   DotCom is entitled to return of the extra $2 million from Payson, under §4A-303(a). Payson *is* entitled to the amount of DotCom's payment order ($4 million) under §4A-402(c), but no more. Payson will have to recredit DotCom's account with the $2 million that it mistakenly added to the amount of the funds transfer. Payson would then have to recover the $2 million that its mistake has cost it by going against BC&W, once again "to the extent allowed by the law governing mistake and restitution."

3b. Here the mistake is again on Payson's part. It issued a duplicate payment order following one that properly executed the payment order received by Payson from DotCom. Under §4A-303(a), the situation is treated like one in which the originator's bank mistakenly issues a payment order in an amount greater than the originator instructed. Payson can retain payment from DotCom only for the first payment order it sent out. It will have to seek restitution of the second $4 million, which it has itself paid out of its own funds and which has been credited to BC&W's account, from BC&W directly.

3c. Under the cited subsection, if a receiving bank (here the originator's bank) mistakenly executes a payment order it has received (here from the originator) for an amount less than the amount of the sender's order, it is entitled to the amount of the sender's order ($4 million) if it "corrects its mistake by issuing an additional payment order [here for $3,600,000] for the benefit of the beneficiary of the sender's order." If Payson does not correct its error, then it is entitled to payment of only $400,000 from DotCom's account. In that case BC&W will, of course, have been only paid one-tenth of what it is owed by DotCom. It will, we have to assume, complain. At this point DotCom presumably issues another payment order for the remainder to be sure that it has paid its supplier what it is owed. Under §4A-305(b), Payson could be held liable to DotCom for any expenses incurred in this second corrective payment order and also for any "incidental expenses" (for example, any late fee it must paid to BC&W for not having its payment in on time because of the bank's initial improper execution). We look at §4A-305 in more detail in Example 4.

4a. Yes. The mistake was on the bank's part. Under §4A-303(c), DotCom, the customer and the originator, does not have to pay a thing for the improperly executed order and is entitled to recredit of its account for the full amount. This is another example of the much-needed security the customer receives from Article 4A's money-back guarantee of §4A-402.

4b. Under §4A-305(b), because Payson's error resulted in noncompletion of the funds transfer, the bank is liable to DotCom

> for its expenses in the funds transfer and for incidental expenses and interest losses . . . resulting from the improper execution. Except as provided in subsection (c), additional damages are not recoverable.

So DotCom could gets its fees back and recover any incidental damages it has incurred, but would normally not be able to recover any consequential damages from the bank for the improper execution. Under subsection (c),

> In addition to the amounts payable under subsections (a) and (b), damages, including consequential damages, are recoverable to the extent provided in an express written agreement of the receiving bank.

So, unless the initial funds transfer agreement entered into between DotCom and Payson, or some other written agreement entered into later between these parties, specifically obliges Payson to pay for consequential damages in the event it makes an improper execution, DotCom will have no right to insist on payment of any such damages. As you can well imagine, it would be the rare instance in which a bank would agree to pay consequential damages even for its most blatant mistakes. The pre-Article 4A history of this issue and the Article 4A drafters' justification for dealing with the problem as they have is given in Comment 2. As you will read, the position taken by the banks in the negotiation leading up to the final version of Article 4A — that protection for them from the obligation to pay consequential damages was essential to keep wire transfers not only "fast and final" but also "cheap" — was respectfully deferred to by the drafters.

4c. It is your obligation to tell Winona Windfall that the money is not hers to keep. Payson State Bank will have a right to recover it from her in restitution.

5a. No. Under the rule of §4A-207(b)(1), San Francisco Federal was entitled to accept the payment order it received and credit the $75,000 to the landlord's account unless it actually was aware that the name and number of the payment order it received referred to different parties. Here it was presumably not aware of the discrepancy; had it been so, it would not have accepted the confusing order and would have asked for clarification from the party sending it the order. As matters stand, San Francisco was perfectly within its rights to credit the amount to the landlord's account.

5b. No. The Palo Alto bank has made no mistake. It executed the order as received from its customer, Horseshoes. Unless a security procedure was in place that should have detected Smithy's error (and it is hard to imagine what that might be) and the Palo Alto bank failed to carry out its part in observance of this procedure, the bank has no liability for executing as it did the payment order received from Smithy.

5c. Your first reaction to this question might have been to say that Horseshoes is entitled to restitution of the $75,000 mistakenly paid into the account on the theory of restitution, just as earlier we saw that Larry Luckowski and Winona Windfall would have had to return the money mistakenly wired into their accounts. There is a crucial difference here, however. In this instance, the party into whose account the money was wired was in fact owed something by the originator. Can the landlord argue that it is entitled to keep the $75,000 in return for discharging Horseshoes to that extent from Horseshoes' obligation to pay the rent that is in arrears? The issue is not addressed directly by Article 4A. That article defers to "the law governing mistake and restitution" of the jurisdiction the common law of which applies to the transaction. Comment 2 to §4A-303 does seem to acknowledge that "in unusual cases" the law might allow the actual beneficiary of the last payment order, in this case the landlord, to keep all or part of the amount mistakenly paid into its account. Is this such a case?

The law of restitution has had to deal with this question of when the recipient of a mistaken payment may actually retain all or part of that payment since long before the wholesale wire transfer came on the scene. Mistaken payments can and have been made by check or cash for just about as long as those means of payment have been in use. Different jurisdictions have adopted slightly different rules to handle the situation. In some, the recipient of the mistaken payment may retain the amount that has come into its possession only to the extent that it has relied to its detriment on the receipt of the funds. The *Restatement of Restitution* sets out a different rule, which has come to be known as the "discharge for value" doctrine (even if the term isn't the best one could think of to explain the situation).

> This defense [to an action for restitution] arises where there is a preexisting liquidated debt . . . owed to the beneficiary by the originator of the payment. If the originator or some third party erroneously gives the beneficiary funds at the originator's request, and the beneficiary in good faith believes the funds have been submitted in full or partial payment of that preexisting debt . . . and is unaware of the originator's or third party's mistake, the originator or third party will not be entitled to seek repayment from the beneficiary of the erroneously submitted funds [citing to a treatise on contracts].

Bank of America National Trust & Savings Ass'n v. Sanati, 11 Cal. App. 4th 1079, 14 Cal. Rptr. 2d 615, 19 U.C.C.2d 531 (1992). The California appellate court, which also took note of the treatment of the issue in the *Restatement of Restitution*, held the discharge-for-value rule to be applicable California law, even if in the instant case it did not bar recovery in restitution (because the recipient of the mistaken payment had not established that the originator owed her a preexisting liquidated debt). In the oft-cited case of *Banque Worms v. BankAmerica International*, 77 N.Y.2d 362, 570 N.E.2d 189, 568 N.Y.S.2d 541 (1991), the Court of Appeals of the State of New York held that the discharge-for-value rule applied to suits for restitution of mistaken payments, at least in cases involving "the unique problems presented by electronics funds transfer technology." Most recently, the Mississippi Supreme Court applied the discharge-for-value rule to a case involving a mistaken funds transfer that ended up putting money into the hands of a legitimate creditor of the originator's in *Credit Lyonnais New York Branch v. Royal*, 745 So. 2d 837, 39 U.C.C.2d 205 (Miss. 1999).

In the case before us, the landlord would have to establish that Horseshoes did owe it a liquidated debt, but that should not be hard if the struggling firm was behind in the rent. It would also have to show that it took the $75,000 in good faith believing the money to have been sent it by the tenant in at least partial fulfillment of what the landlord was owed. Why would it think otherwise? All that it would know, or that the bank's records would reveal to it if it cared to inquire, is that the Horseshoes firm had wired the amount of $75,000 directly into the account where Horsehoes was suppose to wire rental payments. Would the landlord not be reasonable in believing that its tenant was intentionally sending it this money to get caught up, at least to some partial extent, on the overdue rent? That being so, the discharge-for-value rule, if applied to the situation by the court in the jurisdiction whose common law governs this aspect of the transaction, would bar Horseshoes from recovering any of the money from its landlord. True, Horseshoes will be that much less behind on what it owes in back rent, but how is it going to make payment of the $75,000 Ironbars is still insisting upon if it is to continue to deliver Horseshoes' much-needed raw material. We leave that question for Smithy and his colleagues at Horseshoes Incorporated to worry over. Nothing in the law of payment systems gives a ready answer to the question of how to come up with the money to pay an obligation when you don't have it readily on hand.

Table of U.C.C. Sections

Index